ALSO BY BRIAN MOYNAHAN

The Russian Century

Claws of the Bear

Comrades

RASPUTIN

RASPUTIN

The Saint Who Sinned

BRIAN MOYNAHAN

DA CAPO PRESS
A MEMBER OF THE PERSEUS BOOKS GROUP

Library of Congress Cataloging in Publication Data

Moynahan, Brian, 1941–
    Rasputin : the saint who sinned / by Brian Moynahan.
        p.   cm.
    Originally published: New York : Random House, c1997.
    Includes bibliographical references and indexes.
    ISBN 0-306-80930-3
        1. Rasputin, Grigori Efimovich, ca. 1870–1916. 2. Russia—Court and courtiers–Biography. 3. Russia—History—Nicholas II, 1894–1917. I. Title.

DK254.R3 M69   1999

                                                                                    99-045454

First Da Capo Press Edition 1999

This Da Capo paperback edition of Rasputin is an unabridged republication of the English-language edition. It is reprinted by arrangement with Random House.

Published by Da Capo Press
A Member of the Perseus Books Group
http://www.perseusbooksgroup.com

FOR THE SCARLETTS

Preface

Grigory Rasputin, holy man and intimate of the Russian royal family, was murdered in the basement of a St. Petersburg palace in 1916. To his many enemies he was the incarnation of evil genius; he died because they held him to be the real power behind a throne that his malign influence was destroying. Within a few weeks the three-hundred year-old dynasty was swept away and a way of life perished with it.

Rasputin remains. He is the great survivor from the drowned world of the Romanovs. To some, he was once a saint; he is more often thought of now as "the mad monk." He was not mad, or monk, or saint. He is a complex figure, intelligent, ambitious, idle, generous to a fault, spiritual, and—utterly—amoral.

In his prime, when the censors forbade any public mention of him, newspaper editors were happy to trade heavy fines for the guaranteed increase in circulation Rasputin brought. After his death the memoirs of those who knew him—leading politicians, a defrocked priest, secret police officers, women admirers—became a mini-industry. His murderer, Prince Yusupov, was able to restore some of the fortune seized from him by the Bolsheviks with best-selling accounts of the killing and a slander suit against the Hollywood producers of a Rasputin movie. Eighty years on, Rasputin still inspires books, movies, and rock songs. The basement where he died is a tourist attraction.

Why? His life was remarkable in itself. He was peasant, prophet, and party-goer, a combination that is not common. He had apparent psychic powers, attested to but lacking medical explanation. He was, too, for all the medieval trappings that surrounded him, curiously modern. His skills as a spiritual leader and manipulator of souls match those of the latter-day guru; keep the sex, change drugs to drink and rock 'n' roll to wild Gypsy music, and in his blend of charisma and outrage he is the precursor of the modern superstar. Ra-Ra-Rasputin . . .

But it is in the ageless struggle between good and evil, so strong a motif in his existence, that his fascination truly lies.

Rasputin bewitches because his life is both romantic and repulsive. It can be seen as an actual fairy tale. Born in a Siberian cabin, he makes his way to the distant capital of a great empire and there wins the trust and affection of the tsar and empress. He has gifts of healing and saves the life of their hemophiliac son. Or he can be read as a study in wickedness; he is a hypnotist, who casts his spell over the innocent women he seduces and who leads Russia and its besotted rulers to revolution and ruin.

He is much more than an exhibit in an antique freak show (though it suited Russian Communists, with their belief in the impersonal forces of Marxism, to treat him as such). He was a legend in his lifetime—of few people is that old cliché more apt—and his legend did fatal damage to the reputation of the Romanovs and to the fabric of Russian autocracy. So did the reality that lay behind it; by the end seasoned diplomats and foreign correspondents had not the slightest doubt that, as his killers and the Russian public suspected, Rasputin's influence was corrosive and immense. He is a historic personage.

It is the purpose of this book to show Rasputin, and the society on the edge of extinction in which he operated, in his true colors, not as a moral monochrome but rainbowed, as he was, and recognizably and fallibly human.

—

All dates are given here in the Julian calendar that was in use in Russia throughout Rasputin's lifetime. It was twelve days behind the Western Gregorian calendar in the nineteenth century, and thirteen days behind in the twentieth. Thus, for example, the date of December 16, 1916, given for Rasputin's death corresponds to December 29, 1916, in the Western calendar. This applies to events outside as well as within Russia. Rather than consistent transliteration from Cyrillic to the Roman alphabet, common usage is given for family names. First names are anglicized where, as with the tsar, for example, this is appropriate. *Tsar* and *emperor*, *tsarina* and *empress* are interchangeable; Nicholas is most commonly referred to as tsar, his personal preference, and Alexandra as empress, hers. I am indebted to Dr. Igor Bogdanov of St. Petersburg for his great help in skilled translation and painstaking research.

Contents

RASPUTIN

CHAPTER 1

"Proshchaitye, Papa"

It snowed hard in Petrograd in the hours before the murder.

The fall of 1916 matched the war, bleak and endless, gray skies robbing the city of its energy in the brief hours of daylight. Foul winds drove down the quays by the Neva River, pungent with chemical fumes from munitions factories. Families from territories lost to the Germans huddled in sheds near the railroad stations. Their lamentations hovered in the air, they died of typhus and simple exhaustion, "blown away like gossamer." Two in three streetlamps were unlit. The sidewalks were no longer swept. They filled with rubbish and slush and, from four each morning, with long lines of ill-clad men and garrulous women, waiting for bread.

The city's buildings, in faultless lines of pink granite and yellow- and green-washed stucco, had risen from bogs and marshes on piles driven by gangs of forced laborers two centuries before. When onshore winds raised the level of the Neva, alarm bells warned people to flee to higher stories before the floods poured into basement rooms. Now the city was drowning in its own ill humor.

"Rasputin, Rasputin, Rasputin"; one name pounded like surf on a crumbling shore, in the food lines, salons, rooming houses—universally. "It was like a refrain," a Petrograd lady wrote. "It became a dusk enveloping all our world, eclipsing the sun. How could so pitiful a wretch throw so vast a shadow? It was inexplicable, maddening, almost incredible."

Grigory Rasputin was a muzhik, a dark peasant from a distant Siberian bog, a creature who had shat in the open like an animal when he was a boy, who still sucked soup from the bowl and ate fish with his fingers, whose body gave off a powerful and acrid odor, who could scarcely scrawl his name, but (what a but!) who it was rumored had the ear—enjoyed the body—of the empress; who, with her, appointed the mightiest officials of state; who treated fawning "duchesses, countesses, famous actresses, and high-ranking persons" worse than servants and maids; who was plotting a separate peace with Germany; who could see the future. Inexplicable, indeed! Incredible, except that he was visible, a shaggy figure with a sable coat thrown over peasant boots and blouse, seen about town, catching cabs, dining at Donon's, reeling out of the Gypsy houses in Novaya Derevnya blind drunk in the early hours. His very eyes betrayed his identity to strangers. The ballerina Tamara Karsavina, the most beautiful dancer of her generation, who had not seen him before, recognized him instantly in the street through their "strange lightness, inconceivable in a peasant face, the eyes of a maniac."

The censors did their best to hide him. They daubed ink over newspaper columns with stories that referred to him; the black blotches were called caviar. Readers knew whom the caviar was protecting, and they invented stories of their own. A society hostess, irritated that her guests talked of nothing else, put up a printed sign in her dining room: "We do not discuss Rasputin here." But they did; nothing would stop them. The talk was at the top. "Dark Powers behind the Throne! German influence at Court! The power of Rasputin! Infamous stories about the empress!" the British ambassador's daughter, Meriel Buchanan, noted of drawing room conversation in her diary. It ran unbroken to the city's lower depths. "The filthy gossip about the tsar's family has now become the property of the street," wrote an agent of the Okhrana secret police.

Crude cartoons passed hands of Rasputin emerging from the naked empress's nipples to tower over Russia, his wild eyes staring from a black cloud of hair and beard. Gambling dens used playing cards in which his head replaced the tsar's on the king of spades. A caricature icon showed him with a vodka bottle in one hand and the naked tsar cradled like the Christ child in the other, while the flames of hell licked at his boots and nude women with angels' wings and black silk stockings flew about his head. A photograph of him with a collection of society women was reproduced by the thousand. Mikhail Rodzianko, a leading politician, said he was horrified to find that "I recognized many of these worshipers from high society"; he himself had "a huge mass of letters from mothers whose daughters had been disgraced by the impudent profligate."

———

The country could no longer tell the real from the false because, the red-haired poet Zinaida Gippius thought, it had become a large lunatic asylum. It looked normal enough, like an asylum on open house day, but in fact the inmates were all mad. Nowhere was this more obvious than in the capital. Its name had been changed from St. Petersburg to the non-Germanic Petrograd at the start of the war. Gippius rechristened it Chertograd, "Devil-town."

For the rich, the young poet Boris Pasternak wrote, city life was "gay with the brilliance of a florist's window in winter." The Americans had yet to join the First War. Though they were doing well enough against the Austrians, the Russians were bleeding against the Germans, more even than their French and British allies. People shut the fighting out of their minds, "dancing a 'last tango' on the rim of trenches filled with forgotten corpses." The heartrending sensuality of the tango, the novelist Alexis Tolstoy thought, had become a death march for a city "tormented by sleepless nights, stupefied and deadened by wine, wealth, and lovemaking without love." Morphine stolen from military hospitals was openly for sale in cabarets. Prohibition had been declared with the onset of war. Underpaid officials were easily bribed to ignore it, and even the pretense of pouring vodka from a teapot had disappeared. Officers over-staying their leave drank cocktails in the American bar of the Hotel de l'Europe with the teenage prostitutes who teemed in the lobbies.

Nightclubs were full of "heroes of the rear, legal deserters." No stigma at-tached to the "gray ticket men" who had bought exemption from the front, some of them through Rasputin, for a few hundred rubles. A British secret agent, Robert Bruce Lockhart, found his own conduct "puerile and reprehensi-ble." He drank too much, with men for whom he felt contempt. He was ashamed and unhappy, adrift with a senseless ennui. "There is a sort of sick-ness in the soul," wrote the poet Alexander Blok. Above Russia's deathbed hov-ered "crows, a raucous, swirling scum."

The suicide rate tripled, when in other countries at war it was falling. Two out of three victims were under twenty-eight. Marriages collapsed as elderly men "discard[ed] their wives and flaunt[ed] their successors in the eyes of soci-ety." The grand mistress of the court, Madame Narishkina, calculated that half her circle were divorced. "Have you observed that no one understands the story of Anna Karenina nowadays?" she said of Tolstoy's great novel. "Today, Anna would immediately have divorced her husband and married Vronsky and there the story would have ended." Movies of robbery and murder were blamed for a crime wave. The bishop of Vyatka sought out Empress Alexandra to show her photographs of looted shops and bloated bodies. Men back from the front boasted openly that they had become atheists. The bishop blamed this on their contact with "intellectuals and Jews." Others thought that the church was daily losing its hold because of its servility to the despised autocracy that ruled Russia.

The poor of Petrograd were stacked like cordwood in rooming houses. In the Vyborgsky factory district, the living had less space than the dead in the municipal cemetery. "Complete darkness," an observer wrote. "The ceiling is so low a tall man cannot stand upright. A specific smell. Legions of cockroaches and bugs. No double window frame and it is piercingly cold." Work accidents were commonplace. "I, for one, never enter the factory without first making the sign of the cross," said the manager of an explosives plant. Workers were prey to intestinal and lung disease, and to speculators. Flour had doubled in price since the start of the war, sugar had risen four times, aspirin fifty times. "It is said in all directions that merchants and shopkeepers are building up huge profits at the expense of the people," the secret police reported.

Spy fever was endemic. It was the easiest explanation for defeat. The head of the Okhrana was told by a government minister, in all earnest, that two aides-de-camp of the German kaiser had been seen strolling past the shops of the Nevsky Prospect without a care in the world, "dressed as civilians with their coat collars turned up." Not a day passed in the zone of armies, the French ambassador complained, "when a Jew isn't hanged on a trumped-up charge of spying." Jews were deported in scores of thousands from the areas behind the front, "wandering over the snows, driven like cattle by platoons of Cossacks, abandoned at the stations, camping in the open around the towns and dying of hunger, weariness, and cold." In the Baltic provinces German barons were accused of signaling to the German fleet from the towers of their castles. A baron was said to have treated the crew of a German aircraft to a feast before waving them off with one of his cows aboard as a present.

A "devastating chaos and elemental anarchy" was approaching, the Okhrana warned. In two years the government had had four prime ministers, four war ministers, and six ministers of the interior. Rasputin's hand was seen behind each appointment. His minion Boris Stürmer was prime minister in the fall of 1916. Stürmer, a "shallow and dishonest creature who emits an intolerable odor of falseness," excited disgust. He maddened the genial American ambassador, David Francis, by gazing at himself in a mirror during appointments with enraptured admiration, twirling the waxed ends of his mustaches. "Absolutely unprincipled, double faced," his fellow conservatives said, "a complete nullity, finished at fifty." Rasputin was held to have gifted the second most powerful position of state, that of interior minister, to Alexander Dmitrievich Protopopov. He strutted in high boots and an operatic uniform he had designed himself. "A small, gray-haired man, with restless nervous movements and bright wild eyes that shifted all the time," a contemporary wrote, adding that he was possibly syphilitic—he suffered from hallucinations, leg ulcers, and paresis, a partial form of paralysis characteristic of syphilitics—and "certainly not quite sane."

—

The autocrat of all the Russias, Nicholas Alexandrovich Romanov, was 490 miles to the south in the provincial town of Mogilev. It was a pleasant place, with views across a wooded valley to the Dnieper River. Its Jews had been deported, however, and replaced by a transient population of staff officers, and the town had acquired a melancholy that suited the word from which its name was derived, *mogila*, "a grave." The Bristol, a four-ruble-a-night hotel on an avenue of leafless chestnuts, had been commandeered for the Stavka, the supreme army headquarters. The tsar took daily walks by the river with his English setters. In the evenings he watched movies. His favorite was a twenty-two-reel detective serial called *The Secrets of New York.*

He had appointed himself commander in chief the year before. Despite five million casualties, and the loss of Warsaw and his Polish territories, the tsar was confident that the army remained loyal. He followed its movements on maps hung in the hotel's café chantant. He was happy—"my brain is resting here," he wrote—for he was far from the intrigues of Petrograd. His army was, in reality, in such psychosis that fresh troops arriving in the line seemed demented. "It was not that they screamed or did anything violent," an officer remarked. "They simply marched into camp, shoulders hunched, heads down, and if they looked up as they passed, their faces wore a vacant expression that is the beginning of insanity."

In the fall offensive of 1916, at Kovel on the central front, a Guards army of the Semyonovsky and Preobrazhensky regiments attacked across open, marshy country seventeen times in three months. The Preobrazhenskys, the British military attaché Gen. Alfred Knox wrote, were "physically the finest human animals in Europe." Since Peter the Great first dressed them in bottle green uniforms and insisted that each man stand over six feet tall, every tsar had been honorary colonel of the regiment. The commander of the assault, Gen. Alexander Bezobrazov, was thought by his peers to be "of limited intelligence and unbelievably stubborn." One of his corps commanders, the tsar's uncle Grand Duke Paul, was a fine dancer, a skilled philanderer, a dashing figure in close-fitting strawberry britches and short hussar riding boots; alone of four brothers, he would soon prove loyal to his nephew. Unfortunately, however, he "knew absolutely nothing about military affairs." The commander of the other corps suffered from a defect, too; whenever in danger he "lost all presence of mind and was unable to conduct operations because his nerves could not stand the sound of rifle fire."

The guardsmen were sent into a swamp. German aircraft strafed them as they struggled in the mud, then refueled and rearmed, and returned to feast on the bottle green mass. "The wounded sank slowly in the marsh, and it was impossible to send them help," Knox wrote. "The Russian Command for some unknown reason seems always to choose a bog to drown in." In less than a fortnight four out of five of the empire's finest troops were lost. Half-trained re-inforcements were ordered to continue the assault. They advanced in long, thin lines, dressing to the left, officers at the head, sergeant majors behind to shoot deserters. They made no attempt to maneuver; their officers did not think them capable of it. So many corpses lay in no-man's-land that the Germans re-fused a truce to bury them. Despite a terrible stench of putrefaction, the heaps were a physical obstacle to fresh Russian assaults. By the time the offensive was called off in November, the Russians were bombarding their own jump-off trenches to force their men into the attack. The bodies were swallowed slowly in the quicksands. Months later an officer posted there, Prince Obolensky, found that "still above the sand one could see the tops of their bayonets."

As the casualty reports from the "Kovel pit" flooded back to the Stavka, Nicholas was obliged to dismiss Bezobrazov. He did so unwillingly. "What an honest and well-bred man he is!" he wrote to Empress Alexandra. "I have given him leave for two months. . . . I have promised that if some vacancies occur in the Guards Corps to appoint him there!"

The tsar's troops no longer thought of themselves as Russian soldiers; "they were just men who were going to die." They told each other that the government had been paid a billion rubles by Berlin to ensure that as few of them as possible survived the war. Their most special hatred was reserved for the German-born empress; they thought that she was in league with the enemy, that she talked to Germany on a radio concealed under the eaves of her palace, that she passed se-crets to her sister, Princess Irene of Prussia, that to accept a decoration from her meant certain death. They were sure that she was sleeping with Grigory Raspu-tin. When Nicholas attended medal ceremonies to award the Cross of St. George, they laughed and called it the "Georgiy cross": "Tsar with Georgiy, tsa-rina with Grigory." They called her Nemka, "the German woman."

Through the fall Alexandra rarely left the Alexander Palace at Tsarskoye Selo, the "tsar's village" a half-hour train ride from the capital. Her nerves trou-bled her; she lay for much of the day on a chaise longue in her mauve boudoir, its carpets, curtains, and pillows of that color, its furniture mauve and white, a Scottish terrier at her feet. She despised Petrograd and its scandalmongers. To her Russia was the countryside, uncomplaining, loyal, eternal; stands of birch on the plain, a stream, a village, a windmill and white and gilt church, log huts along a road of mud or snow. Rasputin, the honest peasant in blouse and boots, simple and holy, her Friend, was its personification. Her mail from the villages, she told a rare visitor, reassured her that "the real Russia, poor, humble, peas-ant Russia, is with me. If I showed you the telegrams and letters I receive every day from all parts of the empire, you'd see it yourself."

The missives were suspiciously similar. "Oh our beloved sovereign, mother · and guardian of our adored tsarevich," many began, "save us from our enemies, save Russia!" They were forged by the secret police on the orders of Protopopov, Rasputin's friend. Genuine letters intercepted by the Okhrana told a different tale. The muzhik was naturally meek and fatalistic, the court grand master had warned; he would accept an injustice but continue to ponder it. At some point he would demand an accounting; "and, when the muzhik ceases to be meek, he becomes terrifying." That point was being reached. "Perhaps the landowners are getting rich, various rogues are getting richer, but the people, the common people, are being beggared," a writer from Irkutsk complained. The peasants were growing "more furious every day." In the sweet-scented wilderness of rural Russia, Alexander Blok wrote, were "twisted, unhappy, and browbeaten people with ideas and beliefs from before the Flood."

The mood on the streets became "violent, unprecedented" in October. The Okhrana said that it was no longer possible to prosecute all who made "overt and brazen insults" against the tsar and his empress. The numbers were too great for the courts to cope. Sending a letter by diplomatic bag to avoid the censors, Robert Wilton, the London *Times* man in Petrograd, warned that the dynasty was in danger: "I hear that banners inscribed 'Down with the Romanovs' have been found in workmen's houses." Strikers murdered a foreman in a French-owned vehicle plant. Troops from the 181st Infantry Regiment who were called in opened fire on the police instead of the strikers. At the front shell-shocked men were shot for cowardice; in the capital the authorities were too frightened of their own garrison to impose the death sentence on mutineers. Every day the police arrested soldiers for picking pockets at streetcar stops. The military dared not punish them, the Okhrana chief complained, and the thieves were back on the streets within hours.

On October 26 a French spiritualist and magician called Papus died. Years before he had conducted séances with Nicholas and Alexandra at which he had conjured up the spirit of Alexander III, the tsar's dead father. Alexander had warned—so Papus claimed—that revolution would one day strike Russia with unparalleled violence. Papus said that he could avert the prophecy, but only as long as he lived. Now he was gone, and shortly before his death he had written about Rasputin. "Cabalistically speaking," he said, "Rasputin is a vessel like Pandora's box, which contains all the vices, crimes, and filth of the Russian people. Should the vessel be broken, we will see its dreadful contents spill themselves across Russia."

At the start of November, Vladimir Purishkevich, an arch reactionary, the self-styled "most extreme of the Rights," dined with Nicholas in Mogilev. He had gone there to warn the tsar that Rasputin was savaging the reputation of the monarchy. He hoped the tsar's aides would back him up but found their "self-love" was too great for them to risk their careers by speaking out. Disgusted, he returned to Petrograd to attack Rasputin openly in the state Duma, Russia's parliament. He compared him to False Dmitri, a horror figure in Russian history, a pretender to the throne, with facial warts and malformed arms. Purishkevich railed at the "filthy, depraved, corrupt peasant" to whose advice "Russia's empress listens above all others."

"It cannot be that Rasputin's recommendation is enough for the most infamous persons to be nominated to the highest posts," he went on. "Ministers! If you are true patriots, go over there, to the tsar's Stavka, fall at the tsar's feet and ask that Russia be redeemed from Rasputin and all his followers, great and small." A young aristocrat, Prince Felix Yusupov, a onetime transvestite married to the tsar's niece, listened to the speech. He was much impressed and arranged to meet Purishkevich.

With "disquieting news coming to us from all sides," the Okhrana chief worked on a plan to use police and Cossacks armed with machine guns to put down an uprising in the city. He suspected that Duma members and the army high command were plotting to overthrow the tsar and murder Rasputin. He intercepted mail sent by suspects and was alarmed to find that they were beginning to use special confidential messengers. Gray skies devoured the outlines of buildings, and bitter winds muttered in the streets.

Nicholas reviewed the Guards Brigade at the Stavka in early December. One officer had accidentally cut off the ear of his Irish hunter with his saber. He fastened it back on with a little screw, like an earring. It fell off in front of the tsar. It was thought a bad omen.

On December 8 the Union of Towns, an important municipal body, went into secret session. It passed a resolution: "The government, now become an instrument of the dark forces, is driving Russia to her ruin and is shattering the imperial throne. In this grave hour the country requires a government worthy of a great people. There is not a day to lose!" Secrets were no longer kept. The resolution was circulated in roneoscript in thousands of copies. "Dark forces" was simple code for Grigory Rasputin and those about him. A pamphlet, written in poetic, old-style Russian, made the rounds. It was addressed to "Father Grigory, new saint of the devil, reviler of Christ's teachings, ruiner of the Russian land, defiler of wives and maidens." Its refrain urged Rasputin to rejoice: "Rejoice at the tsar's dulled mind, rejoice at the tsarina's delectation . . . at their daughters' seduction . . . at Protopopov's promotion . . . at voluptuousness, at the wagging spine and shaking hips . . . at the propagation of dark forces . . . at the German stronghold. Rejoice, foul receptacle of Satan!"

"Oh, how terrible an autocracy is without an autocrat!" a leading monarchist, Vasily Shulgin, loyal, patrician, wrote in his diary. "The tsar offends the nation by what he allows to go on in the palace . . . while the country offends the tsar by its terrible suspicions." The empress was sleeping badly; she had a dream in which she lay on an operating table while a surgeon cut off her arm.

Frantic debauchery—he liked the word *frantic* enough to be using it as a nickname for a young woman he was trying to seduce—had turned Rasputin's sturdy frame "gaunt and cadaverous." The increasing malevolence of the anecdotes circulating about him kept his bodyguards on edge in December. He was said to be a German spy; he used a radio to talk to Berlin; he was fucking the tsar's beautiful daughters as well as the tsar's wife. His underpants flew over the royal palaces in place of the double-headed imperial eagle. At night he drove in a black car across the Palace Bridge and fired shots at random, killing and wounding for pleasure; he was the first drive-by killer.

He was at risk himself, and he knew it. "Do you know that I shall soon die in terrible pain?" he said, or so the French ambassador reported. "But what can I do? God has sent me to save our dear sovereign and Holy Russia. Despite my terrible sins I am a Christ in miniature." His name was becoming a byword for evil, Meriel Buchanan wrote, "though many people, held in a kind of superstitious dread, dared not pronounce it, believing that by doing so they brought down ill luck on their heads. 'The Unmentionable,' 'the Nameless One'—so they would whisper."

———

Then came the snow.

It fell all morning on Friday, December 16, in thick, spinning disks, throwing a blanket over the dirt and topping the yellow- and green-washed buildings with a brilliant white crust. Rasputin went to a bathhouse with a guard of Okhrana men. He drank heavily at lunch and went to sleep in his apartment. In the late afternoon the skies cleared and the temperature fell. The sun glowed and the empress noted the "wee pink clouds" that reflected it. The scummy floes drifting on the Neva became a solid, luminescent sheet beneath the untainted air. The curse of the ghastly autumn was broken, Meriel Buchanan wrote, "and the golden spires and snow-covered roofs shone beneath a cold, clear sky."

The night was windless; the stars were out and sound carried. Maria Rasputin heard a car driving down Gorokhovaya ulitsa. It braked outside Number 64, a five-story brick apartment house a block away from the Fontanka Canal, one of the three main canals that bisected the heart of the city, their frozen waters colored by the pastel stucco and classical lines of the buildings that fronted them. Maria lived in a comfortable third-floor apartment with her younger sister, Varya, and her father, Grigory. She was seventeen.

She pulled back the curtain and looked down through the double window. A lone figure got out of the backseat; his greatcoat collar was turned up, and the flaps of his fur cap were down, so she could not make out his face.

The man slammed the door of the black limousine. Footsteps ringing on the hard snow, he passed to the yard and the back of the house. It was 11:00 P.M. Visitors who came late to see Maria's father often used the back stairs; a couple of Okhrana agents were always stationed at the front. The rear doorbell of the apartment sounded. Maria climbed back into bed beside her sister and fell asleep. She was used to her father's odd hours.

She woke when she heard Rasputin call to the maid for his boots. She slipped out of bed into the hallway. It was dark, and she almost bumped into her father.

"Oh, Maria!" he said. "Did we awaken you?"

"Yes, Papa, but no matter. Are you going out?"

"I must go, Marochka," he said, using the affectionate pet name.

"You should not. You know what Minister Protopopov said?" She referred to the interior minister. The Okhrana agents cooling their heels downstairs were Protopopov's; the minister had put them on particular alert, because his men had gotten wind from informers in a gambling house of a plot being mounted against his benefactor. Protopopov had called earlier—he visited Rasputin most evenings—and had made the Siberian promise not to go out.

"Yes, I know," Rasputin said. "But it's an important matter."

Maria was frightened for her father. She had seen him stabbed in the stomach by a woman two years before. She knew, from girls at school, from glances in the street and allusions in the newspapers, that others wished him ill. Her unease increased when she caught a glimpse of her father's visitor. He was in Rasputin's study, lounging against a desk strewn with papers and bowls of fruit and bottles given by admirers. He was a young man, tall and slender—"rather prettier than handsome," she thought—and he had unbuttoned his greatcoat to show his finely cut evening clothes. He still wore his fur cap, as though to prove that a prince had no need to uncover his head in front of a muzhik.

"I am very tired," Rasputin said to the young man. "Also, I have been quite ill. Must it be tonight? Can it not wait?"

"No, Otyets Grigory, it cannot wait."

Rasputin sighed. "Very well, moy malenki, give me a moment to change into a fresh blouse." Otyets is "father"; moy malenki is "my little one." The intimacy between the older man and his visitor was confirmed when Rasputin went into his room and Maria saw him root through his chest of drawers and pull out his favorite blouse. Its blue satin was embroidered with gold sunflowers; Empress Alexandra had stitched it for him herself.

When he had been a wanderer in the boggy vastness of western Siberia, Rasputin had told Maria, he had spent a whole year searching for God without once changing his clothes. He had given up women, and alcohol, too, at various times. Now he was back on them—Maria was used to the womanizing, but his heavy drinking worried her because it combined with the lingering effects of the knife attack to undermine his health—but he had become fastidious.

This was his third change of clothes on Friday. He put on his finest pair of breeches, the blue velvet ones. Maria and the maid Katya helped him on with them, Maria with her finger to her lips so that her sleeping sister would not be wakened. He tied a golden sash around his blouse. Maria watched him splash his favorite cologne on his ears and neck and comb it through his beard; the young man would later say that Rasputin smelled of cheap soap.

Katya brought his boots. She smiled when he struck a pose for her, and his tiredness lifted. He put on a beaver overcoat, a present from a wealthy Petrograd banker and speculator, Ignati Porfiryevich Manus, whose niece had been moribund with fever until Rasputin's healing intercession had revived her. He made to leave.

"Papa, Papa." Maria flew to him and clutched his arm, with a premonition of evil. Words would not come, but she thought he understood. He kissed her and wiped away her tears with his fingers.

"Do not fear, Marochka," he said. "Nothing can happen to me unless it is God's will." He helped her into bed and kissed the sleeping Varya on the cheek. He made the sign of the cross over his children, right to left, in the Russian style. Then he went.

Maria cleared the window of frost. Footsteps snapped in the snow. The young man gripped Rasputin by the arm and half helped, half-pushed him into the limousine. The door slammed, and the wheels spun briefly on the ice as the car sped away. Maria fell into disturbed slumber, waking herself at some point to cry aloud, "Proshchaitye, Papa." Farewell, Papa.

————

The murder was a sensation. The story was broken by six words, complete with screamer, in the evening edition of the *Stock Exchange Gazette:* GRIGORY RASPUTIN HAS CEASED TO EXIST! Alive, he had been protected by the censor. His obituarists had fewer constraints. They turned the death of the "court pilgrim—debauchee" into a great political event. Newspapers doubled their print runs, splashing the forbidden name in their largest typefaces. Telegraph operators on the railroad network slipped the news into routine reports of train movements. Travelers in sleds took it from the rail depots to frozen villages.

The bridge from which the victim's body was dumped into the Neva became "a place to take a walk for nearly all of Petrograd. People come here in automobiles and in carriages. Some stay for a long time at the railings." Sightseers tried to get into 64 Gorokhovaya ulitsa. Police sealed off the house. A hearse pulled up, and the crowd hissed with disappointment when it discharged wreaths and yards of mourning crepe instead of a corpse.

A cabaret artiste addressed her audience as she went onstage: "Let me congratulate you with great joy." The audience applauded. Society ladies wrote to the presumed murderer to thank him for saving Russia, and they lit candles for him.

In the backwoods peasants cursed the killer. "They say that beside the tsar was an ordinary peasant like them," a Kostroma landowner, Prince O, told a diplomat. "He defended the people against the court and they killed him." A woman of noble family, overjoyed at the assassination, expected the wounded soldiers in a hospital she visited to share her elation. They were hostile and silent. "Yes," one of them told her, "only one peasant managed to get as far as the throne, and it was him that the nobility murdered." The French ambassador recalled that the dead man had claimed to have a vision as he passed the Peter and Paul Fortress, whose iron-bound punishment cells had housed a glittering clientele of opponents of the regime. "I see many people tortured there," Rasputin had said. "Not individuals but whole crowds; masses, clouds of bodies, several grand dukes and hundreds of counts. The Neva will be red with blood." The editor of *Kolokol*, Skvortsov, wrote that ordinary Russians regarded the murder as a sign of evil.

Other journalists reveled in it. They discovered that the body had been taken in great secrecy in a metallic casket from the mortuary of a Petrograd clinic to a chapel a few miles from the city. From there, they said, it was driven in a Red Cross automobile to the Nikolaevsky railroad station for transportation to the deceased's home village in Siberia. They found out that the postmortem was carried out by a professor from the military medical academy and that none of the clinic's own staff were present.

They reported with glee that "today in Petrograd an interesting photographic card passed many hands on which Rasputin is shown in the company of his high-ranking women admirers." Among them, they noted carefully, was the empress's favorite, Anna Vyrubova. They wrote openly of the victim's lusts, and his fulfillment of the crude peasant dream: "If I was tsar, I'd steal hundreds of rubles and eat fat all day long." Fate had given Rasputin all he had ever wanted, they said: "A lot of vodka, a lot of mutton, a lot of embroidered shirts, a lot of money, and a lot—too much—of 'woman supply.' "

They got things wrong—the dead man was a fish eater who disliked meat, and his remains were in Tsarskoye Selo—but they excited horror well enough. They described a "vaudeville of state" in which a "gilded slush" of ministers, bishops, princes, and princesses had danced attendance on the lowborn Siberian. "But why did they dance?" they asked. "Why didn't the princes and counts hold back the women of their circle, who so readily, with such a mystical reverence, paid Rasputin their 'women's dues'?" They refrained from naming the empress in the context of Rasputin's "dues"; it was a detail they could be sure their readers would supply for themselves.

They said he was a criminal. "He has been sued in court for horse rustling," reported *Russkoye Selo*. "He has been sued in court for perjury. He has been condemned to be flogged by a local court." The Moscow newspaper referred to the khlysts, an outlawed religious sect with a line in orgies and flagellation. "He staged khlyst prayers over a pit," the newspaper continued, "and showed 'corporal bitterness' in convents." That meant whipping nuns. His influence, unprecedented in a Siberian, unthinkable in a peasant, was explained. "He was cheap," said *Russkoye Slovo*. "He was elementary and simple and comfortable in all respects. Imagine a patron who is able to 'fix' an affair for a small consideration or for 'women supply.' . . . Old foxers, intriguers, dodgers, and political rogues said: 'If there was no Rasputin, he ought to have been invented!' "

Why was he dead? "In this drink-sodden, low-class intrigue," theorized the obituarist Alexander Yablonsky, "there were reefs that Rasputin did not see. He did not notice that he had gathered a coalition of all sorts of hatreds around himself. He did not notice that he was but false teeth in somebody else's mouth, and he did not realize what sorts of nuts were being cracked by those teeth . . .

"For Europe, Rasputin was an anecdote, not a fact," Yablonsky concluded. "For us, however, he was not only a fact. He was an epoch."

Grischa

The epoch was difficult to date. The victim's place of birth—a village of rough wooden cabins set in forests and marshes on a Siberian river-bank—was known. His age was uncertain. Rasputin was illiterate until he was well into his teens. The notes he scrawled in his prime—biblical sayings, jerky and half-formed thoughts for women admirers, requests for favors—were unpunctuated and hard to read. He kept no diary. His life was full of gaps, impulses, and wanderings. He was pious and lustful, crystal and mud; his great sleight of mind enabled him to conceal the sinner from those he wished to see only the saint. The censor saw to it that little was written about him while he was alive. Much of what came later was more concerned with exploiting his mystique than with establishing facts. If he knew his date of birth, and most Russian peasants did not, he made no effort to record it. It did not concern him; he was not an astrologer.

It came to be of interest only after his death. His daughter Maria, with legend most likely in mind, claimed that a fiery meteor burst across the night sky as Anna Egorovna, wife of Efim Aklovlevich Rasputin, a carter and farmer, gave birth to her second son. Maria gave her father's birth weight as seven pounds and the date as January 23, 1871. That date corresponds to January 10 in the Julian calendar used in prerevolutionary Russia. The same day appears in the register of baptisms in Tyumen, the nearest city to his birthplace, with the year as 1869. If this is correct—it is the most likely—then he was three weeks short of his forty-eighth birthday when the black automobile collected him for his last ride.

Reporters covering the murder at the time put Rasputin's age at fifty. Six months later the new provisional government set up an Extraordinary Commission of Inquiry to examine Rasputin and the decay of the autocracy. Evidence from witnesses who had known Rasputin in Siberia and elsewhere was collected by its chief investigator, F. P. Stimson, a respected lawyer from Kharkov. Stimson wasted few words on his subject's origins, and he used different dates.

"Grigory Efimovich Rasputin was born in the sloboda Pokrovskoye of Tyumen district, Tobolsk province, in 1864 or 1865," he recorded. "His parents were healthy, nobody insane among his kin, and they lived the way average peasants live." It was understandable that he added four or five years to Rasputin's age. His subject had raddled himself with drink and women in his final months.

—

Grischa, as he was called, began life as a sturdy infant. He stood at six months and toddled at eight. It was as well, for rural Siberia was primitive and no place for the weak. He had a one in five chance of dying before he reached his teens, of diphtheria, cholera, influenza. The nearest doctor was in Tyumen, seventy miles away by river or by Trakt 4, the rough road linking Tyumen and the provincial capital in Tobolsk. Years later, with a deep stomach wound from the first attempt to murder him, his oxlike constitution alone pulled him through the journey. Medicine in Pokrovskoye was no more than vodka for antiseptic, herbal teas for fevers, and slabs of raw meat to draw the infection from wounds.

The village was on a bank high above the Tura River. A landing stage of wooden poles and planks stuck out beyond the reeds for riverboats to Tyumen and Tobolsk, 120 miles to the north. Twice a month yellow and black prison barges with cages of iron mesh passed the village on their way to Tobolsk, a reminder of Siberia's use as a dumping ground for convicts and exiles. Cleared pasture, water meadows, and fields of black earth stretched back from the bank for two miles before running into marshes and forests of poplar, aspen, larch, and birch. The unpaved main street was a mile-long river of dirt without sidewalks or shade trees. Pigs routed along it. It was lined on both sides by cabins built of double planks against the cold, painted green and red, and caulked with oakum, behind stout limed fences. The roofs were shingled with bark. In spring and autumn the farm carts mired to their axles in mud. In summer they dragged clouds of dust and midges behind them. Crude sleds, frames of wooden poles lashed together with rope, were used in winter.

The only building of note was a stone and wooden church with a gilt onion dome. The *kabachok*, the village tavern, served rough Siberian vodka and beer; Rasputin's addiction to sweet wines came after he left the village and began to visit monasteries where wine and Madeira were drunk. A general store sold salted fish, farm tools, plows and harrows, lamps and oil. Horses were hitched to posts outside it. The barns and cattle sheds were in the village, and the countryside was empty.

Its monotony reminded Western travelers of "the sadness of the sea," a waste across which dirt tracks wound like the wakes of ships. The earth was monochrome until, like sails looming out of a sea haze, a church pierced the gloom in whirls of color. Beside it the village was "like a hem of rubbish thrown about." Though native Siberians like Rasputin were lyrical about their land, even the most high-spirited of men from European Russia fell prey to melancholy there. "In the summer our lives were made wretched by midges," the revolutionary Leon Trotsky wrote of his exile. "They even bit to death a cow which had lost its way in the woods. . . . In the spring and autumn the village was buried in mud." In winter cockroaches "filled the cabin with their rustlings."

Cattle, corn, and cartage brought Pokrovskoye a modest prosperity. The region was known for its butter and wheat. Though Trakt 4 was deeply rutted in summer and humped with ice mounds in winter, its travelers brought in rubles. Villagers lodged them, and hired out horses and *telegas*, unsprung carts in which passengers lay on hay with their knees to their chins to protect their spines against the incessant jars and twists. A telega, the American journalist George Kennan wrote, "will simply jolt a man's soul out in less than twenty-four hours." Bargemen and boatmen worked the river after ice melt.

Efim Rasputin, Grischa's father, was a newcomer to the village. The villagers gave him the nickname Novykh, the "new one"; his son was sometimes to sign himself Grigory Novykh after he learned to write, or, more accurately, to scribble in a large and unformed hand. It was often said that the root of the name Rasputin was *raspoutstvo*, Russian for "debauchery," and that it was foisted on the family as an accurate slur. The Rasputins themselves said that it came from *raspoutye*, "crossroads," a more likely derivation since the name was uncommon but not unique. It was rumored that Efim had gotten drunk while working as a coachman at Saratov on the Volga, lost or sold his horses, and fled to Siberia.

The story was typical. Siberia was founded on runaways, religious dissenters, bankrupts, cutthroats, the swill of the frontier. Every few months convoys of convicts, gray columns with yellow diamonds sewn on their coats, shuffled in chains out of European Russia to cross the Ural Mountains west of Pokrovskoye. They were on their way to the huge holding prison in Tyumen, where they were crammed 160 to a cell to await transport to distant mines and logging camps. The air, Kennan found, was "laden with fever germs from unventilated hospital wards, fetid odors from diseased human lungs and unclean human bodies, and the stench arising from unemptied excrement buckets." A third of the fifteen thousand prisoners who arrived at Tyumen each year in Grischa's childhood did not survive to continue their journey; Siberians were aware of the lethal power of the distant tsar. Drivers like Efim, *yamshchiki*, were often ex-convicts and formed a distinct fraternity of chancers and smugglers. A group of Americans who crossed Siberia at this time employed six drivers, all of whom they found to be convicted murderers.

His fellow villagers knew Efim as a driver plying Trakt 4, with sidelines in farming and horse trading, and a drinker. In summer he wore a cotton blouse and coarse woolen trousers with sandals made of the plaited bark of lime trees. He added a sheepskin coat, an armiak cloth jacket, felt boots, and a fur cap above his basin haircut for winter. Grischa stayed faithful to peasant fashion in the days of his fame, though his boots were made of dressed leather and the empress embroidered his silken blouses.

Efim was comfortably off by village standards, rich by those of peasants in European Russia, whose crude, chimneyless huts were built of logs. His single-story cabin was double planked with four rooms, furnished with rough wooden benches. He had money enough to afford glass in the big windows, in place of the stretched animal bladders used by the poorest peasants. He had oil lamps, too, and not tallow candles, in front of the icons in the main room. Low barns ran around a muddy yard, pungent with animal and human dung heaps, where cattle and horses wintered. The family slept in their clothes on wooden shelves near a log-burning brick stove, with piles of bug-infested sheepskins for a mattress. A samovar simmered on the stove for tea; Grischa always thought coffee a sign of great wealth. He ate bread—white bread, he proudly recalled, rather than the brown bread suffered by peasants in European Russia—and fish and cabbage soup, from metal bowls. He chewed wild garlic against scurvy. Though the peasants shat in their yards, the village had a bathhouse where they sweated in a steam room and beat the dirt from their skin with birch twigs. Rasputin loved bathhouses, though he always retained a musty peasant odor that society ladies found "thrilling."

———

Grischa did not start talking until he was two and a half. Then the words tumbled out with vivid imagination. Recovering from a bout of fever, he told his mother that a "beautiful lady" had sat at his bedside to soothe him. He helped with the livestock, rounding up cattle and herding them in the yard. He learned to ride in the arched bareback Siberian style. He had no schooling.

He collected kindling in the forests and played hide-and-seek with his elder brother, Mischa. Siberian children played brodyagi and soldiers. *Brodyagi* were escaped convicts. Each summer several hundred went loose until they were betrayed by bounty hunters or gave themselves up at the onset of winter. October was the high point of the year. At the village fete the children danced to an accordion, the girls in scarves and best dresses, while their parents sat mellow with vodka. Peddlers in black frock coats and black waistcoats with glass buttons sold cheap colored prints of the tsar and famous generals and views of St. Petersburg. It was a rare reminder of the Russia west of the Urals.

When the Russians had first penetrated Siberia three centuries before, the Cossack brigand Yermak Timofeyovich defeated the Tartars not far from Pokrovskoye. The frontier had long since passed east, but the region was still called Zatatarskoe Beloto, the "marsh beyond the Tartars." It remained a place of superstition and legend, of miraculous icons and holy manifestations, where hunters flew through the air by telepathy. Spirits were said to live in the forests. *Leshii*, with bluish skin and goggle eyes, imitated birdsong, whistled and clapped, and protected convicts. The water spirit, *vodyanoi*, caused the Tura River to flood when it got drunk. In the cabins lurked the hairy *domovoi*, breaking windows or protecting the house according to its mood.

Little Grischa, his mother said, became so rapt in staring at the sky that at first she feared he was "not quite right in the head." Then, along with his imagination, he developed powers. He had a way with animals and became a horse whisperer. Efim Rasputin had a favorite story of how his son's gift first showed itself. Efim mentioned at the midday meal that a horse had gone lame and might have pulled a hamstring. Grischa got up from the table and went out to the barn. His father followed and saw him place his hand on the hamstring. Grischa stood in silence, eyes closed and head thrown back. When he was done he stepped back, patted the horse, and said: "You're all better." Efim led the horse out into the yard and walked it up and down. Its lameness had gone.

The boy became a sort of "spiritual veterinarian"—his daughter's phrase—to the livestock of Pokrovskoye. He talked to sick cattle and horses, whose joints were distended by the strain of hauling carts on potholed roads, and cured them with a few whispers and a comforting hand. He extended his healing from the beasts of the field to the villagers. He eased away bad backs and fevers. Word spread that he was gifted with precognition and clairvoyance. He discovered missing objects—a ring, a rake, a plow. A horse was stolen. A meeting was called to discuss the theft. Grischa pointed at one of the richest peasants and declared that he was the thief. The villagers followed the man home, found the horse in his yard, and, in the Siberian fashion, beat him half to death.

Sitting in the warm, while his mother baked bread in the big stove, Grischa often suddenly chirped out, "A stranger is coming." A traveler would be seen on the trakt within an hour. He also predicted deaths among the peasants, a less welcome gift that had his father muttering about the work of the *dyavol*, the devil.

This, at least, is what his daughter Maria wrote later. The provisional government inquiry found village witnesses to have a much less charitable view of her father. "They note that Rasputin's father drank vodka heavily," the investigator wrote. "As a boy Rasputin was always dirty and untidy so that boys of his age called him a 'snotter.' " It served her father's memory well, of course, for Maria to establish that his gifts were clear even in childhood. Some of her claims stretch belief to the limit; here they appear to sit oddly with those of his fellow villagers. The mature Rasputin, however, had the same genius as the child for creating apparently irreconcilable impressions; his character was magnetic, in the sense of polarity, repelling or attracting those who came within its field. There is no reason to disbelieve his daughter's family recollections of his early ability to soothe; no reason either to reject the villagers' account of a layabout in the making. Both traits run through his adult life.

———

When he was eight, Grischa lost his brother Mischa. The boys liked to swim in the river, whose waters, dark and rusty, were fed by bogs thick in iron salts. On airless August days they splashed in the shallows where the cattle drank. Picnickers took their spot one day, and the brothers went farther downstream. Mischa drifted out into the torpid current, dragging Grischa with him. A farmer pulled the boys out, but Mischa developed pneumonia. The Pokrovskoye midwife struggled to cope. Ten-year-old Mischa died.

Grischa became depressed, alternately moodily quiet and hyperactive. His mother found him difficult. "I never knew what to expect next," she told her granddaughter. The boy wandered among the forest larch and birch or made a pest of himself around the house. He had no friends to take his brother's place, and no stimulations to feed his imagination and intelligence. The outside world was guesswork. He had never seen an electric light, a steamboat, or a railroad train. He knew they existed—peddlers sold pictures of them—but none had yet reached Siberia. It was so vast, stretching north to the Arctic, south toward China, east for 4,000 miles to the Pacific, that Siberians lived on the outer margin of Russian consciousness. Tyumen was 2,543 versts from St. Petersburg—some 1,670 miles away—and, until the Trans-Siberian Railroad reached it in 1885, the journey took six weeks.

Grischa's horizons were bound by the dull rhythms of the village and fieldwork. In the long winter the fields were frozen. Arctic air advanced from the Kara Sea in a crystal mantle, and dawn and sunset were chilled into bands of salmon pink and violet blue. By day the sun melted the snow on the cabin roofs though the air temperature remained below freezing. At night it could plunge to fifty below. When southwesterlies blew, violent storms dumped thick snow on Pokrovskoye, the falling flakes mingling with those blown from the ground in a maelstrom that blinded those foolhardy enough to venture outdoors. In spring the fields were plowed and planted, and firewood cut. In August, with temperatures sometimes climbing into the nineties, the men cut the wheat and rye with scythes in another brief burst of labor while the women followed with sickles to reap what was left. The grain was threshed with flails, iron chains attached to wooden handles. In the fall a string of cyclones brought heavy showers, and the village was mud bound. The cycle of drudgery then repeated itself.

Russia was alive elsewhere. It was throwing up great writers, musicians, and new industrialists; its revolutionaries were famed through Europe for their intensity and love of violence. The empire was still racing east at a thousand miles a decade, engorging the khanates of Central Asia. In Pokrovskoye, eternal silence was master. St. Petersburg was the dark side of the moon. Politics were irrelevant to the peasants; no politician came calling, they had no vote. Newspapers meant nothing to men who could not read. As to ideas, no university existed in Siberia's 4.6 million square miles and none would until 1888. Grischa was listless and bored.

Monotony and vast and freezing distance often conspired to make Siberians religious. The beauty of the Orthodox service, the hypnotic chants, the ecstatic Easter "Christ Is Risen! Christ Is Risen!" fell on arid minds like mystic liquid. Wandering pilgrims in rags, *stranniky*, passed through Pokrovskoye on the trakt, tapping on doors and asking for a night's lodgings as they made their way east to the Abalatsky Monastery or northwest to pray before the relics at Verkhoturye. Icons, the face of the Virgin or a saint blazing from a background of somber oils, were paraded at every event; they followed the dead to the cemetery and newlyweds to the marriage bed. On Sundays incense and the priest's rich vestments replaced shabby work clothes and the interminable odor of farm animals. Singing and ceremony—Grischa always loved to sing—were bridges to the unimaginable outside world, which he craved. Candles caught the gleam of the icons and the bright kerchiefs of the women. Illiterate, bookless minds filled with stories of damnation and salvation.

At a service when Grischa was fourteen, the village priest, Otyets Pavel, read a passage from the Bible that impressed him. "The Kingdom of God cometh not with observation," the priest said. "Neither say they, Lo here! or Lo there! for behold the Kingdom of God is within you." His parents walked home for their Sunday meal. Grischa wandered off to the woods and experienced ecstasy under a big larch tree.

He lay on the ground, lost in meditation. A scintilla, a spark, grew in his mind, "nearer and nearer, brightening as it came, until what had been a soft golden glow suddenly erupted in a blinding white flash." The boy prayed, tears wetting his face. Then he raced home to tell his mother: "I can only say . . . I almost saw God." She was frightened, fearing blasphemy. "Only great saints can see God," she told him. "Whatever you do, don't tell your father. He'd certainly punish you." Years later Rasputin took his own children back to the larch tree. He told them how he had realized, on that Sunday, that "God is here, inside, this moment—forever."

Efim Rasputin worried about his son. Grischa did little work on the farm, although he was a strong, sturdy lad whose voice acquired the low tones and unstressed, booming vowels of the Siberian accent as it broke. He mooned about, without friends. Sometimes he got into fights with other boys who called him *malodushni*. It is curious that they used that word, "coward," for Rasputin showed great nerve in adult life. He was shrewd, though, and skilled at tactical withdrawals; perhaps the boys used it in that sense. He did not feel lonely. "God is my companion," he told his mother of his religious experience.

———

As an adult Rasputin often referred to his childhood flashes of insight into the divine. His religious intensity was natural in a country shot through with Christian fervor, and Siberia gave those whom it did not cow a matching wildness and grandeur of spirit. His sense of the presence of God was unforced and simple, a part of his belief in himself, as strong a streak in him as his sexuality. The evidence of his first sexual experience comes secondhand, from his daughter. She maintained that it was a pseudo-rape at the hands of a general's wife, and that it affected him deeply. The investigator noted nothing more than a healthy interest in village girls. The alleged incident took place when Grischa drove a grain cart to Tyumen.

The woman in question was Madame Irina Kubasova, the striking daughter of an artillery colonel, who had married her off at eighteen to his commanding officer to settle his gambling debts. General Kubasov was forty years older than his bride. He resigned his commission, quit his regimental quarters in Moscow, and retired to his estate outside Tyumen to enjoy her.

He saw a young blonde in a carriage in the main street, and followed her in his cart until she disappeared through the crested iron gates of the Kubasov estate. He sat on a wall for some time before driving home. He saw the carriage outside a fashionable clothes shop on his next visit. A lady's maid crossed the street. "My mistress bids me give you this message," she said. "In one hour, you are to take a seat upon a certain wall. I think you know the place."

Grischa drove out of town and sat on the wall, swinging his feet, gazing across lawns that were as large as the Rasputin farm. A pond lay beneath a slope, crossed by a rustic footbridge that led to a summerhouse. Irina Kubasova arrived in a "cascade of golden curls . . . a dress of some pale green material, tight in the bodice to show off her sensual breasts." Maria Rasputin described how her father was led to the summerhouse, where, reaching down the front of his trousers, Kubasova "grasped him gently, releasing him for a moment, then touching him again." She went into the next room, telling Grischa to come to her quickly.

Stripping off his clothes, Grischa followed her into a darkened chamber, where she lay, still fully clothed, on a sofa. She raised a shapely arm and said, "*Teper!*" "Now!" At this, four maidservants burst into the room from behind the heavy curtains. A fifth girl stepped forward with a bucket of cold water and threw it over him. The maids, urged on by their mistress, were on him "like a pack of she-wolves tearing at a stray lamb, teasing and tormenting him, touching his outthrust organ in those lascivious ways that only as a group would they have dared employ." It was a divertissement, a cruel game played by a bored young woman. Once they had finished with him, the girls carried Grischa out and threw him on the ground in front of the summerhouse. One of them, Dunia Bekyeshova, took pity on him and left him his clothes.

Humiliated, "his whole being one amorphous mass of unadulterated misery," the sixteen-year-old returned to Pokrovskoye in his cart, shivering in a blanket on the rough wooden seat. The episode left him with nightmares, in which the women became she-wolves who tore at his flesh, urged on by Irina Kubasova. His mother knew something was wrong; but he was too ashamed to tell anyone, sitting hangdog in the barn with only his favorite horse, Ivan, for company.

—

The incident did no long-term harm to Rasputin's remarkable sexual self-confidence; he enjoyed a natural and easygoing affinity with women until his death. Shortly after the incident a young village widow, Natalya Petrovna Stepanova, took a wanderer into her cabin and her bed. She was spotted by the local gossip, the *splyenitza*, who alerted the village. Efim Rasputin was one of those who caught her in flagrante and hauled her off to Otyets Pavel. The priest proclaimed the punishment for a woman caught in sin; she was to be stripped naked and whipped out of the village.

Her dress was ripped off—Maria says by Efim Akovlevich, Rasputin's father—her hair was shorn with shears, and she was tied to the saddle of a horse. The horse dragged her between a double line of vengeful villagers, eyes popping with lust, lips drawn back in snarls, who beat her with sticks and leather straps. Years later, Rasputin told his daughter, he was "still horrified at the memory." Bleeding and unconscious, Natalya Petrovna was pulled out of the village. Grischa found her in a field. He comforted her. As he touched each of the wounds in turn, the bleeding stopped. The bruises disappeared. He washed the mud from her and built her a shelter. Later he brought her an old dress from home, a pair of shoes, a kerchief to hide her head, and a can of borscht.

The following day Grischa attended a village wedding. Two boys gave him vodka; unused to the fiery spirit, he almost choked on it. The lads talked about finding a woman. Grischa, drunk, said he knew where one was. He led them to Natalya Petrovna's refuge. Their noisy arrival terrified her. Grischa insisted they leave her in peace, before rushing off awash with tears and guilt.

Slowly his mysticism returned. After his farm work he went to the forest to pray. "I have been dreaming about God since early childhood," he recollected to a journalist from the paper *Novoye Vremya* two decades later. "When I was fifteen, in my village, in the summertime, when the sun shone warmly and the birds sang heavenly songs, I walked along the path and did not dare go along the middle of it. I was dreaming about God. My soul was longing to fly to afar. I often wept and did not know where the tears came from and what they were for."

His youth passed in "some kind of meditation, a kind of dream." He believed in the good, he said, and he was loved in the village. He had long talks with his comrades "about God, about nature, about birds." He often sat with the old men of the village, listening to their stories about the lives of the saints, about selflessness and great deeds, about the tsars and Ivan the Terrible . . .

When he was eighteen the brilliant heavenly light returned to him. He was plowing when it exploded from the furrows, becoming a vision of the Virgin, surrounded by throbbing light, her hand above his head in a gesture of blessing. Trembling, he led the plow horse back to the barn. It was, he told his daughter, his "awakening."

———

Moments of prayer and generosity ran side by side with epic debauchery in Rasputin's later life. It is no surprise that the introverted, sensitive boy and the forest mysticism he described to *Novoye Vremya* were strangers to the investigator. His witnesses remembered a lout, a hardnose with a swagger. "Rasputin started to drink vodka at fifteen, and after his marriage at twenty started to drink more," he reported. Villagers gave evidence that the "snotter" was also a thief.

At age nineteen he met a girl from another village to whom he was to remain faithful, in his own fashion, for the rest of his life. They met at a festival at the Abalatsky Monastery; they both loved to dance and sing. She was three years older, a pretty girl with dark eyes and blond hair, Praskovya Fedorovna Dubrovina. They married following a six-month courtship. The year is uncertain; the investigator did not give it, but it was probably 1889. She was a tolerant woman. Her new husband continued to spend his evenings in the *kabachok*, the tavern. Grischa remained a slob in village opinion, with his father's taste for knocking back cheap Siberian vodka from wax-topped bottles, and an eye for anything left lying around.

"He was known to the villagers as a man who liked drinking and leading a depraved life," wrote the obituarist Alexander Yablonsky. "His usual pastimes were drinking, debauchs, fights and vile abuse. . . . He used to go to Tyumen to get bread or hay and came back home without money, drunk, beaten, and often without horses." The tutor to the imperial family, Pierre Gilliard, made no bones about Rasputin's thieving. "Like everybody else, he looked around for things unguarded or forgotten and stole them," he wrote. "Soon he distinguished himself with boldness in these ventures while his dissipation gave him the reputation of a reckless reveler."

A witness, E. I. Kartavtsev, gave similar evidence. He was sixty-seven years old at the time of the investigation and a neighbor of the Rasputin family in Pokrovskoye. "I caught Grigory stealing my fence poles," he said. "He had cut them up and put them in his cart and was about to drive off when I caught him in the act. I demanded that Grigory take them to the constable, and when he refused and made to strike me with an ax, I, in my turn, hit him with a perch so hard that blood ran out of his nose and his mouth in a stream and he fell to the ground unconscious. At first I thought I'd killed him. When he started to move I made him come to take him to the constable. Rasputin didn't feel like going, but I hit him several times with a fist in the face, after which he went to the constable voluntarily."

Soon after the theft of the poles, Kartavtsev said that a pair of his horses were stolen from his meadow. "On the night of the theft I guarded these horses myself," he told the investigator. "I saw that Rasputin approached them with his pals, Konstantin and Trofim, but I didn't think much of it until a few hours later I discovered the horses were not there. Right after that I went home to check whether Rasputin was in. He was there the following day, but his pals had gone."

Others characterized the teenage Rasputin "as a sly, impudent man, of wild, loose, and effusive nature." When drunk he showed off by harnessing his father's horses and galloping them around the yard. He "used foul language in front of not only strangers but his parents as well." It was a habit he kept; he used drunken oaths to shock people he wished to unsettle, and admitted as much to *Novoye Vremya*. "When life touched me," Rasputin told the newspaper, "I used to hide somewhere in a corner and pray secretly. I was unsatisfied, couldn't find an answer to many things. And I was sad and I took to drinking."

After the thefts of the poles and the Kartavtsev horses, the villagers met to discuss exiling Rasputin and his comrades to eastern Siberia. Konstantin and Trofim were expelled from the community for horse stealing. Rasputin survived, but he faced charges of stealing the poles in the local court. He was also accused of stealing a consignment of furs that went missing as he was driving them by cart to Tyumen; he counterclaimed that he had been attacked by robbers. He abruptly left the village for Verkhoturye Monastery, more than 250 miles to the northwest, a place famous for its relics of St. Simeon the Just. The visit was decisive; all witnesses say that he was profoundly changed on his return. They do not agree on why he went. "Soon God brought me to reason," he said himself. "I gave up drinking, I followed another path."

Rasputin always denied being a thief. Slyly, he told his daughter that, since he was convinced that other people shared his second sight, and so could track down any stolen object, he could never bring himself to steal. She believed his departure was the result of giving a ride to a young divinity student in his cart. He told the student of his mystic experiences. Deeply impressed, the student urged him to do God's bidding and go to the monastery to seek advice from the monks. In an agony of indecision, Rasputin knelt in front of the family icon in the early hours to pray for guidance. His wife found him. The young couple talked it over and decided that he should leave for the monastery.

Rasputin spun a similar story to the imperial family. He told them, the tutor Gilliard reported, that he was hired to drive a priest to the monastery. The priest found the lad to have an eager intelligence and natural gifts. He made Grischa confess to his sins and tried to make him devote his ill-used ardor to God. "These persuasions impressed Grigory so much that he was filled with the wish to abandon his dark and dissolute life," Gilliard wrote. "He stayed in the Verkhoturye Monastery for a long time." In the Yablonsky variation, Grischa was hired to drive to Tyumen by a young theological student, Miletiy Zaborovsky, who later distinguished himself as rector of the Tomsk seminary. As they drove, "Zaborovsky made a strong impression upon him and held this influence upon him for a long time." It was, Yablonsky says, this telega fare who inspired Rasputin to leave for the monastery.

The truth seems simpler. At the time, the investigator reported, Rasputin "said he had to do it instead of his father, who had made a vow to walk to this monastery on foot, but that was a pretense." Witnesses told him that Rasputin had stirred up so much trouble for himself that he thought it best to make himself scarce. Better a stint in a monastery than a criminal record.

CHAPTER 3

Monastery Man

The three months Rasputin spent at the monastery were a watershed. The investigator found that his time at Verkhoturye "ends the first, early, wild, and loose period of his life," after which "Rasputin was to become a different person for a long time." After he returned villagers saw a new quality coexisting with the lust and cunning. They found it difficult to define, but it was abnormal, remarkable. He had found his mission in life.

The monastery was a walled complex of white-painted chapels, cells, refectories, and domes in the eastern foothills of the Urals. It was one of the oldest in Siberia, for Verkhoturye had been the Russian gateway into Siberia three centuries before. Hermits lived in huts in the surrounding forests in simplicity and self-denial. They ate black bread and water, and slept on bare mud in celebration of poverty. These retreats were called *skites*, and their occupants, holy men with a special grace from God, were known as *staretsy*, "elders." They were often former strannik wanderers who settled in forest glades to meditate and pray. Pilgrims from across Russia visited them for advice and spiritual healing. Grand dukes and Guards officers, "plebeians and the most nobly born," sought out the starets Father Ambroise in the Optina Pustyn, a famous hermitage in Kaluga province, to confess to him their sins and sufferings and to listen to his advice and teaching; so did Fyodor Dostoyevsky and Leo Tolstoy.

A *starets*, Elder Zosima, was described by Dostoyevsky in his novel *The Brothers Karamazov* in terms similar to an Indian guru. "The elder takes your soul and your will into his soul and will," he wrote. "Having chosen an elder, you surrender your will and give it to him in complete obedience, with complete self-abnegation." The person who offered such obedience attained in return "a total freedom, that is, freedom from himself, and to avoid the lot of those who live without ever finding the self within themselves." The obligations to the elder were of a different order from the vows of obedience practiced in monasteries; the binder and the bound were indissolubly linked in perpetual confession.

Rasputin lodged in a stone-floored cell at Verkhoturye, sleeping on a narrow wooden cot with a thin mat on a base of woven cords. He made daily expeditions through thick woods to the skite of Makari, a renowned starets who had eased the souls of important men in his travels across Russia. Makari was a fifty-year old who had squandered an inheritance on drink, cards, and whores before being struck by a sudden aversion to pleasure. He wore penitential chains and kept a flock of raucous chickens, torturing himself with hunger before overcoming temptation and presenting the eggs to the monastery. Rasputin told him of his own lusts, his shame, the light he had seen in the Pokrovskoye Forest, and his fear that it was mere hallucination.

Ideas, half formed but vivid, tumbled from him. Makari found a troubled and powerful character at the onset of manhood; Rasputin listened, rapt, to his stories of St. Petersburg. He noted the starets's stock-in-trade, what his daughter called "that strange force of will . . . that almost magnetic glance," which he was to acquire so strongly himself. For his part Makari sensed the young peasant's spirituality and intensity. Like Zosima, who formed "close soul-attachments precisely to those who were more sinful," he listened to the peasant's confessions with sympathy. They prayed together, successful starets and acolyte. Makari told Rasputin that God was everywhere, not simply in holy places. "My son, I have seen that your vision was real," he assured Rasputin. "The Holy Mother did come to you, and you must follow her."

To be a starets was thought a noble calling, an expression of selflessness. To a sly man, and references to Rasputin's "foxiness" match even those to his eyes, it was a career, the most brilliant open to a peasant and the one most suited to Rasputin's temperament. A handful of his peasant contemporaries hauled themselves out of the ranks of the army to become generals; a few became writers and scholars; rather more succeeded in commerce. Rasputin was indisciplined, unbookish, and no tradesman. The church offered little to an ambitious and religious peasant with a wife. The married "white clergy" served as parish priests, confined to the villages; paid a pittance of sixty rubles a year, they extracted what more they could from baptisms, weddings, and funerals, and by saying prayers for the souls of the dead. They were distinguished from their parishioners only by their clerical habits and the length of their beards. The heights of the Orthodox hierarchy were reserved for the celibate and educated "black clergy."

No barriers, however, applied to staretsy. Dostoyevsky's Elder Zosima was a former army officer from a landowning family. Others were peasants, and some, the "holy fools," were half-wits. The requirements were self-confidence, insight into unhappy minds, and the ability to calm them; Rasputin possessed all of these. A good starets dressed himself up in philosophy, complex or homespun, but the fundamental skill was to seek out nervous and troubled people and lead them by the nose. Certainly effort and sacrifice were needed to acquire the carapace of a holy man. Rasputin's exceptional persistence and physical endurance were equal to the prologue as a pilgrim, roaming on foot from shrine to shrine. The eventual rewards were glittering: influence, fame, mastery, the temporal exploitation of spiritual gifts. Rasputin discovered his career.

—

After absorbing all he could from Makari, Rasputin returned to Pokrovskoye. The visit had changed him. "It left anguish in his soul," the investigator concluded, "in the form of extreme nervousness, constant restless, jerky movements, incoherent speech, the permanent interchange of extreme nervous agitation and subsequent depression." The lout had found God and turned manic depressive.

Sophisticated enemies were to recognize the tensions caused by extravagant gifts of insight and persuasion to a wayward mind. "His remarkable intelligence was in search of some unknown religious path," wrote the politician Mikhail Rodzianko. "It is clear that his soul lacked firm Christian principles, therefore in his outlook on life there were no corresponding moral virtues." He had qualities of perception and spirituality, Rodzianko conceded, but these were present in "a man entirely free from any morality, greedy for profit, brave to the point of impudence."

His fellow villagers had a plainer view. They thought Rasputin was crazed. "I went with my mother to Tyumen and on the way met Rasputin returning from Verkhoturye," the witness Podshivalov said. "He seemed to me to have become a madman. He was coming home then without his hat, with loose, flowing hair, and he sang something all the time and gesticulated." His neighbor Raspopov saw him praying in the village church. "Rasputin impressed me as a man not in his right mind," he recollected. "Standing in the church, he stared wildly and looked about him and very often began singing in a loud voice."

Rasputin was so unhinged, the obituarist Yablonsky said, that he would appear in church before the priest arrived, take his place in the choir, and strike his head on the floor until blood flowed. "He started to speak mysteriously, incoherently, laying claims to prophecy and foretelling," Yablonsky added. "When asked something, he would be silent for a long time as if thinking hard, and then, sort of half awake, utter a few mysterious desultory phrases."

That Rasputin became "a 'new' man" was beyond dispute; the investigator reported that he "gave up drinking, smoking, eating meat, he started to shun people, he prayed a lot, he learned to read church Slavonic." He stopped smoking and meat eating for good; drink was another matter. He committed parts of the Bible—phrases, verses, half chapters—to memory and mumbled them as he walked. He pored over the intricacies of the Orthodox liturgy. The villagers did not know why. Some thought that the beating he had taken from Kartavtsev was responsible. Kartavtsev himself claimed that his victim "became somewhat strange, even doltish." They did not yet suspect that the "snotter" was a guru in the making, an apprentice starets.

———

Within a month of his return to the village, Rasputin set out on new pilgrimages. It was a rite of passage for a starets to undergo hardship and self-denial as proof of spirituality. A classic route involved isolation in a forest skite or a cell in a hermitage; though he was often misdescribed as one, Rasputin was not a monk, and he was far from solitary. He was bursting with curiosity about people and places. The pilgrim trail was the natural place for him to win his holy spurs. "During a number of years Rasputin visited scores of cloisters in Siberia and Russia," the investigator noted. "From his journeys he sometimes returned with two or three women wanderers clothed in monastic garments."

He became a strannik wanderer, a raw-boned young man, his face pale and intense, with a nose that seemed slapped on with a trowel. His farmboy wrists were thick, his fingers slim and long, playing constantly with his beard. He wore a sheepskin coat, boots, and a peasant cap, and carried a backpack with a spare blouse and bark sandals, a cross and Bible, water bottle, knife, icon, and an emergency loaf of bread. His feet were bound to the calf with strips of cloth, and he muttered, "*Kyrie eleison, Kyrie eleison*," "Lord have mercy, Lord have mercy," to their rhythm as he walked.

A ragged army of similar believers and mystics traversed the empire, bowed with fatigue, plodding with staffs in their hands. Some went barefoot in winter with chains on their legs, rejoicing in the trail of blood they left on the snow. They worried the police. The Okhrana chief Vassilyev thought they represented the "out-and-out anarchist element among Russian peasants"; the strannik, he said, "possesses no ID papers or else false ones, he conceals his real name with the utmost persistence, and thus succeeds in avoiding all social obligations." They survived thanks to sympathizers in the villages, who "supplied them secretly with food and lodging in dark cellars," asking in return that they light candles for them in some distant holy place, or bring holy water the next time they called.

Passing through these hidden rooms, the wanderers became *podpolniky*, "underground men," free from official identity and earthly restraint. It was

Vassilyev's duty to suppress them, in the interest of public order, but he admitted that "in practice this was uncommonly difficult." Ordinary folk admired their fervor and endurance. Russians had a special feeling for the Sermon on the Mount—"Blessed are the meek, for they shall inherit the earth"—and pitied those in need. They remembered the robbers next to the crucified Christ and thought them *neshastnye*, "unfortunates." It was an honor to give a strannik food and shelter.

Rasputin spoke later of his wandering years to his daughter and to a monk, Iliodor, who took verbatim notes of his conversations. In them the pilgrim talked of the hope of "finding the road to salvation" that drove him to abandon his happy existence in Pokrovskoye, where, he said, "I loved the world and everything in it. . . . I drove, I fished, I plowed, and my life was pretty easy for a peasant." He walked up to thirty miles a day, often along riverbanks, where he felt close to nature and to a Savior who had walked on water. He was often hungry and did not change his underclothing, or touch his flesh with his hands, for six months at a time. "I did this for the sake of experience and trial," he said.

Storms, wind, and rain passed over him. He fasted on hot days and worked with peasants in the fields to pay for food, at times rushing into the bushes to pray. He slept in doss-houses, cloisters, and peasant cabins, often walking for three days at a stretch, eating little. The trakts had post stations every twenty miles with fresh horses for richer travelers; there he bedded down in the stables. On lesser routes he slept in the rough between villages. Sometimes he wore penitential chains. "I found greatest comfort in daily readings from the Gospel," Iliodor quotes him, "though I did more thinking than reading." He was attacked more than once by wolves, but they did him no harm. His only dread was of the devil. "The evil one disturbed me, saying, 'You are exalted, you have no fears,' " he claimed.

He wandered as far as Mount Athos, two thousand miles from Pokrovskoye, descending the Volga and crossing the Caucasus Mountains and the Black Sea for the Greek peninsula, whose ancient monasteries clung to rocky sea cliffs amid stands of pine and oleander. It was the holiest fastness of the Orthodox Church. Since the eleventh century it had been the preserve of bearded men, for no man with a smooth face and no female of any sort was allowed entry. Even cows were excluded; the cattle grazing in the steep fields were all bulls. Seeing a young novice being ravaged by monks in the woods, Rasputin found "nothing but dirt, vermin, and moral filth," and turned back for Siberia.

Occasional sightings were reported back to Pokrovskoye. Rasputin's age made him stand out, for it was unusual for a strannik to be in his prime. For most, wanderings were an interlude between the end of their working lives and death. They sold their farm tools and livestock, distributed the money to their children, and set off for the holy places. They were working for their tickets to heaven; Rasputin was preparing for life. He was seen in a monastery in the Urals; he appeared among the fishermen of the upper Tura, helping them bring in their nets, teaching them psalms, and revealing that he was sent to them by God. Other accounts had him holding strange ceremonies with girls in forest deeps, weaving crosses from boughs, kissing the women, and then dancing and singing. The caresses and songs, he said, cheered the Lord.

He developed the inner hardness typical of the strannik. Okhrana agents found it impossible to interrogate men toughened by hunger and distance, and made impervious to temporal authority by their faith. A fresh complaint, more serious than theft, had been received by the police. A veil dancer with a travel-ing circus, Lisavera Nikolaievna Bul, claimed that Rasputin had attempted to murder her in September 1900. She told police in Tobolsk that she had seen him forcibly interfering with two young girls in a field. When she intervened to protect them, Rasputin attacked her, and she had to flee and hide. The police had their doubts—the alleged incident had taken place several hundred miles from Tobolsk and Bul claimed to have covered the distance to the provincial capital at impossible speed—and Rasputin breezily denied any knowledge of it.

His self-confidence, already remarkable, was further strengthened by the fund of stories he picked up on the road. He transfixed listeners with his talk of holy places, the silence of the Siberian forests, and the feral beauty of the open steppe; of boats laden with sheep and fruit on great rivers and Tartar town bazaars flashing with primal colors—all recounted with "that absent look in which seemed mirrored the lands he had visited and the strange adventures he had met."

Praskovya ran the farm while her husband was away. She did it well enough to afford two servants, Katya Ivanovna, a tough, leathery woman, and Dunia Bekyeshova, the pretty ladies' maid who had taken pity on poor Grischa and left him clothes during the summerhouse humiliation by her mistress. Maria Rasputin says that Dunia had fallen in love with her father and was happy sim-ply to be in his home. He roamed so widely that Praskovya took him for a stranger on his sudden reappearances. He entered the kitchen without knock-ing, smiling through the tangle of his beard. Then his wife would cry "Grischa!" and fall into his arms.

He returned often enough to father three children, his son, Dmitry, in 1897, and the girls, Maria and Varvara, in 1898 and 1900. While he was in the village he practiced the healing of souls. The men laughed at the idea of his becoming a starets. The women were less sure. They began calling on him for advice, bringing with them hysterical girls, lame widows, sick children. Sometimes they went with him to pray in the forests, where they made crosses in the trees. He calmed them, listened, inspired serenity. News spread that Pokrovskoye har-bored a healer who was a reader of thoughts and an interpreter of inner secrets.

He also dug out a pit—some called it a chapel—under the stables in one of his barns. He explained to Iliodor that he built it and hung it with candles and icons he had collected on his travels because it felt good to pray there, kneeling on the beaten earth. He cried with anguish and penitence, chanting, "Lord have mercy upon us," and when his mood changed wildly sang psalms and songs of jubilation. "Whenever I was free during the day I'd return there, and I found that my thoughts did not scatter in that narrow place," he told Iliodor. The nature of those thoughts, and of what took place in the chapel, perverted, perhaps non-Orthodox, became matters of mystery and concern that spread as far as the provincial capital, Tobolsk. Rasputin was gaining a reputation.

Meetings were held in the "chapel under the floor." They were attended by a small circle of admirers, including his brother-in-law Nikolai Raspopov and two sisters, Katya and Dunia Pechyorkins. Villagers told the investigator that their attempts to find out what was happening were "without success, for it was impossible for a stranger to get to these gatherings." Strange rumors were afloat. Before the meetings the Pechyorkins girls were said to wash Rasputin in the bathhouse, "drink the water in which he washed," then carry him to the dugout, where they "sing church verses and dance."

The journalist "E.S.," who interviewed villagers for the magazine *Svoboda* shortly after Rasputin's murder, wrote of sex orgies taking place under the barn. "As soon as the stars appear in the night sky," he was told, "Rasputin and his household and admirers bring logs into a pit and set a fire." A basin with incense and roots was placed in a tripod over the fire to give off a thick scent of lust. "Holding each other's hands," E.S. continued, "men and women go around the pit and sing, repeating one phrase: 'Our sin for the sake of repentance, O God!'" Sighs and moans were heard as they ran around the fire, faster and faster. "The fire dies out, and Rasputin's voice is heard in the darkness: 'Test your flesh.' Everybody throws himself on the ground. A melee takes place, and an unrestrained orgy starts, the so-called 'mutual sin.'"

Rasputin's healing sessions were already a challenge to the authority of Father Pyotr, the new village priest in Pokrovskoye. The priest seized on the subterranean chapel as evidence that his rival was a blasphemer. His insistence that Rasputin had created a cult of "sacrificial praying" persuaded the bishop of Tobolsk to launch an investigation. It was the first in a series of attempts to discover whether the young Rasputin had strayed into heresy during his wandering years.

———

The question became critical once Rasputin was close to the throne. Conventional Russia had a particular horror of cults. The reasons were partly moral—

official reports stressed that cults led to "monstrous scenes of sensuality"—and partly political. Since Peter the Great, reformed Orthodoxy had been the state religion of Russia. The tsar had spiritual as well as temporal authority, and to leave his church was tantamount to sedition.

Priests swore an oath of loyalty to the tsar. They were often police informers, obliged to override the secrecy of the confessional and report any member of their flock who expressed treasonable or rebellious views. This included membership in a cult, for which Rasputin was investigated. His later status as the "Friend" of the imperial family thus had a particular resonance; the head of the church was consorting with a suspected heretic.

Siberia was a dumping ground for sectarians and cultists, with whom young Rasputin could have come into contact. The most numerous were the Old Believers, *staroviery*. In the mid-seventeenth century Russian Orthodox liturgy had been reformed to bring it back in line with Greek Orthodoxy. The differences were arcane and largely numerical—the Russian cross had eight points to the Greek four; the Greeks extended three fingers to make the sign of the cross against the Russians' two but the leader of the staroviery, Arch priest Avvakum, accepted Siberian exile and death at the stake rather than submit to Greek practice.

Thousands followed him across the Urals. Many were burned in fires set by police agents or by themselves, for they believed that Moscow was the third and last Rome; the changes in Orthodox liturgy were evidence to them of the rule of the Antichrist and the beginning of the end of the world. The persecution continued as the investigation into Rasputin began. A bishop, Methodius, who had given the sacraments to an Old Believer, was transported to Siberia in irons and then, manacled to a horse, ordered to ride for seven hundred miles to his place of exile. He died, aged seventy-eight, on the track. Old Believers, however, were known and respected for their sobriety, discipline, hard work, and financial acumen.

Rasputin showed no signs of these qualities, and he made the sign of the cross with three fingers. There were other, more bizarre sects; they revealed the intensity of the Russian soul but, with a single exception, no obvious links to Rasputin. *Raskolniks* held the government and all its works to flow from the Antichrist. The first Russian census was held in 1898, while Rasputin was wandering. The people of one raskolnik village dug four tunnels when they heard of it. As the census takers approached, they held their own burial service and jumped singing into the tunnels, walling them up to die of suffocation. Strangling was the preserve of *dushtely*, who cut short the pain of the terminally ill by choking them from "motives of human pity and retrospective pity for Christ and His Calvary." In another extreme of sacrifice, a peasant, transported to Siberia for slaying his wife and children under the inspiration of Abraham's near-slaying of Isaac, nailed his feet and left hand to a cross before driving his right hand back onto a nail placed in the crosspiece. He was found under a crown of thorns, declaring that he was dying for the sins of the world.

Communities of Siberian *skoptsy*, "eunuchs," believed that sexual abstinence was a prerequisite for entry into Paradise. Their biblical reference was Matthew 19:12: "For there are some eunuchs, which were so born from their mother's womb; and there are some eunuchs, which were made eunuchs of men; and there be eunuchs, which have made themselves eunuchs for the kingdom of heaven's sake," Matthew quoted Jesus. "He that is able to receive it, let him receive it." The skoptsy held that the first apostles were castrates who had undergone baptism by fire. They cut off their testicles to achieve a similar state of grace, destroying the infected tissue in the wound with a branding iron. Some strove for perfect purity by having the penis itself hacked off. Skoptsy were prosperous and law-abiding, but a visitor was unnerved by their high-pitched voices, "womenlike hips," and beardless faces.

Dyrniky, "holers," prayed to the sky through holes in the roofs of their cabins. *Kamenshchiky* defied the sins of the world in remote mountain fastnesses. *Bezpopovty* thought that the world would soon end, so corrupted was it by the priesthood. They knelt for hours, their mouths opened to the rainy sky to receive drops of blessing they believed were distilled in heaven. Worshipers of the Holy Ghost breathed deeply as they prayed, hoping to inhale the third person of the Trinity. The famous portrait painter Borovikovsky collapsed through breathing too intensely during one of these prayer sessions. Members of the sect claimed that he had died of a surfeit of the Holy Ghost. Communities of *dukhobory*, "spirit warriors" known as Siberian Quakers, were pacifists who stripped naked when Cossack recruiting sergeants came calling.

—

Rasputin was no pacifist, castrate, or priest hater. Elements in his life, however—lust, power over women, the chapel-pit—provided ready ammunition for those wishing to link him with the cult that provided the most vicarious thrill of disapproval, the *khlysty*. The word, meaning "whips," repulsed and thrilled respectable Russia. Khlysty existed in small groups called arks, each of which was led by a "pilot." They drew their name from the birch rods they used to flagellate each other to reach ecstasy. Their number was officially put at 120,000; the cult was illegal, and this figure, and much of the supposition about them, was guesswork.

The cult had strong Siberian roots, running back to the seventeenth century. It was founded by an army deserter, Danilo Filipov, who denied that a barrier existed between the human and the divine. He claimed to be a living God and declared his follower Ivan Suslov to be his Christ. Filipov was exiled to

Siberia. Suslov was crucified on the Kremlin wall in Moscow. In khlyst legend he rose from the dead and was again tortured, flayed, and crucified; the shroud in which the body was wrapped turned into a second skin, and he rose again from the dead before ascending to heaven in 1718 at the age of one hundred.

In its early stages self-denial was central to khlysty. Filipov laid down twelve commandments. His followers were forbidden to drink alcohol, to swear, or to marry; if already married they had to abandon their wives and call their children "sins." They could then take "spiritual wives," but no sex was permitted. If a man could be divine, however, as they believed, it followed that he was beyond sin. A cult leader named Radaev was the first to exploit this teaching by using his supposed divinity to pleasure himself. He told his disciples that chastity was no more than the sin of pride. He did not act of his own will, he said, but through the urgings of God. If he wished to have sex with a woman, she was obliged to consent because his demand expressed the will of God. The Radaev line was attractive to charismatic men who imposed themselves as "pilots" or "Christs" on obedient flocks. Arks were established, whose members were appointed Holy Mothers, apostles, angels, and prophetesses by their pilots.

Pilots admonished their followers to lead blameless, sex-free lives between rituals. These were held in forest clearings or secret dugouts beneath barns and cabins—hence the interest aroused by Rasputin's underground chapel. The rite began with singing and drumming in air heated by bonfires. Urged on by drumrolls, the members of the ark danced themselves into the state of *radulnlu*, "frenzy," necessary to ensure their possession by the Holy Spirit. As this was attained, with the help of birch-branch whips, they began to prophesy and to shout nonsense words in what they called "the language of Jerusalem." Possessed, they shook, stamped, and fell to the ground until—using sin to drive out sin—they began indiscriminately to fuck. This they called the love of Christ.

Khlysty were secretive, since conviction of being one of them brought a long prison term and an uncomradely flogging by a prison warder. Okhrana interrogations of cultists confirmed, however, that they believed that man could be reunited with God during his lifetime, and that Christ was constantly reincarnated to walk on earth in the form of a peasant. They insisted that sin was necessary for unity with God, for without sin there could be no repentance, and without repentance there could be no redemption. "This doubtful view of morals led them to all manner of extremely grave sexual excesses," the Okhrana's Vassilyev wrote, "which over and over again brought them into conflict with the authorities of both church and state."

Horrified churchmen were told by ex-khlysts of ceremonies where the bonfire became a pillar of flame that, surrounded by swallows, soared into the sky; where the pilot took women by falling on them "in the form of a sweet-smelling cloud," and where there was no sin. Others spoke of dancing around boiling cauldrons that gave off a golden steam. A pilot described how the devil had come to him each day in the guise of an angel, bringing books from heaven that revealed all the thoughts and sins of his novices. Armed with this insight, the pilot explained that he had easily convinced the novices of his saintliness and the need to obey his demands for sex.

The head of the tsar's secret service, Gen. Alexander Spiridovich, described how half-naked khlysts knelt in front of the pilot and the Blessed Mother to be whipped, before forming a moving circle and turning the rods on themselves while chanting:

> *I whip. I whip. I search for Christ.*
> *Come down to us, Christ, from the seventh heaven,*
> *Come with us, Christ, into the sacred circle,*
> *Come down to us,*
> *Holy Spirit of the Lord.*

The celebrants wore white or black robes of calico, "tunics of fervor" that commemorated the robe worn by Ivan Suslov during his crucifixion. They began their rites with chanting. First a man started to beat his feet in rhythm to the song; a woman joined him. As they became sexually aroused, the others waved their robed arms like strange white birds. After this came the "fervor of David," in which the chanting and the rhythmic shaking of the body became more urgent as the khlysts sensed the approach of the Holy Ghost. They began to whip each other, crying, "Mortify my flesh!" As they approached hysteria, the pilot took a woman, and "all surrendered to debauchery, without regard to age or parentage." Spiridovich, a sober and professional policeman, estimated that there were khlyst arks in at least thirty Russian provinces at the time of Rasputin's wanderings.

———

The only evidence that Rasputin fell in with khlysty during his roamings came from his daughter Maria. Lodging with a peasant family whose daughter was ill with fever, he soothed the child and was invited by the grateful parents to a ceremony they were holding that night in a barn. The father, a stocky man with a short, blond beard, was a khlyst pilot. He wore a black robe. A fire was lit, and the devotees danced around him in increasing frenzy.

Commanding them to love one another, the pilot dropped his robe. Rasputin, "not," his daughter said, "wishing to be conspicuous," also stripped naked. As a woman flung herself on the pilot, Rasputin was tugged to the ground by the pilot's wife. Women outnumbered men, so he had "to serve double, even triple duty" until the pilot, equally exhausted, donned his robe and announced the ceremony to be over. The congregation dressed and walked home with "an air of respectability." Rasputin left the family the next morning, kneeling to pray in a hidden spot for fear that the night's sex had offended God. "To his great joy," his daughter wrote, "he found that prayer came easily." Finding that meditation flowed so easily after a khlyst orgy, Rasputin concluded that the khlysts were "obviously on the right track."

Maria Rasputin, writing many years after her father's death, had a vested interest in supplying her audience with the erotic and the bizarre. Other of her claims—that her father took part in a black mass in which the Lord's Prayer was recited in reverse while wine was poured into the navel of a girl lying naked on an altar; that another khlyst pilot lectured her father on world religions, stressing the erotic nature of Hindu temple statuary and convincing him that early Christians believed in "love feasts"—seem fanciful.

It is possible, however, even likely that Rasputin came across khlysty in his time on the road; khlysts were numerous enough, and all Russia had heard of them. In his conversations with Iliodor, he admitted that his fellow stranniky had developed a lassitude toward evil, and that "only one in a hundred" of them followed in the true footsteps of Christ. "It is good to wander, but not for many years," he said. "I met pilgrims who wandered for a lifetime, and it happened that the enemy [the devil] had sown his heresies among the poor souls."

Certainly Rasputin shared the khlyst philosophy that sin is a necessary part of redemption. It provided a convenient justification for his lifestyle, and he was often recorded using it as an excuse for his excesses. The journalist from *Svoboda* quoted a remark Rasputin made as a young man that was classic to khlyst thinking: "I hold myself a higher being and one can be saved only through me," villagers in Pokrovskoye cited Rasputin as saying. "To achieve this, one ought to merge with me, body and soul. Everything that issues from me is a source of light, which absolves from sin." As an older man Rasputin told women that making love to him would purify them of sin; it was an explicit part of his seduction technique.

If he borrowed freely from the khlysty, however, no formal proof that Rasputin was a member of the cult was established. Father Beriozkin, the leader of the bishop of Tobolsk's investigating party, found no evidence to substantiate Father Pyotr's charges when he arrived in Pokrovskoye. Women who had taken part in prayer meetings in the underground chapel denied that any orgies had taken place. They said that Rasputin simply prayed, fasted, and "served God in the deepest contrition and submission." Police visited the cellar and found only icons and candles.

Rasputin became powerful enough to ensure that later investigations were short-lived. After his death the provisional government inquiry took a worldly view of his early escapades; it found that he suffered "terrible explosions of sensuality" but dismissed the cult accusation as unprovable. His conquests were ascribed to the easy virtue of Siberian women; Western travelers described how posses of them staggered about after village fetes with ribbons in their hair, blind drunk, setting straw bales alight and jumping over them, throwing snow at men and trying to drag them to the ground, "slipping over together shrieking on the ice, throwing up their legs, and revealing the most remarkable sights."

The bishop's men duly returned to Tobolsk, leaving Father Pyotr in angry silence and Rasputin as a peasant worthy of ecclesiastical interrogation, set aside from the herd of Pokrovskoye. The suspicion, however, lingered, its destructive capacity intact.

CHAPTER 4

Breakthrough

Rasputin liked to leave Pokrovskoye in the late spring and return in the fall to spend the winter. It was a pattern that stayed with him for much of his life. Siberians love their winters for the clarity of the sky and the purity of the air. His traveling season also meant that he avoided the hard labor of plowing and harvesting; his father jeered that he "turned pilgrim out of laziness." His summer expedition of 1903 took him to the holy places of Kiev.

Half a million other pilgrims visited the old capital of Orthodoxy that year. They lodged in great communal dormitories, eating bread and drinking holy water, kissing the gold cross on the sarcophagus of St. Sergei, and trembling "as in fever" when they approached the catacombs of the Pecherskaya Monastery, which housed the remains of a hundred saints. "The silence seems to breathe," Rasputin recalled, "and the saints sleep simply without silver shrines in oak coffins. . . . They were martyred by barbarians, now we torture ourselves. . . . These sanctuaries were hewn from the rock by the hand of God." He was overcome by a sense of his own worthlessness, and his soul "filled with a great sadness" as he reflected on the vanity of life.

He was in a more boisterous mood when he met Aron Simanovich, a jeweler to whom he made these remarks, a compulsive gambler and influence peddler whose family had shops in the city. Simanovich had no interest in run-of-the-mill pilgrims, but he instantly recognized the young Siberian as an exceptional character. He found a "real Russian peasant," a robust fellow of medium height, with heavy, thick, chestnut hair that fell to his shoulders and gave him a monkish look. His beard was tangled, but he carried a comb to slick his oiled hair over a bump on his forehead. It was his eyes that set him apart from the pilgrim mass; they "riveted a man and at the same time caused an unpleasant feeling."

The future interested Rasputin very little, Simanovich thought; he was "altogether a careless man and lived only in the present." He did not like regular work because he was "a lazy man," but he was physically strong. He prayed "little and unwillingly" but talked incessantly about God. He enjoyed having long conversations on religion, and his lack of education did not prevent him from philosophizing. The spiritual life interested him greatly. "He differed from other doubtful personalities, clairvoyants, foretellers, and the like by an amazing willpower," Simanovich noticed. "His strong personality required the exposure of power. He liked to give orders and to be in command over people." This "yearning for power" was a key to his character and career. Rasputin needed to have influence over people; only the profession of starets offered it to him, a peasant. Simanovich later became his close confidant; eventually he became his biographer, writing with considerable insight into his character. He recognized that the young Rasputin was masterful and mentally tough, and he marked him down as a future contact for a third reason, equally important to a man dealing with the vanity and foibles of the rich: "he was a connoisseur of the human psyche."

On the long return to Siberia, Rasputin stopped at the midway point in Kazan. The ancient Bogoroditsky Convent in the city had been built to house the icon of the Black Virgin of Kazan, whose darkly sensual and majestic features were said to have been dug up from the earth to perform miracles for those who prayed before her. The icon was so precious that it had been moved first to Moscow and then to St. Petersburg, but a likeness remained in Kazan that reminded Rasputin of his vision in Pokrovskoye. The city itself had been the Tartar capital, a place of mosques, before it was sacked by Ivan the Terrible; Tartars in blue and silver coats and red leather slippers still haggled with Chinese and Turks in its markets. Rafts of timber floated down the mile-wide Volga, and barges filled with southern convicts were hauled upriver on their mournful passage to Siberia. Twenty-kopeck whores worked cheap bars built on stilts along the waterfront. Houses of lavender, crimson, and chocolate stood on high slopes above the river. They were decorated with belvederes, straggling annexes, balconies, pigeon houses, the courtyards overgrown with grass. Kazan was a city of ideas; Leo Tolstoy and Lenin had studied at its university, where Nikolai Lobachevski had originated the theory of non-Euclidian geometry.

Here Rasputin met society people for the first time. Yablonsky said that this happened after he fell in with the widow of a rich merchant, Madame Bashmakova, on his pilgrimage. "Bashmakova had just buried her husband and was in great sorrow," the obituarist wrote. "She took him to Kazan and introduced him to prominent merchants." She may have; she could also have been a creature of hearsay. Yablonsky is alone in citing her as the person who brought Rasputin out of peasant Russia and gave him his first scent of the world above it. The secret police, whose meticulous reports became the only reliable guide to a shapeless life, were not yet interested in him; he was another ragged figure with backpack and Bible to them. It is plausible that Bashmakova provided the breakthrough. Such women—"nervous, with wretched soul, with a grief they could not get rid of"—were to become a vital part of his circle. The church could not give them the religious consolation they craved, but Rasputin's skills as a starets "almost always brought elevation, interest, and, to a mournful soul, cheerfulness, hope, solace, and even joy."

He was able to exploit the high-strung, those with inner tensions that inhibited their powers of observation. His time with Makari in the forests of Verkhoturye was paying handsome dividends. His critics, such as Georgiy Chavelski, chaplain to the armed forces, allowed that "you couldn't not notice him." His personality and speech bore the imprint of "something mysterious," with piercing eyes in deep sockets and an unkempt beard. His movements remained jerky, and his speech, laced with references to God, was "abrupt, nebulous, and enigmatic." His opinions were bold, audacious, imperative; he expressed them with absolute conviction, regardless of the person he was talking to. "All that surprised and astounded some," said Chavelski, "and subjugated others."

Rasputin made a deep impression on Kazan's clerical elite. Father Michael, a teacher at the theological academy and a future bishop, introduced him to Andrey, the bishop of Kazan, and to Archimandrite Chrisanthos, a fashionable preacher and the head of the Orthodox mission to Korea. Rasputin was passing the point where he was seen as a simple pilgrim. Those who admired him now thought of him as a starets, exceptionally young, perhaps, but full-fledged; those who did not called him a *yurodivye*, a holy fool. The clerics found him natural and sincere. It was an important breakthrough, in terms of class and intellect; Andrey was born a prince, while Father Michael, a lean and nervous Jewish convert, was a leading church thinker.

Social superiors and the rich did not inhibit Rasputin; he retained the wanderer's indifference to authority. They were more easily malleable than the poor, particularly if they had a religious bent or a melancholy for him to work on. They had rarely—the women almost never—spoken at any length with a peasant, and never on a subject as intimate as the soul; factors and land agents dealt with the ex-serfs on country estates that their owners visited only for a few months in the summer. Yet nine out of ten Russians were peasants. The image of the devout muzhik was sentimental—even patriotic—bedrock to such people; unchallenging, inferior, a person they could patronize with a warm glow of charity. Rasputin, who never dressed or behaved as anything but a peasant, with a fierce pride in his origins, was the ideal made flesh. "In his natural coarseness they perceived only the simplicity of a man belonging to the lower classes," the imperial tutor Gilliard wrote. "They were enraptured with the 'naïveté' of this simple soul."

Rasputin talked to the clerics of his visions, the forces that drove him to seek salvation on the road, his struggle to attain God. The merchants' ladies found him exotic, animal. "A striking attitude, simple and imaginative speech; eyes that seemed to pierce you," one recollected. "A strong and powerful character; this, and the fact that the starets seemed to have the gift of hypnotizing those around him." Rasputin exercised the slick charisma of the khlyst pilot on them with effect. "I do not know of any instance of any lady actually giving herself to him or joining him in orgies," a horrified Kazan worthy wrote. "But I do know of a most respectable lady, a wife and mother, who, though greatly surprised, yielded to Rasputin's request that he share a bed with her. It is true that they were not alone and that matters went no further, but the fact remains that share his bed she did."

Temptation and denial; they were becoming Rasputin's stock-in-trade. In another incident he stressed temptation and salvation, a headier brew. "I was walking down the street and I witnessed the following picture," a respectable Kazan matron, the mother of twenty- and sixteen-year-old girls, wrote in a letter published in the magazine *Svoboda* after the murder. "Grigory Rasputin comes out of the bathhouse with my two daughters. One should be a mother to comprehend the horror and madness that seized me. I stopped and could not utter a word. I was just standing like this, silent. 'The real light of salvation has shone now'; those were the words of the starets." A bathhouse, salvation— conquest.

Provincial Russia was quiet and lethargic, overlaid with "the torpidity of peace, the calm on land which is found at sea." The governor's mansion and the Orthodox cathedral stood above Kazan, stolid and authoritarian, while the sluggish river ran at its foot. In its streets gendarmes saluted passing officials like metronomes; "half the population of Russia," a visiting Scotsman wrote, "seems made up of officials engaged in governing the other half." Rasputin broke its placid calm—a matron bedded, girls led astray, the acrid whiff of sex, and the man a peasant!—but the outrage did not reach Bishop Andrey. Rasputin's indiscretions were wild and unconcealed, but they did not pierce him in the eyes of those who believed in him; they smashed against the piety of his exterior. The bishop wrote to Archimandrite Feofan, inspector of the St. Petersburg theological academy, to tell him that he had met a man of God.

It was a gracious and trusting favor. Feofan was a thin little figure, tubercular, black hair sticking to a bony skull. But he was a man of influence, spiritual adviser and confessor to the empress, a saintly and trusting thinker with a penchant for yurodivy and peasant prophets. Andrey suggested that Rasputin visit the archimandrite in St. Petersburg. He supplied a letter of introduction.

———

Rasputin returned to Pokrovskoye from Kazan in the early fall. The evidence of E. A. Kazakova is the earliest in a number of statements recorded by the investigator on his relations with his women admirers. She confirmed the strange goings-on in the village bathhouse and the khlystlike pattern of his modus operandi. She first met him on September 19, 1903, the day her sister Raisa Alexandrovna was buried. (Did Yablonsky mistake Kazakova for Bashmakova, and dead sister for dead husband? Perhaps, though capitalizing on grief was a constant in Rasputin's career.)

She testified: "A man in peasant clothes came to my apartment and, after kissing a lay sister who was reading the psalm book, asked if he could see me. When I came out to the stranger, he introduced himself as Grigory Efimovich Rasputin. He kissed me and said that there was something he wanted to talk to me about. I was extremely surprised by such behavior and said it was the day of my sister's funeral and I had no time to talk. He left."

Madame Kazakova was intrigued enough to make inquiries about the pushy peasant's conduct in Pokrovskoye. "I had private information that Rasputin preached in the village," she continued. "He told young girls that wanderers visit holy places in the disguise of novices, and that they rape girls and forbid them to say anything about it. To avoid these temptations, according to Rasputin's teaching, they had to kiss him until it was disgusting to be kissed."

Rasputin went to see Madame Kazakova again in October. "I asked him first thing whether it was true what I had heard about him," she said. "At first he said it was the teaching of the devil. But then he started to concur with this teaching. He said that the person confessing of sins to him should not be ashamed as he takes on the sin of the person.

"To verify the thoroughness of confession, he invited young girls and women to go with him to the bathhouse. Rasputin said that by kissing women and girls, he strengthened them against passion, while he himself looked on all people as his relatives."

———

In December, Rasputin prepared to take up Bishop Andrey's introduction and make a preliminary reconnaissance of the capital. All Russians who felt their imagination mired in the darkness of the provinces strove to visit the city. It was the symbol of success, vibrant with riches, floating on the waters of the Neva "like a bark overladen with precious goods." Country folk turned their steps to it by instinct. "It is as if Petersburg all by itself, with its name, its streets, its fog, rain, and snow, could resolve something or shed light on something," a provincial wrote. They swept into it on a huge wave, more than a thousand a week, most to become factory drudges, sleeping under rags on wooden shelves, a handful to succeed beyond their wildest hopes.

"He did not come to St. Petersburg by railway," Aron Simanovich said, "but on foot, and barefoot." It is a pretty legend, but no more. By 1903 the Trans-Siberian Railroad linked Tyumen with Moscow, where travelers transferred to the St. Petersburg line. Regular steamers sailed from Pokrovskoye to Tyumen, and the journey time from the village to the capital was cut from several weeks to four days.

The Trans-Siberian was cheap, fifteen rubles, or about $7.50, for a thousand miles. Immigrants attracted by grants of 140 acres of free land were pouring into Siberia at a rate of half a million a year. The railroad laid on seatless boxcars for them, "stables on wheels," Bassett Digby of the Philadelphia *Public Ledger* reported, packed with bearded ruffians with "flat, animal faces and wild, bloodshot eyes, one's conception of a shipwrecked crew after ten years on a desert island." On outward journeys from Moscow, the first car behind the locomotive had armed Cossacks at each end and heavily barred windows through which manacled hands stretched out; it was the arrestante wagon, transporting convicts and politicals to Siberian exile. The degree of degradation in fifth class shocked Digby, but Rasputin was inured to squalor, and the ticket was within his meager pocket.

He had an open and imaginative mind. He was fascinated by new inventions. He became a heavy user of automobiles, the telephone, and the telegraph, and bought himself a gramophone. Once he could afford it he traveled first class on trains, seducing women in sleeping compartments.

CHAPTER 5

Peter

Rasputin came to St. Petersburg like a projectile from the medieval past, tattered, black, muttering. The signs of his years on the road were unmistakable. He wore a cheap gray coat, with beggars' pockets that bulged as if full of food. His trousers were threadbare; the seat "flapped like a torn old hammock," the monk Iliodor wrote. They hung over peasant boots that were blackened with tar; it became part of his seduction technique to leave traces of tar on the skirts of fashionable ladies whom he embraced, as a keepsake. Ragged, dirty hair, with a rough middle parting like a tavern waiter's, ran into a tangled beard that looked like black sheepskin pasted onto his pale face. His lips were blue and sensual; above them his mustaches protruded "like two worn-out brushes." His eyes were steel gray, deep set under bushy eyebrows, sinking into pinpoints when he was angry. His fingernails were filthy and turned in; his hands were pockmarked. His body gave off "an indeterminate disagreeable smell."

Peasants—most peasants—found St. Petersburg awesome, foreign, almost astral after the villages; it sucked them in as unskilled laborers and gave them the witless faces of zombies. "Apart from muscle power, nothing significant is required—neither literacy, skill, nor even quick-wittedness," an observer wrote. "To carry iron, to load and unload wagons, to fetch and carry all kinds of heavy weights, to dig and prop up pits, these are some of the tasks of the chernorobachi. But his chief task is to survive on seventy kopecks a day." They clung to country practices, messing together in factory barracks, chewing sunflower seeds, whose black husks lay on the sidewalks like a carpet of flies, ambling past the glittering shops and hotels on their hours off with doltish wonderment.

From the moment of one's arrival at the Nikolaevsky railroad station, in its heart, the city clearly demonstrated Peter the Great's purpose in building it. It concentrated the power of the giant land, in politics, commerce, the arts; but it was not Russian, or truly European. It was moored at a swampy extremity of the empire it ruled, on a level with Greenland and southern Alaska, damp with sea fog in winter and hazed with the smoke of burning forests when summer lightning struck. Everything in it breathed falsehood, the novelist Nikolai Gogol thought; "the foreigners who have grown fat there no longer look like foreigners, while the Russian inhabitants have become somehow foreign, and are no longer either one thing or another." It had a smell, insistent, penetrating—"of leather, of sheepskin coats, of cabbage soup and sunflower oil"—and its crowds, Tartars in brilliant embroidered jackets, portly, turbaned mullahs, Kalmyks in shaggy caps, coachmen in long, padded gowns of sapphire blue and low, squashed top hats, seemed "so strange and unknown" that foreign visitors asked themselves if this could still be Europe.

It was built above water, bisected by canals and the smooth, gunmetal waters of the Neva. Its great architects, Rastrelli, Rossi, were Italian; the water, and the painted baroque palaces and avenues they set in angular formal gardens, provided its nickname, the Venice of the North. Its streets were wide and perfectly straight. The Nevsky Prospect ran for two and a half miles, flanked with palaces, churches, and arcades, green, red, and ocher, from the monument to St. Alexander Nevsky to the high, gilded spire of the Admiralty. The Morskaya, with luxury shops and hotels, opened onto immense twin squares dominated by the marble and granite Cathedral of St. Isaac. The colonnade of the Kazan Cathedral was modeled on St. Peter's in Rome. Tsars prayed before its miraculous icon of the Virgin of Kazan in time of war.

The skyline was even and linear, pierced by domes and spires and the new chimneys of power plants and factories; the bright facades were colonnaded and balconied, the prodigious squares artfully positioned. It was unmistakably a city built to a prescription by autocrats. It was dynastic, too; statues of Romanovs glared blindly at its flat horizons. Peter the Great reared his horse above a rock in the Senate Square, sitting astride Russia, Pushkin thought, "on her haunches rearing." He was dressed as a Roman emperor—fittingly, for *tsar* was a corruption of the Latin *caesar*. An embankment of pink Finnish granite faced the Neva along its southern bank. Along it ran the physical evidence of Romanov power: the barracks of crack infantry regiments, the artillery school, the imperial stud, foreign embassies, courthouses. The brownish ocher of the Winter Palace and the Hermitage fronted the river for five hundred yards; here the family housed a magnificent collection of paintings and antiquities that spilled into basements. The windows of Nicholas II's study looked out over the cobbles of the palace square to an elegant crescent, a third of a mile long, which housed the general staff and the finance and foreign ministries.

On the northern shore, a golden spire soared as a landmark over the river and the Cathedral of St. Peter and St. Paul. Generations of Romanovs were buried there. Close by was the fortress, its thick walls surrounded by water, in whose cells, their windows covered with iron sheets, generations of their enemies had languished. The summer palaces, parks, and gardens of the Romanovs were spread on the coast and inland, at Peterhof, Gatchina, Tsarskoye Selo. The city was bright with the colors of Romanov soldiers: Knights Guards in silver breastplates; Horse Grenadiers, whose silk-covered helmets ended in strips of yellow and red that floated in the wind. Others reflected the vastness of the empire: the Heir Apparent's Cossacks, in light blue uniforms, descendants of freebooters who had fled from serfdom in old Muscovy to the free lands of the lower Don and Dnieper, specialists now in repression, charging strikers in their short-stirruped style and sabering Jews in pogroms; Caucasians in red cloaks; Mongol troopers, their faces broad and flat, "with little black eyes, distant from each other like [those of] the Chinese."

Aristocrats and diplomats met at the Imperial Yacht Club on the Morskaya; with 150 members, it was the most exclusive in the empire. Tennis players, and less distinguished sailors, used the River Yacht Club on the Dvortzovaya Naberezhnaya. Good food, political chat, and cards had been offered at the nearby English Club since 1770. Trotting races were held in Semyonovsky Square in fall and winter; the summer racecourse was on the Kolomyagskoye Chaussée. Skaters traced patterns in the Ice Palace of the Aquarium. Photography was popular; the imperial family were keen amateur photographers, and Rasputin loved to have his picture taken. Kodak had a busy shop at Bolshaya Konyushennaya. The winter circus and the all-year cirque moderne were often sold out. The five public theaters were thriving.

Many foreign businessmen were based in the city. Anglican, Lutheran, and Roman Catholic churches catered to them; there was a British-American Congregational chapel. Watkins's English bookshop on the Morskaya provided them with books, and they played golf on a nine-hole course. Russia's economy, the fastest growing of any major country, was fueled by investment from abroad. British and French investors held millions of rubles in "Russian Fives," high-yielding government bonds. Four out of five of the country's share transactions were handled in the stock exchange at the tip of Vasilevsky Island, next to an animal market where rare birds from Central Asia and dogs from the northern ice fields were sold. The city's banks controlled the mines and oil wells that Western engineers were sinking to slice out the mineral wealth of Siberia, the Don basin, and the hot shores of the Caspian.

The big hotels were European in standard but not in price. The Europe on the corner of Nevsky and Mikhailovskaya had rooms with baths from 7.5 rubles, about three dollars; dinner in its sumptuous rooms cost 3 rubles. The Cubat and the Bear were the grandest restaurants. The Donon was a favorite with a small garden for summer. Dinner cost 2.5 rubles, a dollar. Germans ate at Leinners on the Nevsky. Dominique's French restaurant was a haunt of officers—it had a billiard room. Filippov's on the Nevsky was the fashionable place for fast food, pies, and pastries. The rich traveled by *troika*, three-horse sleighs and carriages, glamorous and expensive, from 8 to 20 rubles by distance. *Izvoshchiks*, one-horse cabs that took two passengers, with hoods and rubber tires, cost 20 kopecks a quarter hour. Streetcars, electric, steam, and horse driven, were three kopecks a ride; city transportation suited the poor.

The poor were ill served in other respects. Students were a distinct group, a "university proletariat" with thin, pinched faces, in blue caps and shabby greatcoats, aged prematurely from hunger and exhaustion. Livelier souls formed circles to plot revolution and carry out assassinations; the Okhrana devoted much attention to spying on them. Vladimir Ilyich Lenin's elder brother had been hanged for planning to kill the tsar with a bomb concealed in a medical dictionary; three government ministers had been murdered by students since the turn of the century. In the slums of the Vyborg district, families of workers shared small rooms, *kamorky*, each marking out its space with blankets, sleeping on cots that touched each other. The streets were "ashy and indistinct," turning the passersby into shadows. The faces of the "gray human streams" who toiled in the industrial plants were "utterly smoke-sodden . . . with bluish veins." Single men lived on plank shelves that reached to the ceilings of dormitories, their diet black bread and cabbage soup with cucumber, fresh in summer, salted in winter.

A vigor strode the city; it was busy with the future, a world center of ballet, petroleum chemistry, opera, physiology. It had become a rage in the West, for its ballet, for its fabulous Fabergé jewelery, for its caviar and the vodka used in newfangled cocktails. Young Vaslav Nijinsky was starting his career at the imperial ballet school, from which Fokine and Pavlova had recently graduated; Diaghilev was editing *Mir Iskousstva, World of Art*. The great bass Fyodor Chaliapin, born in a slum, was bringing an actor's craft to opera for the first time. Prokofiev had just entered the conservatory, to be taught by Rimsky-Korsakov, as Rachmaninov had been before him; Gorky's play *The Lower Depths* was attracting the interest of Stanislavsky and his new "method" acting. Ivan Pavlov was about to win a Nobel Prize for his experiments on conditioned reflexes at the Institute of Experimental Medicine; Dmitri Mendeleyev, formulator of the periodic law, was still professor at the university's chemistry faculty.

It was, too, a nervous time, of extreme thoughts, fear, of the poet Valery Bryusov's Pale Horse, whose apocalyptic rider charged with a deadening shriek into the storm of cars, buses, whirling signs, cracking whips, and screaming newsboys. "Time quivers and the Look is Terror," Bryusov wrote. "In letters of fire the Horseman's scroll spells Death. The crowd tramples madly. Terror stays no one." Then the sudden dream of destruction passed; "only a woman from a whorehouse and an escaped madman still stretch their hands toward the vanished vision."

———

Rasputin took to it, without fuss. The city, restless and satiated, was ready for him. Its summer nights were "phosphorescent, crazy, voluptuous," the novelist Alexis Tolstoy wrote, and in the long winter darkness, green tables flashed with gold and couples embraced behind its windows as troikas galloped outside. A new fever had come with the boom, and the city craved sensation. The law courts were crowded "with hysterical women, listening eagerly to details of bloody and prurient crimes."

Hatred and contempt stalked the rich-poor divide. Nijinsky had come from a poor family. When he won five hundred rubles in one of the new gambling clubs, he picked up six pinched-faced whores on the Nevsky. He had often pitied them, and he wanted to celebrate his good fortune by buying them dinner. They snatched and wolfed the food, slobbering wine from the bottle. He was so disgusted that he could not eat; he flung his winnings at them and left the restaurant. "It is too terrible," he said. "I won't do it again."

War with Japan was close; the interior minister welcomed the prospect of a "small victorious war" to keep Russians' minds off revolution, and strikes crippled big engineering plants. The end of the world was approaching, the philosopher Vladimir Solovyev thought. He could smell it, like "some obvious but quite subtle scent—just as a traveler nearing the sea feels the sea breeze before he sees the sea." Dawn and sunset glowed with a wash of surreal rose as the sun caught a veil of ash thrown high in the atmosphere by a volcanic explosion in distant Martinique. Malice was on the streets. This caused in society, and particularly in high society, a "heightened nervous and sensual life, weird combinations of religiousness and sensuality." Spiritualism in hot rooms behind closed curtains vied with prayer in church. It was a time of séances, table rapping, tarot cards, of "neo-Christianity," where soul was united with flesh.

Credulity lurked below the surface cynicism. Holy fools, clairvoyants, and magicians were snapped up by hostesses to be put on display in their drawing rooms. A provincial simpleton, Mitya of Kozelsk, half deaf, half dumb, deformed and dwarfish, with two stumps for arms, entranced aristocrats and churchmen with his screechings and crippled walk. The monks of Optina Pustyn, Dostoyevsky's monastery, had thought him blessed; a sexton, Egorov, claimed that, by praying before an icon of St. Nicholas, he was able to detect the divine meaning behind Mitya's yelpings and howling. Egorov became his interpreter and brought him to the capital. A highborn girl from the Smolny Institute, the best school for young ladies in Russia, married the dwarf in a fit of religious exaltation.

It was to Rasputin's advantage to be crude, a "man of the people," a *varnak*. This was the slang for Siberian settlers and deportees, from the letters *V, R, N,* and *K* which were branded on the foreheads of convicts with irons, denoting "thief," "robber," and "punished by knout." The knout was a whip of raw elkhide that could flay a man's backbone open. Siberians were famously indifferent to it and the authority that wielded it. They treated high-ranking Russian officials as equals, to the latter's astonishment; they were untainted by the serfdom that, though it had been abolished shortly before Rasputin's birth, still cowed the peasants of European Russia.

The lands east of the Urals were too vast for the capital to comprehend. Russian exiles bound for Siberia were allowed to stop at the boundary post that marked the separation of Europe and Asia. Many put their lips to the western side of the cold brick pillar before dragging their fetters into Asia; one scratched the single word *Maria* on it, the American journalist George Kennan wrote, as if in crossing the Siberian line he was leaving "not only home and country, but life itself." When Siberians crossed the Urals in the opposite direction, they spoke of "going to Russia." No Russian ruler had ever visited their homeland. They were thought exotic, prey to strange cults and criminality, thrilling and dangerous—qualities for which the salons of St. Petersburg yearned. Rasputin stepped into a cultivated soil, the investigator thought, "and it dragged him in."

He roomed at a monastery lodging, gave his letter of introduction to Feofan, and delighted him. The frail little archimandrite talked to him in front of an audience of theological students on the problem of sin. Rasputin argued that sin was indispensable to God. "How is that possible," Feofan asked, "when our Savior and all the great saints of the Orthodox Church have denounced sin as the work of Satan?" Rasputin's reply was khlystlike and daring. "Certainly our Savior and the holy fathers have denounced sin, since it is the work of the Evil One," he said. "But how can you drive out evil except by sincere repentance? And how can you sincerely repent, if you have not sinned?"

He sensed a weakness in the archimandrite and allowed his voice to rise with anger. "Away with your Scriptures!" he shouted. "Truly, I warn you, stop this useless labor so that you can stand before the Lord. . . . Stop brooding over whence sin comes, on how many prayers a man must say a day, how long he must fast to escape from sin! Sin, if sin lurks in you. . . . Sin, then you will repent and drive evil from you. So long as you bear sin secretly within you, and fearfully hide it with fasting and prayer, so long you will remain a hypocrite and hateful to the Lord. The filth must be expelled, do you hear, little father?"

Feofan mumbled a defense, but Rasputin fixed "bright, glittering eyes" on him and beat him with words "like a shower of stones" until the archimandrite's feeble body began to tremble. When Rasputin had finished, Feofan bowed his birdlike scholar's head, and said simply: "Yes, little father, that is correct, you speak the truth." The unworldly cleric had heard, from gossip current among the capital's mystic dabblers, that Rasputin had predicted a recent three-month drought. The Siberian made so forceful an impression on him that he now attributed to him rainmaking powers. Grigory, he told his students, like the prophet Elijah, could shut the sky, creating a drought until "he commands the heavens to open" with teeming rainstorms. It was a sad fact in St. Petersburg, Prince Dzhevakov, a high synod official, wrote, that society and priests "preferred to take a sinner for a saint than run the risk of taking a saint for a sinner."

Feofan showed off his new discovery to Ioann of Kronstadt, a priest at the Andreevesky Cathedral on the fortress island of Kronstadt. This was the base of the Russian Baltic fleet, a ninety-minute steamer ride from the city. Ioann had a large following of "ecstatic pilgrims, hysterical women, and beggars living on church handouts." Confession in Russia is heard immediately before communion. The crowds waiting for communion were so great that, to break the logjam, Ioann ordered his followers to call out their sins in unison. The cathedral echoed to sobbing and the shouting of sins. He published mystical material in the popular magazines *Groza*, "Thunder," and *Mayak*, "Lighthouse." His disciples called him the "incarnation of God" and referred to his first follower, a mystic called Porfiriya Kiseleva, as "our Lady." Ioann was an extreme monarchist who had been summoned to pray at the deathbed of Tsar Alexander III a decade before. Although his intercession had failed, the red-bearded priest remained much in favor at court.

Rasputin went unannounced to a service at the cathedral, taking communion with beggars and pilgrims. His inner spirituality was so intense—or he made it seem so, for Rasputin was always master of his emotions—that he trembled and rocked on his feet. Ioann recognized this in the same terms as Makari. "My son, I can feel your presence in God's house," he told the rough Siberian. "The divine spark is within you." Rasputin told of his vision of the Virgin, and Ioann blessed him as a true starets.

Ioann passed Rasputin along the clerical network to dine with Bishop Hermogen of Saratov on December 16, 1903. The bishop was a big-shouldered ex-lawyer, a fierce and bushy reactionary with a taste for prosecuting any writer he found to have liberal tendencies. Also present was Hermogen's protégé Sergei Trufanov, a fiery preacher and Jew-baiter who had adopted the monastic name of Iliodor.

These were powerful potential allies. Hermogen's dislike of liberals made him popular at court. Iliodor was theatrical and puritanical. He attracted huge congregations for bitter, flowing sermons that stigmatized intellectuals as "all Jews" and praised the Russians as a God-bearing people who should shun the corrupt West. He dressed a big doll in a Jewish caftan and had it carried in procession to a bonfire for burning. He despised the nobility as a block between the peasants and their beloved ruler; this endeared him to the tsar and ordinary Russians alike. He was raising money to build a monastery called Mount Tabor at Tsaritsyn on the Volga; its focus was to be a great tower set on a hill built of excavated earth from which he would harangue the masses with his "sermons from the Mount." The violence of his attacks on governors and police chiefs outraged the government, which he said was in Satan's clutches, but he enjoyed the protection of the tsar.

Hermogen and Iliodor took the shabbiness and dirt that Rasputin exuded as signs of inner holiness. He made an excellent impression on them. He flattered them. As they began talking, Rasputin seized the bishop's hand and cried: "I like thee." Hermogen burst out laughing with delight that the peasant had used the familiar pronoun to a bishop; the new starets, simple and open, seemed the muzhik of a reactionary's dreams. Rasputin turned to Iliodor and patted him on the shoulder. "Here's a man who prays deeply," he said. "Oh, how deeply he prays!" They were photographed together, Hermogen sitting in good humor in the center, Rasputin gazing warily at the camera, neatly dressed in a black cassock but with peasant boots beneath the hem. Iliodor's face is taut, his lips pursed and his eyes cold and quizzing.

—

The three already looked a trio. Vassilyev, who was to watch Rasputin meeting new people when he became the secret police chief, admired his technique. Rasputin was boastful and offhand with those he thought unimportant, talking in riddles and leaving them bemused. But with those he thought of consequence, he was observant and attentive. He strained to follow the thread of a discussion, his head thrown back with concentration. He often made intelligent deductions and was careful never to put questions that would reveal his ignorance. He fitted in easily with extreme monarchists. In politics, Vassilyev said, he was "neither a Left nor a Right"; his instincts were sometimes liberal, sometimes authoritarian, but monarchy was always "a kind of religion" for him. He could not conceive of Russia without a tsar. His fundamental principle was "pacification of the enemies of the tsar." Political parties, policies, and ideology went "far beyond his horizon." His most acute sense was an intuition of who could secure his advancement and who was hostile.

The capital seethed with new ideas, with Reds, socialists, anarchists, Slavophils, Communists, nihilists. Sixteen thousand "politicals" had been sent into Siberian exile in 1901 alone. Leftists had no use for a peasant with an age-old line in mysticism. The establishment—corrupt, lethargic, fearful of its privileges, prey to intriguers—was more fertile ground. Reactionaries made no demands on Rasputin. He had only to express a fear of God and love of the tsar for them to embrace him as a "true Russian," untainted by city thought, a loyal blockhead of the type they earnestly prayed would save them if—when—"Red Peter" turned on them.

It was an easy role, and profitable. He was introduced to Countess Ignateva, a society hostess and dabbler in right-wing politics. She was married to Count Alexis Pavlovich Ignatev, a former interior minister and right-winger who figured prominently—soon enough, fatally—on the death lists of socialist assassination squads. An "unstable person of limited intelligence," she was well placed to help Rasputin infiltrate the capital. Her "black salon"—black for reaction, Black against Red—was a haven for the autocracy's nervous hirelings. Bankers and arms dealers intrigued to win contracts for the coming war against Japan. Officers and would-be ministers, egged on by fanatical priests, worked on half-baked plans to reconquer Constantinople for Orthodoxy. Occultists held séances in her drawing room and claimed that the freshly canonized St. Serafim of Saratov hovered above the table, ringed in fire, to proclaim that a great prophet had come among them. Her guests mixed autocratic politics and mysticism, a combination ideally suited for Rasputin.

He spoke in curt, almost incomprehensible phrases; he made no attempt to adapt his manners to polite society; he fascinated during his brief visit, especially the women. Some saw him after his return to Pokrovskoye. Madame Kazakova visited him again in the village in May 1904, with her daughters Ekaterina and Naria. His fame and his women admirers were growing. "I saw Rasputin surrounded by a number of important-looking ladies," she testified to the investigator. "They regarded him as a great righteous man. They cut his nails and sewed them up to remember him by. Rasputin shamelessly embraced and kissed these ladies while walking around." She grilled him on his morals. "He said there's nothing to be ashamed of," she concluded, "because all people are his kinsfolk."

The Pokrovskoye priest obtained letters written to him by wellborn admirers named Berlandskaya, Silvers, and Manchtet. Father Pyotr remained convinced that Rasputin was a secret khlyst, and he filed the letters carefully for a future ecclesiastical investigation. They show that Rasputin's intelligence readily detected the ladies' unhappiness; a few words, a comparison were enough to lift it. The case of Khionia Berlandskaya was typical of the "nervous women with wretched souls" who clung to him. Her husband had killed himself, and "she grieved, ascribing his suicide to the fact that he had learned about her infidelity to him." She was inconsolable until she met Rasputin. He told her simply that Christ himself could not prevent a disciple from hanging himself, she wrote, and her burden disappeared. Those who came to see Elder Zosima entered trembling and afraid, Dostoyevsky had written; but they "always came out radiant and joyous, and the blackest of faces turned to happy ones." Rasputin had acquired that skill, though his intimacy with his soul companions seemed to go further than the aged elder's. In their letters Berlandskaya and Manchtet wrote that acquaintance with him opened a new era for them and that they were the better for it. They also casually remarked what Rasputin had taught them. "In this respect they use one and the same phrase," the investigator said, "that Rasputin taught them 'holy sacraments.' "

The investigator admitted that one could only guess at the meaning of these "holy sacraments." Evidence from other witnesses provided the clue. A woman who had baked communion bread at the Pokrovskoye church testified that, as she was going down into the subterranean chapel with him, Rasputin had once come close to raping her. He assured her that it would not be sinful, for "the Holy Trinity was within him." Sex, it seemed, was an essential part of the holy sacraments.

—

Though he cannot have been aware of the significance of the first, two key events in the rise of Rasputin occurred later in 1904. On July 31 the empress gave birth to a son, Alexis, and—on some unrecorded date during his summer wandering—the Siberian met two sisters, grand duchesses, the daughters of the king of Montenegro. They were meddling, dubbed "the crows" by society for their striking black hair and raucous chattering. They dabbled in the supernatural and wizardry, and they had position.

Though their father was "widely renowned for his cupidity and lack of scruples," the sisters were ladies of the highest society and intimate with the tsar and empress. Militsa, known as Montenegrin Number One, was married to the tsar's cousin, the weak-chested Grand Duke Peter. Montenegrin Number Two, Anastasia, was married to Prince George Leuchtenberg, who returned to Biarritz shortly after the ceremony to resume a long-standing liaison with a courtesan. She was already on close terms with the tsar's tall and dashing soldier cousin Grand Duke Nicholas Nikolayevich, whom she later married after her divorce from the prince. Not having much in the way of husbands, the sisters devoted themselves to social climbing and the occult.

Militsa was the cleverer of the two, with a voguish interest in Oriental religions and mystic and ascetic literature. She learned Persian to be able to read Persian mystics in the original and had written a brief book, *Selected Quotations from the Holy Fathers*. The sisters were dark and stylish, with knowing, haughty eyes and an avaricious slant to the mouth. They nagged officials constantly for handouts; after her husband lost heavily in stock exchange gambling, Militsa damned the finance minister Sergei Witte for his "insolence" when he refused to repair the damage with funds from the State Bank. They were more skillful in building a friendship with the imperial couple. They treated Alexandra with exaggerated deference—"they bowed, they scraped"—and nursed her when she was ill with dysentery, doing "the work of chambermaids," emptying her chamber pot and changing her linen.

The sisters were infected, Witte wrote, by "that disease known by such names as spiritualism and occultism." Grand Duke Nicholas was equally inclined to mysticism. "One cannot call the grand duke mad," Witte said. "Neither can one call him normal." He once asked Witte whether he thought the tsar was human or divine. When Witte said human, the grand duke said that he "was neither, but something in between."

Bored, seeking new sensations, the sisters made an incognito pilgrimage to Kiev and stumbled across Rasputin. This, at least, is the claim of Aron Simanovich; others said that Feofan introduced the starets to the sisters, and the investigator accepted this version. Simanovich, however, insisted that he was in Kiev himself when the Montenegrins put up at the Mikhailovsky Monastery. One morning they glimpsed a simple wanderer chopping wood in the monastery backyard. It was Rasputin, earning his board and lodging. They fell into conversation with him; Rasputin told them of his adventures, the monks and monasteries he had visited. He said that he often preached at railroad stations and steamship landings. He was proud of his talents as a preacher and said that he could outargue educated theologians.

The sisters were intrigued; they invited him for tea. There was fire as well as persuasiveness in his stories, and "his gray, penetrating eyes were shining so suggestively that his listeners were seized by an admiration for him." When he found out the identities of his new acquaintances, he made special efforts to win their favor. He rarely boasted of his gifts, but Simanovich suggested that he made an exception for the sisters, telling them that he could cure all manner of diseases, and that he could foretell the future and divert impending disasters. He had "realized immediately," Simanovich wrote, "what brilliant opportunities were opening." He was on his best behavior, looking at the ladies intently and bowing deferentially to them.

The meetings continued; the sisters stood Rasputin to treats, pastries, and candies. He loved sugar in any form—sweet wine, cakes, buns; he sucked his tea through lumps of it. Simanovich noted of his mouth that "instead of teeth there showed some black rootlets." Far from repelling the Montenegrins, however, he swayed them into "a kind of mystic worship." Their hearts were "searching for a wonder worker," and they were convinced that one stood in front of them. He excited them. Forecasting the impact that Rasputin would exert "upon the nervous and mystically inclined tsar and tsarina," Militsa saw in him a new weapon for strengthening her hold on the imperial couple. She had plans to introduce him at court.

CHAPTER 6

Blood Royal

The Montenegrins' target was the empress. The sisters knew her and her weaknesses well. They had already introduced her to one holy man, Dr. Philippe, a Frenchman with striking similarities to Rasputin; he had started well—brilliantly—but had fallen from grace, and they were looking for a successor. The key to Alexandra was her grandmother, Queen Victoria. The English monarch was a dynastic breeding machine. Her nine children and thirty-five grandchildren included kings of England, the German kaiser, the queen of Spain, and Alexandra, empress of Russia. Victoria died three years before Rasputin first went to St. Petersburg, but she bequeathed him a legacy. She was a carrier of hemophilia.

The disease impairs blood clotting. Victims are unable to synthesize factor VIII, a protein that enables healthy blood to coagulate. The slightest wound can produce prolonged bleeding. Internal bleeding can begin for no apparent cause, with such violence and pain that joints become deformed. Hemophilia is almost invariably sex-linked, transmitted through the female line to male infants only. Victoria had passed the disease on to two of her five daughters, who in turn passed it to their sons. Care was taken to protect the victims from accidental knocks and falls—some were dressed in bizarre padded suits—but most were dead by age thirty.

Alexandra's parents were Prince Ludwig of Hesse, ruler of a grand duchy of wine valleys and forested hills on the banks of the Rhine, and Victoria's daughter Princess Alice. Mother and daughter had much in common, in events and in character. Both were married in mourning to foreigners. Both were ill at ease in their adopted countries and disliked at court; they remained deeply in love with their husbands, a rarity in arranged dynastic alliances; they suffered from the nervous debility and exhaustion then labeled neurasthenia. Each had a hemophiliac son.

Alice married her German prince when she was nineteen. The ceremony was overshadowed by the death of her father, Prince Albert, six months before. Queen Victoria wore black; "Alice's wedding," she wrote, "was more like a funeral." When Princess Alice arrived in Darmstadt, the little capital of Hesse, a relative wrote that she was thought "a foreigner, come from distant England." Her marriage was happy, though, and she had seven children. The sixth was born in June 1872, three years after Anna Egorovna had given birth to Grigory Rasputin in her Siberian cabin. The infant was christened Alix—" 'Alix' we gave for Alice as they murder my name here," her mother explained. She was not known as Alexandra until she left for Russia. Rasputin had no known godparents; Baby Alix had the future rulers of England and Russia, Edward VII and Alexander III, their wives, an English princess, and the duke of Cambridge.

Hemophilia was already known to be in the family. Alice's younger brother Leopold had developed telltale bruises and bleeding shortly after his birth, and constant hemorrhages had lamed him. Alice proved to be a carrier. Her son Friedrich Wilhelm, "Frittie," cut his ear when he was two and bled continuously. A year later he ran across his mother's room while she was practicing Chopin's Funeral March on the piano and tried to steady himself on the bow window. It was unlatched, and he fell two stories into the garden. He died of a brain hemorrhage that evening. On each anniversary of his death, Alix was taken to the crypt where he was buried.

Alix was happy as a small child—nicknamed Sunny, a "sweet, merry little person, always laughing and a dimple in one cheek"—until her mother died. The children developed diphtheria, which proved fatal for the youngest, four-year-old May. Alice embraced her surviving son, Ernie, when she broke the news to him; the British prime minister, Benjamin Disraeli, called it "the kiss of death," for she caught the disease. Exhausted and depressed from childbearing, she succumbed to it. At six Alix was motherless; a brother and sister had also gone. The Darmstadt palace was dark; her mother's room was left as it had been when she was alive, her bed draped with black crepe. Little Sunny became moody and listless. "Poor old Grandmamma will try to be a mother to you," Victoria wrote to her. Alix spent much of the year in England with her, in castles still in mourning for her grandfather, whose bed was turned down each night and whose chamber pot was scrubbed each morning, as if he had used it.

While young Rasputin played pitch and toss with pig knuckles in the dirt and learned the essentials of peasant survival—how to hold a scythe and drive a cart—Victoria taught Alix the arts of ruling. She was drilled in deportment, learning to hold her head high and still for ten minutes at a time; she did the cercle, practicing social graces by touring a room and talking to pieces of furniture as if they were people. She was painfully shy outside the family—an excellent pianist, with a real flair for Wagner, she reddened with embarrassment when her grandmother made her play for visitors at Windsor—and she covered it with a contrived hauteur that, though undeniably regal, brought her little sympathy.

Her tutor, "Madgie" Jackson—a woman of "hard ways and crabbed, bad temper," Victoria thought—encouraged Alix to reject the meek role expected of women and their exclusion from politics. The girl became self-willed and stubborn, alert to ideas and confident in her own. She knew that women could be powerful and historic figures; her grandmother ruled over a quarter of the world's population. She was well grounded, in the arts, in languages, in mathematics, and in morbidity.

Alix made her first visit to Russia in 1884, at the time Rasputin was suffering his alleged torment at the hands of the lascivious general's wife in Tyumen. She attended the marriage of her elder sister Ella to the Russian Grand Duke Serge, dining with her tsar-godfather Alexander III on June 8. Her second cousin, the heir apparent, Tsarevich Nicholas, noted his first meeting with her in his diary that evening: "I sat next to little twelve-year-old Alix, and I liked her awfully much," he wrote. He was sixteen, a handsome young man, whose neat and regular features were relieved of a certain bland weakness by striking blue eyes. It was a happy year for Alix, but it held a distant warning. Her hemophiliac uncle Leopold was wintering in Cannes when he accidentally struck his head and died of a brain hemorrhage.

She returned to Russia five years later, this time in winter, to sledge with Nicholas by torchlight on structures of wooden planks and scaffolding sprayed with water to form ice hills. They ate blinis and caviar, and a ball was held for her. Alix had become a beauty, tall and slender, with striking chestnut hair and blue-gray eyes, and, an observer wrote, "a singular wistful and sweet sadness that never goes quite away even when she smiles." Nicholas, now a Guards officer, fell in love.

Alix was back in Russia the following summer, staying with her sister Ella on Grand Duke Serge's Ilinskoye estate on the Moscow River. She went rowing, picnicked on cold boar and smoked sturgeon, and picked wild berries in the woods. She disliked cities and was nervous in society; the hay-scented, green-shadowed countryside she saw now remained for her the real Russia, as she thought the peasants, dusty figures in linden-bark sandals who bared their heads and knelt as her carriage passed, true Russians.

Although she did not meet Nicholas on this trip, the cousins remained constant. Alix refused to marry Eddy, the eldest son of the Prince of Wales;

Nicholas said that he would rather enter a monastery than become engaged to the German kaiser's ugly sister Margaret. He parted from his young mistress, a striking ballerina, Mathilde Kschessinskaya. They agreed to meet near a barn on the Volkhonsky Highway to say good-bye. She came out from St. Petersburg by carriage; he rode his horse from the nearby army camp where he was stationed. They wept. "When the tsarevich departed for camp," she wrote, "I remained by the barn and watched him go until he was no longer in sight." At the end of 1891 Nicholas wrote in his diary: "My dream is to someday marry Alix H[esse]. I have loved her for a long while." He was to remain faithful to her for life; death did not part them.

Alix's father died in 1892—he collapsed in front of her at lunch; she took to her bed with hysteria—and her brother Ernest became grand duke of Hesse. Nicholas attended his marriage in the spring of 1894 to represent Russia. Alix was at the station to meet him, and they dined by candlelight that evening to a string quartet playing Mendelssohn. Nicholas saw her alone the next morning and proposed. She looked "particularly pretty, but extremely sad." The bride of the Russian heir was obliged to be Orthodox; she wished to remain a Lutheran, and sobbed to him: "No, I cannot." Her cousin Willy, the German kaiser, reminded her that other German princesses—Catherine the Great, her own sister Ella—had converted on marrying Russians. He said it was her "bounden duty" to do so.

Willy seized Nicholas the next day, took some flowers from a vase, and thrusting them into his hand, sent him off to propose again. Alix was waiting for him in a room overlooking the palace garden, the windows closed against a violent spring thunderstorm. She accepted; they both cried like children. "O God, what a mountain has rolled from my shoulders," Nicholas wrote in his diary that evening. "The whole day I have been walking in a dream."

The union, so fateful, was made. Rasputin's reaction, if any, is unknown; Europe's great matchmaker, Queen Victoria, viewed it with foreboding. Her doubts were not about Nicholas—"I like him very much"—but about Russia. "The more I think of sweet Alicky's marriage the more unhappy I am," she wrote, "on account of the Country, the Policy and the differences with us and the awful insecurity to which that sweet Child will be exposed. . . . All my fears about her future marriage now show themselves so strongly when I think of her *so* young and most likely to be placed on that very unsafe throne, her dear life and above all her Husband's constantly threatened and unable to see her but rarely. . . . She has *no parents* and I am her only Grandparent."

In fact, Alix found "the Policy" of her new country much to her liking. Autocracy had been dinned into Nicholas by his tutor Constantine Pobedonostsev, a cold-eyed lawyer in steel-rimmed glasses and bow tie, a reactionary who thought parliamentary democracy "one of the vainest of human delusions," serving only the "personal ambition, vanity, and self-interest of its members." Nicholas was not stupid—he was fluent in five languages, speaking English without a trace of an accent, and he was taught political economy, history, international law, military science, and chemistry by outstanding teachers—but he had no intellectual curiosity and accepted the role of tsar as he received it, by rote. Alix took to absolutism easily, by nature. Otherwise awkward in her new country, she never questioned its system of government, or her place in it, other than to bitterly condemn its spasmodic lurches to liberalism; this acceptance she maintained despite the general loathing of its absolutism, shared by her imperious grandmother, that spread across the English-speaking world and beyond.

Alix was as foreign to Russia in other respects as her unhappy mother had been to Darmstadt. She learned fluent, English-accented Russian—Alexander III sent his personal confessor to Windsor to instruct her in the language and the Orthodox catechism before the marriage—but she arrived as a German princess. Russians, with a historic distaste that stretched back to medieval battles against the Teutonic knights, called her "the German woman." It was unfair, for she was more English than German. English was her mother tongue, and it was her language of love. Nicholas courted her in it, and their letters and notes were written in it. Religion and politics apart, her tastes were English. Like her mother, she bought her furniture by mail order from Maples department store in London and hung her walls with pastoral watercolors of the Scottish highlands. Her favorite writer was the romantic novelist Marie Corelli, the pseudonym of Mary Mackay, who was hugely popular in England— William Gladstone and Oscar Wilde read her—and almost unknown outside it.

Critics detested Corelli as a "self-righteous, sentimental moralist, lacking self-criticism or a sense of the absurd." Alix was pilloried on the same grounds. Petersburg society, malicious and demanding, found her stubborn and provincial. She dressed badly, with her mother's passion for mauve. She was gauche, they said, she danced poorly, she had no small talk. Her French, the language of polite society, was hesitant and stumbling. She represented no great dynastic alliance; she was a poor catch for a Romanov heir. Her new home was not kindly disposed toward her, and her old one was glad to see her go. When the engagement was announced, according to the finance minister Sergei Witte, the Russian ambassador asked the marshal of the Hesse court how Alix had matured since he had first known her as a child. After making sure that nobody could overhear, the marshal whispered: "How lucky we are that you are taking her from us."

———

Alexander III was dying, his body poisoned by kidney failure. Nicholas asked his fiancée to join him at the sickbed in the Livadia Palace in the Crimea. The grand marshal of the court forgot to order an imperial railroad train to wait for her at the Russian frontier as she crossed from Berlin. She caught a standard passenger train, which gave her a rare glimpse of lowborn Russians. The tsar struggled into dress uniform to receive her as a future Russian empress. He was too weak to stand. He sat on a chair in his bedroom, struggling for breath, his great frame shrunken and yellow.

The autocrat in her soul was at once on display. Alix was offended that the tsar's doctors reported first to Empress Marie, ignoring her fiancé's precedence as heir. It seemed not to occur to her that the family was in shock, that none had expected the giant monarch to be felled, that all naturally deferred to the empress in her grief. "Sweet child, pray to God. He will comfort you. . . . Your Sunny is praying for you and the beloved patient. . . . Darling boysy, me loves you oh so very tenderly and deep," she wrote in Nicholas's diary. "Be firm. . . . if the Dr. [Doctor] has any wishes or needs anything, make him come *direct* to you. Don't let others be put first and you left out; you are Father's dear son and must be told all and be asked about everything. Show your own mind and don't let others forget who you *are*. Forgive me lovy."

The words are haunting; Alix wrote them at age twenty-two, when she was an inexperienced princess from an obscure principality, to a man to whom she was not yet married but who would in a few hours inherit one seventh of the land area of the globe. In them she defined the future, for nothing was to change through war, scandal, and revolution. She loved Nicholas, fiercely, but she already found him weak, too ready to "let others be put first." She would scold him, bully him to be firm; she regretted it, "forgive me lovy," but she did it for his sake. She alone, with God, would defend his interests; she would make sure that others never "forget who you *are*." The notes she wrote him—in a flowing English hand, full of underlinings and the hasty abbreviations of a mind that thought impulsively as it wrote, in this Victorian baby language, "darling boysy," with the same allusions to God and prayer, and above all, with the same insistence on his power and primacy—filled volumes by the end. She was his love, his friend, his adviser; she was his absolutism. From this first note her letters show it all. They were a reprise for the Russian empire.

In the afternoon of October 19, 1894, Alexander was given the last rites, rallied enough to say a short prayer and kiss his wife, and expired. Empress Marie collapsed into Alix's arms, an intimacy that was not to resume. Nicholas ran from the room and cried on the shoulder of his brother-in-law Sandro, Grand Duke Alexander Mikhailovich. What would become of him, he sobbed, of Sandro, of Alix and his mother, of Russia itself? "I am not prepared to be tsar," he said. "I know nothing of this business of ruling. I have no idea of even how to talk to the ministers." Nicholas was twenty-six. Death had sought him out before. His grandfather, Alexander II, liberator of the serfs, had been killed by a bomb in the streets of the capital thirteen years before. Leo Tolstoy had appealed to the new tsar to spare the terrorists, to "put forward another ideal, higher than theirs, greater and more generous." Alexander III hanged them. His task was to restore the autocracy, and he did so, with such vigor that the terrorists shuffling in chains to Siberia admitted that theirs had become "a cottage industry."

Nicholas loved his father, the great "Bear" who rose at seven, washed in ice-cold water, wore a peasant's blouse and worn-down boots, who was strong enough to bend a silver ruble in his hand and tear decks of cards in half to amuse his children, who cursed violently and often. The son knew that his younger brother Michael was his father's favorite—Michael could throw a pitcher of water over him and the Bear would laugh, whereas Nicholas would have "got what for"—and that he was in every way his father's reverse. He was slim and slight, dressed beautifully, was exquisitely polite—even revolutionaries admired his manners—and never swore. Fine qualities, no doubt, for the constitutional monarch of a quiet country—his German cousin Willy thought him best suited to be "a country gentleman growing turnips"—but not for a Russian autocrat. Rasputin, who benefited greatly from his character, said that Nicholas had "no insides," no guts.

Nicholas also lacked an instinct to rule. Under his grandfather liberalism had made some strides; jury trials, local government elections, a public state budget were introduced. The terrorist bomb had done that in; his father's years of repression had mirrored Pobedonostsev's dictum that Russia was "an icy desert and the abode of the 'Bad Man,' " which must be governed by a strong tsar contemptuous of the "cheap and shallow ecstasies" of reform. But the essential question of government—autocracy or accountability?—remained. The autocrat needed application and drive to justify his semi-divine status. When Pobedonostsev tried to tutor Nicholas in the intricacies of government, he found his student "became actively absorbed in picking his nose." Victoria made sure that Alix had a grounding in statecraft. Alexander, expecting to live well into the next century, was happy to let young Nicky enjoy the airhead life of a Guards officer; he could catch up on the business of ruling later. Alexander had no illusions about his son.

"What?" he growled when his finance minister, Sergei Witte, suggested that Nicholas be made president of the Trans-Siberian Railroad. "Have you ever had a serious conversation with him?"

"No, Sire," Witte said. "I have never had the pleasure of having such a conversation with the heir."

"He is still absolutely a child, he has only infantile judgments, how will he be able to be president of a committee?"

The young man unfit to run a committee was now to inherit an empire. Sandro felt a sense of "imminent catastrophe" as he watched his future ruler break down. An altar was set up on the palace lawns, and the Romanovs formed a semicircle around it. The guns of the fleet at Yalta boomed as a priest administered the imperial oath of allegiance and Nicholas, weeping, was proclaimed emperor and autocrat of all the Russias, the Sovereign Tsar Nicholas II.

———

The next day, as an autumnal storm swept in from the Black Sea, Alix was confirmed into the Russian church. She wore black; the palace was hung with black. Only the family was present as she renounced the "heresies" of her childhood Protestantism in a firm voice and repeated the Orthodox creed. The names given her at birth—the names of her English mother and aunts, Alix Victoria Helena Louise Beatrice—were swept away. Alix became Alexandra Fedorovna. She was anointed with oil on her forehead, eyelids, neck and throat, and wrists and palms; she then took holy communion with her fiancé and his widowed mother. Nicholas wanted to marry her at once, in private, in the Livadia Palace while his dead father lay in the chapel guarded by Cossacks. His uncles said that a tsar must wed in public.

The journey to Moscow with the corpse took a week as the funeral train stopped in cities on the route for services. Eight black horses with purple bands on their harnesses pulled the coffin through the Moscow streets to the Kremlin, halting outside ten churches while litanies were sung from the steps. "She has come to us behind a coffin," onlookers said of the foreign princess half-masked by driving sleet. A crowd of dignitaries waited at the station as the train slowly drew through dripping fog into St. Petersburg. Sergei Witte watched Nicholas step down with two blondes. At first the politician mistook Alexandra for her aunt, the Princess of Wales. "The young lady who turned out to be our future empress seemed not only less good looking but also less sympathetic than her aunt," he recalled. "Of course she too was pretty then, and still is, but her mouth always seems to be set in anger." The cortege took four hours to cross the city to the Cathedral of St. Peter and St. Paul, muffled drums and church bells tolling. The coffin was displayed in the cathedral for seventeen days. Twice each day Alexandra attended services with her fiancé. She had to kiss the dead tsar's lips; he had not been embalmed for three days after his death, his face was a "dreadful color," and he gave off a terrible smell.

Nicholas insisted that the marriage, planned for the following spring, be brought forward to the week after the funeral. It was his mother's birthday, and protocol allowed court mourning to be lifted for twenty-four hours. His haste was such that his bride had no trousseau. Praskovya Fedorovna Rasputin's wedding five years earlier was witnessed by a few Siberian peasants; no record of it was made. Thousands lined the Nevsky Prospect as Alexandra Fedorovna was driven to the Winter Palace; armed guardsmen were posted every few feet along the route, while secret policemen mingled with the crowds looking for signs of assassins. The bride wore a tiara of diamonds set in platinum, with a wreath of orange blossoms from the imperial conservatory in Warsaw, and a diamond necklace of 475 carats.

It took more than twenty minutes for the wedding procession to pass the three thousand guests in the rooms and halls of the palace, officers drawing their swords to salute her; her mouth trembled slightly, which an onlooker found relieved the "habitual hard expression" that detracted from her classic beauty. "One's feelings one can imagine," Alexandra wrote. "One day in deepest mourning lamenting a beloved one, the next day in smartest clothes being married." The court returned to mourning after the ceremony in the white and gold palace chapel; there was no reception or honeymoon. "At last united, bound for life," Alexandra wrote in Nicholas's diary on their wedding night, "and when this life is ended, we meet again in the other world and remain together for eternity. Yours, yours."

———

The young couple were happy but lonely. Their relations with the other Romanovs started poorly. The dowager empress was Danish. Experienced and practical, she was well placed to help Alexandra cope with the strains of becoming a Russian empress. Instead, she felt that she was losing her son to an obstinate outsider. She insisted that her name be placed first in the daily prayers for the imperial family in the Orthodox Mass. Alexandra resented this, and the tension was obvious in the Anichkov Palace, the dowager empress's residence, where the newly marrieds were at first obliged to live. They shared the dining room, but there was little table talk.

The new empress did not like society, nor did it like her. She was shy and her smile thin-lipped. She preferred the company of children and the old to those of her own age. Prince Sergei Volkonsky, who met her frequently as the director of the imperial theaters, found that "sociability was not in her nature." Her face blotched red with effort when she held a conversation, and she seemed to have a "natural indisposition toward the race of man." People ignored her, Volkonsky said, so that she was "only a name, a walking picture." In return, she despised St. Petersburg; "it's a rotten town," she wrote, "not an atom Russian." Her husband shared her contempt for his capital, his dislike extending as far as its founder, the restless, westernizing Peter the Great. "He is the ancestor who appeals to me least of all," Nicholas told Eugene Botkin, his personal physician. "He had too much admiration for European culture. He stamped out Russian habits, the good customs, the usages which are the nation's heritage."

The couple preferred Moscow; with its narrow lanes, its wooden slums and bulbous, ornate churches, it was more Russian. They brought it calamity when they were crowned in the city in May 1896. During the five-hour ceremony in the Cathedral of the Assumption, the tsar's chain of the Order of St. Andrew fell from his shoulders to the floor. The incident was kept secret for fear it would be seen as an ill omen. The following morning a massive open-air feast was held on the Khodynka Field, the training ground for the Moscow garrison. Free beer and coronation mugs attracted a crowd of half a million, so dense that a patroling Cossack found his horse lifted into the air when he rode into it. A rumor swept the field that the beer was about to run out. As the crowd surged forward people were knocked into deep trenches and gun pits. Those behind trampled forward over them and they disappeared. The crowd gave off a "terrible, long, drawn-out wail," and men and women broke away from its edges "in utter terror."

The official death toll was 1,389; the actual figure was probably higher. Nicholas, deeply shocked, was advised by his uncles that he should attend a gala evening at Moscow's smart Hunt Club as planned. Her eyes red with tears, Alexandra opened the ball by dancing a quadrille with Nicholas. The couple visited the injured in the hospital and gave the family of each victim a thousand rubles, but the folk memory of Khodynka remained, and with it the superstition that Nicholas and his bride would lead Russia to tragedy.

Alexandra's devotion to autocracy was soon noted. True, she had willing material to work with. Nicholas was an inbred reactionary, a lover of old icons, old customs, old ways of spelling. Grammarians argued over whether to scrap the traditional but purely decorative hard sign written at the end of Russian words. "Personally," Nicholas told Dr. Botkin in all earnest, "I shall never trust nor give a responsible position to a man who omits the hard sign." But it was Alexandra who took the blame for it.

Declarations of loyalty were made to the tsar by members of local councils. One, for Tver, expressed the hope that the "rights of individuals will be protected permanently and energetically." Nicholas, taking this as a challenge to absolutism, rebuked the Tver delegates for their "senseless dreams of participation" in government. He added that he would uphold the autocracy "as firmly and unflinchingly as . . . my unforgettable dead father." These remarks, which aroused irritation more than fear, opened him to ridicule at the start of his reign. "A little officer came out; in his cap he had a bit of paper," a delegate wrote sarcastically. "He began mumbling something, now and then looking at that bit of paper, and then he suddenly shouted out: 'senseless dreams'; here we understood we were being scolded for something."

The incident was damaging to Alexandra, whose hand was seen behind it. "What earthly reason was there suddenly to hurl a threat at the head of the entire nation?" Constantine Pobedonostsev, Nicholas's old tutor in absolutism, exploded. He was asked who could have advised the tsar to do such a thing. "Have you not guessed?" he snapped. "Of course, it is the young empress." How could she, when she knew nothing of Russia? She thought she knew everything, Pobedonostsev replied, and she was obsessed with the idea that her husband did not assert himself enough. "She is more autocratic that Peter the Great," he added, "and perhaps as cruel as Ivan the Terrible. Hers is a small mind that believes it harbors great intelligence."

Alexandra was smitten by her new religion. "She completely succumbed to what I call Orthodox Paganism, that is to worship of the form without understanding the spirit," Sergei Witte wrote, ascribing this to the beauty of court services and to her "dull, egotistical character" and narrow view of the world. At every service across Russia prayers were chanted for Alexandra and her husband; Orthodoxy was a symbol of their mastery. " 'If you do not bow down before me, you are my enemy, against whom I will use my autocratic powers because what I wish represents the truth,' " Witte explained her attitude. "Given her psychology, given the fact that she was surrounded by lackeys and intriguers, it is easy to see why she should fall into such illusions."

Alexandra's failure to produce a male heir made her vulnerable to faith healers and mystics. By 1901 she had four children, bonny, healthy, lively, but all girls—Olga, Tatiana, Marie, and Anastasia. The question of the succession became urgent when Nicholas fell ill with typhoid fever. A century past, shortly before he was strangled in a palace plot, the unstable and half-mad Tsar Paul had expressed his hatred of women in general—and his mother, Catherine the Great, in particular—by replacing primogeniture with Salic law. Under this no woman could succeed to the Russian throne unless all legitimate male descendants were dead. To Alexandra's utter despair, constitutional experts advised her that her eldest daughter, Olga, had no claim to the throne. If Nicholas died he would be succeeded by his brother Michael. The imperial couple instructed Pobedonostsev to prepare the draft of a decree to allow for succession in the female line; the tutor found a legal minefield and made little progress.

—

Dr. Philippe, the Montenegrin sisters' French import, claimed to be able to divine the sex of an unborn child. He made other claims, too: that he was a medical man, that he could cure the sick, that he was close to God. Like Rasputin he was a peasant's son and proud of it, and a dabbler in right-wing politics. His real name was Nazier-Vachot, and he had started work at age thirteen in a Lyons butcher's shop. He set himself up as a faith healer when he was in his early twenties. His consulting rooms in the city were soon filled with disturbed patients, whom he treated with a mixture of conventional drugs, prayer, and the laying on of hands. He made enough money to anger qualified medical men, and he was twice prosecuted in France for practicing without a license.

His followers included the Russian military attaché in Paris, Count V. V. Murayev-Amurskii, who thought that the "doctor" had come down from heaven and would reascend there. In 1900 the count introduced him to the Montenegrins, who were wintering in Cannes. He was a "mild little man with a gentle manner and persuasive eyes," which could change from chestnut to a "splendid blue." He appeared clairvoyant; like Rasputin he drew close to people and would "tell you in a few words what was troubling you, and what you did not dare confess to him." He soon cast his mystic spell over the sisters. They invited him to visit them in St. Petersburg.

The following year Militsa arranged for Dr. Philippe to be presented to Nicholas and Alexandra in the château of Compiègne when they were on a state visit to France. He captivated the couple—mystic powers, womb sexing, hints of the divine—and returned to Russia with them. Militsa lived in the Znamenka Palace, very close to the imperial summer palace at Peterhof. Nicholas and Alexandra visited the Znamenka almost every other evening. Here, according to General Spiridovich, the head of the tsar's personal police, they practiced spiritualism with the pseudo-doctor. The Montenegrins promoted him shamelessly, persuading the empress to read the lives of the saints while they chattered on about the similarities to Dr. Philippe. They told the empress that all his acts were blessed by the saintly Ioann of Kronstadt. It was untrue—Ioann complained that he had never said a word to Philippe when they met briefly at Militsa's palace, for the good reason that he had no French and the Frenchman had no Russian—but the empress believed it. The séances continued.

Talk of them raced through the salons of Petersburg. The French ambassador, Maurice Paléologue, was told that Philippe raised the ghost of the dead Alexander III to advise his son on how to govern Russia. Others said that the Frenchman controlled the weather, ensuring smooth seas while the imperial yacht was cruising. Witte was sure that Philippe held "nocturnal séances with Their Majesties"; he remarked that the behavior of the "neurasthenic empress" deeply disturbed her mother-in-law.

It was indeed bizarre. The empress was anxious to reward Dr. Philippe for his services. He wanted official recognition of his "medical" status. Militsa asked the Okhrana's man in Paris, General Rachovsky, to persuade the French government to grant him a medical diploma. Rachovsky protested that this was impossible and prepared a report on Philippe's activities in France. It described him as a clever confidence trickster who exercised power over people with weak personalities. Rachovsky was promptly sacked by the interior minister, Vyacheslav Plehve, who added the vindictive rider that the victim would receive no pension unless he lived continuously out of harm's way in Brussels. Witte castigated Plehve for getting rid of the linchpin of Russia's counterterrorist effort in western Europe. The interior minister shrugged and said that the tsar had personally ordered it.

In France, Baron Alphonse Rothschild complained to Witte that he feared for his huge Russian investments. A country whose court had been penetrated by a charlatan was no place to put one's money, the financier said. Nearer home Prince Elston Yusupov, the richest man in Russia, was walking by the sea in the Crimea when Militsa drove past with a stranger in her carriage. Yusupov bowed, but the Montenegrin made no response. He asked her later why she had cut him. "You couldn't have seen me," she explained, "for I was with Dr. Philippe, and when he wears a hat he is invisible and so are those with him."

Buoyed by faith in his powers, and aware of Alexandra's despairing need for an heir, Dr. Philippe overreached himself in 1902. He convinced her she was bearing a son. She stopped wearing a corset. She grew fatter. An official announcement was made that she was pregnant and would attend no receptions until after the birth. In her ninth month, the capital waited to count the cannon shots that would announce the birth from the Fortress of Peter and Paul. Three hundred rounds would mean a boy, a hundred, a fifth daughter. None came. Alexandra took to her bed. A medical team led by her personal obstetrician, Professor Ott, waited for the first labor pains. When Ott was at last allowed to examine her, he found the pregnancy was a phantom.

Society sniggered; Witte was not so sure it was a laughing matter. If a charlatan could convince the empress that she was pregnant—and she was no girl but the mother of four—then Witte thought that she would believe anything. Once she believed something, her "spineless but good" husband was soon convinced of it, too—and he was a man with unlimited power over the well-being of 140 million subjects. Philippe was indeed an omen. If the empress could fall for one holy man, then by temperament and character it was likely that she would do so again. Rasputin was an accident waiting to happen.

—

Philippe had to go, but he took a handsome payoff. The tsar gave him a Serpollet automobile, the title inspector of port sanitary services, and a diploma from the St. Petersburg academy of military medicine. Spiritualist sessions continued, with Countess Nina Sarnekau as medium. The fixer Simanovich claimed he was carousing in the countess's apartment with influential friends—gentlemen-in-waiting, a provincial governor, the head of the Red Cross, a famous Rumanian violinist—when a palace automobile arrived to take her to the tsar. The countess was drunk but could not decline the invitation to conduct an imperial séance; she left to peals of laughter from her guests, who asked what she would do if the ghosts she raised had also been drinking.

The search for the boy child went on. Archimandrite Feofan, Rasputin's admirer, urged the couple to canonize a pious hermit-monk, Serafim. His bones had been buried sixty years before next to a well in Saratov whose waters were believed to cure the sick, the blind, the deaf, and infertile women. Senior churchmen and the synod were opposed to the beatification. Serafim's body was found to have decomposed, failing the test of miraculous preservation necessary for sainthood. The tsar was warned that Serafim had made an unfortunate prophecy. The monk had foretold that he would be canonized, in the presence of the tsar and his family, but that blood would overwhelm the country shortly after and that millions of Russians would be scattered to the four corners of the earth. Nicholas insisted that the canonization go ahead. When the bishop of Tambov protested, he was dismissed from his see and relocated in Siberia.

An expedition thick with court hangers-on and placemen was mounted to Saratov, a Volga River port, in June 1903. Peasants cured by immersion in the well were paraded for Alexandra to meet. The sighted told her that they were once blind; the nimble that they had been lame. A single ominous note was sounded. A "holy fool" and clairvoyant named Pasha began hitting one of the dolls she always carried with her, shrieking "Serge." Grand Duke Serge had become the hated governor of Moscow after his marriage to Alexandra's sister Ella. Terrorists had not yet kept their vow to kill him, however, and the incident passed almost unnoticed. A gala banquet was held on the eve of the ceremony. Guests noticed that Alexandra was in an excitable state, her breath labored, eyes fixed, red spots on her cheeks. At midnight she left the table and was taken to Serafim's grave by three priests. She prayed at the graveside and then bathed herself in the waters of the holy well.

By the time she knew she was pregnant again, the following February, Russia had drifted into war with Japan. The Chinese empire was a rotting carcass on whose northern province of Manchuria both countries were feeding. The Russians seized the big warm-water harbor and fortress at Port Arthur. Their expansion was given further drive by the completion of the Trans-Siberian Railroad in 1901. It had taken troops eighteen months to toil their way by rough road and river from Moscow to Vladivostok on the Pacific. That was now cut to thirteen days. A group of adventurers at court promoted a scheme for a timber concession on the Yalu River, with their eyes on Korea. The Japanese felt they were being forced into war.

Russia drifted. The foreign ministry, a visitor said, was "indescribable"; everyone in it was asleep. The German ambassador said that he had never seen such laziness. "All officials arrive at eleven or twelve o'clock and disappear at four never to be seen again," he reported. "During office hours they do nothing but smoke and promenade in the corridors." Witte felt that war would be a great disaster; Nicholas dismissed him. "Now I shall rule," the tsar noted—pathetically—in his diary that evening, as though, by sacking him, he had acquired Witte's brilliant mantle. Plehve thought that a "little victorious war" would buy off the threat of revolution at home.

Nicholas, though cautious, had a weakness for war and glory. He had enjoyed his time as a Guards officer. "I am happier than I can say to have joined the army," he wrote to his mother when he was nineteen. He liked mess nights, drinking, and parades. His brother-in-law, Grand Duke Alexander Mikhailovich, thought the life appealed to his "passive nature"—"one executed orders and did not have to worry over the vast problems handled by one's superiors." In 1904 the tsar held the honorary rank of colonel. "His father was a proud tsar and an equable and unaffected nobleman," Witte said icily. "Nicholas II is not a proud tsar, but a very proud and affected Guards colonel."

Nicholas had visited Japan on a world tour when he was a youth. He was so incurious that he found the trip "senseless. Palaces and generals are the same the world over, and that's all I am allowed to see. I could just as well have stayed home." A single incident stood out in his mind. He was being driven through the town of Otsu when an onlooker slashed at his face with a sword. A second blow was parried by his cousin, Prince George of Greece, with his walking cane, but Nicholas carried the scar and a grudge against the Japanese for life. He called them "macaques," monkeys, in official reports. He believed them "an unpleasant, contemptible, and powerless people" whom the Russian colossus would destroy at a stroke.

On a snowy, wet night in January 1904, he and Alexandra sat in the imperial box at the Mariinsky Theater to watch a performance of the opera *Rusalka*. The Japanese ambassador had broken off negotiations and had left St. Petersburg with his staff two days before. Japanese spies in Port Arthur reported that the Russians were not expecting an attack—"they do not maneuver, they do not carry out any gunnery exercises"—and that piles of torpedoes had been left in the open to rust. "War is war, and peace is peace," the tsar told a general plaintively, "but this business of not knowing either way is agonizing." The Japanese decided the issue for him as he watched the opera. Vice Adm. Togo Heihachiro was steaming for Port Arthur with a force of eleven destroyers. Nicholas had been assured by his admirals that the "monkeys" were incapable of handling modern warships; they were "like children playing with toy ships in a bath."

Togo was on a turkey shoot. The seven battleships moored in Port Arthur had their lights burning. None of their great guns was manned or loaded. The shore batteries were so heavily greased against winter cold that they could not fire. The Russian commander, Gen. Yevgenny Alekseev, owed his promotion to having passed himself off as a member of the imperial family wanted by French police for starting a brawl in Marseilles. He had intelligence reports that the Japanese were on the move; he ignored them. No torpedo nets were in place to protect the fleet. Togo's destroyers fired their torpedoes at will into the Russian hulls and turned back to sea. Alekseev was reading a book in his study when he heard the explosions. He told an orderly that he did not wish to be disturbed. News of the attack first reached St. Petersburg from a commercial agent in the port.

The war started well enough politically. Generals and tramps marched side by side down the Nevsky singing "God save the tsar," and when Nicholas drove past Witte's house, he gave him a triumphant and self-satisfied look. The ex-minister thought that war would turn to revolution soon enough, and revolution to anarchy. "How sad for Russia!" he wrote. "How sad for the emperor, that poor, unfortunate man. . . . He is a good man, and is by no means stupid, but he has no will."

It was a military disaster. A Russian minesweeper, sunk by one of her own mines, was lost together with the only log of the minefields she had laid. In March, on a rare foray, the flagship *Petropavlovsk* was blown up by a Russian mine. The remnants of the fleet stayed in Port Arthur. Nicholas was exposed to humiliation. He was besotted by his own autocratic power, a leading senator thought, which "he exercises sporadically, without prior deliberation, and without general reference to the general course of affairs." All was done piecemeal or by chance, on momentary impulse, "through the intrigues of one person or another. . . . There is no policy based on principles, well reasoned and firmly directed, in any field."

A pettiness ran with the tsar's charm. The director of his private office, Prince Nicholas Obolensky, had a regular morning appointment with him and often stayed on for lunch. When he fell from favor, Nicholas changed the meetings to 2:00 P.M. to save himself the embarrassment of not inviting the prince to dine. It annoyed him that his German cousin Willy was a head taller than he. Postcards showing the difference in their height were confiscated. He was fit; he liked sports, shooting, sailing, and tennis; he could still take sets off the Russian tennis champion when he was well into his forties. But he was frightened of his huge Romanov uncles. Grand Duke Alexis filled his admiral's uniform with 250 pounds of flesh. Grand Duke Nicholas Nikolayevich, "Nicky the Long," stood six feet four inches in his cavalry boots. Serge, governor of Moscow, and Vladimir were less intimidating physically but equally demanding and authoritarian. His young cousin Sandro said that Nicholas spent the first ten years of his reign "sitting in his study behind a huge desk, listening with a feeling that went close to terror to the advice and directions of his uncles. He was afraid to be alone with them."

Most of all he was frightened of his wife, now confirmed to be pregnant. Their letters to each other were similar in their endearments—"darling boysy," "sweetest wifey"—but his were placatory and submissive, and hers demanding. When Nicholas ignored his recommendations, Witte several times asked who advised him. "The person whom I trust without reservation," Nicholas replied. When Witte asked him who that might be, he wrote, the tsar "told me that it was his wife." He was tetchy and sometimes drank heavily. His irritations ran to words. When an aide spoke of the intelligentsia, he snapped that the academy of sciences should erase it from the language: "How I dislike that word!" A reference to public opinion in a report had him asking angrily: "How does public opinion concern me?" It was in his nature, Witte thought, to "dislike persons who were firm in their opinions, their words, and their actions." His inferiority complex—the unloved son, the dwarf nephew, the poor speaker—left him uncomfortable with "men who are mentally and morally superior to him." He was at ease only with those he felt more poorly endowed than himself—or, like Rasputin, "people who, knowing this weakness, act as if they were more poorly endowed."

—

By July, Japanese troops had placed Port Arthur under siege. Nevertheless, on July 10, 1904, the guns of the Peter and Paul Fortress in St. Petersburg boomed three hundred times in celebration. "For us a great, unforgettable day on which God's goodness was so clearly visited upon us," Nicholas wrote in his diary. "At 1:15 this afternoon, Alix gave birth to a son." The tsar was certain that the recent beatification lay behind the happy event. "I have indisputable evidence of the holiness and miraculous power of Saint Serafim," he told the synod procurator. "No one can ever shake my faith in that power." A portrait of the saint hung in the tsar's study, and tens of thousands of icons with his features were sent to troops at the Japanese front. "They send us Serafim in place of ammunition," the soldiers complained.

Five days after the birth, Plehve was riding in his carriage guarded by police agents on bicycles. There was trouble everywhere. Troops en route to Manchuria refused to obey orders and ravaged railroad stations while their officers hid from them. A lawyer in Saratov, the new saint's hometown, said that anger at the regime "bursts forth roaring and whistling through every crack and gap." From exile the young revolutionary Leon Trotsky wrote of peasants ravaged "by syphilis and all sorts of epidemics. . . . In thoughtful silence, our village is dying from disease." Plehve opened the traditional safety valve— pogroms against the Jews, who were raped, blinded with stakes, murdered, and robbed—but neither that nor his bicycle escort was enough. Witte reckoned that "thousands of people were willing to give up their lives for the privilege of killing a major official." One of them tossed a bomb into Plehve's carriage. He used nitroglycerin, and only a few bloody traces of the interior minister were found.

The infant was christened Alexis. His father said he had chosen the name to break the chain of Alexanders and Nicholases. The superstitious thought the name an ill omen. Peter the Great had murdered his son and heir Alexis. A story was minted on the birth. The tsar, it ran, held himself responsible for the run of daughters. To ensure a son he urged his wife to give herself to another man. Her choice fell on Gen. Alexander Orlov, commander of her regiment of Uhlan lancers. A widower living high on his late wife's fortune, he was a "jaunty, gallant line officer," handsome, a prince with a taste for strong drink and spiritualism. She had once danced a waltz with him, in breach of imperial etiquette; he was a descendant of Catherine the Great's lover Grigory Orlov. It was enough for tongues to start wagging with malice.

The imperial couple, "quite mad with joy," ignored the talk. The baby had dimpled, chubby cheeks, with fair curls and gray-blue eyes set off by "the fresh pink color of a healthy child." Nicholas insisted that Alexander Mosolov, head of the court chancellery, come to see the tsarevich in the nursery. The baby was kicking lustily in the bath, and Nicholas plucked him out and rested him in his arms. "Don't you think he's a beauty?" the tsar asked, smiling. Alexandra was relaxed and fulfilled, "proud and happy in the beauty of her child."

When the baby was six weeks old, he began to hemorrhage from the navel. It took two days for the bleeding to stop. After three months he started to crawl. He tumbled, and telltale bruises developed on his arms and legs. He cried as the blood formed swellings under the skin. He had hemophilia

Only close relatives and the empress's few intimate friends were told. No outsider knew. Alexandra was ill and suffering; she was thirty-two, and the definitive moment in her life had turned, bleeding, against her. "She spends most of her time in bed," Nicholas wrote to his mother, "lives in seclusion, doesn't care to come to meals, and looks out of her window for hours together." Pregnancies and sciatica had worn her out. She suffered vertigo and anxiety states and canceled public appointments. To the court she appeared her old "cold, haughty, and indifferent self. From this false impression she never fully recovered." When Dr. Philippe had left the court, he presented Alexandra with a bell. He told her to ring it to ward off advisers who did not share her views. He also told her: "Someday Your Majesty will have another friend like me who will speak to you of God." The Montenegrins had one such ready in the wings.

CHAPTER 7

A Man of God from Tobolsk

Rasputin was still in Pokrovskoye when Nicholas saluted the Baltic fleet from the deck of the royal yacht *Standart* as it steamed from the Gulf of Finland for the Pacific. Its mission was to lift the siege of Port Arthur. Nicholas expected it to "reverse the whole course of the war" by sinking the blockading Japanese—he was assured by Father Serafim, a die-hard monk who had assisted at his namesake's beatification, that "only kikes and intellectuals could think otherwise"—but the birth of the heir had not changed his fortunes. Nicholas had been born on the name day of Job the Sufferer, and he accepted ill luck with dull fatalism.

A catastrophe was in the making. Rarely—never?—has a naval expedition been so botched. The commander, aging Vice Adm. Zinovy Rozhdestvensky, called his number two "the sack of shit." The equally obese commander of cruisers was known as "the vast space." Three ships collided almost at once, and the funeral party for a dead petty officer was unable to fire a last salute because the men did not know how to load their rifles. Paranoia sailed with them. "Tonight it will be dangerous," the engineer in chief wrote to his wife while still in the Baltic. "We are passing through a narrow strait and are afraid of striking Japanese mines." Six days out the Russians mistook British herring smacks in the North Sea for Japanese torpedo boats. Their gunnery was so poor that they missed most of the trawlers but put six shells into one of their own cruisers. The nearest Japanese warship was more than ten thousand miles away.

Suez was closed to them, so they steamed around Africa. Rozhdestvensky was obsessed with running short of fuel and piled coal high on decks and around gun turrets. Ventilators and portholes were sealed against coal dust, and men dropped with heat exhaustion in the tropic seas. No gun drills could be practiced without dislodging the coal piles. While he was off the coast of Nigeria, Japanese infantry seized the high ground around Port Arthur and sank the remnants of the Pacific fleet that Rozhdestvensky was sailing to relieve. He reached Madagascar on December 27, 1904, to discover that the Port Arthur garrison had surrendered the week before.

———

Reports of the strikes and riots that were coattailing the military defeats reached Pokrovskoye at the start of 1905. Rasputin was disturbed by them; he began to feel that God "required some mission of him." His wife believed that he had seen another vision of the Virgin of Kazan—he said nothing of it himself—in which she commanded him to go to the capital. His children bid him tearful farewells, and he set out to return to St. Petersburg.

Workers at the big Putilov arms plants in the city struck for an eight-hour day and higher wages. Within a week twenty-five thousand were refusing to work. The city was nervous. On January 6 the tsar took part in the traditional Epiphany blessing of the waters of the Neva from a wooden pavilion set up on the frozen river in front of the Winter Palace. The ceremony dated back to before the Romanovs, when tsars went down to the Moscow River below the ramparts of the Kremlin for the blessing. The guns of the Fortress of Peter and Paul fired a salute. A live shrapnel round was accidentally mixed in with the blanks. "Broken glass shattered from the window above our heads," an onlooker in the palace wrote. "Someone shouted: 'They are firing live ammunition.' . . . Small holes could be seen in the upper portions of the windows." A policeman was wounded. Many thought it was a murder attempt on the tsar; he refused to attend the service for the next five years. It put police and army officers on edge.

Three days later, with icy blasts from the east lifting snow from the streets that whirled in the winter sun, Witte rose with the late dawn and looked out his window. A crowd, or rather, he thought, a procession—workers in padded jackets, students with scarves tied over their ears, women and children in their Sunday best—was marching down the avenue carrying church banners, icons, and Russian flags. No red was to be seen, not a red handkerchief; the procession was restrained. Its organizer, Georgii Gapon, was a young, bright-eyed priest who worked with the poor in the slums of the harbor district. He was also an Okhrana agent; before he was blown to pieces, Plehve had ensured that the workers' movements were infiltrated by the secret police. Gapon wished to present a petition to the tsar, pleading with him to deliver them from the "capitalist exploiters, bureaucratic crooks, and plunderers of the Russian people." He was sure the tsar would accept it. The marchers were on their best behavior;

there were no weapons, not so much as a penknife, and they sang hymns as they walked to the Winter Palace. But their "Little Father" was not in the capital; Nicholas was with Alexandra and the children at Tsarskoye Selo.

"Save us, O Lord, your people!" they sang. "How glorious is our Lord in Zion!" As Witte went out onto his balcony to listen, he heard shots. They whizzed by close enough to kill a porter in a nearby school. Then came a series of salvos. In ten minutes the marchers were running back, some of them carrying dead and women with children among them. Cordons of troops blocked the great avenues leading to the Winter Palace. They had been issued with live ammunition and an extra vodka ration the night before, and were told that workers were plotting to destroy the palace and the dynasty. They warned the marchers to turn back and opened fire when they did not. The worst killings took place in the square in front of the palace. An old man clutching a portrait of the tsar and a child with a lantern were the first to be shot. The company of guardsmen stationed there fired indiscriminately into the marchers.

The light failed, and the sun was consumed in a foggy red circle. In midafternoon a rainbow glistened, and then the wind came up and it snowed in early darkness. At least 150 were killed, and three times that number were wounded. In the evening, obscured in a long cloak, his priestly beard cut crudely in tufts for disguise, Father Gapon fled to Maxim Gorky's apartment. "Give me something to drink," he asked the writer. "Wine. Everyone's dead." He was blue with cold and hysteria. "Peaceful means have failed," he shouted. "Now we must go over to other means." He invoked "my pastor's curse" on the soldiers and on "the traitor tsar." Gorky telegraphed William Randolph Hearst's *New York Morning Journal*: "The Russian Revolution has begun."

Ten days later Nicholas consented to see a few specially chosen workers in a margarine, or ersatz delegation. "I believe in the honest feelings of the working people and in their unshakable loyalty to me," he told them. "Therefore, I forgive them." The workers were less forgiving of him. They spat at members of the delegation and cursed the fifty thousand rubles the tsar donated to the families of victims as "blood money." Gapon had fled the city but left an open letter for Maxim Gorky to read out. "There is no tsar!" it thundered. "Between him and the people lies the blood of our comrades. Long live the beginning of the struggle for freedom!" In the clubs, gloomy nobles and landowners passed on stories: of the tsar's advisers being taken to him concealed in coffins, so frightened were they of assassins, of coming massacres. The slaughter on "Bloody Sunday" ripped the bonds between the Romanovs and the ruled. With a gory bow it ushered in what the dowager empress called the "year of nightmares."

Three weeks after the killings a revolutionary took his revenge on a Romanov in Moscow. Grand Duke Serge, whose name the half-wit in Saratov had cried as she beat her doll, was a rich prize. The bomb was made of nitroglycerin, and it blasted him into slicks of flesh that stuck to the Kremlin gate as he drove through it in his carriage. The assassin, a Social Revolutionary named Kaliayev, made no attempt to escape. Alexandra's sister Ella visited him in prison and offered to plead for his life, on condition that he express sorrow for killing her husband. Kaliayev refused; he said his death would speed the fall of the autocracy. Ella, "saintly and beautiful," withdrew from society into the solace of prayer. She built an abbey in Moscow and became its abbess. Nicholas and Alexandra dared not attend Serge's funeral.

Violence in the cities gathered pace, and there were outbreaks of cattle maiming and barn burning in the provinces. The rich needed reassurance. Rasputin provided it; he was a man of the people, a symbol that the real Russia had not turned on them, a tsar-loving and God-fearing peasant who was also a phenomenon, unique, exciting. He took minds off dark events. The value this gave him was picked up by the sensitive antenna of George Petrovich Sazonov, a political adventurer and journalist of dubious loyalties. A student dabbler in revolution, close to assassination squads, Sazonov had founded *Rossiya*, a leftist newspaper, tapping industrialists for money to ensure good press for themselves. He now veered from left-wing to the extreme right, where the financial pickings were higher. He invited Rasputin to stay in his apartment off the Nevsky and put word out to the capital's religious dilettantes that he had a holy man for their amusement.

Rasputin was soon asked to the salon of a well-known hostess, Varvara Ivanovna Iskul. She invited a writer famous for his works on religious sects, Vladimir Bonch-Bruevich, to watch him in action. Rasputin arrived late, at eight in the evening. He walked straight into the drawing room, though he had never been in the house before, marching along the carpet with a "free, light step." He went up to his hostess and, without any preliminaries, "assaulted" her on her famous collection of paintings and antiques, which crammed the room. "Why is it, Mother, that you hang up so much on your walls, as if it was a museum?" he asked. "Perhaps five starving villages could be fed on this wall alone. Just look how they live while the muzhiks starve." When Varvara Ivanovna introduced him to her women guests, he shot direct personal questions at them. "Is she married?" he asked. "Where's the husband? Why did she come alone?" He turned to his hostess: "If you were together, I'd see how you are, how you live." He talked without a trace of embarrassment, joking and chattering.

The holy man's eyes most drew Bonch-Bruevich's attention. He looked at people directly, with concentration. His pupils "sparkled with phosphorescent light. He sort of groped listeners with his eyes." At times his speech slowed to a drawl. Staring at someone directly in the eye, he told a confused story, as if his mind was far away. Then he suddenly snapped to—"What's the matter with me?"—and hurriedly changed the subject. His stare made a particular impression on all present, especially the women. It flustered them; "they got nervous and then looked at Rasputin timidly, as though wishing to talk to him and to hear him talk." He picked on a single woman, then turned abruptly and talked to someone else. After fifteen or twenty minutes he resumed his little game. He cut himself short in mid-conversation and went back to the unmarried woman he had first stared at. "It's no good, Mother, no good, well," he mumbled. "How can one live like that? You're such a . . . It's no good to be offended . . . you've got to love someone. . . . Well." Then he skipped to another topic and walked about the room quickly, bending and squatting a little, rubbing his hands together.

All this excited the guests. They whispered and said that he had guessed something, that he had said the truth, that he saw a lot. The atmosphere became nervously heightened. "It was the one you can feel in monasteries," Bonch-Bruevich said, "around Elders, 'prophets,' and so forth." Rasputin met the Montenegrin sisters again. Militsa invited him to her palace on the English Quay overlooking the Neva. She introduced him to Anastasia's paramour, the Grand Duke Nicholas Nikolayevich. The tall soldier was devoted to a small lapdog, elderly and panting with exhaustion. Rasputin whispered to the dog, stroking it and praying. Its breathing eased; it licked the Siberian and trotted to its master. The grand duke was impressed.

—

The Baltic fleet decayed in Madagascar. The men got drunk and diseased on runs ashore to the bars and brothels of the Hellville harbor section. A mutiny broke out on the prison ship that accompanied the warships. The ships filled with the reek of animals brought aboard by the men. Instead of ammunition and wireless sets, supply ships from Russia brought thousands of winter uniforms and delivered mail to the battleship *Alexander III* that was addressed to the Alexander III Electrotechnical Institute in St. Petersburg. When it finally steamed for Singapore in March 1905, the fleet could make only eight knots because of the buildup of barnacles and sea grass on the ships' hulls. It was April before they reached Singapore, where a launch brought news that the Russian ground forces in Manchuria had been defeated at Mukden. Steaming on for Cam Ranh Bay in Vietnam, two destroyers rammed each other.

On May 11, as the fleet neared the Tsushima Strait separating Japan from Korea, Admiral Foelkerzam—the number two, the "sack of shit"—died. Rozhdestvensky did not bother to enlighten Adm. Nikolai Nebogatov, Foelkerzam's nominated successor, and the dead man's flag continued to fly from the battleship *Osliaba*. Admiral Togo's fleet was spotted at dawn on May 14, 1905. Battle was joined in the early afternoon. "At this time our formation, properly speaking, was nothing but a heap," Nebogatov wrote. Afraid of colliding with each other, the Russians were outmaneuvered. "I glanced around," a commander on the battleship *Suvorov* wrote. "Devastation! Flames on the bridge, burning debris on the deck, piles of bodies. Signaling, range-finding, and shot-spotting stations swept away and destroyed. And astern, the *Alexander III* and *Borodino* also wreathed in smoke and flame." Four battleships were sunk before nightfall. The sealed coffin of Foelkerzam was found floating among the debris that marked the end of the *Osliaba*. Nebogatov headed north for Vladivostok with the survivors, harried by Japanese torpedo boats. Tsushima was the greatest sea battle since Trafalgar. All twelve Russian battleships were lost, eight sunk and four captured, together with seven out of twelve cruisers and six out of nine destroyers. Five thousand Russians were drowned. The Japanese lost three torpedo boats and 117 men.

Rasputin was an antidote to the war, and salons competed to have him. "The unbalanced society ladies could talk and think of nothing else," General Spiridovich wrote. "They taught him how to dress, to groom himself, to wash—and much more besides." They embroidered silk blouses for him, bought him fine cloth trousers and red leather boots. He learned to pomade his beard but ruined its subtle scent by using cheap, pungent soap on his body.

On June 14 the captain of the battleship *Potemkin*, a martinet and harsh disciplinarian, ordered his crew to eat maggot-infested meat for their midday meal. The men refused, arrested him and the other officers, and seized the ship as it lay in the harbor at Odessa. They hoisted the Red flag while revolutionaries fought with gangs of ultra-rightists in the streets ashore. The sailors tried to help them by turning the battleship's big guns on the city. Their range finding was so poor that they abandoned the attempt and steamed out into the Black Sea. Ten days later they moored in the Rumanian port of Constantza and gave themselves up. Most sought asylum and emigrated to Brazil, Canada, and the United States.

On July 10 news arrived from France for Nicholas and Alexandra that Dr. Philippe had died. They were twenty miles from the capital in the summer palace at Peterhof, whose marble terraces overlooked the sea and a great cascade of waterfalls and fountains in which a gilded Samson tore apart the jaws of a lion. The statue commemorated Peter the Great's victory over the Swedes, happier times for the Romanovs than the string of defeats against Japan. The couple were isolated and fearful. Peasant violence was spreading. On the railroads passengers saw maimed horses and cattle with ripped stomachs hobbling by the track, "mooing or bellowing from pain." At night the steppe was lit by burning ricks and barns.

The constant threat of assassination was unnerving to a girl brought up in secure England and the small-town safety of Darmstadt. Nicholas thought he would share the fate of the Serbian king Alexander, last of the house of Obren-ovich. Alexander had been murdered with his wife two years before, their bodies hurled into the street. The killing "made a particular impression on the tsar," Witte found, "and filled his soul with fear of his own fate." At the end Nicholas and his wife showed bravery enough. For now the common sense that kept them immured in rural palaces at Peterhof and Tsarskoye Selo—scores of their subjects, well-bred girls and youths, intelligent and pitiless, furnished with bombs, safe houses, and false identity papers, wished them dead—was taken for cowardice. "From their fortresses," Witte wrote, "they send telegrams of condolence to the wives of men who have fallen at the hands of foul revolutionary assassins, praise the fallen for their courage, and declare 'my life does not matter to me as long as Russia is happy.' "

They were suspicious of all outsiders, all politicians. "My poor Nicky's cross is heavy, all the more so as he has nobody on whom he can thoroughly rely and who can be a real help to him," Alexandra railed. "He tries so hard, works with such perseverance, but the lack of what I call 'real' men is great. . . . The bad are always close at hand, the others through false humility remain in the background. . . . I rack my brains to find a man and cannot; it is a despairing feeling." When Prince Sviatopolk-Mirsky, the interior minister, tried to warn her that all Russia was against the existing order, she flushed with anger. "Yes," she said, "the intelligentsia is against the tsar, but the people support him." Mirsky warned her that the people were an elemental force: "Today they could slaughter the intelligentsia in the name of the tsar, but tomorrow they could destroy his palaces." Nicholas was forced to sue for peace with the Japanese "monkeys."

As an added humiliation he had had to recall Sergei Witte—huge, ungainly, bold, and coarse, a reminder of his fearsome uncles—and send him to negotiate with the Japanese at the Wentworth Hotel in Portsmouth, New Hampshire. The irascible Witte thought little of Theodore Roosevelt, his "naive" American host; for his part Roosevelt despised the "pitiable" Russian despot. "The tsar is a preposterous little creature," he said. "He has been unable to make war and now he is unable to make peace." Nevertheless, the Russian representative was a superb negotiator. Russia lost only the Liaotung Peninsula with Port Arthur and the southern half of Sakhalin Island; she remained a great Pacific power. Witte regained his reputation; the tsar was branded as the first European ruler to be defeated by Asians.

Nicholas consoled himself at spiritualist sessions with the Montenegrin sisters. Militsa's Znamenka Palace was ten minutes from the Peterhof summer palace, while Anastasia was a thirty-minute walk away at the Villa Sergeievka. The royal couple saw the sisters almost every day at Peterhof, and every other day they went to the Znamenka Palace for a long soiree. Grand Duke Nicholas Nikolayevich, now living with Anastasia and thought of as her fiancé, often joined them. "In Peterhof," the historian A. A. Polovtsev wrote, "they take no account of the situation and what is going on. They constantly vacillate, now doing one thing, then another, undecided, unconfident, holding mystic séances with those two Montenegrins, whose presence is so unfortunate for Russia."

Like his ancestor Alexander I, whose library of spiritualist books he had inherited, Nicholas had a penchant for mysticism. Alexandra shared it. During the summer she gave a book called *The Friends of God* to one of her maids of honor. It was a reprint of a fourteenth-century German work, influenced by the Dominican mystic Meister Eckhart, whose theme was that God on occasion gives divine grace to pious and humble men whom he sends to help the sovereigns he protects. These "friends of God" give the sovereigns moral help and advice on how to rule their people. Rasputin was another visitor to the Znamenka Palace over the summer. He had yet to meet the sovereigns, but the day when, as the dead Dr. Philippe had said, they would find "another friend like me" was not far off.

The couple spent September aboard the imperial yacht *Standart* cruising off the Finnish coast. The 420-foot steam yacht, capable of making twenty-two knots, black hulled with varnished masts and a great bowsprit picked out in gold leaf, carried a brass band and a balalaika orchestra to amuse the family. Security was maintained even at sea: the crew had Okhrana agents among them, and a platoon of the Garde Equipage kept watch for seaborne assassins. Witte returned a hero from New Hampshire. Nicholas received him aboard the yacht and created him a count, but the honor did not conceal the hostility between them. Nicholas wrote sarcastically to his mother that Witte "went quite stiff with emotion and then tried three times to kiss my hand!" The politician felt that the title was awarded "in spite of his and especially Her Majesty's personal dislike for me, and also in spite of all the base intrigues conducted against me by a host of bureaucrats and courtiers whose vileness was equaled only by their stupidity."

This coldness—the sovereigns' contempt for men of ability, their shared conviction that the tsar's mission came from God and that his actions were a matter for God and his conscience alone—was nearly fatal. As they came ashore from their cruise at the beginning of October, their empire started to disintegrate. A railroad strike began in Moscow on October 7. It spread almost as fast as the broad-gauge trains could travel. The wave reached Kursk and Kiev on the ninth, St. Petersburg and Kharkov the next day. "Peter is now cut off from the rest of Russia," Sergei Mintslov, a rare book dealer, noted in his diary on October 12. "Panic is beginning to spread throughout the city. . . . Sausage shops, bakeries, and grocers' shops are all besieged." The price of meat increased by a third during the day. The next morning the St. Petersburg Soviet, a workers' council, was convened. Its leading figure was a wiry and passionate man named Lev Davidovich Bronstein, known as Leon Trotsky.

The Montenegrin séances continued. "The worse things are, the greater the sorrow," Witte wrote. "The greater the sorrow, the more the soul must seek surcease in divination. And there will always be soothsayers, especially for tsars—who say: 'Be patient, you will be victorious and all will be at your feet, all will recognize that only that which comes from you represents the truth and salvation.' " In the last three weeks of October, Anastasia visited the palace on all but two days. Militsa dined at the imperial palace seven times and made many telephone calls to the tsar and empress.

By October 14 the strike had passed over the Urals and the Caucasus into Georgia, Central Asia, and Siberia. Workers with pistols—Brownings and Mausers smuggled in from Belgium—went onto the Moscow streets. Crowds beneath red banners sang the "Marseillaise" and screamed: "Down with autocracy." In the capital almost everyone had stopped working: cabdrivers, telegraph operators, maids and cooks in great houses, doctors, professors, even stockbrokers and the corps de ballet at the Marie Theater. Shop windows were boarded against looters. A destroyer was kept with steam up ready to evacuate the imperial family to Denmark. Murdered policemen, the tsar complained, Cossacks and soldiers, riots, disorders, mutinies—"It makes me sick to read the news!"

"I am sure that the only man who can help you now and be useful is Witte," the dowager empress wrote to her son. "He is certainly a man of genius, *energetic*, and clear-sighted." Nicholas disliked Witte for those very qualities—so different from his own—and for his dangerous liberalism. But fear, and the unraveling events, obliged the tsar to deal with him. "One had the same feeling as before a thunderstorm in summer," Nicholas wrote later to his mother. "Through all those horrible days I constantly met with Witte. We very often met in the early morning to part only in the evening when night fell." Witte had to travel out to Peterhof by special steamboat. Nothing moved on the railroads, and the roads were unsafe. "Snow mixed with rain . . . a rocky journey," he wrote, for the weather had turned bad. "En route, we talked of what a shameful situation we were in, when loyal subjects virtually had to swim to reach their emperor."

The tsar wished to put down the rebellion by force. He gave dictatorial powers to Gen. Dmitri Trepov. The former Moscow police chief had simple views, Witte said: "If people riot, you beat them. . . . For the likes of Trepov there are no complex questions, for such questions are the inventions of intellectuals, kikes, and Freemasons." Trepov issued a famous order to his troops: "Don't use blanks and don't skimp on bullets." The order was fly-posted throughout St. Petersburg, but Trepov warned the tsar that clearing the demonstrators and strikers from the streets would cost thousands of casualties. The other way out,

Nicholas reluctantly admitted, was "to give the people their civil rights, freedom of speech and press, and also to have all laws confirmed by a state Duma—that, of course, would be a constitution. Witte defends this energetically." He drafted a manifesto for a constitutional government. "Man always strives for freedom, civilized man to freedom and law—to freedom, regulated by law and the security of his rights," he said. "The ominous signs of a terrible and stormy explosion each day make themselves felt more strongly."

Army reinforcements moved into the capital on October 15. They set up machine guns in the university and law schools. No newspapers were published. The power stations ran intermittently, the streetlamps flaming with light for a few minutes before turning pitch black again. A huge searchlight shone down the Nevsky. The "revolution" was expected in a few days. Witte prepared a draft manifesto, scribbling amendments to it aboard the steamboat that shuttled him to Peterhof and back. He discovered that Nicholas was holding two sets of meetings, with himself and with Ivan Loganovich Goremykin, an aging bureaucrat with "a sleepy face and Piccadilly whiskers" and a taste for French novels. Goremykin was working on an alternative manifesto; since he thought that the tsar's ministers were no more than his servants, it could hardly coexist with Witte's. It was typical of Nicholas to go behind his back, Witte thought, adding that since the tsar was no Metternich or Talleyrand, his taste for the byzantine led merely to the bloody and shameful. Witte prayed God that "He deliver me from this morass of cowardice, blindness, treachery, and stupidity."

The Montenegrin sisters were in constant touch with the palace, and with Rasputin. On October 17 the tsar called in Anastasia's fiancé, Nicholas Nikolayevich. He proposed making him military dictator. The grand duke took a revolver out of his pocket and said he would shoot himself if the tsar refused to sign Witte's version of the manifesto. The tsar crossed himself and signed. The manifesto made Russia a hybrid, half autocracy, half free. It promised freedom of conscience, speech, assembly, and association. No law could be enforced without the consent of an elected state Duma, a parliament. The tsar retained control of military and foreign affairs, and could appoint and dismiss ministers at will. Alexandra was silent with anger at the loss of power. "The empress sat stiff as a ramrod," Witte recalled, "her face lobster red, and did not utter a single word."

It was not enough for the left. The tsar had granted everything and given nothing, Trotsky said; the manifesto was no more than "the Cossack whip wrapped in the parchment of the constitution." For the right it went too far. "Fear has driven them out of their minds in St. Petersburg!" bellowed Dmitri Pikhno, editor of *Kievlianin*, the only newspaper in Russia to continue publishing during the strikes. "God alone knows what they're doing! They're actually making revolutionaries themselves!" He and others like him organized Black

Hundred gangs, which pogromed Jews under the banner of "Orthodoxy, Autocracy, and Nationality." Membership in the ultra-right, anti-Semitic Union of the Russian People snowballed to more than a million.

—

On October 31, Militsa and her husband, and Anastasia and Grand Duke Nicholas Nikolayevich, dined with the imperial couple and left very late. The next day, November 1, 1905, Nicholas and Alexandra called on Militsa at the Znamenka Palace. Rasputin was there. The tsar made a note in his diary that evening: "We have made the acquaintance of a man of God named Grigory from the government of Tobolsk."

Two days after meeting the rulers—he did not see them again until the following summer—Rasputin acquired his first disciple. Olga Lokhtina, a rich landowner married to a government engineer, had once been a beauty, sad eyed and brilliant, a hostess known for her bitter wit. In her early thirties she was overcome with depression. She became a recluse in her apartment on Grechesky Prospect in St. Petersburg's fashionable Peski district and took to her bed for five years with a nervous stomach disorder. Doctors put it down to neurasthenia, the same handy catchall for nervous women that they applied to the empress. Lokhtina was weak, eating little and crying often.

Rasputin spoke to her gently at her bedside. She was a religious woman, and he assured her that God was with her and would never abandon her. As he soothed her, she later told the investigator, she felt a great warmth and her spiritual crisis lifted, like mist burning off a river under a strengthening sun. She quit her bed and ventured outdoors. She thought her recovery a miracle, like Lazarus arisen, and her healer divine. She fell to her knees in front of him, calling him "Living Christ" and "Lord Sabbath." She began dressing entirely in white, pinning her dress with ribbons that had biblical quotations painted on them. She wore a strange white turban as a headdress and tied a bandeau around her forehead with the word "Alleluia" written on it.

The starets returned to winter in Pokrovskoye, inviting Lokhtina to visit him in the spring. His children were growing, and he enjoyed them. He was a good father. The family sat around the stove in the long evenings, and he took the children on his knee. Maria remembered him telling of "great rivers, . . . Tartar towns with their bright sunshine and narrow streets, . . . markets overflowing with great juicy fruits, . . . wandering pilgrims whose lot he had shared." He lowered his voice to a whisper and spoke of his visions—"a woman of splendid beauty, always with the features of the Holy Virgin, speaking softly to him"—before making the sign of the cross over them. He often prayed in the dug-out chapel, which he filled with icons from his St. Petersburg admirers. The children found the services wearisome but loved to be outside with him in the clear cold of the Siberian winter.

He was proud of little Dmitri's skills with horses. As they galloped across the snows in a troika together, his son learning to feel the reins, Moscow burned. A general strike brought the city to a standstill on December 7, 1905. Panicking Muscovites started a run on banks, withdrawing two million rubles in gold. Barricades were flung up in poor districts and across main avenues on December 9. Maxim Gorky was there, to note that all took part in the "cheerful labor" on the barricades, from "the respectable gentleman wearing an expensive overcoat to the cook-general and the janitor." Contempt for the tsar—still "Bloody Nicholas"—ran across the class divide. Gunmen shot at troops with "bulldogs," Browning pistols. The city's governor-general set up a command post in the belfry of the Stransoi Convent and drew up artillery to destroy the barricades while a machine gunner atop the belfry fired at the defenders, who were slowly forced back into the slum lanes of the city's Presnia section.

The Semyonovsky Guards, a crack regiment commanded by Col. G. A. Min, rushed from St. Petersburg by express train, surrounding Presnia on the night of December 16. The guardsmen were told to destroy every building from which they came under fire from snipers concealed in attics with Mauser and Winchester rifles. Min ordered them to be merciless: "There will be no arrests." A thousand civilians, including eighty-six children, were killed before Presnia fell; a hundred troops were killed. "If such a government cannot be overthrown otherwise than by dynamite," Mark Twain wrote in the United States, "then thank God for dynamite."

The infantry remained loyal and crushed the risings in the cities. Revolutionary leaders were arrested; Leon Trotsky was returned to prison, complaining that the unarmed heroism of the crowd could not face the "armed idiocy of the barracks." Black Hundred gangs, incited by churchmen and ultra-rightists, swept through ghettos with knives and clubs. The Russian empire had the largest Jewish population in the world, more than five million, and pogroms speeded a quarter of them into emigration, largely to the United States. In the great Kiev pogrom of 1905, the banker Alexander Gunzburg shouted at the Orthodox mob: "Have you no fear of Christ?" He was beaten, he wrote, with blows "so powerful that my head was driven into my shoulders and my front teeth split." He escaped to the house of the British consul next door. "The streetlamps are out," the artist Marc Chagall recollected of his Russian childhood. "I feel panicky, especially in front of the butcher's windows. There you can see calves that are still alive lying beside the butchers' hatchets and knives. 'Jew or not?' they asked. My pockets are empty, my fingers sensitive, my legs weak, and they are out for blood. My death would be futile. I so wanted to live." He denied his religion, and the men told him gruffly: "All right! Get along!"

In the Baltic provinces, as the troubles transferred to the countryside, the peasants rose against the German barons, torched their estates, and set up village republics. On Prince Orlov's estates they soaked the tails of their master's thoroughbred horses with gasoline and lit them so that they galloped burning through the night. "It is a fight in the dark, in the mud, with weapons which do not reach," the British ambassador wrote. On one side was the autocrat, "a little man with a snub nose, descendant of an alien and scarcely royal race," and on the other—"nothing at all—but just simply destruction." Witte struggled to cope with the bloodshed, and with the tsar. Nicholas was sickened at the concessions he had made, not from his free will, his cousin Grand Duke Constantine Constantinovich noted, but "torn from him by force."

At Alexandra's urging the tsar wanted them reversed. He was made bolder by the success of reaction and the free use of the gibbet and firing squad by a ruthless interior minister, Peter Durnovo, who thought it the mission of the Russian tsar to be "terrible but gracious, terrible first and foremost and gracious afterward." The rail strike collapsed, unpaid volunteers helped break the post and telegraph stoppage, industrialists felt brave enough to sack and lock out their workers. Cossacks and ex-soldiers were hired to protect country estates. Liberals, who had protested the use of whips on demonstrators in the summer, were rattled enough now to demand that all radicals be shot out of hand. Nicholas noted in a letter to his mother on December 1 that more and more voices were calling for firm action, "which is a very good sign indeed." Witte obtained the largest loan ever floated—almost three billion francs from France at 6 percent—to make the government financially independent of the elected Duma Nicholas so despised.

It was not enough to save the premier. The tsar listened eagerly to Witte's detractors. The Black Hundred leader Dr. A. I. Dubrovin, an ugly figure whose loathings foamed from gutter newspapers subsidized by the secret police, warned that the premier "is acting under the influence of the kikes." Nicholas chipped away on his own account. "As for Witte," he wrote on January 12, 1906, "since the happenings in Moscow he has radically changed his views; now he wants to hang and shoot everybody. I have never seen such a chameleon of a man." It was untrue. Witte had no desire to hang the Russian peasant, whom he thought a "slave," subject to the whims of officials, land captains, village elders, clerks, gentlemen, whose very body "is dependent upon them, for he is subject to flogging." Progress was paralyzed in the countryside. "When things are bad for the sheep," Witte warned, "they are bad for the shepherd."

The shepherd was unimpressed. The day before the Duma was first due to sit, Nicholas asked for Witte's resignation. "I am going abroad at once to take a cure," Witte said. "I do not want to hear about anything and shall merely imagine what is happening over here. All Russia is one vast madhouse." The tsar treated the most able minister in his empire with sly spite. "*As long as I live*, I will never trust that man again with the smallest thing," he wrote. "I had quite enough of last year's experiment. It is still like a nightmare to me." He replaced Witte with the lethargic Goremykin.

——

Rasputin was back in the capital in the early summer of 1906. He stayed in Sazonov's apartment, made his rounds of aristocratic salons, and kept up his contacts with the Montenegrins. The husband of his patroness Countess Ignateva, who had first shown him off to Petersburg society, was assassinated by an anarchist. "Terror must be met by terror," Nicholas wrote. Goremykin was replaced in July by Peter Arkadyevich Stolypin, a tough country squire, big as a bear and as brave, who had put down revolts as governor of Saratov province by walking unarmed into villages and persuading the rebel leaders to lay down their pitchforks and scythes. He treated revolutionaries with a monarchist's contempt. "You want great upheavals," he challenged them, "but we want a great Russia."

Punitive expeditions of well-trained troops led by hardened officers scoured the countryside; some units executed four out of five of the peasants they arrested. Prisoners were tried within forty-eight hours of arrest and executed at once. It was common for a terrorist to be tried and hanged before his victim was buried. The noose was known as the "Stolypin necktie." Stolypin dissolved the first Duma and worked on a new electoral law to ensure that the second would be more docile. Within a month of his appointment, a Socialist Revolutionary murder squad called on him at his summer dacha with armfuls of flowers, and a bomb. It killed the assassins themselves—a young man and a pretty girl—and thirty-one others. Stolypin survived.

The following day, Colonel Min, of the Semyonovsky Guards, was murdered for his work in putting down the Moscow rising. Admiral Dubrasov, the city's governor-general, had already escaped when a bomb thrown into his carriage failed to explode properly. A week after Min's killing the admiral was accosted by a young man while strolling in the Tauride Gardens in St. Petersburg. The man told him to prepare to die, pulled a Browning from his pocket, fired, and missed. He was arrested and condemned to be hanged. Dubrasov wrote to Nicholas asking for mercy, for he could still see the youth's "childish, frightened eyes." The tsar replied that the law was the law, and that not even he had the right to interfere with justice. Since he had intervened to spare the lives of extreme right-wingers convicted of murdering Jews and socialists, Witte thought his reply "childish or Jesuitical." The same month the chief of the prison administration was killed.

Nicholas and Alexandra were safe from murder in their isolated summer palaces. When Stolypin visited them to deliver reports, he traveled by steamer. For the moment, at least, he enjoyed some protection against the various hazards of the premiership, assassins, and the whims of the tsar. He moved with his family into the Winter Palace, where security was better; and, though the omens were not good—the bombing of his dacha had earned him "great moral stature . . . he was unanimously acclaimed master of the situation"—the tsar's jealousy of first-rate men had yet to get the better of him. Neither security nor Nicholas's approbation—"I cannot tell you how much I have come to like and respect this man!"—would last.

During July the sovereigns attended ten soirees, and dined twice, with Militsa at the Znamenka Palace. Anastasia and Grand Duke Nicholas Nikolayevich were present on each occasion. So, on July 18, was Rasputin. This second meeting with the imperial couple was noticed by Spiridovich's palace security. They ran a routine check on him. They found a "peasant of modest allure" and noted that he sometimes attended evening service in the small chapel that lay between Peterhof and the Villa Sergeievka; the empress also liked to pray there and had made donations to it. Rasputin was given a security code name, Blue Shirt, in deference to the light blue blouse he wore with his peasant breeches. It was standard secret police practice to use physical descriptors for people who interested them—they had recently given an obscure oil field agitator known as Joseph Stalin the code name Ryaboi, "Pockmarked"—but they concluded that Blue Shirt posed no threat to the physical security of the sovereigns. The mental state of the rulers—their isolation, the table rapping—was of no official concern to the security services.

A meeting in front of a third party, even one as well connected as Militsa, was not enough for Rasputin. On October 12, Prince Putiatyn, the court marshal, handed the tsar a letter from Iaroslav Medved, a monk and Militsa's former confessor. It was written on Rasputin's behalf and requested Nicholas to grant him an audience so that he could present the imperial family with an icon. Nicholas asked the prince to arrange the visit.

Rasputin came to the palace alone early the following evening. He brought with him an icon of St. Simeon of Verkhoturye, painted on a wooden panel twelve inches high. Nicholas gave his visitor tea and introduced him to the children. Rasputin blessed each of them and gave them small icons and pieces of holy bread. He was remarkably assured. He greeted the children, including the heir, with the traditional Russian triple kiss, cheek to cheek. Nicholas noted in his diary that night: "At 6:15, Grigory came. He brought an icon of St. Simeon of Verkhoturye, saw the children, and chatted with us until 7:15."

After Rasputin had gone, Nicholas asked Putiatyn what he thought of their visitor. Putiatyn replied that the starets seemed mentally disturbed. Nicholas was visibly upset and angry. He turned away and stroked his beard and mustache. Together with drumming on the windowpane and chain-smoking, this was a sign of the ill temper his exquisite manners normally concealed.

The critical meeting—the acceptance into the bosom of the family, the first sight of the heir—had occurred. The appearance of Rasputin, the politician Mikhail Rodzianko declared, and the start of his influence "mark the beginning of the decay of Russian society and the loss of prestige of the throne and the person of the tsar himself." That was with hindsight. For the moment the Montenegrin sisters kept their protégé in the front of the imperial mind.

There were other things to discuss. The Petersburg prefect, F. V. von der Launitz, was shot dead by a gunman at the opening ceremony of the dermatological department of the Institute of Experimental Medicine, where the recent Nobel Prize winner Ivan Pavlov taught. Because he could not be identified, the assassin's severed head was displayed in a jar of alcohol in the capital in the vain hope that someone would recognize it. The "kike-eating" new governor-general of Moscow, Horschelmann, narrowly avoided another murder squad. Gen. V. P. Pavlov, the chief military procurator, who had set up field courts-martial across Russia, was less lucky. He had dealt with cases pitilessly and had received many death threats. He stopped taking walks in public; instead, he took the air in the walled garden of his residence. An unknown gunman climbed the wall, shot him dead, and fled. It was not easy to be a loyal subject of the tsar.

Slowly, Stolypin's dual-track policy, of reform and repression, land hand-outs and hangings, won back stability. The tide of killings in the countryside, and the political assassinations in the cities, ebbed. The table talk in the palace was of other things—miracles, holy men, visions. "Militsa and Stana dined with us," Nicholas wrote on December 9, 1906. "All evening they talked of Grigory to us."

The subject of their conversation, as the sisters knew, had recently passed through the city of Volyn on his way back to winter in Siberia. Rasputin stayed there with a very religious lady—Spiridovich referred to her only as Madame O—at the suggestion of Feofan, who had instructed her in the faith. Madame O, a handsome blonde, met Rasputin at the railroad station. He astonished her by kissing her full on the lips in greeting. Once in the house he looked at her pretty maids "with the leer of a famished wolf." He insisted on a tour, including her bedroom. He sat on the bed and complained about its hardness. She said that she wanted an uncomfortable mattress to mortify her flesh for the sake of her soul. Rasputin laughed. "That's a waste of time," he said.

He asked her—knowingly and insistently—if there was anything she wished to confess. She refused, saying that he was no priest and so could not bless her. "Listen, I know how to fuck really well," he said suddenly. She stormed out of the room. He followed her and suggested, seemingly contrite, that she could become his "spiritual daughter." He asked her to go to Pokrovskoye with him. "Why?" she said. "There are no holy places there that I know of." He scowled and tried a different tack. He told her of the Montene-grins and their husbands, the grand dukes and princesses he knew by their pet names—Stana, Militsa, Petroushka, Nikolashka. She told him that he should show more respect for them. "Why?" he asked. "What good would that do me?"

To flatter her he sent a telegram to Militsa in St. Petersburg; he said that he had found "my ideal lady." Madame O was unimpressed. For a starets her guest had remarkably little interest in holiness. He drank too much, his table manners were disgusting, and he was too lazy to visit the local Potchaiev shrine. He had, she said, the air "of a man who is on to a good thing." She was glad to see him move on to Pokrovskoye for the winter.

CHAPTER 8

The Heir

Militsa wished to be the first to know when Rasputin returned to the capital; she telephoned Sazonov's apartment for reports. The holy man left Siberia early, in mid-March, and she at once invited him to her palace on the English Quay. She had someone important to introduce to him, a young woman, one of Alexandra's maids of honor.

Anna Taneeva was the daughter of the director of the tsar's personal chancellery. "A typical, stupid St. Petersburg lady," Witte remarked, "who also happened to be ugly and shapeless, as commonplace as a biscuit in dough, a young woman who happened to be in love with the empress, at whom she would gaze with ardent, honeymoon eyes, and sigh." The portrait was cruel: "pink-cheeked, full, and all dressed in fluffy fur," Anna had charm and loyalty. If she was oversweet, and her sentimentality cloying, her detractors still allowed her kindliness. What struck everyone most forcefully was her stupidity. It had a heroic quality. She repeated whatever was said to her as though it were a response; conversation with her was said to be like "talking to a gramophone."

Anna had developed what she called a "special religious mood" in 1902, when she was seventeen and suffering a near-fatal bout of typhoid fever. She had heard that people who believed in the power of the prayers of Ioann of Kronstadt would be cured of their sickness, and she asked her parents to call for the priest. "In a state of semi-consciousness, I felt that Father Ioann had arrived and entered my bedroom," she later testified. "He said a Te Deum and laid his stole on my breast. When the service was over, he took a glass of water and blessed it, and poured it over me, to the horror of the doctor and nurse who mopped me dry. I fell asleep at once. The next day, my fever had dropped, my faculties returned, and I began to get better."

Anna's father reported the miracle to the empress. Alexandra visited her sickbed and brought her flowers. Anna was named a maid of honor the following year. She was ill again in the summer, while living at Peterhof with her parents, and the empress brought her a bottle of holy water from the well of St. Serafim. Shortly after Bloody Sunday, she was called to Tsarskoye Selo for a tour of duty. Alexandra gave her a memento—a gray stone medallion in the shape of a heart surrounded by brilliants—and invited her to join the family for the fall cruise to Finland aboard the *Standart*. Their friendship waxed in the intimacy of shipboard life. They played duets on the piano and sang; Alexandra told Anna of her childhood, of Windsor Castle and Queen Victoria, and of how coldly the court had treated her on her arrival in Russia. As they disembarked Nicholas said, "Now you'll be on all our trips." He was glad of a companion who could lift his wife's melancholy. "I thank God for having sent me a friend," Alexandra said.

Anna was present at the palace at least twice a week in 1906, and she joined the family again for a long cruise among the Finnish skerries. "During this voyage the empress complained to me that she had no friends outside her family, and that she felt miserable and a stranger," Anna testified. "Her words somehow brought me close to her, and I started to regard her as my mother." Back on dry land security men noted that Anna was continuously with the empress and that the two "take singing lessons together, read together, and have long meetings."

The fact that Anna was unmarried "irritated the tsarina a little," Spiridovich thought. For five years after Bloody Sunday, Nicholas and Alexandra were not seen in public in their capital. The rulers had become ghostly figures, and there was loose chatter of lesbianism. Alexandra suggested that Anna marry General Orlov, the widower whom some gossips thought was the father of the tsarevich. The general was busy putting down revolts in the Baltic provinces, with notable brutality, and Anna thought him too old for her. But she reluctantly agreed to marry a young naval lieutenant, Alexander Vyrubov.

It was not a love match. Vyrubov's ship had been sunk under him by the Japanese at Tsushima, and he was prey to violent tempers, vodka, and cards. Militsa realized that Anna had accepted his proposal only at Alexandra's insistence, and that the prospect of marriage frightened her. Eager to exploit the young woman's intimacy with the empress, the Montenegrin took her up. They had a mutual interest in mysticism. Militsa lent Anna books in Russian and French—Anna recalled two titles, *Eldership* and *Legends of the Holy Fathers*—that she later testified "proved the existence of men who become prophets thanks to a holy life." It was a fair assumption that she would be ready meat for Rasputin, whom the empress had already described to her. Militsa asked her to come to the English Quay to meet the starets on March 17, six weeks before she was due to marry.

Militsa received her alone in the drawing room. She talked to her for an hour, reminding her that some people were gifted "from above" with the power of prophecy. Anna was sick with anticipation at meeting a living elder; the princess droned on about his virtues; the room was hot, its stuffy grandeur clashing with the icy Neva beyond the windows. Militsa startled Anna by telling her not to be surprised if she kissed Rasputin. "Ask him for whatever you wish," she said. "He will pray for you, he can ask God for anything."

The visitor was announced by a footman. A peasant in a plain Siberian jacket breezed jauntily into the room and gave the princess three hearty kisses on the cheek. He was thin, his face pale, with scarecrow beard and hair. Anna thought him "elderly"—though he was thirty-eight—and was struck by his "piercing, deep-set eyes," which seemed to find their focus deep in her mind and soul.

They paced the room, Rasputin firing personal questions in his staccato fashion. "He asked me about my occupation, where I live, and so on," Anna testified. "And I, anxious about the forthcoming marriage, for I knew my bridegroom very little, asked him whether I should get married." Rasputin looked sharply at her. "He answered that he advised me to do so," she said, "but that the marriage would be an unhappy one." The conversation lasted about twenty minutes, after which she left.

Anna married her lieutenant at Tsarskoye Selo on April 30, 1907. Nicholas and Alexandra attended the wedding, a signal honor that was not appreciated by the chief naval representative, the navy minister Adm. A. A. Birilev. "The empress wept freely, like a merchant's wife marrying off a daughter," he snapped to his friend Witte. "It would have been better if she had waited to shed her tears privately." The bride kissed the hand of the tsar as well as that of the empress. Birilev did not subscribe to the lesbian scenario. He was convinced of a ménage à trois between the two women and General Orlov; "the devil knows what sort of filth was going on," he said. His theory gained wider circulation when Orlov was posted to Egypt—supposedly to spare the cuckold tsar further humiliation—and died en route. "The empress and Anna, so I was told by eyewitnesses, went to the general's grave, left flowers, and wept," Witte claimed, further evidence to him of the "mysterious ties" that bound them.

The ceremony was sad, the bride distracted, the groom's broken nerve evident beneath his officer's brashness. The wedding night was a disaster. The imperial train was lent to the couple to take them to St. Petersburg, and Vyrubov began drinking steadily. When they reached the bridal suite, Anna recalled, the vodka "gave him the courage to be crude. Without any consideration of my feelings or the sanctity of the moment, he practically raped me." He was so drunk, however, that "his mental capacities were far ahead of his physical ones." Trembling with shock and mortification, she refused any further advances. "I only wanted him to go away and leave me alone," she said. "I never wanted to see him again."

The marriage was proved not to have been consummated, and the Orlov ménage à trois to have been fiction, when Anna was examined by doctors in the months after Rasputin's murder and found to be still a virgin. She acquired a new name, Vyrubova, under which she would become notorious, and a fresh hold over the empress. Alexandra felt responsible for the scars—physical as well as mental, for the lieutenant beat his wife—that she had inflicted on her friend by encouraging the marriage. Vyrubov was swiftly given a sea posting. In August, cruising the Finnish islands again on the imperial yacht, the battered bride poured out her misery to the empress—"I will not go back to him"—and remarked on the accuracy of Rasputin's prophecy.

—

As she spoke Rasputin was still struggling to keep up a semblance of inner holiness. He prayed alone while staying at Sazonov's apartment in the capital, and continued to do so while visiting the journalist's summer cottage in Kharkov province in August. "When Rasputin used to spend the night or came to the dacha, the servants said that he didn't sleep at night but prayed," Sazonov said. "When we lived in the dacha, children once saw him in the forest deep in his prayers. The children's story interested our neighbor, a general's wife, who wouldn't hear a good word about him. She went with the kids to the woods and, in fact, although an hour had passed since he'd gone to the forest, he was still praying."

Temptation surrounded him, however. Sazonov was ingratiating himself with the influential Jew-baiters of the Union of the Russian People and their wives. The holy peasant was an ideal lure for rich reactionaries and bored aristocrats. Witte, who knew him well, said that Sazonov "came to act toward Rasputin like the curator of a museum with an outlandish creature on exhibit." A flock of curious high society ladies came to the apartment to look him over. Some were willing to practice "purification by sin" with him. Society women were beginning to show off their independence; they were seen dining out in restaurants and visiting theaters unescorted.

Rasputin's success with cultured young women, so Spiridovich thought, was aided by the fashionable novelists who were exciting their readers with stories of the reconciliation of spirit and the flesh. One of the sensations of 1907, Lidia Zinoveva-Annibal's novel *Thirty-three Abominations*, began with the heroine's lesbian lover describing how she "kissed my eyes and lips and breasts and caressed my body." Homosexuality was in vogue; another book, *Wings*, had racy passages on sex between an older man and a youth. So was incest. The hero of the novel *Sanin* spent much of the book trying to seduce his sister. "If I like, I'll give myself to the devil!" she declared as her brother gazed lustfully at her naked body through a window. Its author believed in sexual pleasure as an end in itself, for "concepts of debauchery and purity are merely as withered leaves that cover fresh grass." Sex clubs opened with explicit names, the Burnt-Out Candle, the League of Free Love. At Ivanov's Tower, an apartment without walls, without clocks, the decadent mystic Vyacheslav Ivanov went to bed at 8:00 A.M. and breakfasted at 7:30 P.M., devoting himself to reviving the cult of Dionysius.

It was not all fun—three characters in *Sanin* killed themselves—but literary fatalism and pleasure seeking flowed into the smart set's affectation of *tryntrava*, the inconsequence of consequence. What difference did anything make? Did it matter if Sazonov's strange creature was a fraud? What if he was repulsive, a lowlife? It added thrill and danger. He was rough trade.

"I? Not in the least," a lady told the French ambassador when he asked if she found the starets charming. "He disgusts me physically, with his dirty hands, his coal-black nails. . . . Ugh! Yet I admit he amused me. He has high spirits and a remarkable imagination. He is even very eloquent at times . . . he has a deep sense of mystery. He can be familiar, scoffing, violent, joyful, absurd, and poetical. And with all that, no affectations. On the contrary, an incredible lack of manners, a staggering cynicism."

When one of Sazonov's ladies was not on hand, to be taken in her own apartment or at Lokhtina's, which he used often for assignations, Rasputin had no qualms about picking up women on the street. St. Petersburg had a policeman for every 150 citizens, a tradesman for each 75, and a whore for every 30. Two thirds of its men, and some of its ladies, used them. White slavers in Odessa brought girls from across the empire to brothels in the capital that reformers thought were no more than "prison houses for sexual slaves." The horrified author of *Children of the Streets* was offered "perverted fulfillment of sexual requirements" by two girls under twelve at five rubles per evening. A few prostitutes of noted beauty and technique made seven hundred rubles a month; most made around forty rubles, three times a mill girl's pay. Rasputin used them, according to his funds, until his death.

He was careful, however, to maintain his aura of spirituality with his religious backers. He did not like going to church, the security men noted; "he went to services only if he had to, and with ill grace." He despised most clergymen—" 'dogs' was the word he used commonly for the most distinguished priests"—but he was subtle and insinuating with those he knew to be important. He went frequently to the Theological Academy. He was at pains to keep up his contacts with its rector, Sergei, blond and energetic, a rising star, and with Veniamin, a brilliant monk-lecturer and mystic, as well as his original supporters, Feofan and Hermogen. All had influence with the empress.

———

Alexandra was exhausted from five pregnancies and the constant worry over her son. His birth, which "should have been the happiest event in the lives of Nicky and Alicky," the tsar's sister Olga wrote, "became their heaviest cross." Alexis was a lively little boy. Pierre Gilliard, the Swiss tutor who was teaching the four girls French, would spot him being taken for sledge rides in the park, careering along the passages, and bursting in on his lessons. Then, "his visits would suddenly cease, and he would be seen no more for a long time," Gilliard wrote. The palace became chill, and the girls were melancholic. When the tutor asked them what had happened, they replied evasively: "Alexis Nikolayevich is not well." Grand Duke Alexander Mikhailovich said that the tsar, his cousin, aged ten years overnight when doctors diagnosed the disease. Life "lost all purpose" for the parents, and visiting them was like entering "a house in which there had been a death."

Alexandra kept the hemophilia secret—"Don't say anything," she told her sister, "people do not need to know"—and nursed her son through his bouts of bleeding, caressing his hand and forehead as he sobbed with pain, his eyes ringed with black as seeping blood swelled into dark bruises on the surface of his skin. Nobody told Gilliard what disease the boy suffered; he deduced it from what he saw. One day the tsarevich slipped from a chair while playing in the classroom, banging his right knee as he fell. By the next day he could not walk. The swelling caused by the hemorrhage spread down the leg; the skin distended and hardened as the blood filled it tight as a drum. Gilliard found Alexandra at the boy's bedside after a bad night. The inflammation was still spreading. "Groaning piteously," Alexis had laid his head in his mother's arms; his "small, deathly white face" was unrecognizable from the romping, handsome boy, with golden hair and his mother's gray-blue eyes, of the days before. At times he stopped groaning and whispered, "Mummy." Alexandra kissed him gently—his hair, his brow and eyes—as though her lips might "relieve him of his pain and restore some of the life which was leaving him." As it struck him that the boy was a hemophiliac, Gilliard saw the empress's double agony—her son's awful suffering made worse by her own hereditary transmission of it. "Now," he wrote, "I realized the secret tragedy of her life."

The Russian people felt no such sympathy. They knew nothing of the drama; they did not see the empress. Apart from the annual cruise to Finland and a spring or fall vacation in the Crimea, Alexandra was closeted almost permanently at Tsarskoye Selo. Two palaces were set in a walled park behind high iron fences. The Catherine Palace was vast and ornate, a blue and gilt rival to Versailles, chandeliered, with exquisite parquet floors and rugs, brocaded silver and turquoise curtains, overlooking terraces, ponds, and statues. Alexandra and Nicholas had chosen to live in the nearby Alexander Palace, a more modest two-story country house with classical facades washed in ocher. The pillared center held state apartments and the rarely used ballroom. The family lived in one wing, court officials in the other. A regiment of Cossack escorts rode around the park and its avenues at intervals of fifty yards by day and night. In the palace itself men of His Majesty's Regiment were stationed in corridors, on staircases, in the kitchens and cellars. Spiridovich's police agents guarded entrances and exits, searching visitors, tradesmen, and staff, cross-referring to photographic files of known terrorists and dissidents.

The dominant color in the rooms the empress used was mauve. The carpets, the drapes, the cushions, the photograph frames in her boudoir were mauve; so were the flowers—lilacs, violets, and orchids—sent daily from the French Riviera, and the cover on the white upright piano. She bought fifty new dresses each season from Paquin and Worth in Paris but rarely wore them, preferring tight-bodiced, full-skirted dresses in cream and mauve, fussily trimmed in lace. She smelled of Rose Blanche perfume and French cigarettes. Nicholas added to her brilliant stock of jewelry each year with new Fabergé creations. For everyday use she stuck to freshwater pearls; on state occasions she so covered herself with diamonds—at her throat, on her breast, her hands, her ears, in her tiara—that the tsar's snide aunt Marie said that she had "*un goût du parvenue.*" The bedroom where she shared a double bed with the tsar was carpeted in mauve. A door led to a small private chapel lit by oil lamps. Another passed to her bathroom, where, true to her Victorian upbringing, the lavatory and the bath were concealed under cloths.

The empress had few visitors other than Vyrubova to lift her spirits; her life centered on her family, and the preservation of her son and the autocracy he would inherit. High society was spiteful to her. When she tried to set up sewing circles to make clothes for the poor, she was ridiculed for behaving like the wife of an English vicar. She gave permission for a charity bazaar to be held in the Hermitage; other charity ladies were jealous, and shopkeepers complained of unfair competition. She was too Victorian, too British, an Englishman wrote; he thought her unpopularity stemmed from "her want of a 'theatrical' sense. The theatrical instinct is so deep in Russian nature that one feels the Russians act their lives rather than live them. This was entirely foreign to the empress's thought." Courtiers and socialites found her earnest and stilted; she thought them false. When it was suggested that she meet new faces, she replied, "Why? So as to hear more lies?"

The vigorous Russia that was emerging beyond the airless world of the court was ignored. The sovereigns insisted that they valued "nothing so much as simplicity and sincerity" in people, Gleb Botkin, the son of their personal physician, observed; at the same time, "without being conscious of it, they actually appraised people almost solely according to the amount of attention these people gave to quite outward and often nonsensical etiquette." Their son had acquired this taste for protocol by the time he was four. Botkin's mother met him at the entrance to the palace, bowed, and said: "How do you do, Your Imperial Highness?" The boy frowned with anger and turned his head away, already aware that none had the right to address him before he had spoken to them.

Alexandra's day was measured and dull. She breakfasted late on bacon and eggs with well-brewed tea. She was seldom up and about before noon, spending her mornings reading or writing letters in bed. She walked with her Scottish terrier, a notorious ankle nipper, before lunch. She was indifferent to food and wine; frugal, she sold unwanted dresses to a secondhand market, first changing mother-of-pearl buttons to glass. She dealt with correspondence in the afternoon before riding in the park in a black landau or the tsar's Delaunay-Belleville automobile. After formal dinner she often listened to music—Wagner was a favorite—or played the piano with Vyrubova. Tea with the tsar at 11:00 P.M. ended the day; then they made love, their relationship still urgent and physical, or she read herself to sleep.

Any public function—a reception, a visit to a theater, a gala—was an ordeal that she avoided whenever possible. The St. Petersburg season lasted from Christmas until Lent. Lapps from Finland camped on the ice in the middle of the Neva and offered rides in reindeer sledges. A woman crocodile tamer thrilled the crowds at the winter circus by putting her head in the reptile's jaws. Hedges of roses, and baskets of daffodils and lilacs, scented the air at the bals blancs for unmarried girls. Outside, heavily padded coachmen chatted in courtyards lit by open fires, the heads of their shaggy horses haloed in the steam of their breath, waiting for girls in fur-trimmed overshoes and fur cloaks, their arms full of flowers and ribbons, to be escorted to their carriages by men in gold and white uniforms and chaperons in pearl gray satin. The dowager empress was often seen in her carriage, a small figure in a black robe protected from assassins by no more than a tall, bearded Cossack riding on the running board.

Of Nicholas and Alexandra, there was nothing. The ballrooms of the Winter Palace were unused, the wheels of the imperial coaches unturned. For the first time in living memory, the tsar failed to bless the waters of the Neva at Epiphany. He was blamed for the severe cholera epidemics that broke out in the summer; the river was heavy with germs, the superstitious said, because the tsar had not purified it. Society had no focal point without the tsar and empress; the glitter was dulled and the unexplained absence blamed on Alexandra's hauteur and hysteria.

She thought her ailments—pains in the back, the chest, the legs, exhaustion—were real and physical. "If people speak to you about my 'nerves,' " she wrote to a friend in Germany, "please strongly contradict it. They are as strong as ever, it's the 'over-tired' heart and nerves of the body and nerves of the heart besides, but the other nerves are very sound. Very bad heartaches, have not what one calls walked for three years, the heart goes wild, fearfully out of breath and such pains." Others were not so sure. Her maid, Madelaine Zanotti, thought she was suffering from hysteria: "When she found herself among congenial people she was always quite well, and never complained about her heart," Zanotti noticed. "But the moment anything displeased her . . . she immediately began complaining. Believing that her heart was affected, she used to spend the greater part of each day lying on her sofa."

Rasputin's first success at the palace flowed from his ability to calm the empress. He also had a natural way with her children. He enjoyed the young, and they, in turn, were enthralled by his stories and the games he played with them. He never patronized them; years later the niece of one of the tsar's doctors recollected him teaching her to "pray with the most wonderful words" and explaining quietly why she should never tear up flowers, because it was cruel to take life by force.

He paid further informal visits to the palace through 1907. He called the tsar Batiushka, "Little Father," and Alexandra Matushka, "Little Mother," the affectionate names used by loyal peasants for their rulers, embracing them with the Russian triple kiss. At court they were submerged by "aristocrats and gentlemen who trick them," so it was natural for them to be captivated by this "true Russian" and to show him off to their children.

The tsar's sister Olga recollected that her brother asked her one evening in the late summer, "Will you come to meet a Russian peasant?" She followed him to the bright, chintzy nursery on the first floor. The children "were completely at ease with him," she wrote. "I still remember little Alexis, deciding he was a rabbit, jumping up and down the room. And then, quite suddenly, Rasputin caught the child's hand and led him into his bedroom." Candles glowed in front of icons on the wall of the modest room, and the tsarevich stood still and silent beside the starets, joining him in prayer.

Afterward Olga took tea with Rasputin and her sister-in-law. His persistent, direct questions set her teeth on edge—"Was I happy? Did I love my husband? Why had I no children? He had no right to ask such questions." Despite Rasputin's insight, for her marriage was close to divorce, she was shocked; the more so for Alexandra merely seemed "uncomfortable" with his impertinence and did not intervene. Olga was glad to leave the palace, and she thought the peasant so pushy that she thanked God he did not follow her to the railroad station and leap aboard her private carriage. Olga felt that both her brother and his wife "were hoping that I would come to like Rasputin." She did not, but she recognized that "a gentleness and warmth radiated from him" when he was with the children. She found it "all most impressive."

A visit by Rasputin during the fall coincided with one of the tsarevich's hemorrhages. He went to the boy's bedside; shortly after the recovery began. "All one knows is that after Grigory examined the child and prayed, the hemorrhage stopped," Spiridovich reported. The starets told the parents, "Be calm, your son will live, and when he is twenty, his illness will disappear without trace." This prophecy was passed on to the security chief by the court doctor, who was told it directly by the tsar. A slightly different version was told by the director of the Imperial Theaters, V. A. Teliakovsky. He was asked by the painter Korovine, "Who is this Rasputin?" "Well," the director replied, "he's a strange fellow. He was taken to the tsarevich, who was ill in bed with a hemorrhage. His veins aren't strong; it's a hereditary illness. When Rasputin went to him, the child burst out laughing. . . . Rasputin did the same. He touched the patient's leg with his hand, and almost at once the bleeding stopped flowing. 'There's a good little boy,' Rasputin said. 'You'll get better. But only the Lord knows what will happen tomorrow.' Now, of course, the family think he's a saint."

The tsarevich's doctors were unable to explain this and Alexis's subsequent recoveries. Some specialists, however, were aware that loss of blood and exhaustion could in themselves so reduce the blood pressure that a hemorrhage would stop. This would occur spontaneously as the crisis appeared to reach its height, and recovery would be noticeable at once. It was not miraculous that Alexis lived; despite medical ignorance of the condition at the time, hemophiliacs could live well into adulthood, surviving repeated hemorrhages. Rasputin's arrival may simply have coincided with the natural onset of self-healing.

Stress increases bleeding, and it is likely that this also played a part. Rasputin had a natural affinity for people undergoing stress. His self-confidence was easily sensed; he had insight and charisma; his presence was calming. There are several accounts of him dealing with hysteria, and with migraines and other severe headaches in adults. These were sometimes accompanied by Rasputin turning pale, sweating, trembling, falling into exhaustion, and other dramatic symptoms of faith healing.

The phenomenon—prayer, intense physical and mental exhaustion, followed by the patient's recovery—is inexplicable, but it was repeated on enough occasions, in his Siberian youth, in Kiev and Tsaritsyn, several times in St. Petersburg, and in front of enough independent or even hostile witnesses, such as the tsar's sister Olga and the head of the chancellery, Alexander Mosolov, for it undoubtedly to have taken place. The physical toll on Rasputin was apparent, too, in his later dealings with the tsarevich's hemorrhages. On this first occasion with the boy, however, he was quiet and natural. The sick boy's affection for Rasputin, the instinctive comfort of prayer, and his sense that his mother's anxiety eased in Rasputin's presence would have relaxed him and thus reduced the bleeding.

Alexandra had a simpler explanation. Rasputin had sought help from God, and God had responded. "The imperial family firmly believed that they owed much of Alexis's improving health to the prayers of Rasputin," wrote Anna Vyrubova, who was herself to be brought out of a coma by the starets in a well-documented case. "Alexis himself believed it."

———

The holy man continued his unholy revels, carrying out his seductions in Lokhtina's convenient apartment. Spiridovich recorded his affair with Elena—the security chief was too discreet to use her family name, but it may have been Timofeyeva—a twenty-six-year-old with "wonderful gray eyes," a gentle creature who broke off her engagement when she became besotted with the starets. At first she tried to resist him, but Rasputin's other admirers did all they could to deliver her to him. "This was the system if someone did not give herself to the starets; it was necessary that she was forced to do what he pleased," Spiridovich observed. The victim was taken away from her home ground to meet him in company, then abruptly abandoned to him. "It was probably in Lokhtina's apartment that he deflowered her," Spiridovich wrote. "The life of the young girl was broken. Submitting to him like a slave, she followed him everywhere as if under a spell." When Rasputin showed her off to the idiot Mitya, the dwarf cackled, "Good morning, Abbess!" She turned to religion when Rasputin left her and she repented. "She took the veil, entered a convent, and died," Spiridovich concluded.

Throughout the fall, Rasputin played with his rich admirers. He lay in bed between mothers and daughters, taunting the flesh to fortify the spirit. He was interested only in the pretty. "Get off, you old crazy, get away, you old carcass," he yelled at an elderly admirer eager to be purified by sin. Others he took to bathhouses for "fervors." These were not to be confused with visits to the Nevsky bathhouses with prostitutes. "They might end in the same fashion, but the goal was different," Spiridovich commented. "If Grigory wanted to see a nude woman, he didn't have to go to a public place. There was no lack of private apartments in the capital where he could find what he wanted."

He varied his methods depending on who he was with, knowing exactly how far he could go. "He attracted some to his bed, and with others he was an angel of virtue"; with the Montenegrins, and above all with Nicholas and Alexandra, he showed "extreme decency and chastity."

———

Rasputin was flush with funds from admirers when he returned to winter in Pokrovskoye. He gave five thousand rubles to improve the church and oversaw the building of a new house for himself, the finest in the village, built of double planks on two floors with high and well-lit rooms looking toward the river. Six double windows overlooked the road, three on each floor, with handsome carved surrounds. The rooms were screened from curious passersby with muslin drapes, which gave the house a solid bourgeois air, as though its owner were a prosperous and respectable local miller. He fenced in the space in front of the house where the sidewalk would have been if rural Siberia had run to such niceties. It gave some privacy. The roof was of corrugated iron, and the eaves had the pretty detail of cross-planing. Metal chimneys replaced the roof-holes that served his neighbors. It was well decorated inside, with rugs, china plates and fruit bowls, icons, a desk, and a dining table. There were two guest bedrooms where Rasputin could play test your flesh with visitors.

He was careful that no women were in evidence when Feofan visited him for two weeks in the spring of 1908. He showed off the house proudly to the churchman, taking him to his old cabin and praying with him in the chapel beneath the barn. Feofan had reinforced his high opinion of the starets when he left Pokrovskoye for Saratov to pray in front of the shrine to St. Serafim. Rasputin accompanied him only as far as Nizhni Novgorod. He had good reason not to go on to Saratov, where the bathhouse seductions of four years before were well remembered. The mother superior at the Saratov Convent boiled with rage when Feofan spoke of Rasputin's holiness. She hurled her fork to the floor and shouted, "That's what should be done with your Rasputin!" Feofan ignored the outburst and made a favorable report to the tsar and empress on his return.

CHAPTER 9

The Go-between

Rasputin was in fine fettle when he returned to the capital in the early summer of 1908, "full of self-confidence, well-dressed in peasant style and shod in high varnished boots." He had no qualms about name-dropping. He bragged of his intimacy with the Montenegrins and their husbands when sober, and with the tsar and empress when drunk. This, and the approving noises from senior clergymen, gave him a high profile. "He begins to think he is predestined to play a special role with the tsar," Spiridovich found, "and that he will save Russia." He was now claiming to have seen Peter and Paul as well as the Virgin in his Siberian visions.

He stayed at Lokhtina's apartment and resumed his round of salons. At the house of Princess Sonia Orbeliani, he fell in again with Aron Simanovich, whom he had first met in Kiev. Simanovich had nearly been killed during the great Kiev pogrom. His shops had been looted, and his business manager and several relatives were murdered. His own life was spared because he was a fixer—he called it "an 'our' man"—for the local police chief, who smuggled him out of the city. As he left, he said, "My family and I saw the corpses of murdered Jews near the synagogue; they had been killed during the service." In St. Petersburg he was promoting gambling clubs and trading in jewels. Gambling, he found, made people "less fastidious when choosing acquaintances and less punctilious of the means of satisfying their passion"; by that he meant that they would mix with Jews and take bribes. Nevertheless, officials subjected him to "all sorts of humiliation and abasement," and he was well aware of the value of friends at court.

Simanovich's first high-level contacts had been made through two gambler brothers, the princes Wittgenstein, who served in the tsar's personal retinue. Both had recently died, one in a duel over a courtesan, the other, married to a Gypsy beauty, when he choked on a chicken bone. As a substitute Simanovich was using Princess Orbeliani. Vivacious, brave, blond, and petite, the princess had charmed the court when she arrived from Georgia a decade before. She had now developed an incurable spinal disease. This aroused the compassion of the empress—who took her for carriage outings and visited her when she was bedridden, arranging for special supports to be made for her back, as leg irons and weighted pulleys were made for the other beloved cripple in her life, her son—and hence the interest of Simanovich. He met Alexandra through the princess, and sold her diamonds at cut rates. Afterward she would check the price with the court jeweler, Fabergé, and, Simanovich wrote, "if he was surprised how cheap it was, the empress was very content."

He was aware of Rasputin's growing list of contacts and was delighted with his reception. "He treated me with respect and showed that he was ready to do a favor in his turn," Simanovich wrote. "I noticed that this muzhik could appreciate good relations. Soon we became friends." He realized that Rasputin had "not a clue about the financial side of life" and thought little about money; his loves were "wine, women, music, dances, and long and interesting conversations." Simanovich took "the trouble of his material well-being," supplying Rasputin with cash and credit. He took care not to treat him as a protégé— Rasputin hated to be patronized—but as a friend whom he helped orient in a new world of politics and power. "I became his secretary, mentor, manager, and defender," he wrote. "He would not undertake anything important without me. I was initiated in all his deeds and secrets." Rasputin's "mighty and sensual temperament" created scandals and excesses, which Simanovich smoothed out by "reprimanding him like a naughty schoolboy." Rasputin responded to this help; "soon I became indispensable to him."

It pleased Simanovich that Rasputin already knew the unhappy Anna Vyrubova; her closeness to Alexandra made her a rich prize. She had set up in a house in Tsarskoye Selo, on the corner of Church and Nobility streets. It was a pretty wooden cottage on a small lot, with a large, enclosed porch, a dining room, a drawing room with an upright piano on which she played duets with the empress, and three bedrooms on the first floor. The windows at the back gave onto the gardens of the local high school and a statue of its most famous student, the poet Pushkin. The front of "Anna's little cottage"—it was always called that—was overlooked by the many windows of the imposing palace police building. A flow of police agents strolled on the sidewalk. Being in it was "like living in a glass house," but it was only five minutes' walk to the Alexander Palace, and a direct telephone line ran from it to the palace switchboard.

Simanovich arranged for Vyrubova to meet Rasputin again at the cottage. "I was very glad to see him and said that I wanted to talk about my unhappy life," she testified. "He gave me his address: Grechesky Prospect, at the Lokhtins'." She was deeply impressed that he had predicted the failure of her marriage. A single impression was enough to make up her "limited, childish mind, for she classified people as 'good' or 'bad'—which simply meant 'friends' or 'enemies.' " She had no hesitation in classifying Rasputin as both good and holy.

Vyrubova was vulnerable to him. Her belief in the power of prayer had remained since her recovery from typhoid. Ioann of Kronstadt, who had performed that miracle, had recently died, and she was seeking another man of God. Her marriage had been "a year of dreadful trials and humiliations," she said; it had left her nervous and suggestible. She was powerfully attracted to Rasputin physically—her color heightened when she was with him, her eyes brightened and she often trembled—but her wedding night had traumatized her, and she seemed unaware of this. Rasputin kissed and caressed her in public. It flattered her, but he went no further, for she was too valuable for him to risk an indiscretion. In any event he lusted for conventionally pretty and fresh women, not the over-larded. He made no sexual advances to her, and she was often heard to say that he was "not like that." He exercised his power over her as a starets, and a "complete enslavement of her will" was rapidly established. They met frequently from the summer of 1908, at the cottage, at her father's town house on Inzhenernuyu Street, and at Lokhtina's

The relationship grew with her accelerating influence at the palace. Infatuated with both starets and empress, Vyrubova was an ideal go-between. If she missed a day with Alexandra—she often called at the palace twice a day—she pouted with hurt, and the empress joshed her, "our big baby," "our little daughter." The friendship alarmed politicians. "Not only the courtiers, but also their wives and daughters, try to get into her good graces," Witte wrote. "Also, she helps some officials gain access to the emperor." Palace staff shared the anxiety. The tutor Pierre Gilliard thought that Vyrubova had "the mind of a child . . . her judgment had not matured," and that her "unqualified adoration" for the empress was dangerous in its intensity.

She talked up the Siberian to good effect. "Their Majesties were among those who believed in the power of these wanderers," she later testified. "Like his ancestor Alexander I, the tsar always had a penchant for mysticism. Alexandra shared the same disposition." Now they shared a new friend; she said that "Their Majesties were convinced that nowadays, as in the time of Apostles, there were people—not necessarily priests—who had the grace of God and whose prayers the Lord listened to."

Only three of Rasputin's visits to the palace were recorded in the *Kammerfurier*, the official court ledger. He used a side door, entering the imperial apartments through a back corridor. He was observed by the palace security men but not by the chamberlain's staff, who logged official visitors. On his arrival, Vyrubova said, he embraced the family three times in the Russian style and chatted informally with them. He told them of Siberia, the needs and desires of the peasants, his pilgrimages—the stock-in-trade of his conversations with people he wished to impress. Nicholas and Alexandra always spoke of the heir's health and the cares and worries of the day. Their marriage was under strain—Simanovich's palace contacts told him that the empress was suffering from "hysterical breakdowns" and sometimes refused to speak to her husband, who himself "drank a lot, looking very bad and sleepy"—and the visits acted as therapy. When Rasputin took his leave, after talking with them for an hour or so, Vyrubova said that he blessed them and always left them "gay, their spirits full of joyous hopes. They believed in the strength of his prayers. . . . Nobody could ever extinguish the faith they had in him."

——

In Siberia, Praskovya Rasputin fell ill with a stomach tumor. A telegram was sent to her husband, and he arranged for a carriage to take her from Pokrovskoye to catch the Trans-Siberian Railroad at Tyumen. He was still on good terms with the Montenegrin sisters. Militsa's husband, Grand Duke Peter, arranged for Praskovie to be operated on in St. Petersburg and paid the surgeon's bill and hospital expenses. She was invited to Anastasia's palace while she was convalescing. Anastasia, now married to Grand Duke Nicholas Niko-layevich, sat her down in an armchair and washed her hands, fussing over her. The grand duchess remained standing while the peasant woman sat. "When my mother protested," Maria Rasputin recalled, "the grand duchess told her that it was not dignified for her to sit in the presence of the wife of Grigory Efi-movich." When she had recovered Rasputin took her for a droshky ride down the Nevsky to the Winter Palace and across the Neva to the Peter and Paul Fortress. The sight-seeing trip exhausted her, and she disliked the city. "I don't want to live here," she told him and happily returned to Pokrovskoye. Maria said that the operation was a hysterectomy and that her parents' sexual relations ended after it.

Rasputin was fond of his wife, and she of him, despite his infidelities. She gave him license; Simanovich said that she paid little attention to her husband's amours and "used to say in such cases: 'He can do what he likes. He has enough for all.' " Usually stubborn, hot-tempered, quick to detect a slight and pick a fight, he was "very complaisant with his wife. They lived in hearty friendship and never argued." He was a loyal family man; though he often fought with his father, he insisted that he also visit the capital. The old man was frightened by the complicated journey and the monstrous new machines—

steamboats, railroad trains—that swept him to Moscow and on to St. Petersburg. His first gesture, staring slack-jawed at the streetcars, motors, and crowds, was to make the sign of the cross in terror. He returned to Siberia within a week.

Kindliness never deserted Rasputin, and, for the moment, he kept his spiritual credentials intact when the mood took him. Prince Dzhevakov, a deputy procurator of the church synod, an intelligent man with a perceptive and sober interest in religion, arranged to meet him in Lokhtina's apartment to sound out his beliefs and methods. The prince was troubled when he glanced around the drawing room. His hostess was wearing her ribboned turban and squatting in a corner. She looked demented. Several other women were gazing at Rasputin with mute adoration. The holy man was suspicious and on edge. "Why have you come?" he asked the prince. "To look at me, or to learn how to live in this world and to save your soul?" At the word *soul*, Lokhtina began crying in a thin, piercing voice: "He's a saint! He's a saint!" "Shut up, imbecile," Rasputin snapped. Then, to the prince's surprise, he turned to him, settled himself, and began to talk of salvation, the discourse confident and lively.

"To save his soul, a man must lead a pious life," he began. "That's what the priests and bishops pontificate from their pulpits. And it's true. Yes, but how do you do it? They tell you: 'Take the *Lives of the Saints*, read it and read it again, and you'll know.' So I did. I read how each saint achieved salvation in his own fashion. But, you know, they abandoned the world, they found their salvation in deserts and monasteries. The *Lives* described the existence of ascetics from a moment when they'd already become saints. I told myself—there's something wrong with that. . . . Don't tell me about their lives after they've become saints. Tell me how they got there. That's the only way I can learn something from them.

"Remember—among them are great sinners, brigands, scoundrels. And suddenly they pop up among the just! How did they do it? At what point did they leave the path of evil for the path of heaven? How did they—mired in spiritual filth—recognize that God exists and come to him? That's what I must be shown. And another thing. Every time you look at the life of a saint, it's a monk. What about ordinary people? They want to save their souls, too. They need help, too. A hand must be held out to them, too."

At this Lokhtina shrieked back into life. "Help us! Give a hand to us!" she sobbed, shaking as she held out her hands to the starets. "You can do anything. You know everything. Christ! You are Christ!"

"Shut up, imbecile," Rasputin roared. "Or else . . ."

"I will be silent. I will be silent," she promised.

Regaining his temper and concentration, Rasputin turned back to the prince. "Laymen must be helped to salvation," he said. "Say a minister of the tsar, or a general, or a princess worries for the soul and wants salvation. . . . So, they're told to take refuge in a desert or a monastery! What about their responsibilities? Their families? Their children? Their duties? No, these people cannot abandon the world. Something else must be done—but they're never told what. Go to church, keep the commandments, read the Bible, lead a pious life, and you'll be saved—that's all they're told. And that's what they do. They go to church, they read the Bible. That doesn't stop their sins from growing every day. It doesn't stop evil from stealing up on them and turning them into savage beasts. You have to show this man who has lost his human form, who has the morals of a wild animal, how he can escape from the pit. How he can breathe pure air. This path exists. But he must be shown it." Rasputin leaned forward to the prince. "And I can show it to you."

The nervous tension in the room mounted toward a paroxysm; Rasputin's listeners sweated, and Prince Dzhevakov felt them straining for wisdom, for a guidance that priests could not give them but that shone from the bearded man with gleaming eyes. Lokhtina relapsed into hysteria, and Rasputin cursed her into silence.

"God is salvation," he continued. "You can see God when everything else is black around you. Evil, sin—all that hides God from you. The room you're in, the work you do, the people around you—they all hide God. You have to do something to see God. . . . But what?" His eyes slipped into a distant focus. "After mass, after prayer, leave the city—on a Sunday or a holiday—go into the deep countryside." He lowered his voice, and his soft Siberian accent stroked his listeners. "Walk, walk until you no longer see the black smoke of the Petersburg chimneys behind you, and the limpid air of the horizon lies on you. . . . Stop and reflect. How small you seem, how insignificant and helpless. And, in your mind's eye, the capital will change into an ant heap where men rush about like busy insects. What happens to your pride, your self-love, your feeling of power? . . . You feel miserable, useless, abandoned. And then—then, raise your eyes to heaven, and you will see God. In your heart, you sense that you have one father, our Lord God, and that it is to God alone that you must give your soul—that it is to him alone that you wish to give it. Only he can protect you and help you.

"A great tenderness will seize you. This is the first step toward God. Later, you will venture further, but for now return to the world. Go about your business while preserving, like the very apple of your eye, what you have brought back with you. Because you have brought back God in your spirit. This emotion that overwhelmed you when you met him . . . preserve it jealously . . . it will be the sieve through which you can sift all the acts of your life. Thus you will transform your worldly deeds into divine deeds. You will save your soul, not through penitence but by working for the glory of God. If you live for your own glory, for the glory of your passions, you will not be saved."

Rasputin returned to his childhood, to the reading in the Pokrovskoye church that had so deeply affected him, and that was so convenient to his message, for it proved the existence of men of God. "This is what the Savior meant when he said, 'The Kingdom of Heaven is within you.' " He paused, a moving, well-calculated silence, and raised his voice for the final blessing. "Find God and live with him and in him. Not just on saints' days and Sundays. . . . Tear yourselves away from your workaday lives. Instead of socializing or going to the theater, go into the deep countryside, toward God!"

The prince was overwhelmed. Rasputin's words, he wrote, "struck me with irresistible force." Piety, for which he had long searched without success, seemed to light the room as physically as the sun burning off a salty Petersburg fog. Dzhevakov had heard many brilliant preachers. Fifteen years later he had forgotten them all. He recalled Rasputin word for word.

At the same time the starets pressed on with his debauches. He behaved with "such impossible caddishness" that Simanovich, a hardened operator with few scruples of his own, was shocked at the deliberate way Rasputin set out to outrage society. He never cursed when he spoke to peasants or to his daughters, but he scolded and jeered at noblemen with particular vigor, calling them "dogs" and saying that they had not a drop of Russian blood in their veins. This was dangerous ground, for three centuries of Romanov marriages with German and Danish princesses had left the tsar with one part of Russian blood to more than one hundred foreign; the tsarevich, suffering with his mother's blood, had less than one part to two hundred.

It mattered little to Rasputin; he lusted for "exciting sensations," Simanovich said, and insulting his social superiors was one of them. He swore at countesses and famous actresses "in the most obscene manner and with words that would have made a stable lad blush. His impudence at times was indescribable." He talked openly to women he found attractive of farmyard sex, stallions and mares, bulls and cows; "Ah, my fine mare!" he called them. "The presence of their husbands and fathers did not baffle him in any way," Simanovich reported. "His conduct would have revolted the most inveterate prostitute." To his great relief, however, Simanovich found that "it almost never happened that anyone expressed indignation. Everyone was afraid of him."

They feared Rasputin's tongue, his reputation, his energy; they fawned on him. He rarely used a knife and fork at the table, helping himself with dry and bony fingers; "big pieces he tore like an animal." He did not eat meat but grabbed at fish, potatoes, and vegetables, which often stuck in his beard. Ladies kissed his hands, soiled with food, and "did not shun his dirty fingernails." He passed chunks of fish and bread around the table in his hands to his women admirers, and they "tried to assure him that they regarded it as bliss."

Simanovich himself found this merely "disgusting," but he was glad to see that the socialites quickly became used to it with "unparalleled acceptance."

The starets could, however, go too far. Grand Duke Nicholas Nikolayevich was shocked when the starets extended his habit of insulting churchmen to include saints. But he was virtuous, eager, and polite on his visits to the Alexander Palace; no trace of lust remained. Before he set out for the palace, Spiridovich discovered, Rasputin behaved "as if he were going to communion." He prayed, took a bath, put on a clean shirt and fresh clothes, and "appeared nervous to the highest degree."

———

The tsarevich was in good health for most of 1908, protected from falls by his minder, a giant sailor called Nagorny, who swept him up into his arms if he became too boisterous, though Rasputin helped him through nosebleeds. He told Simanovich that he prayed with the boy and helped him to relax until the bleeding passed. Once, he said he took a piece of oak bark from his pocket, mashed it up in boiling water, and spread it over the boy's face as a poultice so that only the eyes and mouth were uncovered. It was a Siberian peasant remedy for cuts; Rasputin claimed it was effective. He treated Simanovich for migraines at this time. He stood behind him, took his head in his hands, whispered unintelligible phrases, and then squeezed his head with the word *Go.* The result, the patient said, was "stunning."

When the boy's life was not directly endangered, Rasputin's welcome at the palace was more as a family friend than as a healer. The tsar took to him. Nicholas believed that courtiers and politicians deceived him. "For me, there are honest people only to the age of three," he told Rasputin. "As soon as they reach that age, their parents should be glad that they cannot talk enough to lie. They are all liars." This suspicion bred inconstancy and weakness; Simanovich thought it "the tragedy of his life." As a child Nicholas had had an English tutor, Charles Heathe, from whom he learned a very English sense of self-control and reserve; he hated scenes. He was only fully at ease with others while an army officer in his early twenties; he had enjoyed the easygoing familiarity of the officers' mess, with its rituals of drinking and hunting. An aide-de-camp thought that he had only a "single real friend," General Orlov, whom he had served with in the Guards Hussars. Even that friendship was debased by the scandalmongers, who had nodded and winked over Orlov's supposed affair with the empress.

The tsar knew that he was not respected; "craftiness," his former premier Witte wrote of him, "unspoken lies, the inability to say yes or no and to live up to what one has said, to be possessed of an optimism born of fear, that is, optimism used to shore up one's nerve." He lived in dread of his uncles and his mother, and of the "old court" she maintained as dowager empress. Terrorists kept him away from his own capital; they also prevented him from traveling freely abroad. As the "butcher of Bloody Sunday," he was so despised in Italy that a planned state visit to Rome had to be called off when Italian newspapers called for the "despot" to be met with demonstrations. He finally went in 1909 but met the Italian king in his seaside summer residence at Racconigi, which could be reached by water.

The tsar was conscientious and hardworking enough, but the business of ruling did not intrigue him; it was merely his duty, a family chore. It was becoming increasingly irksome as political parties chipped away at autocracy and the chairman of the Council of Ministers tried to consolidate himself as a Western-style prime minister. Even after property owners dominated the Duma electorate when the franchise was changed by decree on June 16, 1907, he found the Duma's lower house odiously radical.

Nicholas was solitary, cocooned with his wife and children in those dull, mauve apartments. Rasputin amused him; he told him stories of distant parts of his empire he had never seen. The Siberian's self-confidence was catching; he showed his good nature, hid the fangs of his temper. They enjoyed their chats; Nicholas laughed at the earthy Siberian dicta that peppered his new friend's lively talk. These were, or so the tsar thought, purely private conversations of an intimacy he could not show to officials and appointees; he felt safe with Rasputin, not knowing that the peasant was already trading ruthlessly on his imperial connections. Rasputin brought out in Nicholas those private qualities—generosity, forgiveness of indiscretions, loyalty—that suspicion sapped from his professional life. Rasputin had no airs and graces; he seemed honest and simple, a representative of those scores of millions of peasants with whom Nicholas shared no common blood or interests, whom he seldom met, but who he believed loved him. The tsar wished to meet a man of the people, his security chief said, "his people of whom he is ignorant. Rasputin is that." And thus he trusted him.

The idea that peasants were a reservoir of Russian virtues—brave, patient, unvenal—was common to both sides of the political divide. Leo Tolstoy had condemned his own great novels as worthless; he believed that art lay in rural simplicity, gave his fortune to his wife, and was living as a peasant under her roof. The tsar's sister Olga was deeply impressed when she went into the huts on her husband's estates. She found hardship and beggary, and also "kindness, magnanimity, and an unbreakable faith in God. As I saw it, those peasants were rich for all their poverty, and I had the feeling of being a genuine human being when I was among them." Leftists and terrorists felt the same romantic pull. Social Revolutionary students went out in thousands to the villages, searching for an ideal society where all things were shared, confident that in turn they would radicalize the peasants. In practice, they found hostility—men who sold them to the police for a few rubles, who mocked them as *belorucha*, "whitehands," and stripped them naked to see if they had tails or were covered in hair like Antichrists.

———

There was mounting evidence that the tsar's trust in the peasant was misplaced. Okhrana agents reported that Rasputin was visiting bathhouses with "lowlife girls." The police were well aware of his high connections. He was seen "almost running from the platform" at St. Petersburg railroad stations to a waiting automobile that drove him to Militsa's palace. Stolypin was concerned enough to order security chiefs to prepare a file that would enable him to serve an expulsion order to remove Rasputin from the capital for immoral conduct.

Some church leaders were equally alarmed. Bishop Antony Khrapovitzki of Volhynie, a member of the synod, was angry at the attention and favors given to the peasant. He had heard of the debauches in Kazan, and he reminded his fellow bishops that a debauchee could not be a saint. "Grigory is a sly and skillful flatterer, a khlyst, a sot, a lecher, and a layabout," he warned the synod, "and nothing more." He forwarded letters denouncing the starets from Kazan to Sergei, the rector of the St. Petersburg Theological Academy. Bishop Antony was active in a campaign to grant autonomy to theological academies. Rasputin, who never forgot or forgave a hostile act, wrote a note to the tsar condemning the scheme. It was duly killed off. Although Sergei ignored the Kazan letters, Rasputin was made nervous by his presence in the capital. Sergei was named archbishop of Finland and left for Vyborg; he was replaced by Feofan at the tsar's personal instruction. It was the first time that a direct link was made between Rasputin and a senior church appointment.

Toward the end of the year, Rasputin visited Finland with his friend the academy lecturer Veniamin. The Vyborg monks did not find Rasputin a saint, as Veniamin introduced him; they thought him crude and drunken. "What! What!" cried Veniamin. "You don't know Grigory, you don't understand him. I see him walking like a saint, an archangel come to earth." The precaution of removing Sergei had been wise; Rasputin's growing intimacy with the tsar was still vulnerable to scandal. Nicholas did not think of him as a saint. "He is just a good, religious, simpleminded Russian," he told a senior security officer. "When in trouble or assailed with doubts, I like to have a talk with him and invariably feel at peace with myself afterward."

Rasputin's relations with the empress and Vyrubova were more secure. They referred to him as "our Friend," using the capital letter in the sense of a guide and protector sent from God. On the late summer cruise aboard the *Standart*, the empress had gotten to like one of her husband's aides-de-camp,

Sablin. "Her conversations led up to the fact that she was acquainted with Rasputin," Sablin testified later. "She said that there were some people whose prayers had special power due to the pious life they led. Finally, she mentioned that there was such a man in Russia, that is Rasputin, and offered that I should meet him." As to Vyrubova, Rasputin was reporting to Simanovich that she "is devoted to me to the grave" and that "my minutest wish is a law for her."

By the late fall of 1908, the links among the trio were common knowledge in society. A general's wife, Madame A. K. Bogdanova, was writing in her diary that Alexandra and Vyrubova had a "lively amorous correspondence." Most nights when the tsar returned to his study to work at 9:00 P.M., the pair retired from the dining room to the mauve boudoir to discuss the starets. Bogdanova also knew that the empress was meeting Rasputin at Vyrubova's cottage. Her informant, one of the tsar's valets, had been told by Vyrubova's maid that her mistress had a photograph of herself with the muzhik, which she kept in her Bible. "It appears that Vyrubova is friends with some sort of peasant, and a monk to boot," she wrote on November 5. "The peasant has the stare of a wild animal, a repulsive, insolent appearance . . . the peasant is there when the empress calls."

CHAPTER 10

Testing the Flesh

Rasputin recontacted Khionia Berlandskaya, still suffering guilt over her husband's suicide, and persuaded her to return with him to Pokrovskoye that winter. He made love to her on the Trans-Siberian to Tyumen, moving into her sleeping compartment as soon as the train pulled out of Moscow. "He told me that he loved me as a man," she wrote later. "He instructed me to prepare myself as a woman and began to do what a husband alone is permitted to do. . . . He forced me, caressed me and kissed me, and lay with me. He then did all he wanted, to the end." The following morning, he explained that his mission in life was to relieve original sin. He "tested" her again as darkness fell on the slow-moving train, becoming aroused and, she said, "obliging me to acknowledge his excitement." She was miserable and suffering—"Heavens, how can God help to write all this down!"—and she thought that she must be "dirty, impure, and given over to passion . . . for he clearly felt it necessary to subject me to perpetual testing."

Few of his women were as breathtakingly naive as this. Some—actresses, courtesans, bored aristocrats, the mistresses of important men—were quite as cynical as Rasputin and gave themselves to him out of lust and curiosity. Casual sex—and Rasputin's was casual, often a matter of five minutes and a grunted "now, matushka, that's better"—was making inroads with the capital's fast set. If it remained more or less scandalous, and several Romanov grand dukes were living in France and Germany because their liaisons had become known, that added the fillip of danger. Other women slept with him in a matter-of-fact way, hoping to gain advancement for themselves or their families. Nevertheless, Rasputin was aware that to destroy the reputation of a respectable woman like Berlandskaya was to subject her to ostracism and contempt. He had no remorse.

Praskovya Rasputin was chilly when the lovers arrived in Pokrovskoye. She shouted at Berlandskaya, served her small portions at meals, and refused to give her a guest room. Rasputin slept with her on a mattress on the floor; Praskovya removed it and gave her a thin mat. Rasputin found it too uncomfortable to pass a whole night on; he fucked her swiftly when the mood took him. "Ah, this is a heavy stone," he told her of the "sin" he was lifting from her. "I've never known one so heavy." Another disciple joined them, and he made her wash him in the bathhouse in the courtyard. "He was quite naked," Berlandskaya wrote, "and he ordered her in front of everyone and in their sight to wash the parts of his body that are covered up more than others."

When he returned to St. Petersburg early in 1909, Rasputin was short of funds. He rode second class, much to his irritation, while Berlandskaya traveled in third. He ate well but gave her only his scraps.

———

The young widow later made bitter public accusations against Rasputin, but for the moment he was safe. He made a second important contact at the palace when Vyrubova introduced him to Lili von Dehn. She was the wife of an aide-de-camp, Capt. Charles von Dehn, whom the empress had met on the annual cruise aboard the *Standart* and to whom she had become close. Lili von Dehn's son Titi was running a high fever, and doctors feared that he was sickening with diphtheria, then a potentially fatal disease. Vyrubova advised her to see Rasputin and telephoned him to arrange a meeting.

She met him at Sazonov's. He seemed a "typical peasant from the frozen North," in high boots, loose shirt, and a muzhik's long, black coat. Then she noticed his eyes, "shining and steel-like," in a thin, pale face framed in light chestnut hair. Many people described him as tall; she noticed that he was not, "but he gave the impression of being so." His stare unsettled her—"I felt at once attracted, repelled, disquieted, and reassured"—but she asked him to come and pray at her child's bedside.

He arrived with a "quaint creature" dressed like a nun—Lokhtina—who refused to enter the boy's bedroom and sat praying on the stairs. Rasputin knelt and prayed, then bent over the bed. "Don't wake him," she asked, afraid that the strange peasant would frighten the child. "Silence. I must," he insisted, putting his fingers on the boy's nose. Titi woke at once but looked at the starets without a trace of fear, telling him that his head ached. "Never mind," Rasputin said. He turned to the mother: "Tomorrow your son will be well. Let me know if he is not." Titi slipped back to sleep. The next morning his temperature was normal. His doctor was "astonished."

The illnesses that Rasputin relieved for adults—Lokhtina's hysteria, the empress's "neurasthenia"—were psychosomatic. He had undoubted talent. "Taking the head of the sick person in his hands, as if praying, he could suggest what he liked," Spiridovich said. "The patient became calm, and the cure was attributed to the prayers of the starets, which were obviously pleasing to God. It was thus that he operated with Lokhtina and others." Although he was most successful with the suggestible and religious, particularly women, he was also effective with the cynical Simanovich. He used his powers sparingly; he made no claim to be a professional healer, as Dr. Philippe had done. He acted only on request and as a favor to people he knew or as a means to seduction; he seldom boasted of his cures, at least when sober, and was always careful to attribute them to God.

With children the possibility that he was a thaumaturge, a miracle worker, was discussed by doctors. They could think of no other explanation in cases like that of Titi von Dehn. As the tsarevich grew he became more vulnerable to his hemophilia. Shortly after the Dehn case, he fell in the park at Tsarskoye Selo and hit his leg. His aunt Olga saw him lying in his palace room "in such pain, dark patches under his eyes, and his little body all distorted, and the leg terribly swollen." The doctors seemed more frightened than the family and kept whispering among themselves; they were "just useless." As it got late Olga was persuaded to go to her room. Alexandra had a telephone call placed to Rasputin in St. Petersburg.

He reached the palace at about midnight, when Olga was asleep. The next morning Alexandra called for her to go to Alexis's room. "I just could not believe my eyes," Olga wrote. "The little boy was not just alive—but well." He was sitting up in bed, his eyes bright, the fever and the swelling in the leg "quite gone." Alexandra told her that Rasputin had stood at the foot of the bed and prayed. He had not touched the boy. Some claimed that his prayers had coincided with the child's natural recovery. Olga disliked Rasputin, but she was convinced there was more to it than that. The doctors insisted that no attack of such severity could be cured in a few hours. "Secondly," she continued, "the coincidence might have answered if it happened, say, once or twice, but I could not even count how many times it happened!"

Lili von Dehn joined Rasputin's circle. She met him frequently with Vyrubova and saw him when he came to the palace, at this time "on average once a month." Alexandra treated him "with veneration." She called him Grigory when she was with him and Father Grigory when she was not. "I believe in him," she told Dehn repeatedly. For his part, he became angry if he thought people were blocking his access to the palace, and he often said that "Mama is stingy," complaining that the empress gave him little money.

Having seen him save her son, Dehn had no truck with the rumors of Rasputin's seductions. Quite the contrary; she claimed that he saved women from themselves. "I know for a fact," she testified later, "that many women of my world who had affairs and many demi-mondaines were not dragged further into the mire by Rasputin, for—incredible as it may appear—his influence in such cases was often for the best." As an instance of his morality, she recalled how she met him while out walking in St. Petersburg with one of her husband's brother officers. The starets was outraged. "Are you following the example of frivolous society women?" he bellowed. "Why are you not walking with your husband?" To women who sought his advice, he said: "If you mean to do wrong, first come and tell me." If he meant "come and do the wrong with me first," it passed Dehn by. Rasputin's admirers met evidence of misdeeds with heroic suspension of disbelief.

———

Vyrubova traveled to Pokrovskoye at the empress's expense with three other ladies, their maids, and a palace nurse, Maria Ivanovna Vichnyakova, to satisfy Alexandra's curiosity. Subsequent police reports recorded by Spiridovich described the visit, in May 1909, as sordid and ill-tempered. Vyrubova's own account—she used a different date—was of a rural idyll full of prayer and sanctity.

She said that Rasputin met them at Tyumen station in a peasant cart drawn by two farm horses. The house was "almost biblical in its bare simplicity." The guests slept on straw mattresses laid out on the bare wooden floors of the upstairs bedrooms; there were icons on the walls and faintly burning tapers in front of them. She made no mention of the rich furniture mentioned by other witnesses. They ate plain meals downstairs with four peasant friends of their host; "sitting around the table," she said of these guests, "they sang prayers and psalms with rustic faith and fervor."

Every day Vyrubova and the other ladies went down to the river to watch Rasputin drawing in his nets. He had become fisherman as well as farmer. They often had dinner by the river, cooking the fish "over little campfires on the shore," sharing their raisins, bread, nuts, and pastries. They visited Verkhoturye together, saw the relics of St. Simeon, and talked with the starets Makari in his forest retreat. "This aged and pious monk," Vyrubova reported to the empress, "held Rasputin in higher respect than the village clergy."

In the police account Rasputin traveled with the ladies Vyrubova, Madame Orlova, the mother of the dead general, Rasputin's conquest Elena Timofeyeva, and a lady Spiridovich referred to as Madame S, possibly Anna Dmitrievna Shipova, a maid of honor in the court of the princess of Oldenburg. People who knew Rasputin well denied it—in seven hundred pages of memoirs, the former premier Sergei Witte made no mention of their meetings, and a future premier would see him only in secret in the Peter and Paul Fortress—while those who did not, seeking to gain advantage, claimed that they did. Some who came across him, like Madame S, were protected by the use of an initial.

The anonymity Spiridovich afforded her is explained by events on the first night outbound from Moscow on the Trans-Siberian. Rasputin and Elena took the two top couchettes of a sleeping compartment, with Madame S on the berth beneath. During the night Rasputin fucked Elena noisily. When he had finished he climbed into Madame S's berth. She grabbed his beard and pulled it as hard as she could before seeking sanctuary for the rest of the night in the corridor. At Tyumen station they were met by two telegas, which drove them off at spine-jolting speed. When the elderly Madame Orlova complained, Rasputin hissed: "Why am I lumbered with you?" They arrived in Pokrovskoye, sore and upset, at 2:00 A.M. Rasputin put Madame S in a separate bedroom. In the morning he ordered her to wash in the river. She did so, weeping with humiliation. A peasant woman who had come to get water tried to comfort her. When she learned that she was staying with Rasputin, the woman shrugged expressively, picked up her bucket, and trudged off to the village.

At lunch Vyrubova asked Rasputin to bless each course. There was little talk after the scandal on the train. After the meal they went for a walk. They met Father Pyotr, the village priest, but Rasputin refused to introduce the women to his old enemy. "No need!" he said angrily. He bought each of them a head scarf in the store. They said psalms when they returned to the house—the two accounts have that much in common—with Rasputin swinging his arms like a conductor. After dinner, at six, Praskovya Rasputin washed her husband in the bathhouse in the courtyard while Elena and Vyrubova looked on. Vyrubova suddenly reddened and cried: "Come here! Come here! The Holy Spirit has descended on Grigory Efimovich!"

As the ladies came out of the house, a dog began to bark. Praskovya Rasputin pushed them back indoors, warning, "Look! Priests are coming!" It was a false alarm. The village priest walked past without looking in. Rasputin came out of the bathhouse, lobster pink, drying his face on a towel. "Ah, you're young," he reproached Madame S, "much too young to be so chaste." She accused him of being a khlyst. Vyrubova calmed him.

He took them by cart to a neighboring village the next morning to meet two peasants he introduced as "my brothers in Christ." They insisted on taking the ladies by the waist to walk with them. When they returned to the house, Vyrubova said that she wanted to send a telegram to the empress. "We are bathed in beatitude," it read. The others objected; the visit had become an ordeal. Rasputin told her to send it, and she did so. In the evening Rasputin had a wire from Grand Duke Nicholas Nikolayevich asking him to return to St. Petersburg for the consecration of a new chapel. Rasputin said they would leave the next morning.

The "brothers in Christ" drove them to Tyumen in telegas. Madame S threatened to tell the empress that Rasputin had made love to Elena on the outward journey. Vyrubova retorted that all his deeds had a "divine character." Rasputin made them sing psalms in the carriage; a Siberian industrialist on the train warned the ladies that these were khlyst songs. A soldier asked Madame S if it was true that one of the empress's maids of honor was traveling with Rasputin. She felt ashamed. At Vyatka, Rasputin tried to kiss her; she slapped him, and he became angry. He said that he had spoken well of her to the empress— "and this is how you treat me. What am I to say about you to her now?"

As they neared St. Petersburg, however, Rasputin's behavior improved and he resumed his role as starets. When he embraced the ladies as the train drew in, it was to mollify them. Vyrubova left without a word. Madame S's husband was on the platform. Rasputin sneered to him that his wife had "done nothing but argue with me the whole time." True to her threat, Madame S wrote a letter to the empress, thanking her for the opportunity of visiting Pokrovskoye but adding that Rasputin merited "neither the favor nor the confidence of Their Majesties." She said that Madame Orlova could vouch for his misconduct.

Orlova was summoned to an audience at the palace, Spiridovich said, but she maintained that nothing untoward had taken place. The problem was Madame S, a "prude who sees depravity where there is none," whose lies were calculated to disgrace Vyrubova and worm her way into the empress's favor. An embellished version of the episode was soon making the rounds. "Vyrubova went to Tyumen to the screwball's place and spent several days there," Madame Bogdanova noted in her diary. "Several ladies' maids were outraged by the screwball. One of them is pregnant, and it seems that Annushka [Vyrubova] is going to bring up the baby."

———

Rasputin's next scandal was religious. He took up the cause of Iliodor, the young monk he had met with Hermogen on his first visit to St. Petersburg. Convinced that the church was rotten, the tsar betrayed, and Christianity dying, Iliodor had moved to Tsaritsyn on the Volga to raise a popular movement to protect Russia against the Jews, Freemasons, anarchists, and church leaders he thought hell-bent on destroying it. He arrived in the city with three rubles and seventy kopecks in his pocket and was given a small chapel on wasteland in an outlying slum district.

He was a Don Cossack by birth, and his sermons were a battle cry against "drunkenness, filth, selfishness, and sordid rapaciousness of all kinds." Bargemen, porters, timber carriers, the scum of the Volga, wept for their sins and "gloried in his bold mouth." He saved alcoholics by holding long services that kept them out of the vodka shops until they closed. He took prostitutes out of the riverside brothels to hear him preach, and shamed their customers by reading out their names. Robert Wilton, the London *Times* correspondent, was intrigued enough to visit Iliodor, finding a congregation of thousands, "a sort of Russian Salvation Army. . . . Desperadoes and a similar class of women flocked to him." With "wax-like fingers and a face transparent from long vigils," Wilton wrote, dressed in white vestments, the monk stood above the dirty crowds like an angel as he harangued them; he "caught the people's hearts, and held them."

Fifty thousand gold rubles were raised by public subscription to build a monastery for Iliodor while the poorest of his flock toiled on the site without wages. It was a dramatic building, like the film set of a medieval fortress, with battlements and wooden towers. It matched the monk's crusading calls for violent counterrevolution against politicians and in favor of the tsar. He denounced the prime minister, Stolypin, for selling his soul to the Jews. He kept a photograph of the "Antichrist" Leo Tolstoy, and the faithful spat on it as they passed. He had made a model of a huge dragon, which he said represented revolution, decapitating it with a sword when his sermons reached their climax. Alarmed officials reported that he was spreading sedition. "I am accused of treason," he thundered in reply from the pulpit. "The government demands that I cease preaching the divine truth. I declare holy war on the synod and the government. . . . I am ready to die a thousand deaths. I ask you, brothers and sisters, to do the same!" He had tunnels built in the clay beneath the monastery; when the provincial governor sent troops with a message for him to hold his tongue, he disappeared. Wilton thought that "the monk's madness has a world of method in it."

After a rabble-rousing performance in the summer of 1910, in which Iliodor openly called on his followers to arm themselves, Stolypin and the synod persuaded the tsar to sign an order expelling him from his Tsaritsyn power base. He was ordered to enter a monastery in Minsk. At this he traveled to St. Petersburg to see whether Rasputin could use his influence to have the order revoked. The two holy men resumed their friendship; Rasputin assured Iliodor he would help. He introduced him to Vyrubova. She knelt before him and kissed his hand. "Well, you saw it with your own eyes!" Rasputin bragged to Iliodor as they left. "What do you think of that!" They arranged to meet the empress at Vyrubova's cottage. She asked Iliodor not to indulge in "demagoguery" but recommended that Rasputin appeal to the tsar.

He did so. In the account Rasputin gave to Iliodor, Nicholas argued that he could do nothing, since he had already given his consent to the order. "You are the tsar," Rasputin replied. "Act like one. You have given your word, and you can take it back. When you threw Iliodor to the dogs to be eaten, you signed your name like this, from left to right. All you have to do is to sign it from right to left. Then you will have acted like a real tsar." Rasputin was always at his most boastful with Iliodor, himself not a reliable witness. It is highly unlikely that Rasputin was so cavalier with a man as sensitive of his position as Nicholas. Nevertheless, to Stolypin's fury, and the growth of Rasputin's reputation, the tsar indeed revoked the order.

———

Nicholas attended celebrations at Poltava to mark the two hundredth anniversary of the victory of his ancestor Peter the Great over the Swedes. He was met with cheers, a sound he had heard rarely since Bloody Sunday, and he assured the French military attaché that they proved both his popularity and the fact that "we are no longer at Petersburg." He said that "the rural population, the owners of land, the nobility, and the army" remained loyal. Those against him, he said, were "composed above all of Jews, students, landless peasants, and some workers." With this comforting but untrue thought, he took his family to spend three months of late summer and fall abroad. They visited the yachting regatta at Cowes on the Isle of Wight, where Nicholas sailed with his look-alike cousin, the future George V of England, and partied with another cousin, German Kaiser Wilhelm. Alexandra visited her brother in Darmstadt and went to the spa at Nauheim to see heart specialists. Rasputin went with Bishop Hermogen to visit Iliodor in Tsaritsyn.

The monk's followers feted Rasputin as the savior of their prophet and an angel of God. He enjoyed himself. A line of women formed in the monastery to seek his advice. He kissed the pretty ones and turned the others away: "Mother, your love is pleasing, but the spirit of the Lord does not descend on me."

He cured two demented souls at Iliodor's request, according to police reports. A carter's wife, "young, beautiful, and buxom," was prey to voices in her head that made her curse and convulse. Iliodor's attempts to exorcise her demons with prayers, crucifix, and holy water failed. She continued to shriek. Rasputin asked to be left alone by her sickbed. After a few minutes the cries ceased. The wife then came smiling from her bedroom, peaceful and content, while Rasputin followed to say that he had cast out the evil spirit, with a "sly, triumphant smirk on his lips." This cure was followed by the treatment of the niece of a rich merchant, Madame Lebedeva. Rasputin said that he could not exorcise her demons in the bedroom where she lay, and he had her carried to an isolated room. He spent several hours with her, reappearing in the late evening while she slept quietly, as though "surrounded by angels." News of "miracles" swept through Tsaritsyn. When he set off for his winter trip to Pokrovskoye, taking the grateful Iliodor with him, Rasputin rode through cheering crowds in a flower-strewn carriage.

Iliodor reported that Rasputin drank heavily on the steamer trip up the Volga and boasted that the tsar thought him "Christ incarnate." He said the starets claimed that Nicholas "cannot breathe without me" and had knelt before him. He said that both tsar and empress had kissed his hand. This was a sign of subservience in Russia—a reason why Iliodor was deeply impressed when he saw Vyrubova greet the starets—and rumors that the sovereigns thus debased themselves to Rasputin were persistent enough for the investigating commission to examine them carefully after the murder. No evidence was found. Vyrubova said in her testimony that—although "the emperor and empress called him simply 'Grigory' and he called them 'Papa' and 'Mama' "— neither ever kissed his hands. They kissed cheeks. Although Iliodor's account was written after he had fallen out with Rasputin, it is doubtful that he invented this out of malice; additional accounts show that Rasputin embellished his palace tales when he was in his cups. His other claims on the steamer ring true. He said Alexandra had sworn to him that she would never waver and "always consider him to be her Friend." He showed the monk blouses embroidered for him by the empress and her daughters, and he told how he freely enjoyed himself with society women, fucking them until he "overcame the flesh" and they became "passionless."

When they arrived in Pokrovskoye, Iliodor found the house to have none of Vyrubova's "biblical simplicity." There were leather sofas, glass bookcases and a piano, potted plants and palms. Amid the icons were photographs, of the imperial family, court dignitaries, and ministers, signed with flattering dedications. The study reminded the monk of a cabinet minister's private room, with heavy leather chairs and a big oak table with piles of telegrams on it. Rasputin gave him a guided tour, pointing out which Romanov or society beauty had presented which piece.

He gave a reception for the monk, inviting village worthies, a couple of schoolmarms, the owner of the general store, the commune secretary and his wife. He dressed up in a raspberry satin blouse, blue trousers, and red slippers. They had candies, nuts, and jam doughnuts. Rasputin walked up and down, hands in pockets, self-important, and led them in singing canticles. He had insisted that Father Pyotr be there; the parish priest did not join in the general jollity. The next morning the priest got Iliodor on his own and told him of Rasputin's "debauchery." "Grigory gets young girls, and he lays them, he lays them," the priest said. "Now he has these airheads from Petersburg who come and see him. They bathe with him, they sleep with him. . . . He's nothing but a drunk and a troublemaker. . . . The villagers think he's a thief, an imbecile. He's always trying to suck up to the bishop. He offered money for the church and the villagers didn't want it—they know how he gets his money. . . . He thinks of us priests as less than dirt. He says that divine grace bypasses unworthy priests and falls directly on the simple. Naturally, that means on him. He has the nerve to say that when he beds a woman, he blesses her and delivers her from carnal desire."

Iliodor, intense, obsessed with moral crusade, his own passions turned inward by his vow of chastity, was troubled by sexuality. He discussed it with Rasputin while they sweated in the bathhouse together. "I am safe from desire," the starets told him. "God has given me this gift in recompense for the penances imposed on me. Touching a woman is the same for me as touching a plank of wood." He explained how this state was achieved. "I direct my lust from here"—he indicated his loins—"to my chest, my head, and my brain. Thus I become invulnerable. And if a woman touches me, she is also delivered from desire. That's why women run after me. They want to pleasure themselves, but they're afraid of losing their virginity, or they're afraid of sin. So they ask me to deliver them from the lusts of the flesh, to make them invulnerable as I am." He described his recent visit to Makari in the Verkhoturye woods. While Makari had prayed in his cell, he had lain naked with the women, spread-eagling them against his legs and thighs and curing them of lust. When they returned to Pokrovskoye, he'd had them bathe him, and they had knelt in front of his nude body and kissed it.

It was, as Iliodor well knew, khlyst talk. The monk claimed that Rasputin sent two servant girls to his bedroom in a vain attempt to "make a khlyst" of him. This is unlikely. Rasputin was no procurer for others; none of his acquaintances makes a wholly credible witness, and Iliodor's later hatred made him less reliable than most. The theme of the bathhouse discourse, however— sex, sin, purification—was one Rasputin returned to often. If he boasted, he had reason to; he was welcomed to the imperial palace and in the beds of highborn ladies. He was forty, and already there was none in the gray and servile history of Russian peasantry with whom to compare him.

On December 6 Rasputin sent a telegram to Nicholas in his and Iliodor's names congratulating the tsar on his name day. They received a reply from Vyrubova: "Very touched by your congratulations. We thank you with all our heart. Anna." Iliodor was "stupefied." A few days later the village postman Mikhail delivered a large envelope bearing the imperial arms and seal. Rasputin read it through, stroking his beard with pleasure, and told Iliodor that it was an autograph letter from the empress. Iliodor asked if he often had such correspondence. He showed the monk a bundle wrapped in blue checked cotton that held letters written to him by Alexandra and the young grand duchesses. It was a dangerous indiscretion. Iliodor purloined some of the letters. To a man at war with the government, they might provide useful insurance.

———

The two holy men left Pokrovskoye for Tsaritsyn on December 15. There was no train from Tyumen until the following morning. Iliodor slept at the monastery, Rasputin spending the night at an admirer's house. They stopped off at Saratov to spend a day with Bishop Hermogen. Iliodor told him that Rasputin bathed with women. "Why do you do that?" the bishop asked the starets in despair. "You mustn't. It won't do." Rasputin appeared to be contrite, but when he was alone with Iliodor, he told him never to mention baths to the bishop again.

They arrived at Tsaritsyn on December 23. Iliodor suggested that he hear Rasputin's confession in his monastery the next morning. Rasputin appeared worried, and the monk asked him if he wished to unburden himself of his sins. Rasputin scratched his nose with his finger and said, "It's got nothing to do with that." "What then?" Iliodor said. "It's about my enemies," he replied. "What's going to happen if they all get together, if they trouble the tsarina's soul, if they stir up a row?" Iliodor assured him that God was with him and would direct his fate. "All right," Rasputin said. "That's all."

If he sensed that the monk was turning against him, he made no effort to mend his ways in front of him. Visiting a rich merchant's wife, he tried to embrace her sister, a pleasing brunette. She slapped him twice around the face, hard. "Well, she landed a beauty on me, the bitch!" he said to Iliodor, half amused, as he beat a retreat. He was taken to see a "holy fool," a half-wit dressed in tatters called Nastia, in the hope that he could cure her. When she saw him she covered her face and screamed, spitting and throwing the contents of a chamber pot at him.

On December 28 Rasputin sent a telegram to the tsar's children, a verse copied from a canticle. The next day he distributed Christmas gifts. He had bought a thousand handkerchiefs, candies, apples, sugar loafs, cheap rings, and holy medallions. A crowd of several thousand came to the monastery. He told the girls that the presents would indicate what was to become of their lives. They rushed forward; he gave most of them rings, to show that they would marry, but he slipped some of them medallions, meaning that they would enter convents. He promised Iliodor fifty thousand rubles to build a convent next to the monastery.

He left on the evening of December 30. A procession escorted him to the railroad station singing "Save Us, Lord." They sang the national anthem as the train drew in. Iliodor blessed the locomotive, and Rasputin blessed the crowd. He asked the local officials who were present to make sure that enthusiastic word of his triumph was passed to the capital. After he had gone Iliodor heard the confession of a twenty-eight-year-old novice, Xenia, a naive woman, "chaste and pious, no beauty but pleasing." She was working for a local tradeswoman to show penitence, and Rasputin had seen her bringing supplies of holy bread to the monastery. She told the monk how she had lost her virtue.

"Father, it happened over Christmas," she said. "While I was getting ready for bed, Rasputin came and told my mistress: 'My good woman, send Xenia to the monastery. I have great need of her.' Of course, I went, even though it seemed strange to need me so late. He didn't beat about the bush. . . . He told me right off to undress. I obeyed. He lay on the bed and said, 'Fine, my little darling, come and lie with me.' I thought, Father, that he was a saintly man whom God had given the grace to purify our sinners' bodies and to heal them.

"He embraced me in such a way that only a tiny place of my body was not covered by him. He kissed me full on the mouth. I cried out to him—'Grigory Efimovich, what are you doing to me, a poor girl?' 'It's nothing, nothing,' he said. 'Stay lying there and be quiet.' I asked him what he was doing with me, and did Father Iliodor know? 'Certainly, he knows,' he said. I asked if Bishop Hermogen knew. 'Of course he knows. He knows everything. Don't worry.' And then I asked, 'Our father the tsar and our mother the tsarina, do they know?' 'Yes, yes! They know better than anyone.' Father, I didn't know what to do, listening to him. . . . He tormented me for four long hours."

By the time Iliodor wrote this account, he was actively seeking to have Rasputin murdered. His story is, however, consistent with others, indicating that the inner struggle between faith and the flesh of Rasputin's early years was almost over. The following year showed that sensuality, and desire for power, had won; spirituality became his greasepaint, the stage prop of a great actor.

CHAPTER 11

Friends and Enemies

Halley's comet reappeared in 1910, and the talk was of imminent apocalypse. Leo Tolstoy died in a railroad siding. The individualist painter Mikhail Vrubel expired of dementia and exhaustion in an asylum, believing that God would give him emerald eyes if he could remain standing for seventeen days. In Moscow, at the fashionable Yar restaurant, Rasputin's favorite, a young man named Praslov approached a beautiful woman sitting at a table with a party of older men in evening dress. She laughed when he asked why she was out so late and in such company. He pulled a revolver from his dinner jacket and shot her repeatedly. Several of those subpoenaed as witnesses committed suicide rather than give evidence; Praslov, who was the woman's ex-husband, was acquitted. In St. Petersburg the titled parents of two young students refused to give them the money for a champagne supper; they forced their way into the apartment of a well-known actress, knifed her to death, and stole her jewelry to pay for their meal. "I've decided to get away," Alexander Blok's mistress told him. "The only thing left to do here is to lie down and die." The poet did not join her, for he enjoyed the "smell of burning, blood, and iron in the air."

The economy was booming with Stolypin's reforms. He sold off state-owned land, including the vast Siberian crown lands to which peasants from European Russia flooded in the boxcars of the Trans-Siberian. He was creating from the most energetic peasants a sturdy yeoman class as a counterweight to radicals, taking, he said, "a gamble not on the drunken and feeble but on the sober and the strong." Russia had the world's highest growth rate, fueled by foreign capital. Moscow industrialists upended their top hats on bar counters and filled them with champagne corks. Distant revolutionaries fell into gloom. In the southern oil fields a Bolshevik agitator called Joseph Stalin, arrested in March for hand-setting strike calls on a flatbed press in the slums of Batum, felt the tide was flowing against revolution.

But Nicholas was tiring of his prime minister—Stolypin was too masterly, too much admired—and Russia was tired of the tsar, and his wife. "In the house of the Romanovs, a mysterious curse descends from generation to generation," Dmitri Merezhkovsky wrote. "Murders and adultery, blood and mud . . . the block, the rope, and poison—these are the true emblems of the Russian autocracy. God's unction on the brows of the tsars has become the brand of Cain."

In Andrei Bely's fashionable novel *The Silver Dove*, the poet hero deserts his beautiful and sensitive fiancée for a pockmarked peasant woman. She was the "great whore. . . . The movement of her breasts, her thick legs with their white calves and the dirty soles of her feet, her big belly, and her sloping, rapacious forehead—all frankly bore the imprint of lust." She thrust herself on the poet, "pawing him and pressing her plump breasts against him—a grinning beast." But she was not his; she belonged to Mitya Kudeiarov, a carpenter and khlyst pilot, whose ark performed dark deeds in the forests. "The Russian earth knows the secret," Bely wrote. "So does the Russian forest. . . . If you are Russian, there is in your soul a red secret—to live in the fields, to die in the fields. . . . There is that in Russia which destroys books and smashes buildings and puts life itself to the fire." Kudeiarov had a double face that "always looks like half a face; one side of it winking craftily at you, while the other is always spying on something, always afraid of something."

Lust, two faces—Rasputin. A provincial girl who searched out the "strange new saint" found the Janus in him; her account appeared in René Fülöp-Miller's 1928 biography, *Rasputin: The Holy Devil*. At first Rasputin reminded her of the peasant preachers she knew at home, his gaze gentle and monastic, his "worthy, simple face" haloed by his light brown hair. Then she saw another man—"mysterious, crafty, and corrupting"—peering out from eyes that still radiated kindness. He sat opposite her and edged closer. The pale blue eyes darkened and bored into her. As he thrust forward his "great wrinkled face, distorted with desire," she was overcome with lassitude. His eyes, deep in their sockets, "furtively roved over her helpless body. . . . His voice had fallen to a passionate whisper, and he murmured strange, voluptuous words in her ear."

She was on the point of surrendering to him when she dimly remembered that she had come to ask him about God; perhaps Xenia would have been saved if she had thought of God instead of Iliodor and the sovereigns. As she struggled consciously against him, her heaviness lifted. He sensed the resistance immediately; "his half-shut eyes opened again, he stood up, bent over her, lightly stroked her girlishly parted hair, and pressed a passionless, gentle, fatherly kiss on her forehead." His face smoothed, and he blessed her, almost humbly; only in the depths of his little eyes could she see "the other man, the sensual beast," lurking.

—

Rasputin was at Vyrubova's cottage several times a week. Alexandra remained ill and nervous despite her visits to doctors in Germany; Vyrubova was with her at the palace every day, and Rasputin called frequently. Until now he had stayed partly in the shadows, as Mikhail Rodzianko put it, "doggedly preparing solid ground for himself." As he felt his power grow, "this wild fanatic throws aside all restraint. His erotic adventures become more impudent and disgusting, the number of his victims and his worshipers grows." The fear of enemies Rasputin had mentioned to Iliodor was justified; he was fast acquiring them.

Stories of the visits to Pokrovskoye appeared in the press in January 1910. They were noted at the Theological Academy in St. Petersburg, together with a letter from Khionia Berlandskaya detailing Rasputin's behavior toward her. Archimandrite Feofan was alarmed at the mounting evidence of Rasputin's misconduct. Although the newspapers had not mentioned the connection with the palace, Feofan thought it his duty as the tsar's confessor to warn him that the peasant philanderer was a danger to the dynasty. "I made up my mind to take a last measure against Rasputin, to openly expose him and to impart everything," he testified later. Nicholas refused to see him and suggested that he meet Alexandra and Vyrubova. "I spoke about an hour and tried to prove the state of Rasputin's spirit," Feofan testified. "The empress objected to this, she worried, she quoted ecclesiastical books, and it was clear that someone, most probably Rasputin, taught her to talk like this." As they parted she told him that saints always suffered such calumny.

Feofan was an early example of the disgrace that pursued those who spoke out to the empress against the starets. He was first dismissed as confessor to Nicholas; when that failed to silence him, he was transferred from the academy to a distant bishopric in the Crimea. Rasputin flirted with the idea of filling the vacant post at the palace himself. Hermogen had remained loyal to him despite Feofan's protests. "He is a servant of God," the bishop warned Prince Dzhevakov when the latter told him that the synod had doubts of Rasputin's sincerity. "It is a sin to judge him and think critically of him." It was necessary for a confessor to be a priest, and Rasputin discussed his ordination with Hermogen. "They'll make me a priest and I'll become the tsar's confessor and stay at court forever," he boasted. In the event, though he obtained Hermogen's blessing and had himself photographed wearing a priest's soutane with a pectoral cross on his chest, he did not have the patience to learn the liturgy necessary for ordination, and the scheme lapsed.

Rasputin fell out with the Montenegrins and their husbands over having extended his habit of insulting churchmen to saints. He was "so disgustingly rude" about Grand Duke Nicholas Nikolayevich's favorite, St. Sergei of Radonege, that the grand duke swore, "I'll never see the devil again!" It was the beginning of a long feud; Rasputin was fortunate that Alexandra's own relations with the grand duke were cooling. He survived, too, a scandal in the palace itself. Maria Vichnyakova, the palace nurse who had been on the Pokrovskoye trip, told the children's governess that during the visit Rasputin had stolen into her room and seduced her and that she had seen him "lying in his underclothes" with Madame Mandshtet on the Trans-Siberian. The governess, Sophia Ivanovna Tyutcheva, advised the girl to go to Alexandra and repeat her allegations. The empress, Tyutcheva later testified, "declared that she didn't believe this hearsay, that she saw in it the activity of dark forces wishing to annihilate Rasputin." She accused the nurse of lying, forbade her to speak to the tsar, and sent her on an indefinite leave of absence to the Caucasus.

Alexandra's anger now fell on Tyutcheva for having encouraged the nurse to complain. A palace messenger ordered the governess to go to the tsar's study at 6:30 the same evening. "Sophia Ivanovna, you can guess why I called for you," he said. "What's going on in the nursery?" She told Nicholas what had happened, adding that she was shocked at the way Rasputin went unchaperoned into the bedrooms of the young grand duchesses and the heir, and at his "gross familiarity" toward them. "Do you not believe in the holiness of Grigory Efimovich?" Nicholas asked her. She replied that she did not. "And what will you say if I tell you that all these hard years I've survived only thanks to his prayers?" he asked. "You survived thanks to the prayers of all Russia, Your Majesty," she replied. It was a diplomatic answer, and it did not satisfy Nicholas. "The emperor started to say that he was convinced all this was a lie," she testified, "that he didn't believe all these stories about Rasputin, that everything sticks to the pure." She felt she had no option but to resign from the palace staff.

It was a serious matter. The governess was the daughter of Fyodor Tyutchev, a metaphysical romantic whose tragic love poems many Russians knew by heart. She had credibility. When she moved to Moscow and told of Rasputin's influence and lechery, she was believed. In her Caucasus exile the nurse Vichnyakova confessed her seduction to Metropolitan Antony, the bishop of Volhynie, at a clinic where he was being treated for a nervous disorder. She detailed Rasputin's involvement at court, pleading with the churchman to save the imperial children from the "devil." Antony requested an audience with the tsar and repeated what the nurse had said. Nicholas told him that it concerned his family alone and that the church had no right to pry.

"No, My Emperor," Antony replied. "It is something that concerns all Russia. The heir is not only your son. He is our future ruler, and he belongs to Russia." When the tsar repeated that he would not tolerate any interference in palace matters, Antony said nervously, "Very good, Sire, but permit me to think that a Russian tsar should live in a crystal palace open to the eyes of his subjects." Nicholas bade him leave; his nerves returned and he suffered a breakdown.

Stolypin was concerned enough to order a report to be made from the dossier the security services were keeping on Rasputin. It left little doubt of his lifestyle; it told of "carousals, his love of women, his relations with dubious entrepreneurs and promoters who exploit him." The head of the police department, Gen. P. G. Kurlov, warned the premier not to show the report to Nicholas; "it might seem to the emperor," he said, "a wish to darken the person who enjoyed his favor." Stolypin ignored him and gave the tsar the gist of the report. Nicholas heard him out in silence, and then, "with characteristic obstinate calm, suggested Stolypin proceed to the business of the day." No action was taken. The dowager empress was concerned enough to summon Vladimir Kokovtsov, the finance minister, to her apartments in the Anichkov Palace. "My son is too kind," she said. "He has not given his answer because he is trying to find some other way out of the situation. He seeks advice from no one. He has too much pride and, with the empress, goes through such crises without letting anyone see he is agitated. . . . My son has so little luck with people."

———

Rasputin was acquiring new friends along with his enemies. Munya Golovina lived with her wealthy mother, the widow of a state councillor, in a fine apartment on the Winter Canal. The girl had recently lost a man she was in love with and was ill with grief when she met Rasputin. Both she and her mother took to the holy man at once. At the turn of the year Munya asked a family friend if he would like to meet the starets. She described him as "a man of exceptional spiritual power who had been sent into the world to purify and heal our souls, and to guide our thoughts and actions." The friend was Prince Felix Yusupov, heir to the biggest fortune in Russia, who was waiting to go up to Oxford.

The prince thought Munya innocent and guileless—he referred to her as Mademoiselle G in his writings to spare her embarrassment—and he was intrigued by her enthusiasm for Rasputin. She thought him an "apostle come straight from Heaven," Yusupov wrote, a man with no weakness or vice who passed his life in prayer. Yusupov accepted the invitation to take tea with Rasputin in the Golovinas' drawing room. A peasant in baggy trousers and great top boots came into the room with short, quick steps, bade the prince "Good evening, my dear boy," and tried to kiss him. When that failed he calmly put his arms around mother and daughter and gave each of them a hearty kiss.

Yusupov was irritated by the peasant's self-assurance; "there was something about him that disgusted me," he wrote. He was of medium height, muscular and thin, with long arms and a scar on his forehead. Yusupov guessed his age correctly at forty. "He had a low, common face framed by a shaggy beard, coarse features and a long nose, with small, shifty gray eyes sunken under heavy eyebrows," Yusupov wrote. He, too, sensed the Janus in Rasputin. "Although he affected a free and easy demeanor," he went on, "one felt him to be ill at ease and suspicious. He seemed to be constantly watching the person he was talking to."

As they drank tea Rasputin quoted the Old and New testaments at random. The prince studied him closely. "He was not in the least like a holy man," he wrote. "On the contrary he looked like a lascivious, malicious satyr. I was particularly struck by the revolting expression in his eyes, which were very small, set close together, and so deep-set in their sockets that at a distance they were invisible." Even close up it was difficult to see whether they were open or shut; the impression was one of being "pierced by needles rather than merely of being looked at." Yusupov was revolted by the starets's "sweet and insipid smile. . . . There was something base in his unctuous countenance; something wicked, crafty, and sensual."

But Munya Golovina and her mother never took their eyes off him, drinking in his every word. After a while Rasputin rose and pointed at the girl. "What a faithful friend you have in her!" he told Yusupov. "You should listen to her, she will be your spiritual spouse. Yes, she has spoken very well of you, and I too now see that both of you are good and well suited to each other. As for you, my dear boy, you will go far, very far." With that he left. A few days later Yusupov met Munya again. She told him, he wrote, that "Rasputin liked me very much and wanted to see me again." Maria Rasputin, in hindsight, claimed her father had described young Felix as "a frightened boy, frightened by the world . . . by his own desires, which I doubt even he understands . . . frightened by the future and torn between many demons." Rasputin had met his murderer. Shortly after Yusupov left for Oxford.

The Golovinas were classified as Rasputniky, the sneering term used for those admirers who thought him divine. Another such was Sister Akulina, a novice he had heard screaming while he visited a convent in Okhits. He had found her lying in her cell, her face to the wall, "her whole body writhing, a deep masculine voice coming from her lips, moving in convulsions." He entered the cell, knelt beside her, and prayed. "I order you to be silent," he said. Her face took on a "glow of serenity." Her fits never resumed. She had asked to be relieved of her vows and had now followed him to St. Petersburg, "openly and unashamedly in love with her master, always taking a place at his feet, ever ready to serve him, running to fetch a glass of water and a piece of fruit, lovingly stroking his hand or kissing his cheek."

Others, the entrepreneurs and promoters of Stolypin's report, were under no illusion that Rasputin was holy. They merely found him useful. Financiers began approaching him in 1910. The journalist Sazonov used his houseguest's influence to raise backing for a financial weekly called *Ekonomist*. Its early editorials attacked the finance minister, Vladimir Kokovtsov. Sazonov suggested that this line would change if the finance ministry placed official advertisements at inflated rates. It was soon praising the minister's "brilliant financial acumen." Sazonov next presented a proposal to the ministry for a grain bank, a project he said was backed by Rasputin and would deal in the rotten grain that piled up on the railroads after the harvest. A bank charter was duly obtained. The ministry further obliged Sazonov by changing the charter to authorize the establishment of a regular commercial bank called the English Bank.

Charters were difficult to obtain; Sazonov promptly sold his for a quarter million rubles. Part of the money was used to finance a new newspaper, *Golos Zemli*. Claiming that Rasputin enabled him to enjoy the confidence of the tsar, Sazonov persuaded the director of the finance ministry's Credit Chancellery to summon the board of the English Bank and suggest that they help the newspaper. The bankers agreed to underwrite it and to grant Sazonov a further hundred thousand rubles. It was astonishing that anyone as corrupt as Sazonov should exert "great influence through the instrumentality of Rasputin," Witte wrote, "but it is nonetheless a fact."

An irrigation scheme in the Transcaucasus, coal contracts, and an unsuccessful attempt by a group of distillers to break the state vodka monopoly were other uses to which Rasputin's influence was put. He was not paid; he played no active role and he had no business sense, but his name was already enough to impress financiers and officials, and he was happy for it to be used. He was motivated by flattery and power, not cash. Those who exploited his name, by contrast—Simanovich and a fellow fixer whom he introduced to Rasputin, Prince Mikhail Mikhailovich Andronnikov—were entirely ruble driven. The prince was a bizarre figure, a snob, vain, with a sharp tongue, witty when he wished to be, and a promiscuous homosexual. He was the publisher of a small-circulation Black Hundred magazine, *Voice of Russia*, which few people read. He behaved as a statesman, however, pomaded and black suited, always carrying an important-looking yellow leather briefcase. He had no regular income, though he spent "immense means" on a large apartment, on drink, on expensive gifts for his lovers. He made his living from character assassination, and blackmail.

Andronnikov knew everyone, and most of their vices and secrets. These he passed on for more information, or for an introduction, or for money. He had been plying his trade when Rasputin was still a wanderer. The industrial magnate A. I. Putilov, chairman of the mighty Russian-Asian Bank, recollected how Andronnikov insinuated himself into the finance ministry and then came to him with details of new contracts and tenders, and "all manner of rumors and suppositions." His clients found him an invaluable political conduit, and they feared him. The prince could "always harm a person that was unpleasant to him." He had a habit of tapping his briefcase as though it were full of dark secrets, instead of the pile of old newspapers that an Okhrana search found it to contain. The prince's burning wish, Putilov said, was to "play a strange political role, to have free access to high dignitaries and thus to satisfy and entertain his vanity."

Cadets at military academies were under standing orders never to enter Andronnikov's apartment, a place of "vice and religiosity . . . at the same time a chapel and a saloon where homosexuals of all Petersburg came to meet each other." It was big enough to have two separate sets of rooms. The prince received respectable visitors in a drawing room furnished with overstuffed armchairs, antimacassars, and oil paintings of country scenes. When the conversation turned to money, he led his guests into a book-lined study in which he kept carefully updated files on leading politicians and their weaknesses. The visitors were unaware that "all manner of crooks caroused in other rooms." These were hung with black silk curtains and decorated with icons and lecterns. They smelled of incense, and a crown of thorns hung on a wall. The prince sometimes wore a chasuble to heighten the religious atmosphere. His bedroom was decorated as a chapel, with an altar and a cross. On the name days and birthdays of his friends, he had a monk come in to hold services. "Crowds of people visited the prince, mostly youth," his valet Peter Ivanovich Kilter testified. "Cadets, schoolboys, young officers, all very handsome. . . . Very often they were brought right from the street and impressed by their slovenliness. All this turned the apartment into some kind of dirty haunt."

Particular favorites were Ensign Smirnov, a brother of the famous opera singer, and a Baron Sripper. The baron lived in the apartment illegally—he was not registered in the capital—and was later arrested for fraud. "All these people used to come to the house as if they owned it," the valet said. "They ate, drank, and stayed the night and slept on beds two by two. Andronnikov behaved suspiciously, absenting himself in the bathroom with the young men." Andronnikov hated women, his valet said, and was visited by only one, an elderly relative of the war minister who "delivered him rumors."

His lobbying technique was crude but effective. "As soon as some Ivan Ivanovich Fintiflyushkin," he explained, using the Russian equivalent of John Doe, "is appointed director of a government department, I send him a letter to say that 'at last the sun of truth has risen over Russia. The crazy government that has led it to ruin has finally understood that the fate of the department in charge of the most important affairs'—in fact it's no more important than a shithouse—'should be entrusted to your noble, educated, and firm hands. A happy era has come, and I, a man ardently loving my motherland, am relieved by this because I believe that an exceptionally successful choice has been made. May God save you. . . . With deepest respect, Andronnikov.' "

At this, the prince continued, Fintiflyushkin would come through on the telephone to thank him for his kind attention. "I warn him to be wise and prudent as he is surrounded by worthless people I won't mention. . . . If he needs support I will render it because of my love for the motherland. Fintiflyushkin is hooked and I have only to show my visiting card to be received and have my problems settled."

The prince boasted that the technique was so successful that he had ministers "bumping their heads" to obey him. Another of his tricks involved his cultivation of the government messengers who carried important correspondence. Orders and medals were distributed in packages each December 6 and January 1. By having the messengers show him the mail, Andronnikov could congratulate the recipients in advance. He sometimes persuaded the messenger to delay delivery—the promotion of the navy minister Grigorovich was an example—so that he could place two telephone calls. The first said that he was striving to arrange the honor, and the second confirmed that it was on its way.

Despite his disapproval of the monks of Mount Athos, Rasputin was tolerant of homosexuals. He had much to learn from the prince on the skills of subverting politicians. The two began to see each other frequently.

———

Rasputin had enough funds now to take his own apartment, at 70 Nickolayevskaya ulitsa. Although he was often invited out, he kept open house, and Simanovich and Andronnikov ensured that there was usually a "diverse society" in his dining room. Guests brought food with them—caviar, choice fish, fruit, and white bread. The table—bare of any cloth—always had potatoes, sour cabbage, and black bread on it, and a boiling samovar. Rasputin's pantry was well stocked. He liked to throw hunks of black bread into a tureen with fish soup bubbling in it and take them out hot to give his guests. Salt and bread, traditional peasant offerings, were kept for important visitors. They often took them away; Rasputin's crusts became status symbols.

His study was the only well-furnished room. It served as his "place of intimate rendezvous with society ladies"; his lovemaking, Simanovich said, was carried out with "impossible simplicity" and speed. He took the lady from the dining room into the study, and a few minutes later saw her out before visiting the bathhouse on the other side of the street from the apartment. He brought his daughters from Pokrovskoye and placed them in a good school. Simanovich noticed that he never swore in front of them. The girls had their own bedroom and never entered a room when guests were there. He had brought the maid Dunia, the participant in the Kubasova pseudo-rape, with him from Siberia. The girls knew that he slept with her, but Maria said she loved her like a mother. "I found the liaison delightful," she said.

Maria was aware of her father's other indiscretions. Rasputin spent an evening of Gypsy dancing with a former Finnish ballerina, Lisa Tansin. The couple got drunk and returned to her villa with other revelers. An orgy ensued in which a naked Rasputin was photographed surrounded by naked women. Returning home in the early hours, unsatiated, Rasputin shared his bed with Dunia. A man later came to the apartment with a package containing the compromising photographs. He said that they would be shown to the tsar unless Rasputin left the capital forever. Dunia advised her lover to counterattack, to be like the woodcutter in the Russian folktale who turned on a wolf slavering to eat him with such a terrible roar that the beast fled.

Rasputin at once took a droshky to Tsarskoye Selo. He told the tsar of the incident at Tansin's villa and showed him the photographs. Nicholas looked at each of them closely, "a frown creasing his usually smooth brow," shaking his head sadly. He said that blackmailers were clearly using Rasputin as a pawn in a filthy game "to weaken my position and destroy the Romanov line." He told the holy man that he had been "foolish, very foolish, but no doubt the temptation was great." No damage had been done, though they might try again.

Rasputin's daughter said she was told this by Dunia. The detail is odd. Why should Rasputin have taken a bumpy, four-hour droshky ride to the tsar when his normal railroad journey took thirty-five minutes? But it was in character for the tsar to be tolerant of lapses. "He often closed his eyes to the escapades of his favorites," Simanovich wrote. "Their behavior even amused him." He recruited Caucasian princes to his personal convoy, though they were "prone to carousing and overindulgence"; he was confident that they would die or kill for him. He often paid their gambling debts; one of them, Prince Dadiani, pawned his epaulets after a drinking bout, certain that Nicholas would retrieve his honor by settling with the men with whom he had been playing cards. Simanovich, who cultivated the officers of the convoy, was playing a noisy game of macao with them in the palace in the early hours when the tsar stormed into the room in his nightgown to complain about the noise. After reprimanding them he gave each of them ten rubles and sat down at the card table to play himself.

It was in character, too, for Rasputin to enjoy having his photograph taken, particularly with women admirers; he did so often. He was an exhibitionist when drunk—he later exposed himself in a well-documented case in Moscow—

and he knew Lisa Tansin. His behavior made him vulnerable to blackmailers, but his character gave him a natural defense. He was brave, and he had little sense of shame.

———

The prime minister, however, was less malleable than the tsar. Iliodor was continuing his fiery preaching. Countess Ignateva, whose salon Rasputin often graced, asked General Kurlov to meet Iliodor on a visit to the capital, so that he could "form a correct opinion" of him. The countess arrived at Kurlov's office late at night with a "tall, lean monk with burning wild eyes." The text of one of Iliodor's sermons, noted by an Okhrana agent, was lying on the police chief's desk. It called on his followers to use violence against the authorities. Kurlov asked the monk how he could reconcile it with his monarchist, right-wing views. "I'm not inciting the people to mutiny," Iliodor yelled at him. "I can think what I like of officials who are traitors to the emperor." Kurlov concluded that the monk was a "downright maniac."

The lunatic was unabashed. For good measure on his return to Tsaritsyn he decided to speak up for his friend Rasputin. He gave two long sermons on consecutive Sundays to crowds of more than five thousand, explaining that there was nothing wrong in Rasputin's kissing women or bathing with them, because he was "protected from desire." The sermons were reported in the press. The synod ordered Iliodor to leave Tsaritsyn and enter an obscure monastery at Novosilsky in Tula province. He refused to go. Kurlov's agents intercepted telegrams from Hermogen and Iliodor to Rasputin asking for his help. Rasputin confirmed that he would seek a favorable result.

Iliodor's flagrant disobedience, and Rasputin's meddling, were sapping the prestige of the church. It seemed "in the depths," in decay. "What is happening . . . cannot help but weaken the influence of the church," Witte wrote, "it cannot help but arouse fears for the future of Russia." Stolypin and the synod procurator, Dr. S. M. Lukyanov, ordered a second investigation into the starets. Stolypin again reported his concerns to the tsar. The prime minister detailed how deeply Rasputin was compromised and demanded that he be removed from court, or so Rasputin himself claimed to his friend Sazonov. Stolypin "told the tsar that, to the great incitement of society, Rasputin went to a bathhouse with women," Sazonov later testified that Rasputin said. "The emperor said to this: 'I know, there he also propagates the Scriptures.' . . . He ordered Stolypin to leave and threw the police department report into the fireplace."

In his own version of events, Stolypin said that the tsar had asked him to meet Rasputin so that he could see for himself that the starets was sincere and misunderstood. As soon as he entered his study, Stolypin reported, Rasputin had tried to cow him with a "hypnotic" stare. "He studied me with his whitish eyes, uttered some mysterious incoherent quotations from the Bible, and gesticulated at me," Stolypin said. "I felt an irresistible disgust rising inside me toward this reptile in front of me. But I knew that he had a great power of hypnosis and somehow he impressed me, in a repulsive way."

Kurlov was also at the meeting. He recalled a thinnish man with a dark red beard and piercing eyes, a "certain kind of cunning Russian peasant," who protested that he was the most harmless and peaceful of people. The premier was unimpressed by the holy man's careful show of innocence. "Getting over my feelings," he said, "I raised my voice and told him outright that I had documentary evidence against him. He was in my hands, I could squash him by bringing him to trial. I ordered him to leave Petersburg without delay, go back to his village, and never appear here again."

Alexandra protested angrily to the tsar when she heard Rasputin's account of the interview; she made no secret of her hostility to Stolypin. Nicholas refused to countermand the order expelling Iliodor from Tsaritsyn despite a flood of telegrams from the monk's followers begging him to do so. Rasputin, judging the ice to be wearing thin, left to winter in Pokrovskoye. It was a timely decision.

The tsar sent a personal envoy to Tsaritsyn to tell Iliodor to submit to the synod. He chose his aide-de-camp Captain Mandryka, an officer in the Fourth Sharpshooters' Regiment attached to the imperial bodyguard. The captain was the godson of the superior of the Balachov Convent in Saratov province and an admirer of Rasputin, a fact that reassured Alexandra that he was the right man to send.

———

Mandryka was welcomed in Tsaritsyn; he was offered bread and salt, and a Te Deum was celebrated for him. Iliodor was not there. Alerted by Hermogen, he had fled to Serdobsk. Mandryka followed him there and told him that the tsar insisted he obey the synod. Muttering with anger, Iliodor reluctantly gave his word that he would go to Novosilsky.

On his way back Mandryka visited his godmother's convent. She was away in St. Petersburg, but the nuns greeted him eagerly. They told him proudly that Grigory Rasputin had stayed at the convent and had chatted with them about his intimacy with the tsar and empress. They showed him a telegram that had arrived for his godmother after her departure for the capital: "One of your godsons is sent on a mission to Tsaritsyn for our affair," it read. "Influence him. Grigory." The captain was appalled that news of his trip had been leaked to the starets, almost certainly by Vyrubova on the empress's behalf. He made inquiries with local police and officials. He was told that Rasputin was a khlyst, a debauchee who violated young girls, abused them, and "chased demons."

The captain arrived back at Tsarskoye Selo on the morning of February 10, 1911. He was at once invited to lunch at the palace. It was Mardi Gras, and the family had blinis. After lunch he took coffee with them and gave his report. He told them all he had learned of the starets—the warning telegram, the baths with girls, the khlystlike philosophy. "They even say," he concluded, "that he enjoys the favor of Your Majesty." With that, the nervous captain burst into tears. Nicholas hastened to get him a glass of water; Alexandra sighed deeply. He left.

The next morning—Vyrubova was quick—Mandryka had a telegram from his godmother: "You've made a mess." He saw her three days later. "You've ruined your career," she told him. "Rasputin is a good man. He must be saved." There were signs that, although Alexandra was cold and distant to the captain, Rasputin was in serious trouble. When Mandryka reported back to the palace at the end of the week, Nicholas shook his hand warmly, gave him lunch, and seemed pleased.

Pilgrim

Rasputin lay low in Pokrovskoye until the end of February 1911. No word came from the palace asking him to return. He thought it wise to resume his wanderings until the tsar's irritation passed. The ruler's quick temper, and his sensitivity to slight, made him dangerous for others to cross. The sovereigns were Rasputin's treasure, his prize and power base; for them, from affection and necessity, he would wait. Great numbers of Russian pilgrims visited the Holy Land, and it was natural for Rasputin to join them. He delighted in journeys; he had a restless and curious mind and a love for landscape. He knew, too, that his pilgrimage would be taken as an act of contrition by Nicholas, and of piety by Alexandra.

He kept them abreast of his progress by sending notes and letters to Vyrubova, and postcards to the empress. To ensure that his reformation was appreciated, he dictated notes on his return for a little book. He called it *My Thoughts and Reflections*, with a subtitle, *A Short Description of My Journey to the Holy Places and the Meditations on Religious Matters to Which They Gave Rise*. It was written out by one of his admirers, probably Munya Golovina, and published privately in a limited edition.

Rasputin went first to the lavra of Potchaiev, a complex of recluses' cells. "I saw men of God, and my heart rejoiced at the sight of pilgrims," he wrote. "These are true believers; you feel the fear of God in their souls and their search for divine truth." He was careful to stress the benefits to his soul; in press interviews he was sharp and to the point, but here his style was cloying and larded with biblicisms, like the romantic novelettes his principal target, the empress, so liked. "I was afraid and trembled, then I became calm and felt myself humble," he wrote of his feelings when he prayed in front of a famous icon. "After each holy place, a new pearl of humility is added to the others."

From Potchaiev he traveled to Odessa and took a pilgrim ship. "Sweet is the night at sea," he wrote. "Sleep comes over you peacefully in the middle of profound thoughts and emotions. . . . O sea of Christ! What marvels are within you. When suddenly you see the shore, you rejoice at the green, at the trees. . . . When high seas toss the boat, the spirit is unquiet. Man loses his consciousness and staggers as though in a fog. . . . The wave is our conscience. However great are the waves of the sea, they always end in calm; but only a good deed can appease the conscience."

He left the ship at Istanbul and was shocked at seeing Turks smoking in the cathedral of St. Sofia. "Oh misery!" he wrote. "God must have been angry with our pride to have given this sanctuary to the infidel. . . . Lord, hear my prayer and return this church to us." He crawled on all fours in the caves and sanctuaries around Ephesus; in Patmos he saw where John the Divine had been imprisoned. In Jerusalem he wept for joy; he found "all just as it used to be," people wearing "the same strange garments as in the Gospels." He put the boot into his old enemies, the homosexual monks of Mount Athos. He noted the many hangers-on in the city, traders in relics and cheap wine, which many drank because it cost a few coppers for a liter. "It is the monks of Athos who offend most, and they therefore ought not to be allowed here."

At the Cave of the Mother of God, lit by torches, Rasputin rejoiced "in Her gladness that the Lord had taken Her body unto Himself." He was careful to denigrate the church establishment that was giving him such trouble—"our bishops are educated but their souls are not simple and the people can only follow simple souls and that is why the temple is empty"—and to include passages on love. "The moment I approached Christ's tomb, I felt it was the tomb of love and I wanted to embrace everyone," he wrote. "If you love, you will never kill, all commandments are subservient to love, it contains all wisdom, greater than Solomon's, and love alone is real, all the rest is scattered fragments." To his admirers, this was the height of religious poetry.

Rasputin's daughter claimed that he had a vision in the Garden of Gethsemane; he saw a corpse and recognized it as himself, collapsed and was helped to an inn, falling into a feverish sleep, where women he had known—Irina Danilova, Natalya Stepanova, Lisa Tansin—mocked him, burning his flesh with irons, until, when he was near death, the Virgin of Kazan made the sign of the cross over him and gestured that he should regain his body. The starets made no mention of it himself—even if it happened, and it is the least likely of his visions, it was hardly suitable material for the empress to read in *My Thoughts and Reflections*—although he did write that he had fasted, eating nothing but rusks as he meditated on salvation. He may have fainted from hunger; he wrote that he prostrated himself in Gethsemane, "afraid to walk upon this holy ground where every little pebble is sacred."

He recovered well enough to immerse himself in the waters of the river Jordan. The Dead Sea fascinated him. "God's punishment is upon it," he wrote. "We were filled with horror and awe . . . not a living creature, not an insect may live there, not a fish even, so that you gaze upon it and weep." In Bethlehem he complained that there were no facilities for Russian pilgrims. He disliked the Catholics he met almost as much as the Turks; he knew the tsar would appreciate such simple patriotism. He found a Catholic Easter service a grim affair. In Russia congregations celebrated the moment Christ's tomb was found to be empty. They left the church behind the priest, surrounding it in a sea of light from their candles. When the priest looked back into the church, triumphantly telling them, *Khristos Voskres!* "Christ is Risen!" they responded with a shout of joy, *Voistinu Voskrese!* "Indeed He is Risen!" Rasputin found Catholicism unimpressive by comparison. "With them, even in church, no joy, no animation, you'd think they had lost someone," he said. "When they leave, you see that their spirit is not joyous. . . . How happy we are, we Orthodox!"

—

While Rasputin was in Bethlehem, Iliodor defied Stolypin and the synod by leaving the Novosilsky Monastery and returning to Tsaritsyn. The provincial governor, Stremoukhov, surrounded his headquarters with troops. Here the monk was protected by howling women and barefoot peasants who swore to kill anyone who laid a hand on him; they vowed not to eat, drink, or sleep until the banning order was lifted. The tsar undermined both his prime minister and governor. The bishop of Tsaritsyn announced Nicholas's decision on April 3, 1911: "The emperor, taking account of the people's supplications, permitted on April 1 Hieromonk Iliodor to come back to Tsaritsyn from Novosilsky."

Stolypin was furious. He suggested to Stremoukhov that he resign in order to shock Nicholas into reason. The governor agreed, and said he would use the opportunity to talk to the tsar as well about Hermogen's and Rasputin's support for the monk. The next morning the governor was telephoned by a man who gave no name—but who was clearly speaking for Stolypin—advising him against making any mention of the "third man" when he went to see the tsar. Rasputin's reputation had reached the point where the Russian prime minister was advising colleagues that it was best not to mention him.

The affair aroused enough international interest for Robert Wilton of the London *Times* to travel south again. He was intrigued that the "Mad Monk of Tsaritsyn," as he called him, with the support of a "strange Siberian," Rasputin, could humiliate a man of Stolypin's stature. The correspondent arrived to find a mass of pilgrims waiting to leave Tsaritsyn by chartered steamers. The atmosphere was charged with hysteria, particularly among the eleven hundred women present. They were divided into groups of fifty, each led by a banner carrier, with knapsacks and pilgrim staffs. Iliodor, in a cassock with a red, white, and blue collar, the national colors, led them singing through the streets. The whole city gathered at the landing to bid them farewell, "bells joyously ringing, crowds shouting hurrah and singing church and patriotic hymns . . . pilgrims, governors and their staffs, the city fathers, the clergy in corpore."

Iliodor defined the purpose of the pilgrimage. "The revolutionaries wished to travel up and down the Volga and bombard our cities, but they failed," he shouted. "Our mission is to bombard these cities with the word of God and the shots of divine truth." With that the pilgrims steamed upriver. They docked at each major town. Processions were led by the fifty best-looking girls, selected by Iliodor, and followed by a group of the best singers. Crowds were drawn by the music and the pretty girls, and Iliodor worked them well. Priests and officials were sucked into the near frenzy, and Wilton saw that they "did the 'Mad Monk's' bidding." Venerable bishops were overawed, and governors kissed his hand. The processions entered cathedrals and churches at all hours of the day and night, while archpriests were "dragged from their homes and forced to put on their vestments and celebrate solemn mass." Any failure to pay Iliodor homage brought "torrents of curses and imprecations." He prophesied the fate of Sodom and Gomorrah to one Volga town he thought "stony" in its reception. He told another that Chinese cavalry would capture it and fly the temple dragon over a church that was slow to open its doors to him. In Kazan he proclaimed the archbishop anathema.

By the time they returned to Tsaritsyn, Iliodor struck Wilton as "bordering closely on real madness" and in need of "imperative medical examination." A bodyguard walked with the monk during his open-air services, brandishing a large pistol. A new standard was carried in front of him, an enormous pole with a shining steel ax and lance hanging from it. "Till now we have only threatened our enemies," he preached. "Henceforth we will shoot. It is war to the death. Arise, Orthodox Russian people, and raise the flag of revolt for the defence of our holy faith, of autocracy and of Russian brotherhood. Look out, Jews and Russian fools."

Bloodshed was close. Iliodor's supporters mobbed people who failed to remove their hats or laughed in his presence. They seized a Russian colleague of Wilton and daubed his face with naphtha. They yelled, "Jew, Jewess," at anyone who remained seated when Iliodor passed, or who used opera glasses to get a better look at him. The monk ordered his pilgrims to raise their staffs and wave them like a menacing forest in the air before, "with a snicker," ordering them down. The only reason the tsar could tolerate Iliodor, Wilton thought, was that he controlled a reactionary "black army" against the "red peril" of the left.

———

Rasputin was back in St. Petersburg at the end of June. As he had hoped his pilgrimage restored him to the tsar's good graces—spectacularly so, for Nicholas now sought his political advice and entrusted him with a sensitive mission. It was the first time that the heart of power was opened to him. He visited the palace several times to give the spellbound Alexandra his account of the Holy Land. Vyrubova, who was present, testified later that she did not know to whom Rasputin dictated his *Reflections* but confirmed that "their content quite corresponds to everything that Grigory Efimovich said. He touched on these topics when he talked to the tsar's family, and present during these talks were the grand duchesses and the heir, who, of course, sometimes left to go to bed."

Rasputin also sought to poison his enemies, Stolypin and Lukyanov, the procurator of the synod. He made quick work of the latter; he braggingly referred to the new procurator, B. K. Sabler, as "my man." The prime minister was a grander and more difficult target, but the omens were good. Stolypin's dislike for Rasputin ensured that the empress turned against him. Already humiliated by Iliodor, he was further undermined when a reform to introduce locally elected councils into the western borderlands was blocked by state councillors who claimed that they were acting at the express wish of the tsar. Irritably, he offered his resignation; Nicholas, equally annoyed, asked what would become of a "government responsible to me" if ministers could come and go as they pleased, and refused to accept it. Stolypin felt weary, and ill with grippe; he knew that he had lost the tsar's confidence and told friends he was sure he would soon be murdered by an Okhrana agent. Nicholas now discussed his replacement with Rasputin.

Two alternatives were open: to restore Witte as premier and appoint Alexis Khvostov as interior minister, or to make Khvostov premier with the current finance minister, Vladimir N. Kokovtsov at interior. Khvostov was a young and little-known provincial governor who had caught the tsar's eye on a visit to Nizhni Novgorod. To ask a man thought an "inexperienced, corrupt, and opinionated nonentity" by one of the few who knew him to become premier or indeed interior minister, the most sensitive and difficult post in Russia, was a breathtaking gamble. Nicholas knew that Rasputin had no administrative insight, but he trusted him as a judge of character. He asked him to go to Nizhni Novgorod to "search the soul" of its governor.

Rasputin traveled to the Volga town, 250 miles east of Moscow, with his journalist-blackmailer friend Sazonov. Khvostov, told that a peasant and an adventurer were requesting an audience, refused to see them. They barged into his drawing room, leaving a trail of dust from their boots on his carpet. He told his manservant to eject them. Rasputin said that the tsar would be displeased when he cabled him about his reception; he complained that he had only three rubles in his pocket and that the governor had not even fed him. Khvostov thought he was mad or bluffing but later rang the telegraph office. He was told that a peasant had indeed sent a telegram to Tsarskoye Selo. It read: "The grace of God is in Khvostov, but he is young and there is something lacking in him." He would do for interior minister, if that was the tsar's wish, but not as premier.

The pair next sounded out Witte on whether he would accept reappointment as premier. He was summering in Biarritz when he received a letter from Sazonov at the end of July. It opened by suggesting that Witte might like to make a financial contribution to Sazonov's newspaper; this was the bribe requested for the offer of the premiership that followed. The letter went on to say that the tsar had decided to replace Stolypin before the end of August and closed by stating that Witte would give a new government the authority it needed. "Are the ones who make this proposal mad," Witte pondered, "or do they think I am such a madman that they can make such a proposal to me?" He found it difficult to believe that "Rasputin now had such influence that a man of Sazonov's shadiness" could tout the highest office in Russia.

A fresh opportunity to influence a key church appointment came with the death of the bishop of Tobolsk. The Siberian bishopric included Pokrovskoye; although Rasputin had survived the diocesan investigation into his alleged khlyst connections, it was important for him to see a sympathizer installed in case of a repeat. His choice was Varnava, the father superior of the Novolugvinsky Monastery near Moscow. The two had met first in the house of Anna Shipova, the possible Madame S of the Trans-Siberian scandal, and later at Prince Andronnikov's apartment. Varnava was an exotic creature in his early fifties. He was the son of a market gardener, uneducated but witty, resourceful, and sly. He had a penchant for young novices, which had led him to Andronnikov. He liked to be photographed. One picture later submitted to the investigating commission showed him lying in a coffin placed on a richly brocaded bed; in another he sat with "a pretty, effeminate novice lovingly clinging to him," his lively eyes showing his natural intelligence while his lower face had "the features of a satyr and goat-legged Pan."

Varnava had enough in common with Rasputin for neither man to believe in the other's holiness, but each had uses for the other. Varnava passionately wished to become a bishop. His lack of education and theological training should have made this impossible, but he "understood that there was a man before him who could make anything come true." Rasputin, for his part, saw in Varnava someone "who, having received by his mercy Tobolsk diocese, will slavishly do there what he wants." The synod at first refused the appointment. Even Sabler was shocked when the tsar insisted on it. "I pointed out to the tsar that Varnava was not prepared for it," he testified later. "He did not know the law, he was illiterate, he might be mocked and undermine the standing of bishops." He sat on the nomination until he received a handwritten note from the tsar: "Remind you of my wish to have Varnava a bishop in Tobolsk in the nearest future." This pressure, and the help of Rasputin's friend the Finnish bishop Sergei, obtained a narrow majority in the synod. The faithful were shocked that the tsar was conniving in Rasputin's corruption of the state religion.

Rubbing salt into the wounded church, Rasputin paid a visit with Lokhtina to Iliodor in Tsaritsyn. It was not a success. He was greeted with less fervor than before. He tried money. He promised to give three thousand rubles for a new pilgrimage Iliodor was organizing; he wired Alexandra for the money, and Spiridovich said that it arrived four days later. When a public collection failed to meet expectations, Lokhtina bolstered it by paying three hundred rubles for a souvenir icon, and Rasputin persuaded a group of local ladies to present a silver tea service. In gratitude a little girl gave him a bouquet of flowers, saying, "Your soul is as beautiful as these flowers." Yet he noticed, with much hurt pride, that his image had disappeared from the banners carried by the faithful. They still had huge photographs of Hermogen and Iliodor, but he had been cut out. He sent a cable to Vyrubova alerting her to this change.

Rasputin gave an open-air sermon that much affected Iliodor. "It was the first time since I had known him that he appeared truly attractive," the monk wrote. "His tall and lean figure, with his rich peasant coat and a cord at his waist, had a particular grandeur when, in the heat of his discourse, he thrust his body forward and supported himself on slender feet encased in varnished boots. From the height of the raised platform, Rasputin seemed to me like a creature of the air ready to take flight, but toward hell and not heaven. His hair and beard, carefully washed, were blown lightly in the wind; they floated elegantly around his head. . . . His voice was staccato, firm, sonorous. His speech was brief and impregnated with gravity and power." Iliodor remembered one passage: "Yes, my enemies have launched attacks on me," Rasputin said. "They think my end has come. It makes you laugh! It's their end that's here. Not mine. Who are they? Worms crawling in a pot of cabbage. Miserable worms and nothing more. They want to knock me down. Well, there's many a slip twixt cup and lip!"

It was significant that Iliodor should see Rasputin swooping "toward hell" and recall the reference to Rasputin's enemies. He was about to become one. The two men visited the Dubrova Convent together. The mother superior honored Rasputin and gave him a candle decorated with flowers that she had made herself. Iliodor noted that the starets "succeed[ed] in visiting several nuns' cells," and that he boasted of having had Sabler appointed as synod procurator and said he would make sure that Stolypin was sacked. When Rasputin stopped off in Saratov to see Hermogen, he found a coldness in this old friend too: the bishop warned him that the evidence of his seductions was becoming hard to bear. Hermogen was at least sane. Iliodor's mental state made his growing hatred especially dangerous.

———

It was, however, one of Rasputin's "miserable worms" who was the first to be done in. Peter Stolypin was expected in Kiev at the end of August to attend the tsar's inauguration of a statue of his grandfather Alexander II, the murdered tsar-liberator. The prime minister knew his days in power were numbered; he was not invited to join the imperial train for the trip to the Ukraine. Rasputin was in town, staying with a member of the Black Hundreds. He was in the front row of the crowd on Alexander Street, near the Kiev Museum, to watch the imperial parade pass through the city on August 30.

The holy man caught Alexandra's eye as her carriage went by, elaborately escorted by police and cavalrymen. He blessed her, and she smiled and inclined her head to him. Stolypin was in the carriage behind, looking tanned after a summer break, but so unprotected against terrorists that he remarked to his finance minister, Kokovtsov, riding with him, "We are superfluous." Rasputin turned pale when he saw him, so Vyrubova claimed. He trembled and cried, "Death is behind him. Death follows him . . . him, Peter . . . it follows him." That night Rasputin's host heard him tossing sleepless in his room; death was "close by," he muttered, and he was powerless in "its bony hand." Simanovich claimed that Rasputin had already told him and the tsar that the "old man," as he called Stolypin, would be killed if he went to Kiev; he also warned that a Jewish pogrom would follow his death.

A police informer called Dmitri Bogrov, who worked the revolutionary fringes on behalf of his Okhrana paymasters, had recounted details of a plot to assassinate the tsar during his stay in the city. The police squandered their resources on this false scent. Bogrov was given a police identity pass to attend a gala performance of Rimsky-Korsakov's opera *Tale of Tsar Saltan* at the Kiev opera house on the evening of September 1, 1911. His task was to spot any terrorist who might slip through the security checks to kill the tsar as he sat in the imperial box with his daughters Olga and Tatiana; the empress, true to her loathing of public events, was absent.

Stolypin sat in the front row of the orchestra stalls. During the second intermission he stood and stretched with his back to the stage. The hall emptied as the audience filled the lobby bars for soft drinks and candies. A young man in evening dress and an opera cloak walked down the aisle. It was an airless night; the summer was so hot that the Ukraine was a desert of parched grass, but the plainclothesmen paid no attention to the man in the cape. He had a police pass. Bogrov fired two shots into Stolypin's chest with the terrorists' weapon of choice, a Browning pistol.

The shots sounded to the tsar like the thud of something dropping. He ran back into his box to see if an opera glass had fallen on someone's head. He noticed a scuffle below him; men in uniform were dragging someone along the carpeting. "Stolypin was standing," he wrote to his mother. "He slowly turned his face toward us and with his left hand made the sign of the cross in the air. Only then did I notice he was very pale and that his right hand and uniform were bloodstained. He sank into his chair and began to unbutton his tunic. . . . People were trying to lynch the assassin. I am sorry to say the police rescued him from the crowd. . . . The theater filled up again, the national anthem was sung, and I left with the girls at 11. You can imagine with what emotions."

The premier survived for five days in agony. Stolypin had given constancy and calm to a fevered country; under him industrial production had almost doubled. The leader of the obscure Bolshevik party, Vladimir Lenin, exiled in Paris, a city he loathed, sat with his disciples in a miserable café on the avenue d'Orléans, drinking sickly grenadine and soda, half-convinced that the chance for Russian revolution had passed. Even the left was stunned by the shooting. "The person who seemed most unmoved was the emperor," Prince Paul Vassily wrote. "He expressed no sympathy . . . beyond some conventional inquiries and official words of regret."

Nicholas called at the nursing home where the premier lay on September 3, but Madame Stolypin refused to let him see her husband. He was told of the death on the pierhead on his return from a trip on the Dnieper. A memorial service was held in his presence at the nursing home. "The poor widow," Nicholas wrote, "stood as though turned to stone and was unable to weep." She well knew of his hostility to her husband; she may have suspected that he had a hand in the murder. Many did, for the use of police agents to murder those who displeased Black Hundred leaders was well established; if these reactionaries did not act on the tsar's orders, they claimed in their pamphlets to act in his interests. Bogrov was hastily hanged, conveniently removing the principal actor, and four police officers were suspended from duty. An official inquiry called for senior officials to be put on trial. The tsar refused to agree; Alexis having recovered from a fresh hemorrhage—Vyrubova later testified to the investigating commission that "a telegram was sent to Rasputin with a request to pray and he comforted the tsar and tsarina with a telegram to say that the heir will live"—Nicholas was "not of a mind to punish anyone" when God had shown him mercy.

No evidence emerged from the dirty half-world of double agents and provocateurs to link the tsar to the killing; some members of court thought that Nicholas had deliberately taken Stolypin to Kiev so that Rasputin's prediction would come true, a convoluted accusation that Simanovich thought groundless. The empress, however, was well pleased and made no secret of it. Alexandra thought that the premier had brought death down on his own head through his contempt for Rasputin. She told her husband's cousin Grand Duke Dmitri Pavlovich that "those who have offended God in the person of Our Friend may no longer count on divine protection." The Friend himself, having predicted his enemy's fall, now prepared to welcome his successor.

—

The appointment was carried out in casual style on September 9. Vladimir Kokovtsov had effectively taken over the government on the night of the murder, drafting three regiments of Cossacks into Kiev to forestall the Jewish pogrom with which the Black Hundreds celebrated such events. Simanovich wrongly attributed this precaution to the tsar, claiming that Nicholas was persuaded into uncharacteristic protection of his Jewish subjects by a telegram Rasputin sent him: "Joy, peace, calmness. . . . Blood of aliens on the earth of the Russian tsar is as precious as that of one's brothers."

Kokovtsov was waiting at the railroad station to see the imperial couple off to the Crimea, where they were to stay in the Livadia Palace, when a courier drove up hastily and asked him to go at once to the tsar. Nicholas took him into his study. He told him that he had decided to appoint him premier, with the young Khvostov, as Rasputin had confirmed, at the interior ministry. Kokovtsov was appalled. "Your Majesty, you are standing at the edge of a precipice," he said. "The appointment of Khvostov will signify that you have decided to jump off." Alexandra was already wearing her hat and was waiting impatiently for her husband to leave. "In that case," the tsar said, "I ask you to take the post of premier and as for interior minister, I'll think about it." With that he climbed into the automobile.

The Crimea had been a special place for Russians since Prince Potemkin had wrested it from the Tartar khans more than a century before. Its warmth lifted their dark and half-frozen northern souls. Roses bloomed at Christmas; it had copses of juniper bushes, promenades of palm trees, chestnuts, baby willows, stands of acacia, terraces with cascading geraniums, orchards and vineyards. The southeastern coast, protected from northerly winds by mountains, was a Romanov redoubt. Nicholas had replaced the old wooden palace at Livadia, where his father had died, with an Italianate palazzo of white limestone and marble. The family was happy here. The tsar rode, played tennis, and swam with Alexis from the Golden Beach, close to the Swallow's Nest, crags that rose from the sea in the shape of a medieval castle. Vyrubova imagined a "race of Centaurs come back to earth" as cavalcades of Tartars in red and yellow rode by in this "earthly paradise." The girls flirted innocently with young officers from the Black Sea fleet. Alexandra relaxed in her high-ceilinged room, with its views to the blue sweep of mountains, its pink chintz light and cheerful despite the obsessive presence of a motif of mauve flowers. She was able to go shopping incognito with Vyrubova in Yalta, a forty-five-minute walk from the palace, a freedom unthinkable in the frigid north.

The empress did not unwind enough to forget politics, however. When Kokovtsov visited the palace she invited him to take tea with her on the terrace. "I notice that you keep on making comparisons between yourself and Stolypin," she said. "You seem to do too much honor to his memory and ascribe too much importance to his activities. . . . Believe me, one must not feel sorry for those who are no more. I am sure . . . when one dies that means his role in the world is ended and that he was bound to go since his destiny was fulfilled. . . . Remain yourself. Do not look for support in political parties; they are of so little consequence in Russia. Find support in the confidence of the tsar—the Lord will help you. I am sure that Stolypin died to make room for you and this is all for the good of Russia." Kokovtsov knew very well that this meddling—the superficial dismissal of political parties, the belief in God and autocracy—had a purpose. The empress thought that Stolypin's end was bound up with his dislike of Rasputin, and she was warning the new premier to turn a blind eye to the starets. "Strange as it may seem," Kokovtsov wrote, "the question of Rasputin became the central question of the immediate future; nor did it disappear during my entire term of office."

The family stayed in Livadia until the end of December. Rasputin arrived in Yalta and put up at the Edinburgh Hotel under the name of Nikonov. He was invited to the palace on December 6, St. Nicholas Day in the calendar of saints, the tsar's name day. The holy man paid several visits; he was happy and self-confident when he left, sending a telegram from Moscow on December 13 to say he was on his way back to St. Petersburg. But his confidence was mistaken. Old friends who wished him harm were awaiting him.

CHAPTER 13

Scandal

Iliodor had gotten to St. Petersburg first. Bishop Hermogen was also in the city, attending a session of the synod and staying at the Iaroslavl Monastery. He was given further evidence of Rasputin's transgressions by Captain Rodionov, a Cossack writer and Duma deputy. The three met with Mitya, the half-wit "fool of Christ," to discuss the starets. They exchanged anecdotes and worked themselves into a moral rage. Hissing with jealousy at Rasputin's success, the idiot passed on as fact the salon rumors that Rasputin was fucking the empress. He said that the lecher must be killed, or at the least castrated. Iliodor turned on his former friend. He wanted Rasputin kept in a locked cell as far away as possible—the prison island of Sakhalin was suggested—while his house in Pokrovskoye was publicly burned.

Hermogen was less extreme; he felt that they should force Rasputin to swear that he would never go to the palace again. At first, he explained later to the newspaper *Russkoye Slovo*, he felt that the starets had a "spark of God," an inner sensitivity and sympathy. "I'll tell you frankly—I experienced it myself," he said. "More than once he responded to the sorrows of my heart. He won my heart like this and, at least at the start of his career, the hearts of others." But by 1911 the bishop had realized, "too late," what sort of person Rasputin was. "He suffered from a particular ailment, a particular lust," he said. "I'd call it an 'ailment of satyriasis.' " It was this that he was determined to unmask.

After the receipt of Rasputin's telegram from Moscow, Mitya and Rodionov pressured Hermogen to go further. Reluctantly the bishop agreed to see the justice minister and inform him of their plan to kidnap Rasputin and lock him in a monastic cell. The minister told him this would be illegal. Rasputin arrived in the capital on December 16. He telephoned Iliodor and suggested he come to Munya Golovina's apartment on the Winter Canal. At their meeting Iliodor asked Rasputin to go on to the Iaroslavl Monastery, where Hermogen was waiting to see him.

Once his victim was in the monastery, Iliodor telephoned Rodionov and Mitya. When they arrived Rasputin sensed trouble and became nervous. He was ill prepared for the meeting; he was outnumbered, in a stone-walled room deep in the monastery. Hermogen was a powerfully built man, six feet tall, and Rodionov, who had been invited as a witness to the bishop's denunciation, was fit and athletic. Mitya suddenly yelled in his spittle-flecked voice: "Ah! Impious one!" He grabbed Rasputin by his penis, the author of his debauchery, and tugged at it, staring wildly and cursing. Iliodor joined in the attack, quoting his victim's own braggings, his voice growing in anger before lapsing into incoherent rage as he accused him of raping the novice Xenia.

The bishop now shouted at him. "You are a liar and impostor," Rodionov reported him as saying. He was waving a large wooden crucifix. "You say you're holy, but you live in sin and mud. It is my fault to have introduced you to the tsar's family. Now I see your true face. . . . By your deeds you soil the name of the empress. With your unworthy hands, you dare to touch her holy person. . . . In the name of the living God, I command you to disappear and no longer trouble the Russian people by your presence at the palace!" Rasputin, "eyes pale," hissed back oaths and threatened "to have done" with the bishop. "So, you filthy debauchee, you refuse to obey the commands of a bishop?" he shouted. "And you threaten me? Know that I, a bishop, curse you!"

The litany of sin, and the vehemence of the curse, left Rasputin cowed and trembling. Both Rodionov and Iliodor asserted this, and Hermogen confirmed it; this was the first and only recorded instance when Rasputin's self-confidence deserted him. The tirades stunned him; they were unexpected, and they came from powerful preachers, for whom denouncing the ungodly was meat and drink. "Is it true?" Hermogen demanded. "It's true," Rasputin quavered. "It's true, it's true." Hermogen punched him in the face and began beating him with the crucifix. Rasputin fought back; his face "lost human expression" as Rodionov drew his Cossack saber and hastened to help the bishop. As he rained blows on the starets, Hermogen roared, "You are smashing our sacred vessels." He pulled him by his hair to a small chapel. He pronounced a death sentence on Rasputin's sources of pleasure and power. The starets was not to touch another woman, and he was never again to go to Tsarskoye Selo or contact the imperial family. Hermogen forced him to kneel and swear it on an icon.

"I tried to reform him," Hermogen recalled to the *Russkoye Slovo* reporter. "I read a prayer of prohibition over him in the chapel. I ordered him to renounce the actions that so ruinously influenced high society and that reflected on the life of the State. Finally, I told him to return to Pokrovskoye. It seemed to persuade him." Rasputin swore obedience. "Good," he told the bishop. "I'll go to Pokrovskoye. I've got plenty of corn and I'll live comfortably there. And I'll never be with people from society again." With that he fled.

He tried to repair the damage the following day. He went to Iliodor. "Save me!" he begged. "Save me!" Iliodor took him back to the bishop, who refused him pardon, turning his back on him with the words "Never and nowhere!"

———

Word of the beating soon got out through the writer Rodionov. The press seized on it to dig up the old allegations that Rasputin was a khlyst. The Moscow newspaper *Golos Moskvy* published a letter to the editor from Mikhail Novosyolov, an assistant professor at the Moscow theological academy and a specialist on illegal cults. It was based on a pamphlet he had written and demanded that the synod, still sitting in St. Petersburg, expose Rasputin as a heretic.

" '*Quo usque tandem!*' " it started.

> These indignant words escape from the lips of all Orthodox men and women against the sly conspirator who betrays our Holy Church, that fornicator of human souls and bodies—Grigory Rasputin, who impudently defends himself under the holy cover of the Church. "*Quo usque?*"—with these words the children of the Russian church are forced to address the synod, seeing its terrible connivance with Grigory Rasputin. How long will the synod, in whose face this criminal comedy is being played, be silent and inactive? Why is it silent, in the face of God's commandment to protect the sheep from the wolves?
>
> Why are the guardians of Israel silent when in letters to me some of them openly call this pseudo-teacher "a pseudo-khlyst, an erotomaniac, a charlatan"? Why is the lewd khlyst allowed to do dark deeds under the guise of light? . . . Where is the ruling hand if it will not throw the impudent seducer beyond the fence that protects the Church?

The reference to the empress's Friend as an "erotomaniac" and a "pseudo-khlyst" created a sensation. Preliminary censorship had been abolished in the post-1905 reforms. Newspapers were now liable to arbitrary fines and to confiscation after publication. Novosyolov's pamphlets were confiscated, and copies of *Golos Moskvy* found in a raid on its printing plant were burned. The paper was heavily fined. The public took it as proof that Rasputin was indeed a khlyst, the lewd pilot of an ark whose members included the empress. The copies that were in circulation "started to sell for fabulous sums of money," the politician Rodzianko noted, "and all the other newspapers started to publish articles about Rasputin and the illegal confiscation of the pamphlet." For the first time the press began to run letters about Rasputin's women victims and published photographs of him with his admirers. "The more zealous the censor and police were," Rodzianko added, "the more they published and the larger were the fines."

Rasputin was in deep trouble. Instinctively, as with the blackmail attempt, he felt attack to be the best means of defense. Nicholas and Alexandra had returned from the Crimea to Tsarskoye Selo for Christmas. He got word to them through Vyrubova that Hermogen and Iliodor had "ambushed" and tried to murder him. He asked that they be expelled from the capital immediately, before they could do more harm. He also worked on Sabler, his nominee as synod procurator. The pressure was effective. On January 3, 1912, Sabler presented to the tsar a synod recommendation ordering Hermogen to return to his diocese in Saratov. Nicholas signed it.

It was an unprecedented punishment for a member of the synod to be expelled from the capital while it was in session. Hermogen refused to go. He cabled Iliodor with the news; the monk, who had returned to Tsaritsyn, told the press. Hermogen demanded his right to trial by twelve fellow bishops, who alone could banish him from the synod under canon law. He was refused. On January 16 he demanded an audience with the tsar. "I am ready to obey the orders of the sovereign," he explained, "but those of Grischa Rasputin, never!" Nicholas let him know via Sabler that he would not see him. The bishop wrote a letter begging him to "pull out the weeds growing around the throne". It went unanswered. He cabled the empress; she did reply, to say that he must submit to the orders of an authority, the synod, that was instituted from God.

On January 17 Hermogen was notified that the synod had stripped him of his diocese and had exiled him to the obscure Zhirovretsky Monastery in Vladimir province. Iliodor was exiled to the Florishchev Monastery, but the exclusion order could not be served on him. He had gone to ground. Hermogen bowed to his fate a week later and left the capital. "Denunciation of Rasputin had a fatal effect on my life," he told the *Russkoye Slovo* reporter. "I was forced to retire from my see. More than that, I was removed from St. Petersburg by force, without having any opportunity to explain myself." He was philosophical about his treatment. "Even we, people grown wise with theological experience, could not realize at first what sort of person Rasputin was," he recollected. "Small wonder that weak women who got into his net could not see it either. . . . As for men, he simply bullied them. He said to those who believe in God: 'If you send me away, God will punish you. Something terrible will happen to your house.' " By that Hermogen meant the tsar; he went on to allude to Sabler and the members of the synod: "With others, who clutched at their position," Hermogen continued, "he said how powerful he was, how much influence he had, and he warned them: 'Watch out, you'll feel bad if you don't obey me.' And they obeyed him."

———

Iliodor soon served notice that he would not accept his punishment meekly. From hiding he issued a memorandum to the press. He entitled it "Grischa" and signed and dated it. "Sabler is Rasputin's creature," it read. "Grischa tells how Sabler thanked him on his knees for making him procurator of the holy synod. Bishop Varnava is also Grischa's creature. . . . Here is my advice on Grischa. He is a khlyst and an incorrigible dissolute. He must be kept away from the tsar and punished, like the depraved soul he is, for having pretended to be a saintly man and coming close to the sovereigns. If Grischa is not distanced, if he is not driven from the light, the throne of the tsars will be toppled and Russia will perish. January 25, 1912. Iliodor."

Delighted newspaper editors published it; the increases in circulation paid for the fines. Nicholas was furious. At a dinner in the Winter Palace on January 29, given in honor of the money-grubbing father of the Montenegrin sisters, he told the interior minister to take "the most severe measures" against any paper that mentioned Rasputin. The next morning, the minister—A. A. Makarov, for the objections to Khvostov had been sustained—raised the question at a meeting with Prime Minister Kokovtsov and Sabler. The synod procurator thought it imperative that Rasputin leave for Siberia at once. They asked the court minister, Count Fredericks, to take the matter to the tsar. Fredericks did so. "Today they want Rasputin to go," Nicholas objected, "and tomorrow they'll think of someone else."

Makarov had a routine audience with the tsar on February 1; Nicholas told him they would discuss Rasputin another time. Kokovtsov tried again on February 3. "I told him in detail the damage that was being done to imperial prestige and how important it was to cut it off at its roots," the premier recalled. "The emperor heard me out in silence. He looked out of the window, as he usually does when he is displeased. Suddenly he interrupted me. 'Yes, you're right,' he said. 'It's necessary to lop it off at the roots and I'll take decisive steps to do that. I'll talk to you about it later, but for the moment let's not discuss it further.' "

He did nothing, and the situation got worse. Iliodor contacted journalists and handed them copies of letters from the empress and her daughters to Rasputin that he had stolen from the blue-checked wrapper on his visit to Pokrovskoye. The letter from the empress was undated but seemed to have been written in 1908 or 1909. "My beloved and unforgettable teacher, redeemer and mentor," it began.

How weary I feel without you. It is only then that my soul is quiet and I relax, when you, teacher, are sitting beside me and I kiss your hands and lean my head on your blessed shoulder. Oh! how light I feel then. I wish only one and the same thing then. To fall asleep forever on your shoulder, in your arms. Oh! what happiness it is even to feel your presence near me. Where are you? Where have you flown? And I feel so miserable, so sick at heart. . . .

But don't you, my beloved mentor, tell Anya [Vyrubova] about my sufferings without you. Anya is kind, she is good, she loves me, but you shouldn't reveal my grief to her. How soon will you be close to me again? Come quickly. I am waiting for you and I am tormenting myself for you. I am asking for your holy blessing and I am kissing your blessed hands. Loving you forever, M.

The *M* stood for Mama.

It read like a passionate love letter, and it was seen as such by those who bought or were given one of the thousands of duplicated copies that were soon in circulation. "Only those who did not know the empress, her moral elevation, the crystal pure nature of her family life," Spiridovich protested, "only profoundly vicious people, fanatics or scandalmakers could find in this letter confirmation of this revolting calumny." But few, very few, knew the empress. It was bad enough that she should write of kissing Rasputin's hands, an act of subservience. Worse were the references to the imperial head nestling on the peasant shoulder, to the imperial body falling asleep in the peasant arms, the mentions of love, torment, and happiness.

Was it all mere literary license? Vyrubova and Lili von Dehn later testified that the empress had never kissed the starets's hands. But why did Alexandra write—and the letter was genuine—that she did? Why did she use lovers' language—"beloved . . . how light I feel . . . I wish only one and the same thing . . . come quickly"—if her affection was purely spiritual? To suggest that it was not, the press stepped up the flow of stories of Rasputin's seductions and cuckoldings.

This letter apart, there was no evidence that Rasputin slept with the empress. The investigating commission did not interrogate her—that was beyond its brief—but, as mentioned earlier, medical examination proved that Vyrubova, also a supposed lover of Rasputin's, remained a virgin. Simanovich, operating in the dark area where indiscretion mingled with blackmail, kept himself abreast of Rasputin's affairs as a matter of professional pride. He had no qualms about passing on the equally scurrilous story that the tsarevich had been fathered by General Orlov, but he mentioned the rumors that the empress was Rasputin's lover only in the context of Rasputin's indifference to them.

Negatives, however, are difficult to prove, and the non-affair was no exception. Alexandra's letters to her husband were published after the revolution;

though they certainly show her to have been deeply in love with him, they were no more emotional than the letter to Rasputin. Married women made love to khlyst pilots without it affecting their marital relations; Rasputin was known to have stayed on friendly terms with at least two husbands whom he was cuckolding. When he was reproached for this, he replied that it was not his fault if high-ranking men made their wives and mistresses run after him in the hope of gaining some benefit. "Most of these women," Simanovich confirmed, "formed a connection with him with the consent of their husbands or relatives."

As to opportunity, although Vyrubova was present when the empress met Rasputin at her cottage, Rasputin frequently made love while his admirers were sitting in the next room. He brought a Siberian woman named Akulina Laptinskaya to St. Petersburg in 1911; she acted as his secretary and occasional housekeeper until his murder, and also gave massages to the empress. "He'd be surrounded by his admirers, with whom he also slept," she testified in 1917. "He'd do his thing with them quite openly and without shame. He'd caress them . . . and when they felt like it he'd simply take them into his study and do his business. . . . I often heard his views, a mixture of religion and debauchery. He'd sit there and give instructions to his female admirers. 'Do you think I degrade you? I don't degrade you. I purify you.' This was his basic idea. He also used the word *grace*, meaning that by sleeping with a man, a woman came into the grace of God."

It was, in fact, Iliodor who unwittingly furnished the most obvious indication that the empress's letter should not be taken at face value. As he fled toward Saratov, hoping to find sanctuary in Hermogen's former see, he drew a Pied Piper's tail of journalists behind him. He kept them well supplied with material and released the stolen letters from the young grand duchesses. They indeed showed how startlingly intimate Rasputin had become with the imperial family—but as friend, confessor, and soul mate, not lover. Olga, now a beautiful sixteen-year-old with chestnut hair and her father's limpid blue eyes, wrote with unaffected charm to Rasputin of her infatuation with a young Guards officer: "Nicholas drives me crazy. Whenever I go to the Sofia cathedral and see him, I'm ready to climb up the wall and my body shakes all over. . . . I love him. . . . I am about to throw myself on him. You advised me to behave more carefully. But how can I do that when I can't control myself? . . . Loving you, Olga."

Tatiana, two years younger, was chatty; she missed playing with "Matryosha," Rasputin's daughter Maria, and she wanted to see the fabled Siberia he had spoken about so often. "My dear and faithful friend," she wrote.

How long will you stay in Pokrovskoye? How are your kids? How's Matryosha? Whenever we get together at Anya's we always talk about all of you. And we so wish to visit Pokrovskoye. . . . Arrange everything as soon as possible, you can do everything. God loves you so. . . . We miss you, miss you. And mama is unwell without you. . . . Oh! if only you knew how difficult it is for us to stand mama's illness. But you know because you know everything. Kissing you heartily and affectionately, my dear friend. . . . Good-bye. Your Tatiana."

Marie, twelve when Iliodor handed her letter to journalists, was girlishly worried about being bad when she wrote it. "Sweet, dear unforgettable friend of mine," she began.

I miss you so. You won't believe it but almost every night I see you in my dreams. In the morning, when I wake up, I take the gospel which I received from you from under my pillow, and I kiss it. . . . Then I feel it is you that I kiss. I am so wicked but I want to be kind and don't want to offend our sweet, good, kind nurse. She is so kind, so good, we all love her so. Pray, unforgettable friend, so that I should always be kind. I am kissing you. Kissing your pure hands. Yours forever, Marie.

Little Anastasia, ten when Russians gloated over her letter, also saw the starets in her dreams. She wondered if he saw her so. "My sweet friend," she wrote.

When shall we see you? Anya told me yesterday that you would come soon. It will make me so happy. I like it when you talk to us about God. . . . God seems to be so kind, so good. Pray to Him so that he helps mama to be healthy. I often see you in dreams. Do you see me in dreams? When will you be telling us about God in the nursery? Come soon. I am trying to be a good child like you told me. I shall always be a good child if you are always with us. Good-bye. I kiss you and you bless me. Yesterday I had a grudge against the little one [Alexis] but then I made it up with him. Loving you, your Anastasia.

It was clear that the infatuation with Rasputin was a family affair, based not on the mother's lust but on a perception of his goodness. He had done his work well. He was the girls' friend; Olga asked his advice about a boyfriend, Anastasia admitted she had gotten fed up with her little brother. He was kind and loving; he helped them to pray, to be good, and he calmed their mother's hysteria and made her well. The relationship was full of charm and innocence. The letters damned Rasputin, not the young Romanovs who wrote them. They revealed the extent of Rasputin's duplicity, the skill with which he concealed his lewdness under a mask of generosity and affection; they sketched the family's utter trust in him—a loyalty as touching as it was misplaced—and explained the "perpetual incredulity" and hostility the parents showed to those who warned them of the other face of Janus.

The public, however, did not see them in this light. Phrases were seized on— "I feel it is you that I kiss" "Do you see me in dreams?"—to show that the grand duchesses had followed their mother into the Siberian's bed. Kokovtsov complained that the letters caused "the most revolting comments. . . . We [he and Interior Minister Makarov] believed that the letters were apocryphal and were being circulated for the purpose of undermining the prestige of the sovereign, but we could do nothing. . . . The public, of course, greedy for sensation, was according them a very warm reception." The girls' letters were genuine, but frankly pornographic fakes were soon in circulation.

—

The storm raged on. The Duma seethed with anger at the treatment of Hermogen. Mikhail Rodzianko, its twenty-stone chairman, a bluff country squire with a powerful presence—"on a still day he can be heard for a kilometer"— found it difficult to keep the excited deputies under control. The most ardent monarchists were outraged at the tsar's behavior. "Where do we go?" the extreme right-winger Vladimir Purishkevich demanded of Rodzianko with horror. "Now the dark forces are destroying Russia's last stronghold—the church. And what makes it even more horrible is that all this seems to come down from the highness of the tsar's throne. A rascal, a khlyst, a dirty illiterate muzhik is playing with our churchmen. What abyss are they taking us into? My God! I want to sacrifice myself and kill this vile creature—Rasputin." It was not an idle threat.

Rodzianko recognized that the crisis was real. If the affair could be limited to Alexandra's "passion for Rasputin's imaginary gift of prophesy and his hypnotic power which eased her nervous sufferings and abated her fears for her family . . . then it would not arouse much alarm." But there was more to it than that. Rodzianko was afraid that Rasputin's closeness to the tsarevich would influence the child's receptive soul, "imparting mysticism and making the heir a nervous and unbalanced person." Respect for the dynasty was being undermined. "Ambitious men, climbers and dark crooks"—the Simanoviches, Sablers, Varnavas, Andronnikovs—were crowding around the starets, flies on the dung heap. More terrible, Rodzianko thought, was that senior officials and ministers had split into "two hostile camps, Rasputin supporters, and the anti-Rasputins. . . . The gradual rise of Rasputin's supporters and their success was tempting, and the desertions from the anti-Rasputins to the Rasputin camp grew apace."

Rodzianko gave the example of a lady, a "happy and exemplary family woman," who visited Rasputin to solicit a position for her husband. "All right, ·

I'll see to it," Rasputin said, openly ogling her. "But come again tomorrow in an open dress with naked shoulders. Otherwise don't bother." The lady left, so Rodzianko said, full of indignation and determined not to submit. Once home she fell prey to "invincible melancholy." The next day she wore a décolleté dress and returned. "Her husband got his promotion eventually," Rodzianko wrote. "It is a documentary story."

It alarmed the Duma president to think of the "repulsive impression" this must make on servants, "for whom there are no alcove secrets," and on ordinary Russians in general. The "gray" people who met Rasputin—"the cabmen who took him and his women to bathhouses, the attendants who gave him separate rooms, waiters who served him during his orgies, the police agents who guarded his precious life"—had no illusions about his holiness. "All they said was 'The masters are up to their tricks,' " and the contempt they felt was helping to tarnish the throne. Rasputin was winning the battle, undermining premiers, ministers, senior churchmen; if it continued Rodzianko was sure it would lead to revolution.

His view was shared by Nicholas's mother. On February 13 she summoned Kokovtsov to discuss the affair. She listened to what he had to say about Rasputin. Then, in tears, the dowager empress promised to speak to her son. "My unhappy daughter-in-law," she said, "does not understand that she is destroying the dynasty and herself. She truly believes in the saintliness of this rogue and we are powerless to stave off this disaster."

Iliodor was continuing to rail against the injustice done to Hermogen and himself, his journey "a triumphal procession." He preached against the synod for a few more days, until he was finally arrested and confined to the Florishchev Monastery; but the damage was done. Rasputin tried to repair it. He spun a pretty tale of sex and hypocrisy to explain his rift with the monk. His daughter Maria and his admirers believed it, but it convinced few others. He said that he had become tired of hearing the monk preach that chastity was all when he did not practice it. He said that, during Iliodor's visit to Pokrovskoye, he had caught him sneaking a look at the maid Dunia while she was stripping to wash. When he had reminded Iliodor of this, in Tsaritsyn the previous summer, the monk had spluttered: "You . . . you . . ." "Come," Rasputin had sneered. "Confession is good for the soul." "Go! Leave me!" Iliodor had yelled back. "You are no friend but a vicious enemy. . . . You are the sinner, not I. My life is blameless. Who knows what yours has been?"

The Rasputin explanation for Hermogen's hostility was equally far-fetched. Maria claimed that her father had found a hole in the accounts of the Union of True Russians, the right-wing league in which the bishop was involved, and was about to expose his fraud when the beating intervened. Its purpose was to kill Rasputin before his allegations against the lecher-monk and the embezzler-bishop could bear fruit.

Rasputin mentioned none of this when he tried to stem the flood of hostile press articles by giving an interview of his own to the newspaper *Novoye Vremya*. It was published on February 18, 1912. The paper called him Grigory Rasputin-Novykh. The journalist signed himself I. M-v. This was Ivan Manasevich-Manuilov, part journalist, part Okhrana informer, and a full-time intriguer with a penchant for high living and antiques. He wrote it up directly from shorthand notes, catching the jumpiness, the sudden switches in subject, the phrases left to hang in silence.

Rasputin started, like the celebrity he was, by complaining about the press. "Newspapers are like birds," he said. "Once they start singing, they won't stop. They chirp. . . . They hoot. . . . They hurt. . . . They exalt. . . . Some kind of intoxication, a whirlwind. If you get caught in their path, there's no mercy. They'll beat you to death. . . . And why, no one will ask." He slipped skillfully into the role of the little man beaten up by bullies: "Why did they assault me, the little one?" he asked. "What do I signify, me among the big and the strong? One blow, and I'm gone. No one will remember me. They all pounced on me like one. A kind of wild dance. . . . Who could I hit? I'm not strong enough. . . . They've made me out as some sort of athlete. . . . Look at me. . . . I don't even know the ABC. . . . I spell like a little kid. And here, they're all big, clever, learned, and distinguished."

A pause, and some self-satisfaction entered his voice. "Maybe I'm not a little one . . . a bit bigger," he admitted. "Otherwise they wouldn't be interested . . . would not shout in a mighty voice all over Russia. Looks like I stuck in their throat." He became the people's champion. "When everybody was silent as the grave, I, the little one, weak one, spoke up," he went on. "My voice is small but there are people who hear me and want me to speak. . . . I say all I know, all I feel. . . . I say it simply. People with good souls, with pure designs, do not need many words."

He returned to the beating in the Iaroslavl Monastery. "They pounced on me from all sides," he said. "Slanders. . . . Dirty tricks. . . . Bishop Hermogen took it all for granted, that it was true, he didn't understand anything and started shouting. . . . I don't bear him malice. Who gives himself up to malice, walks out on God. . . . And they have given themselves up to malice. . . . With covered eyes, with closed ears they walk about and shout and stigmatize Grigory." He said that a man under the power of lies was worn out and floundered like an animal. "God deprived Bishop Hermogen and Iliodor of wits," he said. "Where has the bright wisdom gone? . . . The sun has come down. . . . It's not seen anymore. . . . Only the darkness, black darkness. They run against each other, break their foreheads. . . . Make a hubbub. Malice has gained the upper hand over the heart."

The delivery became more staccato, more disjointed and consciously poetic; the guru was hitting form. "You have to weep. Hot tears, that's what's needed," he said, flinging in an obscure aside: "And then, monks. . . . Associates. . . . Going into intrigue worse than simple people . . . into politics . . . into the whirlwind of passion where the right does not know what the left is doing. Love is needed . . . and tears. And there's no love, no tears. Where's the selflessness? There's strength in selflessness. . . . The bad, it's like the wind. . . . It makes noise, it hoots. . . . Everyone listens to it." But not the good, not Grigory— "those who are higher, who have pure soul, they won't listen and they step off the malice."

The journalist, dashing down shorthand notes, was barely able to keep up with the jerky flow of ideas—"My thoughts," Rasputin said, "they are like birds in the sky, they fly and often there's nothing I can do with them." He changed tack again, this time into an admission. "I'm sinful," he said. "Great sin more than once tortured me and it was stronger than I. Hermogen knew everything. For him, my soul was open. . . . I went to him with the good and the bad and he spoke of his love for me. There was great solace in his words and in bitter moments I often found joy . . . when I talked to him of all my sins and he listened to me kindly and ordered me to go to Jerusalem."

He followed this lie—there is no evidence that the bishop suggested the pilgrimage—with a confession. It was all that the readers of *Novoye Vremya* dared hope for. "But sin entangled me," he said. "I made a mistake. . . . It was three years ago. . . . Bishop Hermogen knew everything. . . . I was deluded! My women admirers were in the village. . . . They thought they were superior to everyone. Gold, diamonds, and money obscured their brains. They walked about like peahens. . . . I thought I had to humble them . . . to humiliate . . . when a person is humiliated, he understands much. I wanted them to experience all this." After the innuendo came the revelation: "I made them go to a bathhouse with me. . . . There were twelve women. . . . They washed me and they have gone through all the humiliations."

Twelve women, a bathhouse, every form of humiliation—it was as far as he could go. The retraction followed instantly. "Wicked people said that I hurt them, that an animal spoke up in me," he said. "They lie, they impudently lie. They tell bad, dirty things. . . . There wasn't anything like this. . . . I was deluded, I was thinking wrongly. . . . I paid dearly, very dearly for my mistake. They all pounced, especially the local priests. . . . There was no sin. Sin is darkness. . . . All my life I escaped the darkness. I was looking for the sun . . . each ray made my soul quiver."

He spoke of sin and forgiveness, his favorite line, always reliable: "Sinful man, nearer to God," he said. "He always thinks about God, he prays . . . and will be pardoned. His soul is in secret prayer, he is in eternal contrition. The sinner will be the first to present himself in front of God." Suddenly, he was silent.

The journalist had time to look up and see Rasputin smoothing out his beard with jerky movements of his long and bony hand. The eyes were small and colorless; they looked sideways and did not like to be looked into. There was "something nervous in all of him."

"I gave all my soul to Iliodor," Rasputin continued. "But they have forgotten that for me there is nothing superior to the power of God and that of the tsar." The twin pillars of Orthodoxy, God and tsar; it would go down well at Tsarskoye Selo. "All this distresses me. My soul is anxious. Wicked people say that I did harm to the bishop and Iliodor by winning over big men. I know my place. Am I, the little one, to push myself forward? If I'm called, it's only to talk. . . . Big men live as in a dungeon. Lies all around. . . . Everyone with wants, looking for profit, and I don't want anything, I don't need anybody."

He denied that he had ever wanted to be a priest. He'd never even dreamed of it; he hadn't the literacy and the power of concentration that a priest needed. He'd never preached, he claimed, or spoken in public. He almost didn't know his ABCs; perhaps it was for the better, because there was happiness in simplicity. What he liked best was being in Siberia and healing and doing good. "They all love me in my village," he said. "They open their sick souls. I comfort them. Words mean a lot for a sick soul. A person will come to me with black thoughts, giving everything up as hopeless, and then he leaves and, behold, he's in better spirits. . . . A smile on his face. . . . Like the sun on a black day."

A maid interrupted—"Grigory Efimovich, there's someone . . ." Rasputin said he was busy. Whoever it was should call back in the evening. "They say I live wrongly," he went on, whining now. "Libertine. But I live modestly. I've got a household. Two good maids. Kind wife. We get on well. In God's manner. . . . I don't know any women. They've covered me with filth from all sides. But filth won't stick to what is clean."

The journalist was unimpressed by this declaration of innocence. He asked Rasputin whether he had many women admirers. "Women admirers . . . many, very many." The journalist noted that his interviewee was smiling maliciously behind his beard. "Didn't count them. Women, they're poor. They're oppressed. All their life they're in chains. They need consolation. They remember it for a long time. All sorts of them visit me. Many a tear I've seen. Tried to ease their grief." There were men, too, who visited—about twenty of them. "All these people are for me. They'll all stick up for me. They won't let anyone hurt me."

———

The next question was ideal for the starets—what impression was Petersburg making on him? He aimed his reply directly at the palace. He knew well that

Nicholas and Alexandra despised the city; he knew, too, their belief in autocracy and in the love that peasant Russia had for them.

"Clerks all around," he said of the city. "Toadying. One eats another. They've pushed truth into the corner here . . . it's afraid to peep out. But Russia needs truth. It must rule. It's strong. Everybody is in a hurry here. . . . Urgent matters. . . . Live in intoxication, that's what they do. . . . They say good words and don't have any notion of what's good. . . . Hypocrites. . . . It's so painful. . . . I wish that God could make it so that truth wins."

He fashioned himself as the little man, the loyal peasant-thinker. "And sometimes I hear untruth and I feel like raising my voice all over the great Russia," he said. "Then I look at myself. . . . Ridiculous, all this. . . . Little one, that's what I am. What can I do? Can I make anyone listen to reason? All sorts of big people here, they lie. . . . They invent things and are listened to. . . . People are strangled in this big city. They think about everything. But they forget about God."

He was pleased with himself. He leaned forward on the arm of his chair, a light shining in his small eyes. He smoothed out his dark-colored blouse. "They've told me here about the ecstasy." Suddenly he laughed out loud. He waved his bony hand. "What sort of ecstasy is that? They all lie. . . . They cheat. And when someone spoke up sincerely, from his heart, they started to cry: ecstasy." He was talking of religious ecstasy, a subject close to khlysts and the sects, and he was careful to circumscribe it. He was guarded, too, when the journalist asked him about visions.

"No, I haven't had them," he said, carefully going on to confirm his spirituality. "But when I'm alone, in the quiet, I feel kind of ethereal. . . . I can hear my heart beat. . . . Begin to feel easy. I start to think about the deeds of the saints. I want selflessness so much." He emphasized the word *selflessness*, and slipped in a claim of personal modesty. "But I'm small. . . . Not fit. Just dreams, that's all. . . . And dreams, they are like flowers. . . . I've been trying my strength. . . . Tortured myself severely more than once. I want so much to be nearer to God. All dreams. And once a man is deprived of God, what'll be left?"

He took a swipe at séances. There is no evidence that Rasputin ever summoned up spirits, or felt the need to; he won his admirers through force of personality, not by tricks. He had fallen out with the Montenegrins by now, and judged it safe to mock table rappers. "You fly in your dreams to God and you feel so warm at heart," he said. "Everyone is looking for it. And the sinful think that it's enough to tap with one's fingers on the table so that a vision appears. . . . Foolishness, all foolishness." He finished his appraisal of the soul with a burst of phrases. "Devotees, they are different. . . . They have visions. . . . The sick . . . must be cured . . . must pray. . . . When I was twenty, I had all these thoughts but my chest ached. . . . I went to the holy places, to Verkhoturye. . . . Prayed there hard. . . . Felt easier afterward."

Without effort he switched to politics and the state of Russia. Again, beneath the babble, the aim was true. He slipped the knife into the Duma and its politicians, and twisted it with words he knew were sweet for Nicholas and Alexandra. "I've heard somewhere that I was the enemy of the state Duma," he mocked. "Am I, really? I've never been to the state Duma. . . . What's going on there, I don't know, don't want to know. . . . May God judge them. . . . All I think is about Russia, like a son about a mother."

He dropped in a reference to his powerful patrons, a clear warning that he was protected by the palace. The politicians, he said, "don't like me having top people among my acquaintances. But they came to me by themselves. . . . I didn't go into any sort of politics and never will. But the state Duma assaulted me, the little one. . . . They've got big deeds to do but all of a sudden—me. As if the power is in me and I'm in the way. . . . I don't hinder. And when I have to speak, I talk about truth, about ways to God, about human lies. . . . About the soul."

A mirror for the empress, he accused the politicians of ruining the empire. "They have to think in the Duma, and they rush about like women and in this chaos forget about the empire," he said. "I don't really represent anything. Shall I really go against what they want from above? No, I'm not this kind of person. . . . I've never had thoughts like these. I want everything to be good. But there's a kind of whirlwind instead. . . . Destroys our house. The whirlwind is not good. One can do something only when it's peaceful, calm."

He leaned forward. "Strength is needed." He meant the tsar, the autocracy. "Do you understand?"

The interview was over. "I'm leaving for Siberia now," he said. "Want to stay for a while in my own place." It was a bravura performance, never resting long enough to be trapped on any topic, mixing confession with defiance, a shrewd mind digging itself out of trouble. Throughout it, those brilliant little eyes were fixed on the palace.

Miracle at Spala

The tsar issued a ukase forbidding newspapers to mention Rasputin's name; the edict broke the terms of the 1905 manifesto and failed to gag the politicians. Kokovtsov warned Nicholas of the risks he was running by seeing the starets. Maria Rasputin claimed that the audience was overheard by her playmate, Grand Duchess Marie. In her version the tsar spoke of Rasputin's "great service" to the throne; the premier replied that he knew of the heir's miraculous recoveries but said that Rasputin gave the credit to God and not himself. "Ah yes," the tsar said. "But why did God choose to act through him?"

The premier recollected only telling the tsar that the flood of stories of "orgies and disgraceful conduct" was no ordinary gossip. He said that "respectable newspapers call Rasputin a thief and swindler." When the tsar said that the press was beneath contempt, Kokovtsov reminded him as gently as he could that it molded public opinion. "The public does not run the country," the tsar retorted. "It is run for their benefit, and I am the one who decides what is best for them." Nicholas concluded by asking Kokovtsov to see "the simple peasant" who, "by a strange power," relieved the sufferings of his son.

Kokovtsov did so. The peasant strode into the premier's study and sat himself down in an armchair. "I was struck by the repulsive expression of his eyes," the premier wrote. "Deep seated and close set, they glued on me and for a long time he would not turn them away as though trying to exercise some hypnotic influence." When tea was served Rasputin dipped a handful of biscuits into his cup and ate the soggy mass before again fixing his "lynx eyes" on the premier. "I was getting tired of his attempts at hypnotism," Kokovtsov recalled, "and told him that it was useless to stare at me so hard because his eyes had not the slightest effect on me." He thought Rasputin a "typical Siberian convict, a tramp who had cleverly taught himself to play the fool and who carried out his role according to a tried-and-tested recipe."

It was a grave underestimate. This Siberian had seen off Stolypin, a man the British ambassador considered "the most notable figure in Europe"; though the same source thought Kokovtsov "the best type of the old bureaucracy," he was easier meat and Rasputin knew it. Like his murdered predecessor the new premier demanded that the starets leave the capital for good. Rasputin told Vyrubova that he was offered a sweetener of 200,000 rubles—"a fortune beyond the dreams of avarice to a Russian peasant," she wrote admiringly, "but he declined it, saying that he was not to be bought by anybody." He agreed to return to Pokrovskoye for a while and did so a few days later. It was hardly a concession, for he regarded Siberia as his sin bin, a place to take to when a cooling-off period was needed.

He made sure it was the premier who would suffer by letting Vyrubova know that he did not enjoy the grace of God. Alexandra, so friendly when they had met in the Crimea a few months before, made a point of ignoring Kokovtsov the next time she saw him; she deliberately talked to minor officials and "passed Kokovtsov with averted face, thrusting out a hand for him to salute." The premier was well aware of the implication. "From that time on," he wrote, "though the tsar continued to show me his favor for another two years, my dismissal was assured."

On February 26, 1912, with the starets already on his way back to Siberia, Rodzianko obtained an audience with the tsar. He thought his mission so important that he first prayed for strength in the Kazan cathedral. He was hot with shame that a royalist like himself should have to speak of such matters to his sovereign. "I beseech you, Sire," he said, "as Your Majesty's most loyal subject, will it be your pleasure to hear me to the end? If not, but say one word and I will be silent." Nicholas would not meet his eye but murmured, "Speak." He reminded the tsar that Hermogen's career had been ruined for telling the truth about Rasputin, whom he was sure was a khlyst. "How can the Orthodox Church stand by in silence when Orthodoxy is being destroyed and defiled by this rogue?" he asked. Nicholas replied that he had nothing against Hermogen. "I think he is an honest and sincere archpastor . . . and a staunch man serving the dignity of the Church," he said. "He will soon be taken back. But I had to punish him because he openly refused to obey my command." Rodzianko thought it typical of the tsar's weak character that he should have no personal argument with the exiled bishop. Nicholas asked him if he had read Stolypin's report on the starets; he had not. The tsar suggested he do so and then prepare a further report.

The Stolypin material was with a synod official, Mikhail Damansky, who handed it over with great reluctance. The next day he called on Rodzianko to demand it back, saying that he had been sent by a "very exalted person." Rodzianko asked if that was Sabler, the synod procurator. Damansky replied that the person was incomparably more important; it was, he snapped, the empress herself. If that was so, Rodzianko said, then she should be reminded that she was as much her husband's subject as Damansky was. Rodzianko had been told to prepare a report; he would do so. He refused to hand back the material—provoking a hysterical outburst by Alexandra, who thought he should be hanged for his impudence—and included it with further details of Rasputin's Siberian youth in a second report. The tsar did not so much as glance at it. Rodzianko asked for further audiences. They were refused on the ground that Rasputin was a personal matter for the family, not politicians.

A debate on the budget for the synod was held in the Duma on March 9. Alexander Guchkov took advantage of it to thunder an accusation: "I feel like saying, like crying out that the Church is in danger and the State is in danger too. You all know what serious drama Russia is experiencing. In the center of this drama—a mysterious tragicomic figure, a ghost or survivor through the darkness of centuries, a strange figure in the light of the twentieth century," he said. He did not mention a name; if he had the new ukase would have prevented his speech from being reported. In any event such detail was superfluous to the person who obsessed all St. Petersburg. "In what ways has this man reached such heights that the senior holders of Church and State power bow to his influence? You must ask—who is playing the master at the top? Who is wielding the ax that fells some policies and people, and promotes others?" The man was not alone, Guchkov warned; he was surrounded by "unnoticed individuals greedy for distinction . . . obscure tradespeople, shipwrecked pressmen, contractors."

It was the first attack on Rasputin by a public figure in a public place. A single deputy criticized it, an old reactionary who shouted: "These are old wives' tales!" Inevitably, the tsar took the taunt that the ax of power was carried by another as a personal insult; he ordered the interior minister to have secret police agents shadow Guchkov as a potential enemy of the state. "Conduct of the Duma is profoundly outrageous," he wrote, "and especially disgusting is the speech of Guchkov. . . . I will be very glad if my displeasure reaches these gentlemen. It's not always that one should bow and smile to them." He told Kokovtsov. "I simply suffocate in this atmosphere of gossip, inventions, and malice."

Guchkov did not let the matter rest. The moderate Octobrist party he led commissioned Vladimir Bonch-Bruevich to research the allegations that Rasputin was a khlyst. Bonch-Bruevich, who had already observed Rasputin in a

St. Petersburg salon in 1905, was an expert on sects who had studied Dukhobors, the "Siberian Quakers," in emigration in Canada; he would be a Bolshevik commander during Red October and nationalize Russia's banks. His report concluded that Rasputin was an Orthodox believer, although he showed sectarian habits of speech and thought; Guchkov claimed that Bonch-Bruevich wrote him a private letter in which he described Rasputin as a scoundrel and a practitioner of his own brand of sectarianism but not strictly speaking a khlyst.

Metropolitan Evlogi, another Duma member at the time, read the dossier that Damansky had reluctantly handed to Rodzianko. It did not prove Rasputin to be a member of the sect—in particular, a case against him in 1902 had been dropped by the prosecutor for lack of evidence—but Evlogi found that parts of the dossier appeared to be missing. After the murder the Commission of Inquiry made a final attempt to decide the issue. There was firm evidence that Rasputin took baths with women, and Professor Gromoglassov, who held the chair of religious sects at the Moscow theological academy, was asked to comment on it. He found that in parts of Siberia it was "common practice for men and women to take baths together" and that there was no definitive proof of khlyst activity.

Villagers found Rasputin uncharacteristically meek on his arrival in Pokrovskoye; no fashionable women came with him, and no bathtime frolics were recorded. A Siberian Duma member, Sukhanov, found that he seemed chastened by the scandal and that the villagers mocked him. He was soon protesting his innocence and warning of Duma "revolutionaries" in cables to the palace. "Dearest father and mother," he wired. "See how the devil gains in strength the evil one. The Duma serves him it is the fault of revolutionaries and Jews. And what is it they want? To get rid of the Lord's anointed as soon as they can. And Guchkov is their ringleader he speaks slander and mindless rebellion. Father the Duma is yours do as you want with it." Rasputin was later to show considerable sympathy to the Jews; for now he was severely rattled, and he chose his words to appeal to the anti-Semite and the reactionary in the tsar. In another cable, he urged: "The rebel Iliodor must be broken. Or this cur will eat us all up. . . . He will stop at nothing. File his teeth. Be harsh with him. Lock him up good. Yes. Grigory."

Alexandra recalled the starets to St. Petersburg a few days after Guchkov's speech. The two met at Vyrubova's cottage; Rasputin also had talks there with Witte, who was hoping to use him to make a political comeback. The imperial family left for a holiday in the Crimea on March 16. Rasputin smuggled himself aboard their train, probably with Alexandra's help, but the tsar had him put off before it reached Moscow. He made his own way to Yalta, arriving there on

March 20, 1912. The local paper, *The Russian Riviera*, carried a news item. "Yesterday, at two in the afternoon, Grigory Rasputin arrived in Yalta by automobile from Sevastopol," it ran. "He is staying at the Hotel de Russie." The newspaper was correct—he was indeed staying at the resort's finest hotel—but it was fined for breaking the ukase in mentioning his name.

The interior minister, Makarov, arrived in Yalta the same day and was astonished to find that the starets was no longer in Siberia. Police removed Rasputin's name from the hotel register, but a local news photographer had taken his picture outside the hotel, and this was printed as a postcard, which fashionable visitors to the resort sent to their friends. The city mayor, Ivan Dumbadze, a bustling, excitable Georgian, was persuaded by right-wing friends that Rasputin's presence was a provocation. They urged him to "drown the dirty adventurer" in the Black Sea. Dumbadze sent a cable to the Okhrana suggesting that he have him thrown overboard from the tourist steamer that ran between Sevastopol and Yalta. He received no reply. Stefan Beletsky, director of the police department, said later that Dumbadze had another plan, to lure Rasputin to a clifftop near the town, rob him, and throw him into the sea "as if he were the victim of brigands."

Rasputin returned unscathed to Pokrovskoye after Easter. He was now escorted by a *konspirativnykh filverov*, a team of undercover agents. The premier had asked Beletsky to maintain surveillance on him at all times, partly for protection and partly to note his activities. Beletsky stationed a plainclothesman in the village; since Rasputin was friendly with the postmaster, the agent had to travel to the next telegraph office to send his reports. Rasputin was not inhibited by his shadows; he enjoyed his time with his family, singing psalms around the samovar in the evening and taking them for a steamer trip down the Tura River to Tobolsk, where they prayed before the relics of St. Ivan.

Far to the east in Siberia, miners in the Lena goldfields went on strike. As they marched in an orderly demonstration to the manager's office, a drink-sodden police officer told his men to fire on them. Two hundred were massacred. A young deputy, the radical lawyer Alexander Kerensky, made a name for himself by heading a Duma inquiry into the killings; a wave of strikes followed this "second Bloody Sunday."

—

In August the Romanovs gathered outside Moscow to celebrate the centenary of the battle of Borodino during Napoleon's disastrous invasion of Russia. There was a reminder of the distant Siberian. The tsar cut Rodzianko when he passed him on the battlefield. "He looked askance at me," the politician complained, "and did not acknowledge my salute. I understood that the cause of his dissatisfaction with me was my report on Rasputin." Kokovtsov was alarmed that the tsar's belief in divine right was degenerating into a mysticism that was impervious to advice from working politicians. He had suggested that some of the many restrictions on Jews—barred from some schools, universities, and professions, and from living in many Russian regions—should be lifted as part of the celebrations. Nicholas agreed that the arguments were convincing. "An inner voice keeps insisting more and more that I do not accept responsibility for it," he said, however. "So far my conscience has not deceived me. . . . I know that you, too, know that the tsar's heart is in God's hands. Let it be so." Guchkov's speech had already confirmed Nicholas's conviction that the Duma, despite its large royalist majority, was implacably hostile to the dynasty.

The premier feared that the tsar's "intimate circle"—by which he meant Alexandra, Rasputin, Vyrubova—had only a dwindling interest in a government as such. "In its place," he wrote, "emerged with increasing force and clarity the purely personal nature of the emperor's rule, while the government increasingly came to be considered as a wall cutting off the ruler from his people." The comment was the more damning for the dapper, loyal, and hardworking man who made it.

The imperial trains—there were two, one a decoy to confuse terrorists—rumbled west after Borodino. Alexis, now eight, his hair auburn, his features delicate and handsome, was so well that there was a false hope of recovery. The train stopped at Smolensk for a reception with local worthies; the boy got hold of a glass of champagne and chattered away to the ladies before complaining that he could "hear my tummy rumbling." The girls were perfecting their German and French to add to their English and Russian.

They stayed first at Bielovezh, a hunting lodge set in forests rich in game in eastern Poland. The girls rode along woodland paths with their father. Alexis was not allowed to ride for fear he would fall. But he slipped while jumping into a boat to go rowing on a lake and hit his left thigh. The bruise hurt for several days, but he appeared to recover. The family moved on to Spala, a rustic hunting lodge set in magnificent forests cut by streams and sandy paths. Guests rose at seven each morning to the notes of a hunting horn and picnicked in glades while a military band played hunting airs. In the afternoon the men hunted—stags, all of ten points or more, elk, bison—and shot snipe and partridge. At dusk the day's bag was laid out on the lawns in front of the lodge for the guests to examine the ranks of antlers by the light of flaming torches. The forests were dark, the paths narrow and yellow under the tangled trees; the windows in the wooden lodge were so small that lamps were left burning through the day. Pierre Gilliard had begun tutoring the heir in French. He was struck by the pallor of his charge, who was carried everywhere by the sailor Nagorny.

At the beginning of October 1912, Alexandra took her son for a carriage drive to get him some fresh air. She cushioned him between herself and Vyrubova. The paths were rough where roots cut through and rains had scooped out the sand. "Before we had gone very far we saw that indeed he was very ill," Vyrubova recalled. "He cried out with pain in his back and stomach, and the empress, terribly frightened, gave the order to return." He had begun to hemorrhage. The return drive was "an experience in horror." Each jolt brought the boy "the most excruciating torture," and he was almost unconscious with pain when they reached home. Eugene Botkin, the stout court physician, found telltale swelling in the upper thigh and groin. As the blood continued to flow unstemmed, the leg drew up to the chest until there was no longer space to fill and the swelling became as tight as a drum.

For the next eleven days, "dreadful sounds" echoed down the dark corridors outside the heir's room. A stream of doctors—the surgeons Fedorov and Rauchfuss, the hemophilia specialist Vladimir Derevenko, the pediatrician Ostrogorsky—worked without success to stem the bleeding. No painkillers were given to the child; his parents did not wish him to become addicted to morphia. The screams were so penetrating that some of the household staff put cotton wool in their ears. Though normal life seemed impossible, it continued; the secret of the imperial blood was maintained. "One shooting party succeeded another," Gilliard wrote, "and the guests were more numerous than ever." The tsar hunted with Polish nobles each day.

One evening, the two youngest grand duchesses performed two scenes from Molière's *Bourgeois Gentilhomme* for the visiting hunters in the dining room. Gilliard watched Alexandra chatting gaily to her guests before suddenly running upstairs, holding the long train of her dress in her hands, her face "distracted and terror-stricken." She returned a few minutes later, her smiling mask intact apart from a single despairing glance she threw at the tsar. The scene brought home to Gilliard "the tragedy of a double life" in which the condition of the heir to the great empire was concealed from his future subjects, for fear it would encourage the millions who wished the dynasty ill, and depress and confuse the loyal.

All night Alexandra sat beside the bed where her son lay on his side, his left leg drawn up so sharply toward his chin that he could not straighten it for almost a year after. His face was "absolutely bloodless," Vyrubova said, "drawn and seamed with suffering while his almost expressionless eyes rolled back in his head." Alexandra "never undressed, never went to bed, rarely even lay down for an hour's rest." She dozed fitfully on a sofa next to the bed, woken by his cries to soothe his forehead, her golden hair becoming streaked with gray. Nicholas could scarcely stand the strain; Vyrubova noticed that once, seeing his son's agony and hearing the screams, "the poor father's courage completely gave way" and he rushed to his study in tears.

The parents, and the doctors, expected the boy to die at any time. On October 6, Dr. Fedorov examined him and warned that the stomach hemorrhage was likely to bring on a fatal abscess. "The days between the 6th and the 10th were the worst," Nicholas wrote to the dowager empress. "The poor darling suffered intensely, the pains came in spasms and recurred every quarter of an hour." Alexis stirred in his delirium, and when he sat up the movement brought a rushing recurrence of pain and he cried to God to have mercy upon him. He also thought he would die; "when I am dead build me a little monument of stones in the wood," he begged his mother, asking for his grave to be in the light under a blue sky.

There was no church at Spala; a big green tent was raised in the gardens and outfitted as a chapel. Cossack escorts, servants, and huntsmen begged the court priest Vassilyev to hold a Te Deum, and Polish peasants joined them, weeping through the service. Bulletins were sent to St. Petersburg confirming that the tsarevich was gravely ill. Prayers were said for him throughout Russia, and worshipers in the Kazan Cathedral in the capital maintained a vigil by day and night. The cause of the illness was not mentioned; people muttered that Alexis had been wounded by a revolutionary's bomb, that he was mentally abnormal, an epileptic.

Alexandra was twice convinced that the end was imminent. At lunchtime on October 10 she sent a note to the tsar from the sickbed to say that the suffering had become so acute that she was sure the boy was dying. Though he pulled through that crisis, his condition the next afternoon was so alarming that Vassilyev administered the last rites as Nicholas and Alexandra prayed at the bedside. The medical bulletin dispatched to St. Petersburg for October 11 needed little amendment to announce the death of the heir. A single hope remained. "The empress declared that she could believe that God had abandoned them," Vyrubova recalled, "and she asked me to telegraph Rasputin in his home in Siberia, to pray for the child."

That the empress should wait so long before calling on Rasputin—allowing one apparently fatal climax to come and go—is significant. It suggests, strongly, that Alexis's illness was not the basis of her obsession with Rasputin; it is another reminder that her need for a holy man, for a personal guru, for intercession with God, went back to Dr. Philippe and the days before the birth of her son. Rasputin had already survived public scandal, allegations of rape and lewdness, the criticism of two prime ministers, the contempt of the Duma, the hatred of churchmen, and a vitriolic press campaign—all this before he was called on as a last resort to save the heir. It was not Spala that made him inviolable; to the empress, if not to the husband she so dominated, he was already that. Her fatal attraction stemmed from the soul, from her hysteria, mysticism, and isolation; it was cemented by Rasputin's skill and her own obstinacy and autocratic pride. Hemophilia merely—post facto—confirmed it.

———

On the afternoon of October 11, Rasputin was walking on the banks of the Tura River when he clutched his heart and said, "Oh, no!" Maria was alarmed for him, but he reassured her that there was no need for worry on his account. "It is the tsarevich," he said. "He has been stricken." A telegram from Alexandra arrived in the village that evening. He prayed in front of an icon, his face gray and sweating with effort, then went to the village telegraph office. He sent two cables to Spala. In the first he said that the illness was not serious but that the doctors should not be allowed to tire the boy. The second told her to have no fear. "God has seen your tears and heard your prayers," he wired. "Do not grieve. The little one will not die."

When Alexandra received them the tsar was discussing funeral arrangements with members of his suite. She relaxed immediately. "I am not anxious now," she told Vyrubova. The next day the hemorrhaging stopped. "The pain subsided," Vyrubova wrote, "the boy lay utterly wasted and spent, but it was obvious now that he was going to live." Recovery was slow and involved the use of mud baths and a steel triangle to strengthen wasted muscles and straighten the crippled leg; his mother sat reading with him for days, his body slowly filling out and regaining color as Nicholas played tennis and went rowing with Vyrubova. But within a month Alexis was able to return to Tsarskoye Selo. The roads to the railhead were smoothed and sanded by hand, and the imperial train steamed slowly without once using its brakes on a track whose points had been specially oiled to prevent any jars or bumps. The tsarevich had survived.

The drama was quickly forgotten by the public; photographs of the heir were carefully composed to conceal the damaged leg. Her child's survival merely deepened Alexandra's existing conviction that Rasputin was a miracle worker, but Nicholas had had doubts. The main effect of the incident at Spala was to drive out his reservations.

The honor in which the rulers held Rasputin was extended to his family when he returned to St. Petersburg in the fall to put his daughters into school at the smart lycée Steblin-Lamenska. The girls were sent for by the headmistress during morning school. They were told that they were to be presented to the empress and her daughters at Vyrubova's cottage. Maria put on a frock with a sailor collar for the railroad ride to Tsarskoye Selo. The empress was dressed in black; she had a fixed look on her face, proud, gentle, and "profoundly sad." A "vague fear or uneasiness" clung to her; it made Maria tongue-tied. The girl felt she had to say something. "Is it true, little mother," she faltered, "that you have hundreds of servants?" She blushed deeply when she realized that it was a stupid question, but the empress answered sweetly: "Yes, my child, I have lots of servants, but I could do without them if necessary." She patted her cheek.

Maria got on well with the grand duchesses, sitting primly on a sofa with them like "great ladies at a reception." She felt that, as their parents with her father, they were intrigued by meeting an ordinary person. They were prisoners in the palace, bound by etiquette; the life of an ordinary girl "who went to school with other children, and once or twice a week to the movies, sometimes the circus, seemed to them the rarest and most enviable of wonders." They talked of "their little preferences for this or that handsome officer, with whom they danced, played tennis, walked, or rode. These innocent romances were a source of amusement to Their Majesties, who enjoyed teasing the girls about any dashing young officer who seemed to attract them. The empress discouraged association with cousins and near relatives, many of whom were unwholesomely precocious."

The demonstration of royal friendship was soon repeated when Rasputin and Maria were invited to dine at the Alexander Palace. They were asked to use a side entrance in a vain attempt to cover up the relationship. "He went upstairs by a small staircase," Vyrubova commented. "He was received in the private apartments and never in the public drawing room. . . . More than once I pointed out to the empress the futility of the course pursued. 'You know that before he even reaches the palace, much less your boudoir, he has been observed . . . by the police at least forty times?' " Alexandra agreed with her; she realized that there could be no palace secrets but continued to try to shield her visitor.

It was Maria's first visit to the palace. She watched her father embrace the tsar and empress; Alexandra caught her in midcurtsy, hugged her, and, she recounted, "gave me a most motherly kiss." The thirteen-year-old was introduced to the tsarevich, and the young grand duchesses made her feel at home at once. They ate from a table crammed with red and black caviar, meatballs, prawns and herring, with bottles of vodka and wine. At the end of the informal supper they had an ice cream so delicious that Maria asked for the recipe. She wrote it down under the heading "Ice Cream Romanov." It suited her father's sweet tooth; it was made of two and a half pounds of sugar, ten egg yolks, a quart of light cream, one large vanilla bean, and a half pint of whipping cream. She played with Grand Duchess Marie, who was nearest her age; "we became fast friends." She recalled her father discussing Iliodor with the tsar, warning him that it was not in Iliodor's nature "to remain within the walls of an ancient monastery while the world burns outside."

———

He was right. Iliodor was not silent in his cell at the Florishchev Monastery. In September the government had forcibly closed his own monastery in Tsaritsyn. It sent him off into a new fit. He wrote a violent letter to Sabler: "You have bowed down before the licentious khlyst Grischa Rasputin as if he were the devil. You are a traitor and apostate. Your filthy hands are unfit to hold the most holy tiller of God's church, the bride of Christ. They should be shining the devil's boots in hell. I say this from a sense of priestly duty." He followed it by detailing Rasputin's depravity in a letter to Vyrubova.

Iliodor signed a letter to the synod on November 20 in his own blood. "Either indict Rasputin for his horrible crimes or unfrock me," he challenged. Sabler and the synod duly expelled the monk from holy orders in mid-December. He was ordered to be held under house arrest in his native village, Bolshaya Stanitsa, in the Cossack territory of the Don. On his way he wrote in the space reserved in a hotel register for the guest's religion, "My own. Iliodorian." He resumed his secular name, Sergei Trufanov.

Back wintering in Pokrovskoye, Rasputin fretted that his enemy was no longer safely tucked away in a monastery. He sent a rambling telegram to Maj. Gen. V. N. Voyeikov, the palace commandant: "Now there are millions of wasps so believe that in matters of the soul we must all be trusted friends, a small group perhaps but all of one mind while they are many but scattered and their rage shall have no power." He was more specific with the sovereigns. "Dearest papa and mama," he cabled. "Iliodor is joined with demons. He is a rebel. They used to flog monks like him. Yes, the tsars flogged them. Now bring him to heel." In another, he said, "The police must keep an eye on this accursed one." He had good reason for that. Iliodor was obsessed with castrating him.

CHAPTER 15

Before the Storm

Rasputin was back in the capital for the tercentenary celebrations of the Romanov dynasty in March 1913. Each Easter, Nicholas gave Alexandra an exquisite Fabergé egg of gold, silver, and jewels. For this special year the egg had miniatures of the Romanov rulers and their wives, and a blue steel globe showing the expansion of their territory. The first Romanov tsar, Michael, grandnephew of Ivan the Terrible, had ruled a narrow and barren compression between Europe and Asia; the Poles had recently sacked Moscow, and Russian adventurers barely had crept east of the Urals. Nicholas Romanov now ruled an empire that stretched from Poland to the Bering Strait, reaching along the Turkish, Persian, Afghan, Mongolian, and Chinese borders, until it ran into the foggy waters of the Sea of Japan. More than a hundred nationalities were his subjects.

It rained in torrents in St. Petersburg throughout the festivities. Society hoped that the imperial family would venture out of its seclusion, but no balls were held at the Winter Palace. The nobility and the diplomatic corps were asked to *baise mains*, or court receptions; Nicholas and his mother attended without the empress. Politicians hoped in vain that the tsar would make some concession to democracy in his speech to the Duma. An amnesty was announced, but it covered only common criminals. Political exiles, Prince Paul Vassily wrote, "men of culture and the highest civic and private virtue, were left to their sad fate . . . and despairing memories." People muttered of Rasputin. A special one-ruble coin was struck. It showed Nicholas in the foreground with the bearded Michael Romanov behind; he was, they said, a look-alike for the starets.

A solemn Te Deum was held at the Kazan Cathedral on March 6. The crowds lining the streets were "strangely silent" as the sovereigns passed them; they cheered only when the young grand duchesses smiled at them from under their flower-trimmed hats. The cathedral was full. Rodzianko had reserved seats for the Duma leaders close to the front; since Michael had been elected tsar by the people, the burly man insisted, it was right that the people's elected representatives should be treated with dignity at the service. He was waiting in the cathedral porch for the arrival of the imperial family when a sergeant at arms rushed out to tell him that an "unknown man in peasant dress and wearing a pectoral cross" had barged into his seat and was refusing to budge. Rodzianko guessed his identity.

"Sure enough," he wrote, "it was Rasputin . . . in a magnificent Russian tunic of crimson silk, patent leather top boots, black cloth trousers, and a peasant's overcoat." The pectoral cross was hung on a fine gold chain; it was a gift from the empress. "What are you doing here?" Rodzianko bellowed. "What has it got to do with thee?" Rasputin asked, using the familiar pronoun. Rodzianko was not amused. "If you 'thou' me," he roared, "I'll drag you out of the cathedral by the beard. Don't you know I'm president of the Duma?" Rasputin's stare had "an unknown power of tremendous force." Rodzianko did not succumb to it, feeling an "almost animal force" in himself as he worked himself into a frenzy. "Clear out at once, you vile heretic," he said. Rasputin knelt and prayed. Rodzianko kicked him in the ribs and was about to seize him by the hair when Rasputin turned to him and said: "Lord, forgive him such sin!" He got up and left by the western door of the cathedral, where a Court Cossack helped him on with his coat and put him in an automobile that sped him away.

The service Rasputin missed was conducted with great aplomb by Patriarch Antiochus, a great bearded figure in a jewel-studded miter, and the choral singing was superb; but the empress was clearly nervous and the tsar's stern gravity gave no sense of rejoicing. In the evening they went to a gala performance of Glinka's *A Life for the Tsar* at the Mariinsky Theater. Meriel Buchanan, in the British ambassador's box, was so close that she could see the fan of white eagles' feathers the empress held begin to tremble compulsively. The English girl noticed that a "dull, unbecoming flush was stealing over her pallor," while her labored breathing made the diamonds on her bodice glitter with "a thousand uneasy sparks of light." She gave way to her distress, whispered a few words to the tsar, and hid herself at the back of the box. She was seen no more that evening.

A wave of resentment ran through the theater. Women looked at each other and shrugged their shoulders, while the men muttered under their breath. It was always the same story, Meriel Buchanan thought. "The empress hated St. Petersburg, disliked its society, its people, anything to do with it," she wrote. "She refused to take her proper place by the emperor's side, would not put her own personal feeling in the background and make herself pleasant." Her father, the ambassador, told her that Alexandra hid herself through real torment or affliction, and not by whim or fancy. That was true; on her rare public appearances Alexandra showed all the symptoms of panic attack: panting, faintness, and distress. But the "disagreeable impression remained in people's minds," Buchanan observed, and no amount of argument could make it disappear.

The empress repeated the performance at a big ball given for the family in the Assembly Hall of the Nobility. As tradition demanded she opened it by dancing a Chopin polonaise with her husband, her face grave and unsmiling. She felt so ill that she had difficulty staying on her feet. It was the social debut of her eldest daughter, Olga, and the beautiful grand duchess swept through every dance in a simple pink chiffon dress. Alexandra caught Nicholas's eye; an onlooker thought he was "only just in time to lead her away and prevent her from fainting in public." Even Vyrubova thought that, for all the brilliance of spectacle, the mosaic of uniforms, gowns, jewels, and headdresses, there was "little real enthusiasm, little real loyalty. I saw a cloud over the whole celebration in St. Petersburg."

The Romanovs hoped that the provinces would show more warmth. They went by river steamer to Kostroma, the Volga town where Michael had been three centuries before when he heard he had been elected to the throne. Nicholas's sister Olga described the loyal scenes that greeted them as "bordering on wildness." Peasants waded chest-high into the river to catch a glimpse of the tsar; in the towns workmen fell to the ground to kiss his shadow as he passed. Alexandra took it as confirmation that Rasputin's Russia loved them with all its simple soul. The voyage, she said, showed that government ministers were cowards. "They are constantly frightening the emperor with threats of revolution," she told a lady-in-waiting. "Here—see it for yourself—we needed merely to show ourselves and at once their hearts are ours." Kokovtsov, the principal "coward" who went with them, was not convinced. The premier thought that the interest was no more than "shallow curiosity." If the peasants waded out into the shallows, it was because Nicholas never showed himself on deck, keeping out of the biting wind—and rifle range—below. He feared the tsar did not realize how much the country had changed since a Romanov could rule it by whim.

———

The financial boom continued—the 1913 harvest was not to be equaled for more than fifty years—but the country was out of sorts, at once churlish and light-headed. A vandal slashed Ilya Repin's great painting of Ivan the Terrible. It was no isolated act, a journalist wrote, but a sign "of times with no values, no education, and a total absence of moral sense." Million-ruble fortunes, the novelist Alexis Tolstoy wrote, "appeared as if out of thin air. People doped themselves with music . . . with half-naked women . . . with champagne. Gambling clubs, houses of assignation, theaters, movie-houses, amusement parks cropped up like mushrooms." There was an epidemic of suicides in the capital. Twenty-two were mentioned in the press in the first ten days of April, ten of them on April 10 alone. Only two were aged more than twenty-five, and twenty were girls.

Romanovs joined in the philandering. The tsar's cousin Grand Duke Andrei was living with Nicholas's former mistress, the ballet dancer Mathilde Kschessinskaya; his brother Michael had married a twice-divorced commoner the year before and was living in Bavarian exile as a result; his sister Olga was divorcing. In May the crowned heads of Europe met in Berlin for the marriage of Kaiser Wilhelm's daughter Victoria Louise to the duke of Brunswick. At the state banquet in the Berlin palace, the German kaiser, the tsar, and England's George V wore one another's uniforms—the kaiser the dress uniform of the British Royal Dragoons with the Russian Order of St. Andrew at his breast, Nicholas in Prussian Dragoon uniform and displaying the Hohenzollern—and escorted one another's wives. It was the last meeting of the three royal clans before a war that would destroy two of them.

There was a glittering finality, too, to the last full summer of peace in St. Petersburg. At the Hotel de l'Europe the black barman acknowledged orders for newfangled cocktails in a soft Kentucky accent. In the "phosphorescent, crazy, voluptuous summer nights," the rays of the midnight sun drifted into gardens and lit "long-haired students discussing with girls the transcendental values of German philosophy." Stravinsky's mold-breaking *Rite of Spring* had a sensational premiere. Futurists dressed in cardboard clothes with flowers painted on their faces chanted a poem of one word, *Smekh*, "laughter," and its derivatives. Igor Sikorsky built the world's first four-engined aircraft at the Russo-Balt plant. It cruised above the city, with sixteen people and a dog aboard in a passenger compartment with a sofa and washroom.

Simanovich was making a fortune. "My self-confidence was growing," the gambler-fixer wrote. "I saw that many persons respected my relations with court circles. My requests and wishes were coming to be satisfied in government offices. . . . A lot of people wanted to be useful and complaisant to me. For my part, I tried to be pleasant to them." Rasputin was proving to be a formidable ally. Vyrubova was constantly asked by the empress to take him messages about Alexis's health. Simanovich wrote that "his fabulous success with the royal couple was making him an idol. All the Petersburg officials were excited. One word from him was enough for them to receive high honors or other distinctions. Everyone sought his support. . . . There was no need for special knowledge or talents to make a brilliant career. Rasputin's nod was enough for that."

The holy man's protégé was in "the best relations with all the fast livers of the capital," mistresses of grand dukes, ministers, financiers. "Society ladies, courtesans, famous actresses, and cheerful aristocratic women—they were all proud of their relations with him," Simanovich reported with delight. "They were blinded by his success." With Prince Andronnikov's help, he knew all the scandals, the "liaisons of high-ranking persons, nocturnal secrets of high life." Friendship with Rasputin, and the discreet interest of Simanovich, gave those on the make "the chance to know many secrets and to fix their affairs."

Rasputin took to entertaining them at the Villa Rhode, a restaurant-cum-nightclub on a tree-shaded lane in the suburbs. It was known for its music-hall singers and Gypsies; it was popular with "big names and titles," the ladies often trying to outperform the entertainers. The villa was a wooden plank building in the Russian dacha style, set in a muddy garden behind a stout fence, with heavy double windows and a small winter conservatory projecting from the first floor. An annex had been added to one side for private parties. Adolph Rhode, the proprietor, used this for Rasputin when he telephoned to make a booking. The table was set with flowers and fish and candies, his favorite dishes, and large supplies of Madeira, a powerfully fortified Georgian wine, stronger than the Portuguese original.

Rasputin's nights at the villa had a ritual. He first telephoned women he was interested in. Simanovich said that the invitations were always accepted; women took advantage of them to "solicit for their friends, lovers, and relatives. Very many ladies thus enriched themselves as Rasputin was very complaisant in such cases." There was usually a minister or potential minister present. Rasputin began by drinking steadily, amusing his guests with random quotations from the Bible and stories of his Siberian youth. As he got drunker he described how he watched the stallions in the yards enjoying themselves with the mares. He liked to grasp a woman guest at this stage and leer: "Come, my lovely mare." If the gentlemen present muttered at this, he turned and scolded them: "Yes, yes, my dears, I know you, I can read your souls."

After eating greedily with his hands, he usually called for a Gypsy choir. The Gypsies sat on a semi-circle of chairs, the men with guitars in brocaded shirts and bright colored trousers, the women singers in colored silks with kerchiefs on their heads.

The British agent Robert Bruce Lockhart, later to see Rasputin in a notorious nightclub incident, found Gypsy music "more intoxicating, more dangerous, than opium, or women, or drink"; plaintive, melancholic, half lyrical and half sensuous, the singing "will drive a man to the moneylenders and even to crime." The guests drank the *charochka*, in which tankards of champagne were filled to the brim, emptied, and left upside down on a plate to show that no drop remained.

Rasputin filled his pockets with notes that he gave to the ladies—scrawled maxims: "Go not from the way of love, for love is your mother"; "I gladden you with the light of love"; "God send your soul humility"—and gifts for the Gypsies: candies, silk scarves, ribbons, powder compacts, and perfumes. He tempted the Gypsy singers to filch the trinkets, crying merrily, "The Gypsies are robbing me!" He loved to dance with them, lithe and light in his heavy boots; Simanovich said that "even professional dancers found it hard to compete with him." If he became completely drunk—"Siberian drunk"—Rasputin's warning apparatus failed him and he went too far. He sometimes boasted that the empress was a "second Catherine" and that she and not the spineless Nicholas was the real ruler of Russia; since his guests knew of his influence over Alexandra, it was an unsubtle way of reminding them of his own power. A young Guards officer, Obrasov, once boxed his ears for so insulting the tsar, though most thought it no more than the truth.

———

Rasputin had a sobering influence, however, in the fall of 1913. After they had successfully defeated their former Turkish masters, cross-hatreds broke out among the Balkan states. They were fueled by Austria, which annexed Bosnia and was determined to prevent Serbia from gaining freedom from Austrian tariffs by breaking out to the Adriatic. Bulgaria, though exhausted by its war of independence against the Turks, attacked its onetime Christian allies in Serbia over Macedonia. Although a diplomatic peace was imposed in London, Austria brought its three corps on the Russian frontier in Galicia up to wartime strength. Tensions ran high.

Kokovtsov warned Nicholas that conflict with Germany, a disaster that could sweep away the dynasty, was approaching. The tsar was unimpressed; he replied with a shrug: "All is in the will of God." Inflammatory speeches were made in the Duma, and the press whipped up Slav nationalism. Rasputin was frightened by the talk of impending war. In an interview published in the *Petersburg Gazette* on October 13, 1913, he said that Christians should not kill each other, neither should they kill Turks. In contrast to the supposedly Christian people of the Balkans, he said, "the Turks are more fair and peaceful on religious things. You can see how it is—but it comes out different in the newspapers." If there was to be war, then "let the Turks and foreigners eat each other. They are blind, and this is their misfortune. They will gain nothing and simply advance the hour of death. While we, leading a harmonious life, will once more rise above others. . . . Fear, fear War."

Rasputin was given credit for preserving peace by one newspaper, and by Alexandra. "He always said the Balkans were not worth fighting over," she reminded her husband later. By contrast, Rodzianko was telling the tsar to "profit from the general enthusiasm. The Straits [Constantinople] must belong to us. War will be accepted with joy and serve only to increase the prestige of the imperial power."

Iliodor equally dreamed of violence in his Cossack village. He planned to start a revolution in October. "I planned the assassination of sixty lieutenant governors and forty bishops throughout Russia," he claimed. "I chose a hundred men to execute this plan." It failed; he had no posse of men, but he had gathered a group of women to carry out the castration of Rasputin. One of them was Khioniya Guseva, a twenty-six-year-old, once a handsome prostitute in Tsaritsyn who had turned to religion and Iliodor when she became disfigured by syphilis. She tended him in the village and swore to mutilate the starets who had ruined his life. "Grischa is a true devil," she said. "I will stab him. I will kill him as the prophet Elijah killed the 450 false prophets of Baal. Rasputin is worse than them. . . . Father, bless me so that I finish him." Iliodor hung a knife on a chain around her neck. "With this knife, kill Grischa," he said.

———

The new year of 1914 was greeted with church bells, vodka, flags, and bands. Alexandra remained in seclusion, but her daughters Olga and Tatiana appeared in public, Olga more beautiful still than her tip-nosed sister, with dark hair and amber eyes. Countess Shuvalov gave two balls, one all in black and white, the other the Ball of the Colored Wigs, with the guests in red and green and blue wigs and turbans. Balls at the German and Austrian embassies were well attended, tension or not. Crowds packed the Ural Stone Shop with its carved animals of jade and amethyst, and bought lacquered boxes and wooden toys at the Peasant Shop. Fabergé did good business. Couples hurtled down ice slopes on sleds. Dancing bears and vendors of hot toddy and apple and cinnamon tarts took to the frozen river.

But it still seemed a place open to catastrophe, Anna Akhmatova thought; there was something menacing about its "frightening sunsets, the frightening moon." Nicholas had not forgotten the humiliation of his forced signature on the October 1905 manifesto. He continued to chip away at the Duma and his minister. He was urged on in this by his wife, and by Prince Vladimir Meshchersky. The prince had been a childhood friend of Alexander III and had traded on this to extract a government subsidy of eighty thousand rubles a year to support himself and the good-looking young men who surrounded him, and to publish a Black Hundred newspaper called *Grazhdanin*. His catamites prospered as he introduced them to "luxury and dirty work." Meshchersky advised the tsar that the best way to reduce the influence of the prime minister was to appoint his own man as interior minister. He pointed out that it was the interior minister, not the premier, in "whose hands at present lies control over all rights and freedoms."

Nicholas appointed Nikolai Maklakov, a young provincial governor and "slapdash reactionary," to the post. Maklakov was inexperienced and unknown; he said of his new post that "for me it was like a clap of thunder from a clear sky." He had, however, the virtue of loathing the concessions of 1905. He felt that "one leg had been lifted" by them, and that ever since Russia had suffered "a drunkard's walk, tottering from wall to wall." He urged the tsar to carry out a coup d'état against the Duma; he should make a threatening speech in the assembly, to be followed by its dissolution and the abolition of its legislative powers. Nicholas found himself "pleasurably surprised" by the idea, but the rest of the cabinet was opposed to it and the plan was dropped.

This appointment irritated Rasputin, who had played no part in it. He was jealous of Meshchersky's influence. He had his own homosexual fixer-prince, Andronnikov, and he resented the interference enough for the tsar to write to Meshchersky advising him to "visit Grigory . . . he is angry with you." Meshchersky died before he could take up the invitation; Rasputin and Andronnikov ensured that they gained a hold on the new interior minister by finding a place at St. Petersburg university for his slow-witted son. They also worked on Major General Voyeikov, the palace commandant. "Much respected Vladimir Nikolayevich," Andronnikov wrote to him on January 19, 1914, with standard flattery. "Following Your energetic, tireless, and creative activity since long ago, I was indescribably happy to learn that the Emperor chose You. Now one can be quite calm that our dear Emperor will be guarded by firm, reliable, and good hands. . . . I would be very grateful if You would give me the opportunity to call upon You in Tsarskoye Selo at Your convenience so that I may personally inform You of some questions that might interest You." The two duly met, and from then on Voyeikov received "a mass of notes showing in an unfavorable light this or that statesman objectionable to Andronnikov."

The tsar's next reshuffle was entirely to Rasputin's liking. On February 12, 1914, Nicholas dismissed Kokovtsov; the premier had proved too independent, too hostile to Rasputin, and too sympathetic to the Duma and constitutionalism. Nicholas did not have the courage to sack him face-to-face; instead he sent him a letter, "for," he said, "it is easier to select the words when putting them on paper than during an unsettling conversation." The dowager empress saw Kokovtsov a few days after his fall. "My daughter-in-law doesn't love me," she told him. "She doesn't understand that my only desire is my son's happiness. But we are going in great steps toward a catastrophe, and the tsar listens to no one save flatterers." She asked him to see Nicholas and tell him all that he knew and feared. "I told her that no one would listen to me or believe me," Kokovtsov recalled. "The young empress thought me her enemy."

The tsar wrote to Kokovtsov to say that he would be replaced by "a man fresh for the work." This turned out to be Count Ivan Goremykin, a tired, ill man in his mid-seventies who expected to die at any minute. "The Emperor cannot see that the candles have already been lit around my coffin," he remarked on his appointment, "and that the only thing required to complete the ceremony is myself." He likened himself to an old fur coat that had been packed away in camphor and was being taken out now merely for the occasion. He was cynical, read French novels and watched "Piccadilly weepers" at the theater, and was often found asleep in his office. The court marshal, Count Paul Benckendorff, said that the tsar "neither wanted nor expected him to do anything."

To appoint a half-dead premier in a stable country would have been remarkable. To do so in turbulent Russia, menaced by foreign war and internal revolution, was utter folly. It was shared by husband and wife, and by the starets. For Nicholas, Goremykin seemed an ideal, a throwback deep into the autocracy of the previous century. "I am a man of the old school," Goremykin said without shame, "and an Imperial Command is for me a law. To me, His Majesty is the anointed one. . . . When the decision of such a man is made . . . his faithful subjects must accept it whatever may be the consequences. And then let God's will be done." This attitude delighted the empress, who called him Old Man with affection. "He sees and understands all so clearly and it is a pleasure speaking to him," she said. Goremykin's wife was an admirer and visitor of Rasputin's. She supplied him with boiled potatoes delivered from her kitchen with such speed that they had no time to get cold, and with fish soup, apples, and croissants. "She knew how to cook potatoes ten different ways," Simanovich said, "and in this way she really won Rasputin's favor."

———

Rasputin and Prince Andronnikov worked closely together. The prince sent flowers and candies to Vyrubova, while Rasputin's flattery of Goremykin was underpinned by pamphlets Andronnikov wrote in French and Russian to praise the premier's policies, and by gifts of cigars and pheasants. An "infinite number" of requests were satisfied. Distillers and sugar manufacturers won state subsidies, bankers were given oil concessions, civil convictions were quashed together with "appointments, transfers, pensions, awards from all the institutions, and so forth."

The starets moved into a new apartment at 64 Gorokhovaya ulitsa. Simanovich and his contacts paid the rent. The street was in the western section of the city, running from Admiralty Square to Zagorodniy Prospect. The dull brick facades were streaked with dirt and soot, and it had a dark air to it: the long overcoats worn by plainclothes police agents were called Gorokhovoyo coats. The murderer in Dostoyevsky's novel *The Idiot*, Parfyon Rogozhin, had lived in one of the suviving old buildings on the street, a large, gloomy, three-story house, dirty green, hiding in a dark corner, with thick walls and few windows. Newer apartments had been built since for tradespeople, successful clerks, and minor officials.

It was handy to the railroad station to Tsarskoye Selo, and Number 64 had two entrances. The building had double doors on the street leading to a dank courtyard. The main staircase led past the doorman and the concierge's room up to the apartments; a back staircase led discreetly from the courtyard. The common parts smelled of cabbage, hot sheep's cheese, and black tobacco. Rasputin's flat, Number 20, was a walk-up on the third floor. It had five rooms and a kitchen. The hall led into an anteroom and a corridor with rooms off it. On the street side there were a dining room and Rasputin's bedroom and bathroom. He rarely used the bathroom, preferring to go to a bathhouse across the street.

No one was admitted to the bedroom when Rasputin was not alone there. It was a room, a police agent said, that could "tell many tales . . . disheveled petitioners of the lower classes ran from the room screaming, cursing, and spitting, while attempts were made to pacify them and get them out of the flat." Okhrana agents were posted outside the concierge's room and in the street, from where they had occasional glimpses of Rasputin's activities. Akulina Laptinskaya, Rasputin's "secretary" who helped him move into the new apartment, liked to entertain him in the bedroom with the curtains undrawn. "Owing to the absence of blinds," an agent noted, "her erotic exercises with Rasputin presented an attraction for the street." On the courtyard side was the large room used for receptions. The furniture was heavy and bourgeois, stout wooden chairs, overstuffed sofas, a wooden table. Here he held court. His study was next to it, the kitchen, and the rooms of his daughters and maid. His telephone number was 646-46.

———

The mood in the city changed during Lent. "Absolutely no one wants war or adventure," Count Benckendorff wrote, "but the feeling that war is inevitable has grown and grown in all classes." Men in long brown coats scattered yellow sand on the sidewalks and set bonfires to thaw the ice. In late March the frozen river broke with cracks like pistol shots, and icebreakers churned through the blocks of ice. Then, at last, the guns fired from the Peter and Paul Fortress, and its commandant met the city governor in midstream to proclaim the river open to navigation. Tugs towed landing stages to fix in position on the docks for the passenger steamers. It was spring.

Rasputin hoped to celebrate by seducing a provincial lady, Vera Alexandrovna Zhukovskaya, who had come to Gorokhovaya ulitsa seeking spiritual advice. She was shown into his study by the maid-mistress Dunia. A bed was against the wall covered by a shabby silk coverlet, a washstand next to it, and a lady's writing desk, with some pencils and dirty pens and a gold watch with the double-headed Romanov eagle engraved on it. A table and two chairs were in the middle of the room. A lady's vanity table with a mirror was in front of the window. A large photograph of the altar of St. Isaac's Cathedral was next to it, pinned with ribbons—she remembered that the khlysty also put ribbon-encrusted icons next to windows.

Rasputin came in. He pulled up a chair opposite her, close enough for him to put her legs between his knees. "What good things have you to say to me?" he asked. She replied that there was little in life that was good. He stroked her face, and replied, "Listen to what I am going to say to you. Do you know the psalm 'From my youth up the lusts of the flesh have tormented me; Lord Jesus Christ do not condemn me therefor'? Do you know it?" She said she knew it very well.

He pressed her knee firmly and told her he would explain. "I tell you that people may sin up to the age of thirty; but then it is time to turn to God, do you see?" he said. "And when you have once learned to surrender your thoughts completely to God, you may sin again, for that is sin of a special kind—do you follow? And as far as sin generally is concerned, you can be freed from it again by repentance. Only repent of everything, then everything is good again." He asked her to go to communion. She refused. He began stroking her hands and shoulders. She would not understand his words, he said; she had to be convinced by deeds. "Only come to me often, little honeybee, love me and then you will understand everything. Love is the most important thing." As long as she was a stranger to him, she would ignore his words; once she loved him, all would be clear. He kissed her on the corner of her mouth, so rapidly and simply that she could not object.

The telephone rang. He went to answer it. "Now I shall not let you go again," he said when he returned. "Once you have come to me you will not escape again! Understand clearly, I will do nothing to you, only come, my juicy cherry." He asked her for her telephone number. While she wrote it down he squeezed her shoulders and whispered into her ear, his breath warm: "Well, and what more have you to say to me?" She was repelled and pushed him away. "I came to you so that you could give me advice," she said. "You know well, don't you, where the truth is and where sin is?" He told her about his friendship with Grand Duchess Militsa—it was a name he dropped often—and how she also asked about sin and did not understand it.

"Only he commits sin who seeks sin," he said. "But in him who merely passes through it, sin has no part. If you like, I will show it all to you. Go next week to communion, and then come to me while you still have Paradise in your soul. Then I will show you sin, so that you will not be able to stand on your feet!"

"I don't believe that," she gasped, feeling remote and incredulous. He whispered, like a magician, his mouth open with lust: "Do you want me to show you?"

He had gone far enough; in an instant he changed and his eyes became "kind, friendly, and passionless." He asked her gently and with assumed surprise, "Why do you look at me like that, my darling?" He kissed her with "priestly dignity." In place of the khlyst—insistent, lascivious, seeking out weakness—she saw an honest peasant with meek eyes. He got her to promise that she would return on Saturday evening.

—

On Saturday she was shown into the dining room, crowded with women and a nervous young man in a morning coat, von Pistolkors, whose pregnant wife gazed at Rasputin with devotion. Madame Golovina acted as hostess and kept the conversation going. Her daughter, Munya Golovina, wore a thin silk dress and a white hat with violets; she also had a look of submissiveness. Vyrubova was there, big, full-figured, and blond with a bright red, sensual mouth and a face that was "equivocal, deceptive, and at the same time seductive." The Grand Duchess Militsa sat with her hands in an ermine muff; she was dark, her black eyes sad and lifeless, and she was silent.

Rasputin passed the women boiled eggs from the mess of food on the table—tarts, bowls of fruit, peppermint cakes, black bread and gherkins, a bottle of wine. They grasped them eagerly. Vyrubova passed him some bread and gherkins, which he ate with his hands, wiping them on the tablecloth before pawing his guests. He talked spasmodically about the church and the clergy—"I cannot exactly swear that I love them particularly but there are believers even among them"—and warned them that Olga Lokhtina was coming. She had missed the way, he said, and broken away with Iliodor, but he was sorry for her—"the mad bitch."

She arrived on cue, "improbably bright, broad, pale pink, puffy, disheveled, absurd," shrieking, "Chr-i-st is ri-s-en!" She wore pleated skirts of different colors that swooped like wings as she staggered around the room. Beneath them she had a pair of old boots Rasputin had discarded. She wore a Siberian wolf-skin cap, which Rasputin had also worn, and one of his cast-off red peasant blouses. Little bags were strapped onto her shirt, with scraps of food and old gloves that had belonged to him. Her face was covered with veils pinned with gaudy ribbons; only her "delicate, sad, and beautiful mouth" could be made out.

She had brought Rasputin a cake—"white outside, black inside"—which he tossed back onto the table. At his rejection she took his head and kissed it wildly, stammering, "Oh my dearest . . . vessel of all blessing, . . . Ah, you lovely beard. . . . You delicious hair . . . me martyr . . . you my adored one . . . my God . . . my beloved!" Rasputin, half-choked by her embrace, snarled at her: "Away! Satan! Away, you devil, you monster!" She redoubled her incantations: "And yet you are mine, and I have lain with you. I have lain with you. . . . You are my God! I belong to you and to no other. . . . However many women you take, no one can rob me of you. You are mine!" Rasputin snapped at her—"I hate you, you bitch, the devil is in you"—and threatened to break her jaw. It had no effect. "I am happy, happy, and you love me," she said, her ribbons and frilled skirts shaking. "Soon I will lie with you again." He pushed her, and she shouted: "Now, strike me! Strike me, strike me!" She was frenzied; the onlooking women felt chilled and afraid. When Rasputin hit her on the chest, she tried to kiss the spot, but her chin prevented her and she ran around kissing the air, kissing her hands, and kneading her breasts. Eventually she calmed down and lay on a sofa.

When Zhukovskaya asked Rasputin why he insulted the crazed woman, he replied—kindly again—that she had deserted the church. The other ladies had remained silent, their eyes veiled from the hysterical scene, though their faces were red and their breath came in gasps. Then Madame Golovina turned to Lokhtina, saying, "I cannot understand why you deliberately make Grigory Efimovich angry." Lokhtina demanded soup; she said she had eaten nothing all day and had given the last of her money away to her chauffeur. Munya Golovina fetched her a bowl of soup. Rasputin told her to take it away, but she persisted. "What are you doing?" her mother asked her. "Why do you anger Grigory Efimovich?" Her daughter whispered, "Mama, please let me alone, say no more about it."

The telephone rang at intervals, and Rasputin left the room to answer it. Lokhtina resumed her masochistic wail: "Carry me off, beat me! Insult me as you like, spit at me. . . . And now I will lie with you, I will lie with you immediately." Munya Golovina cleared the dirty dishes as though she were a maid. When Rasputin was called to the telephone again, Lokhtina took advantage of his absence to slip into his bedroom. He rushed in after her, and the ladies listened to the sounds of blows and screeches. When Lokhtina reappeared her veils were torn; Rasputin was breathing heavily, and he wiped his sweating face on the sleeve of his cornflower blue blouse.

Madame Golovina complained that the tension was making her ill; she would need bay rum drops to revive her. The room was thick with sex, hysteria, religious longing. It was clear to Zhukovskaya that those present "must either depart or shriek, fall into convulsions, and smash things." Vyrubova rose first, and the others followed her to the hall. Rasputin made the sign of the cross over them and bade them farewell. As Vyrubova took his hand and kissed it, Zhukovskaya noticed that she moaned and the whole of her body trembled.

At the beginning of April the imperial family left for a two-month visit to the Crimea. War tensions were growing; Nicholas was hundreds of miles away from his capital, with no reliable radio link, dependent on communications by post and courier. Spiridovich attributed this irresponsibility to Alexandra's state of "extraordinary nervousness," which could be relieved only amid the gardens and relaxed family life of the Livadia Palace.

Rasputin joined them, staying at the Hotel de Russie in Yalta. The visit turned into scandal. He bragged of his intimacy with the family to the hotel staff. Newspapers remarked that Vyrubova's carriage was often seen outside the hotel. Tourist shops did a roaring trade in Rasputin postcards. Nicholas, irritated, suggested that the starets collect his daughters from St. Petersburg and spend the rest of the summer in Pokrovskoye. He agreed. After he left Yalta, Khioniya Guseva came looking for him. When the hotel told her he had already gone, she set out in search of him.

His daughter Maria was now fifteen. She played little games with men when she was bored. She telephoned numbers at random. If a man replied she chattered away to him, telling him that she adored him and arranging a rendezvous on the steps of the Hotel de l'Europe. She would giggle from across the street as the man paced up and down waiting for his mysterious admirer. At the end of May a man played a reverse trick on her. He rang her up, asking for her by name and telling her that he was hopelessly in love with her, and requested a meeting. She told him that she could not see him because she was leaving for Siberia with her father. The caller asked her carefully for the date of her departure.

Maria left St. Petersburg with her father on June 4 for the four-day journey by first-class sleeper and river steamer to the village. As the Trans-Siberian reached the Urals, a British Royal Navy battle squadron steamed past the imperial yacht *Standart* and moored in the Kronstadt naval base. The British had long viewed Russia as the land of whip and exile, but the threat of European war and fear of German strength had persuaded them to ally with Russia as well as France. The visit was a sparkling affair. Eight hundred guests were invited to a ball aboard the battle cruisers *Lion* and *New Zealand*, which steamed up the Neva to the Nicholas Bridge. The young grand duchesses, returned from the Crimea, stole the hearts of the crews as they clambered around the gun turrets. Alexandra met her nephew Prince George Battenberg, who was serving aboard the cruiser, but she did not allow the girls to stay on for the ball. It was a "white night," when the summer sun scarcely slipped below the horizon and turned the smooth, gray waters of the Neva to gold. The linden trees were out, the fields filled with bluebells and cowslips. Guests were greeted by an arch on the gangway of HMS *New Zealand* with the word *Welcome* in huge letters; the mayor of St. Petersburg proposed a toast: "To the finest navy in the world." The supper was abundant, the champagne half frozen to the Russian taste; the ship's band played dance music. After the warships left the family began its summer cruise along the Finnish skerries.

Aboard the steamer *Sokolovsky* on the river from Tyumen to Pokrovskoye, Maria Rasputin was approached by a "dark gentleman" who introduced himself as Davidsohn. He came from the Jewish ghetto in Vilna and was now a journalist on the popular daily *Birzhevye Vedomosti*. He admitted that it was he who had telephoned her, and that he was determined to follow her home. She did not much care for him and was not pleased when she saw him disembark at Pokrovskoye. He lay low, however, while the Rasputins caught up with friends and local gossip.

CHAPTER 16

"I've Killed the Antichrist!"

Two killings were being planned. Two thousand miles to the west, on Sunday, June 15, 1914, in the Russian calendar, the heir to the throne of Austria and Hungary drove in a motorcade through the streets of Sarajevo with the province governor. Archduke Franz Ferdinand had been watching army maneuvers in the Bosnian mountains. He was wearing the braided blue tunic and green-feathered cap of an Austrian cavalry general. Sarajevo was a provocative place to wear such a uniform. Bosnian Serb nationalists were set on expelling the Austrians and linking up with independent Serbia. A bomb was thrown as the motorcade neared the city hall. It hit the back of the archduke's automobile but exploded behind it. A young Serb from the Black Hand terrorist group was arrested as he ran away.

The archduke, badly shaken, interrupted the mayor's welcome. "To hell with your speech!" he shouted. "I come to your city and I am welcomed with bombs." He left at once for the governor's mansion. The driver of the lead car forgot the route, and the motorcade was briefly stalled. Another Serb, a nineteen-year-old student called Gavrilo Princip, stepped out of the crowd and fired what diplomatic incompetence and territorial greed transformed into the first shots of the First World War. The archduke's wife, Princess Sophie Chotek, was hit in the stomach. The flowers on her picture hat caught in the strappings of her husband's tunic as she sagged onto his chest. "Sopherl! Sopherl! Don't die. Live for our children!" the governor heard him moan. He remained sitting erect, but the governor saw a stream of blood pumping from his neck. He was carried into the governor's mansion as waiters proffered glasses of chilled white wine on silver salvers for the reception that was to be held in his honor. "It's nothing," he said, and died.

———

The following day, June 16, was soft and balmy in Pokrovskoye. Rasputin spent the morning trotting some newborn colts in the farmyard. He went to church with his wife and children. He was in excellent spirits as he ate a big meal of fish for lunch. He amused the table with tales of how he liked to offer raw country vodka with a kick like gasoline to pompous officials in St. Petersburg. They felt obliged to drink it; he said he called it Rasputin's revenge. After lunch Maria went to a friend's house to show off some snapshots she had taken in St. Petersburg.

What followed next was recorded by the deputy prosecutor of the Tobolsk district court. At around 3:00 P.M. a postman brought a telegram to the house. Rasputin "made up his mind to send a telegram in reply and, coming out of the gates into the street, called for the postman." A woman standing by the gates, identified as Khioniya Kozmishna Guseva from the city of Syzran, Simbirsk province, bowed to him and begged for a coin. Her face—"of repulsive ugliness, her nose was crushed and misshapen"—was covered by a shawl. "You shouldn't bow," Rasputin told her kindly. "Taking advantage of the moment," the prosecutor continued, "Khioniya Guseva drew a sharp dagger out of her coat and struck Rasputin in the stomach." The knife entered the lower abdomen, and Guseva drew it upward to the navel.

As she pulled out the knife for a second thrust, Rasputin stretched out his hand with a coin. Confused, she took it and dropped it. Rasputin picked up a stick lying on the ground and hit her over the head. Angry villagers seized her and threatened to drown her in the river. "Let me go!" she yelled as they beat her. "I've killed the Antichrist!" Holding his entrails in his hand, Rasputin staggered back to the house. The prosecutor measured the distance; it was 108 steps, and Rasputin moaned as he ran: "Oh, what a pain I have." His wife swept the remains of lunch off the table in the kitchen and laid him on it. His son, Dmitri, rushed to the post office to send telegrams alerting the Tobolsk governor to the murder attempt and asking Dr. Vladimirsky, the best surgeon in Tyumen, to gallop to Pokrovskoye at once. Maria rushed back to the house, almost fainting as she saw a large pool of blood turning brown in front of it.

The door was banged as she helped her mother cut away her father's breeches and blouse from the area of the wound. She opened it to find Davidsohn. She knew in an instant, "like the burst of a skyrocket," why the journalist had flattered her over the phone, why he had wanted to know the date she was traveling, why he had been on the steamer . . . why he was now at the house. He had a story to write; he wanted to see for himself that the victim was dead. It was never established whether Davidsohn was a part of the conspiracy; certainly he had wind of it. Maria slammed the door in his face and shrieked, "Haven't you done enough?"

It was after midnight when Dr. Vladimirsky arrived in a troika with three exhausted horses. Rasputin refused ether and was conscious as the doctor cleaned the abdominal cavity and stitched the ripped intestines. He clasped a cross and muttered prayers. The doctor was in a dilemma as he prepared to transfer his patient to Tyumen at first light. If he drove fast on the pitted road, the bouncing might reopen the wounds and the patient could bleed to death. If they traveled the seventy miles slowly, the delayed shock could be fatal.

Vladimirsky called for the five fastest horses on the Rasputin farm. The starets had loved horses since he was a boy, and the cash from admirers he had invested in them now helped to save him. Three were harnessed to the troika, the two spare horses allowing the doctor to change them every hour. Rasputin was laid between Maria and the maid Dunia so that their bodies cushioned his from the shocks as the troika careered along the trakt. He slipped into a coma, coming around once to mutter, "He must be stopped, he must be stopped." Maria thought he was referring to Nicholas and the threat of war, or so she wrote later. The journey took six hours.

The starets was critically ill for ten days. Skillful medical treatment helped—the empress gave Vladimirsky a gold watch in gratitude—but Rasputin's great physical and mental toughness were crucial. His body absorbed debauchery; it withstood the knife wound.

———

Connecting the murder in Sarajevo with the attempt in Siberia became part of the Rasputin legend. Maria claimed that, in muttering the words "he must be stopped" as he lay semi-conscious on the troika, her father had foreseen the coming war and sought to warn the tsar to keep Russia neutral. How could he have known of events in the Balkans? Maria claimed that the telegram he had received moments before the stabbing was from the empress, bidding him return to St. Petersburg because of the archduke's assassination. The archduke died shortly after noon Central European time the day before the stabbing. It is known that Kaiser Wilhelm of Germany was informed of the killing aboard his yacht *Meteor* three hours later. Alexandra was on the imperial yacht *Standart* several miles off the Finnish coast. It is technically feasible that she received news of the death as promptly, weighed its implications, and radioed a message from the yacht for transmission to Pokrovskoye by telegram. But Sarajevo was not yet feared as a prelude to war; the tutor, Pierre Gilliard, who was on the yacht, reported that Alexandra's only concern was with Alexis. The boy had twisted his ankle as they boarded the yacht. The ankle swelled as it hemorrhaged, and Alexis wept as Gilliard read to him to distract him from the pain. Rasputin's instant precognition of war was almost certainly an invention.

It was a convenient one, however, for it offset the new scandal caused by the stabbing. Guseva was at once identified as a former prostitute and an admirer of Iliodor. It was also said that she had been Rasputin's lover, that he had spurned her, and that she had tried to castrate him by stabbing him low in the stomach. The newspaper *Russkoye Slovo* claimed that she was the sister of a terrorist named Grigory Zaitsev, who had been arrested for murdering a policeman in St. Petersburg in 1907. Taking him to Siberian exile the following year, his convict convoy passed through Pokrovskoye on its way to the holding prison in Tobolsk. He was allowed to meet his sister, who was staying with Rasputin. The starets offered him money; he refused to accept it and rebuked Rasputin for his lewdness and bad influence. He tried to convince his sister to walk out on Rasputin, the newspaper said, but she remained faithful, "and it was only a few years afterward that she recalled the words of her brother and made up her mind to kill Rasputin."

There was no doubt that it was Iliodor who had encouraged Guseva in her murder attempt. He fled from his village immediately after he heard the attempt had failed. Disguised as a woman he slipped over the border to Finland; once he was safely out of Russia, he admitted his involvement. Guseva herself told police interrogators that Rasputin was a heretic who raped nuns. She said that she wished to punish the "false prophet," both in revenge for the fall of Iliodor and to kill "the khlyst in Rasputin's person." The authorities did not want her to repeat such accusations in open court in front of the press. There was no question of her standing trial for attempted murder. Instead she was declared insane and committed to an asylum in Tomsk. Relatives who tried to have her released were told that doctors had found unmistakable symptoms of "psychological disturbance and exalted religiosity."

———

The public was not totally robbed of scandal, though. Davidsohn filed a sensational account of the wounding for *Birzhevye Vedomosti*. Another journalist, signing himself S. P., wrote an account of a surreal interview in Rasputin's hospital ward in the daily paper *Russkoye Slovo* that caught the starets's vivid phrasings, the restlessness of his mind as it darted between subjects, the philosophizing and cunning. The staff put him into a white hospital gown. He met Maria Rasputin outside the ward. She refused to let him in, so he asked if he could see Akulina Laptinskaya, who was also nursing the patient. It was a sensible request. She was amenable to rubles; the investigating commission was to characterize her as "a sly and calculating woman, who demanded money from visitors."

Laptinskaya came to the door of the ward. The journalist noticed her tranquil gray eyes; she had the transparent shadow of a knowing smile on her face. He asked to see the patient and explained that he had come all the way from St. Petersburg. She hesitated—rubles passed hands—and agreed. The ward was all white. The bed was covered with a fiery red satin blanket. Strong, bony fingers played with it. Rasputin's head lay feeble on the pillow. He stretched out a hand. "Hallo, sit down," he said. "Here's my wife and my father."

The father was thickset, shaggy, clumsy. He looked awkward in his white hospital coat; he reminded the journalist of linen aired on an elm stump. Praskovya Rasputin had a sad, withered face. The journalist thought she had the kind of eyes the wives of celebrities—artists and writers—have; they share the grief of the failures and the troubles of hard labor but are not able to share the joy of success.

"I was in Pokrovskoye," the journalist said. Rasputin's fingers started to move restlessly and swiftly, as if they were spinning a web. He dropped his head to one side and looked at his visitor slyly, showing the whites of his big, light eyes. The eyes were blue, the color of a flax field in blossom. "Eyes of a woman," the journalist noted. "Sinful eyes. Eyes of Jean Baptiste by Leonardo da Vinci."

"Like the village?" the starets asked, holding out his hand in the journalist's direction and pecking at him with a long finger.

"No, I didn't. People live better where I'm from."

"In Russia!" Rasputin snorted. "The muzhik in Russia is not a muzhik but a martyr. In Perm province, it's all right." Perm was the closest province across the Urals. "But no farther. They eat potatoes out there. Our muzhik eats white bread."

"Filling, but dirty," said the journalist, who was no admirer of Siberia. "Cream with cockroaches. Shit in the yards up to one's knees. They say you can't stay for long in the yard here calling out your cow: cow dung gnaws around your legs."

"Dirt," said Rasputin. "Princes come out of dirt. Sow oats in the dirt, and you'll become a prince. All Russia, my dear, comes out of dirt. All Russia is out of dirt. Cockroach. . . . How can you do without a cockroach? It whispers, whispers, whispers . . ."

Rasputin showed the whites of his eyes, the whites only. His face was pale. He raised his eyelids and looked at the journalist sharply, piercingly, turning a lock of his beard with a finger. "Dirty you say, my dear . . ."

"And two floors," the journalist said of Rasputin's house in Pokrovskoye. "What do you want two floors for if you live on one with an empty chamber?"

"My dear, you can't live on the first floor," Rasputin said, indicating his wife. "Praskovya Fedorovna here has five cows, and thirty sheep, and a pig with sucklings, and hens. . . . And what about the chamber? Let the chamber be there. A guest comes. Joy comes with him. Let the chamber be there for guests. Shit. . . . Throw your cleanliness into shit and trample on it. Chamber. There's a chamber . . ."

He closed his eyes and was silent for a moment. He went on in a different, calm voice, without rambling.

"This thing that happened to me. The stick was small, the knife was big." He started to tell how the Noseless One had assaulted him; that is what local people were calling Guseva, because of the way syphilis had disfigured her face. "The stick was small. . . . I keep close to the fence. And I hold the wound. I'm afraid to let it go, I hold it with my hand. . . . And she follows me with the knife. The way I see it, I'm not going to make it. Then I look down and see a chip on the ground—a small stick lying there. I pick it up and I touch her lightly with it on the shoulder. She gets scared and backs off."

His head dropped back on the pillow and he looked sideways, craftily. "The knife was as big as that. Her hand trembled. See?" He demonstrated. "She approaches me and I give a *pyatachok*, five kopecks. Alms. Her hand trembled. Otherwise . . . You can defend yourself with alms. The stick was small."

Laptinskaya signaled for the journalist to go. Rasputin started looking for something. "This *pyatachok* . . . she threw down the *pyatachok*," he said. "Threw it on the ground, right there. Conscience. That's conscience. She threw the *pyatachok*. A boy found it and brought it to me. My *pyatachok*. Came back to me. Here—where is it?—my *pyatachok*."

He rummaged around under the blanket. He looked angrily at Akulina. She smiled amiably and arranged his pillow.

"Here it is," Rasputin said triumphantly. "She dropped it. And she dropped the knife, too . . ."

———

Alexandra was told of the murder attempt aboard the *Standart* the day after it happened. Gilliard noticed unusual excitement among the retinue. A colonel told him that a woman had knifed Rasputin in the stomach and that the wound might be mortal. There was a great commotion; "people whispered no end, mysterious meetings took place." The whisperings stopped immediately at the approach of "anyone supposedly belonging to the Rasputin circle"—by that Gilliard meant Vyrubova or the empress and her children. The prevailing hope on the yacht was that the starets would die and the family would "at last be set free from this pernicious creature." They were not convinced, however. Gilliard said they thought that "the soul of this cursed muzhik was sewn on his body" and that he would live.

That did not include the empress, of course. She sent a stream of telegrams from the yacht to the Tyumen hospital. They were all more or less the same,

Gilliard said: "We are frightened by the war that threatens us. Do you think it might start? Pray for us. Encourage us by your advice." The Austrians were threatening Serbia, and Berlin had sided with Vienna. Alexandra was deeply worried that her birthplace would soon be at war with her country of adoption. Nicholas shared her yearning for peace; "one had to see him," Gilliard wrote, "to understand what tortures and moral trials he had to suffer."

Rasputin's early replies were ambivalent. "Do not worry too much about war," he cabled the empress from his sickbed on July 3. "When the time comes you will have to declare it, but not yet, there'll be an end to your troubles." He was noncommittal on July 6: "My dears, my precious ones, do not despair." As Alexandra's cables became more desperate, he shifted against war. "I believe in, I hope for peace," he cabled her later in the day. "They are doing wicked things, we are no part of it, I know how you suffer, it is very hard to be apart from one another." As he sent this message, the *Standart*'s summer cruise ended. Alexis, still in pain from his ankle, was carried gently ashore in Nagorny's arms.

The following day, the *Standart* lay to off St. Petersburg to await the arrival of French President Raymond Poincaré aboard the battleship *France*. Over lunch Nicholas chatted with Maurice Paléologue, the French ambassador, about the Serbian crisis. The tsar said that he did not believe that Kaiser Wilhelm wanted war. "If you knew him as I do!" he said. "If you knew how much theatricality there is in his posing!" The battleship steamed slowly toward them in a silver light, her wake white against an emerald sea, shore batteries firing salutes that merged with the thunder of the "Marseillaise" and the cheers of spectators on an armada of pleasure boats. A state banquet was held for Poincaré that evening in the Peterhof Palace.

———

The Zaria, the army's summer review, was held at the Krassnoye camp outside the capital two days later. The weather was cloudless and intensely hot, and the tart scent of forest fires hung in the air. Ambassadors and their families were present, and Meriel Buchanan listened to the chatter on Paris fashions—wider skirts and no sleeves, trying unless one had pretty arms—and complaints about dishonest cooks and the price of vegetables. "I wonder after all what an army is for," a woman said. "It's so immense, isn't it?" An officer looked up at her. "Just a toy for kings and emperors to play with, Madame," he said. "Rather dangerous toys," she replied.

The capital was airless when the guests returned from the review. Riots had broken out in the Vyborg slums, and some barricades had been thrown up. The manager of a big factory was shot by a terrorist. Cossack patrols were out on the streets. The windows of a streetcar were smashed. Kaiser Wilhelm thought Russia was in "the mood of a sick tomcat." The thud of hooves came closer, and horsemen with sloping lances rode by, rank after rank, weary and dusty, sent directly from the review into the city as a precaution against insurrection. Buchanan recognized one of the officers, a boy she had danced with during the winter, and he saluted her and called out a laughing good night before he and his horse were swallowed by the twilight haze.

Poincaré left on July 10. He gave a farewell dinner aboard the *France*. Alexandra exchanged pleasantries with Paléologue. "I'm glad I came tonight," she said. "I was afraid there would be a storm." The ship's band struck up an allegro with brass and drums. She put her hands to her ears; with a "pained and pleading glance" she pointed and said, "Couldn't you?" The ambassador signaled to the conductor to stop. The royal party transferred to the *Standart* as the *France* raised steam. Paléologue and the tsar watched the battleship and its escorts speed westward, their wakes sparkling across a calm and moonlit sea. Nicholas again reassured the ambassador that Kaiser Wilhelm had no stomach for adventure and that the only wish of Emperor Franz Joseph of Austria was to die in peace.

—

He was no better a judge of emperors than of men. While he was speaking Austria gave Serbia an ultimatum. It said that the archduke's murder had been planned in Belgrade and carried out with a revolver supplied by Serbian officials. It demanded the dismissal of anti-Austrian officials and the suppression of all Serb nationalist groups and anti-Austrian propaganda. Austrian officials were to be granted free access to investigate the murder. Serbia was given forty-eight hours to reply. The text reached Serge Sazonov, the Russian foreign minister, at 10:00 A.M. on July 11. "It means war in Europe!" he exclaimed.

Sazonov warned the tsar by telephone that the brutal Austrian note must have been worded in agreement with Berlin. The Serbs could not conceivably comply with it; the note was a prelude to military action. Sazonov added that the Germans were "certainly in the most advantageous position owing to the supreme efficiency of their armies." They wanted a war because they thought they would win it.

Nicholas was not impressed. A few minutes later the finance minister, Peter Bark, had an audience with him. "He said he thought Sazonov was exaggerating the gravity of the position and had lost his nerve," Bark recalled. The tsar told him that no one wanted to start a general European war over the Balkans. He thought it unlikely that the note had been sent after consultation with Berlin; "the German emperor had frequently assured him of his sincere desire to safeguard the peace of Europe." The cabinet was less optimistic. The same afternoon it decided that, if Austria refused negotiations with Serbia, Russia would mobilize four military districts in the hope that this would warn off Vienna and not provoke Berlin.

Rasputin was well enough to sit up in bed and write. He was now fully alert to the danger of war—the only senior politician to share his insight and foreboding was Sergei Witte, long out of office—and accurately foresaw disaster. He was not a pacifist in the sense of rejecting all war, but he sensed that the particular war in prospect, against the Germans, a people he admired, would prove a cataclysm. He sent a scrawled, misspelled letter to Nicholas, headed by a cross. "My friend, I saw again—a terrible storm menaces Russia," he wrote. "Woe, disaster, suffering without end. It is night. There is not one star . . . a sea of tears. And so much blood. I cannot find words. The terror is infinite. I know that all want war of you. . . . You are the tsar, the father of your people. Do not let fools triumph. Do not let them do this thing. If we conquer Germany, what will become of Russia? When I think of that I see an awful martyrdom. Russia drowned in her own blood . . . Grigory."

Nicholas did not reply. He continued the royal round of prize givings and hospital visits, and played tennis and canoed with his daughters. On July 13 he received the master of the horse of the court of the obscure German dukedom of Mecklenburg-Strelitz, who had come to fulfill his traditional obligation to inform the tsar that his duke had died; Nicholas gave him lunch. The tsar was not alone in this apparent indifference; Kaiser Wilhelm took a short cruise on his yacht. The joint roles of chief executive and monarch were difficult to reconcile. Neither Nicholas nor Wilhelm truly controlled the slide toward hostilities. Rasputin was to claim that, had he not been in a Siberian hospital ward, there would have been no war. Nicholas did not want war either; but he was driven by his ministers and generals, by Russia's tradition as the protector of Slavs, and by the timetables of mass mobilization.

Rasputin's tantalizing hypothesis needs two ifs, not one; *if* he had been in the capital, and *if* his influence over the tsar had been conclusive. The first did not occur. He was not in St. Petersburg; even had he been, the second is unlikely. The impulses to war were too strong. For all his bluster—"Serbia must be disposed of, and that right soon!"—Wilhelm was as much in the hands of his generals and officials as Nicholas. In Austria, Franz Joseph was eighty-four, tired and freighted with tragedy; his son Rudolf had committed suicide in a love tryst at Mayerling in 1889, his wife, Elizabeth, had been stabbed to death by an anarchist in Geneva ten years later, and now the murder of his heir, Franz Ferdinand, had precipitated the crisis. His chancellor was so set on war that, when the Serbs made an unexpectedly humble reply to the Austrian ultimatum, he hid it.

On July 16, though white flags were flying in the Serbian capital, the Austrians began shelling Belgrade across the Danube. Rasputin cabled Vyrubova: "Let Papa not plan war because war will mean the end of Russia and yourselves and you will lose to the last man." Vyrubova told the tsar, but she admitted that he took little notice of it. Nicholas was, however, doing his best to slow the stampede to war, sending telegrams and a personal envoy to Wilhelm begging him to restrain the Austrians. The cables between the cousins maintained a family gloss—the two monarchs remained on "Willy" and "Nicky" terms—but Berlin had little interest in compromise. The pressure for Russia to aid its fellow Slavs in Serbia was overwhelming.

Sazonov saw the tsar at 3:00 P.M. the following day. The foreign minister told him that the order to mobilize could no longer be postponed; the tsar showed "extreme loathing" for war and was visibly irritated. "Think of the responsibility you advise me to take," he said. "It would mean sending hundreds of thousands of Russians to their deaths." Sazonov persisted; he said that the Austrians and Germans were hell-bent on enslaving Russian allies in the Balkans, and that Russia was being reduced to "pitiful dependence" on the whims of the Central Powers. Nicholas agreed to general mobilization. A message was sent from the Central Telegraph Office in St. Petersburg to all points of the empire: "His Imperial Majesty orders colon the army and navy to be placed on war footing stop to this end reservists and horses to be called up according to the mobilization plan of the year 1910 stop." Red cards ordering men to mobilization points were nailed on signposts.

At midnight on July 18, Count Pourtalès, the German ambassador, delivered a German ultimatum to Sazonov. Russia was to reverse the mobilization order within twelve hours or face the consequences. Pourtalès gave the Russians extra time. He did not return to see Sazonov until shortly after 7:00 P.M. on July 19, but he carried orders from Berlin to declare war even if the Russians proposed further negotiations. After he had delivered the declaration, the ambassador looked out of Sazonov's window at the soaring Alexander Column and the oxblood bulk of the Winter Palace, and wept. Sazonov rose and embraced him. "So the die is cast!" the French ambassador, Paléologue, wrote in his diary. "The part of reason in the government of peoples is so small that it has taken merely a week to let loose universal madness!"

Nicholas and his family were at vespers as Germany declared war. Gilliard was struck by the tsar's exhausted look; he wrote, "The features of his face had changed, and the small bags which appeared under his eyes when he was tired seemed far bigger." In church he prayed that God would still spare his people war, "his whole being absorbed by religious feeling, simple and convinced." Alexandra, at his side, had the sad expression of suffering the tutor had seen when she was nursing Alexis through a bout of bleeding. They returned to the palace at 8:00 P.M. Before going in to dinner Nicholas went to his study, where he read Sazonov's report of the German declaration. He had a short telephone conversation with the foreign minister. He appeared in the dining room—Alexandra had been about to send Tatiana to look for him—and told the family the news. Vyrubova found the empress weeping hysterically in her bedroom later in the evening. "War!" she cried. "And I knew nothing of it! This is the end of everything!"

Shortly after 9:00 P.M. the tsar met his ministers and the British and French ambassadors. He went to his bedroom after midnight and drank a cup of tea with Alexandra. A servant knocked on the door at 1:30 A.M. with a telegram from the kaiser, imploring him not to let his troops cross the German frontier. Six hours before the Germans had declared war; now the kaiser was suggesting that Nicholas could still avert it. He read Alexandra the telegram. "You're not going to answer it, are you?" she said. He replied that he would not. "I felt that all was over forever with me and William," he said. "I slept extremely well. When I woke at my usual hour, I felt as if a weight had fallen from my mind. My responsibility to God and my people was still enormous, but at least I knew what I had to do."

A grand levee was held in the Winter Palace on July 20 to read the manifesto of war. Alexandra turned up the brim of her hat to give the crowds a rare glimpse of her face. A Te Deum was sung by the court clergy. An intensely mystical expression crossed the tsar's face as he prayed, Paléologue thought; Alexandra's breast was thrust forward, her head high, lips crimson, eyes glazed—when she closed them her livid face made the ambassador think of a death mask. All fell to their knees to receive the tsar's blessing. The enthusiasm was boundless. The tsar was mobbed as "highborn ladies, the reserved as well as the exuberant, old and young" rushed forward to catch a glance from the tsar, to touch him, to kiss a fold of his uniform. When he stepped onto the balcony to show himself to the crowd, the ourrahs—the deep-throated, echoing Russian hurrahs—seemed to shake the palace walls. Foreign diplomats climbed on top of their cars on the edge of the square to get a better view. In the depths of rural Russia, the liberal Pavel Miliukov wrote, "eternal silence reigned."

The next morning Count Pourtalès and his staff left St. Petersburg on a special train for Stockholm. The military plenipotentiary left his Stradivarius violin behind in the rush. The imperial rooms at the Finland Station were kept open for them; a senior foreign ministry official ensured that they departed unmolested. Their embassy did not escape so lightly. The mobs who had thrown up barricades a few days before transferred their hatreds from the Romanovs to the Germans on July 22. They burst into the building, tore down tapestries, smashed precious busts and statues from Pourtalès's private collection, and pulled down the famous bronze horses from its roof. The *St. Petersburger Zeitung* and the *Herold,* the capital's German-language newspapers, disappeared, and the favorite German restaurant, Leinners on the Nevsky, closed its doors. Later in the month Nicholas issued a ukase changing the city's German-sounding name to Petrograd. Ambassador Paléologue thought this "a little puerile"—he wondered what would happen if the French changed the name of Strasbourg "and all the other bourgs in France"—but he thought that the collective soul of Russia was showing itself more strongly than at any time since Napoleon's invasion a century before.

On July 23 news came that Britain had declared war on Germany; the red, white, and blue flags of Russia, France, and Britain floated together above the city. The mood was triumphal. "It has been a splendid time," the London *Times* correspondent Robert Wilton wrote on July 25, "and I think these people are out to win. They are now our fast friends for ever." The Duma committed itself unconditionally to the war. Nicholas, for the first and last time in his life, praised it lavishly. "The State Duma has shown itself worthy of its position," he said, "and has truly expressed the will of the nation, because the whole Russian people feels the insult Germany has caused it. I now look on the future with complete confidence." He named his cousin Grand Duke Nicholas Nikolayevich, the giant husband of the Montenegrin Anastasia, commander in chief. Alexandra and Rasputin railed against the appointment of their ex-friend. Pettily, the empress insisted that the tsar should not bid the grand duke farewell at Petrograd's Warsaw railroad station when he left for the front on August 1.

It seemed a crusade, a "duel to the death between Slavism and Germanism." Ninety-six percent of the reservists answered the tsar's call to the colors. Guards officers, foreseeing a victory parade down the Unter den Linden in Berlin, wondered whether they should pack their dress uniforms. Napoleon's invasion, the wars against Turkey and Japan had all been over inside eighteen months. The Russian high command's twin war plans, A and G, like the corresponding German Schlieffen plan, anticipated a result within months. Cheeky and confident postcards were sold of Kaiser Wilhelm as a miserable tomcat:

> *Uncle Fritz has gone quite barmy,*
> *Wants to have a boxing match!*
> *So who leads the German Army?*
> *Willy Whiskers—stupid cat!*

A few were more prescient. Rasputin feared calamity by instinct and Peter Durnovo, a former interior minister, by reason. In a brilliant analysis, later found among the tsar's papers, Durnovo listed Russian weaknesses: "Insufficiency of war supplies," his litany began. "Far too great dependence on foreign industry . . . inadequate strategic railroad network . . . rolling stock insufficient for colossal demands of a European war . . . heavy artillery far too inadequate and there are few machine guns. Expenditures beyond Russia's limited financial means . . . military disasters and shortcomings in supply inevitable."

He moved on to the terrifying consequences of a long war: "Nervousness and spirit of opposition," he wrote. "All the blame will be put on the government. . . . socialist slogans, capable of arousing and rallying the masses . . . division of all valuables and property. Army having lost its most dependable men, and carried away by a primitive peasant desire for land, will find itself too demoralized to serve as a bulwark of law and order. . . . The intellectual opposition parties, lacking real authority in the eyes of the people, will be powerless to stem the popular tide, aroused by themselves, and Russia will be flung into hopeless anarchy." The paper was stunningly accurate; it was ignored.

On the road between the new Petrograd and Tsarskoye Selo, amid an endless line of ammunition wagons, field kitchens, ambulances, and gun limbers, Paléologue noted a departing soldier and a woman—young, delicate, a red and white scarf around her fair hair, a blue cotton sarafan drawn in at her waist by a leather belt, an infant at her breast—fixing each other silently with "mournful, loving eyes." The ambassador wondered how many men would return. Witte, mortally sick with a cerebral tumor, returned from summering in Biarritz convinced that tsardom, "this insane regime . . . this tangle of cowardice, blindness, craftiness, and stupidity," would not survive the test of war.

———

At first the war had "one joyful as well as unexpected consequence," Gilliard said: it removed Rasputin to the background. He was back from Siberia at the end of September, almost recovered from his wound, though he continued to have stomach pains for the rest of his life. But he paid few visits to the palace. In the thrill of war his warnings seemed outdated. Alexis's ankle mended, and the boy was in good health through the winter. The tsar was preoccupied with news from the front; Alexandra was recovering from the shock of a war that had made enemies of her closest relations.

Rasputin was at the palace on October 17. A rare entry in the *Kammerfurier* recorded that he met Nicholas and Alexandra "at 9 1/2 in the evening." Maria Rasputin remembered it as the only occasion when the tsar was cold with her father. Rasputin told the tsar that the only victors in the war would be the ghouls of death and hospitals for the blind and maimed. When it was over crippled veterans would roam the cities and ghettos and villages, despised by those for whom they had fought. Tears streamed down his face as he spoke. The tsar said nothing but slowly sipped a drink. The empress looked pained but made no comment.

The starets was right; Durnovo's predictions were well grounded. A chronic shortage of shells and machine guns developed at once. "With his sly look, his eyes always gleaming watchfully under the heavy folds of his eyelids," Paléologue wrote of the man largely responsible, the war minister, Vladimir Sukhomlinov, "I know few men who inspire more distrust at first sight." The tsar agreed that Sukhomlinov's looks were against him, "but," he wrote, "he is an excellent minister and I trust him entirely." This drawing room soldier, "scented, pomaded, with gold chain bracelets on his white wrists and a secret twist to the pale lips between the short gray beard," spent much ingenuity in maximizing his expense account to keep his wife, thirty-five years younger than himself, in parties and clothes. He had last fought against the Turks, in 1878, boasted that he had not read a military manual in twenty-five years, and held that machine guns and rapid-firing artillery were cowardly. He was so lazy that, after preparing a mobilization plan during the first Serbian crisis two years before, he left for a vacation on the French Riviera. "Why not?" he told his critics. "A mobilization doesn't have to be conducted by the war minister in person." He and his wife were friendly with Rasputin and Alexandra, however. His job was not in jeopardy even when reservists reporting to their depots found only enough .299-inch rifles for two men in three, and some were not issued boots. Signals units had no wire for field telephones, and communications were forced onto radio. Because there was also a shortage of code books, many radio messages, to the joy of German intelligence, were in clear.

The Russians consistently outfought the Austro-Hungarians. Smashing fifteen Austrian divisions, which fled in panic crying, *"Kosaken kommen!"* "The Cossacks are coming!" they rapidly captured Lemberg in Galicia. Austrian officers taken prisoner accepted parole and dined in Russian messes, telling their hosts that they wanted no part of German aggression. The Russian press wrote that the campaign was all but over; against Rasputin's advice, Nicholas visited Lemberg to celebrate its return to its old Russian name, Lvov, riding streets gay with bunting to a thanksgiving service in the cathedral and a gala dinner. He slept in the bed reserved for the Austrian emperor, Franz Joseph, but the visit was not a success. Although Nicholas shared his wife's belief in the loyalty of his peasant-soldiers, he was too shy to approach them in the uniformed flesh. The army was "cold and indifferent" to him. The new governor, a third-rate former hussar officer, conducted a witch-hunt against the Galician Catholics, and they were soon as hostile to their fellow Slavs from Russia as they had been to the Austrians. "Our Friend would have found it better," Alexandra wrote to Nicholas, "had you gone after the war to the conquered country." Rasputin feared that it would soon be won back.

He was correct. The Austrians, demoralized, riven by cross-nationalisms, were one thing. The Germans were quite another. They were better equipped and better led than the Russians, who were frequently obliged to face them, not at a time and place of their own choosing but in response to pleas from the distant French and British. Within a month of the outbreak of war, the Germans were within thirty miles of Paris. To ease the pressure on their allies, the Russians attacked with two armies in East Prussia.

The First Army under General Rennenkampf was to drive southwest parallel to the Baltic coast, drawing the bulk of the German forces, while the Second Army under General Samsonov moved north out of Poland. Samsonov made slow progress in difficult country. When his men broke into the small town of Allenstein, they cheered because they thought they were in Berlin. Hindenburg and Ludendorff, the formidable German generals facing them, feared the two armies would link up and trap them. But radio intercepts of uncoded signals gave them the exact dispositions of Russian units and their objectives. The information was so priceless that the Germans kept asking "anxiously over and over if we should believe them." Aerial reconnaissance and telephone calls from local inhabitants—the Russians had not bothered to cut the lines—confirmed that the Russian commanders were unable to coordinate their armies' movements.

As Samsonov drank a toast to his "victory" in Allenstein, the Germans cut into his flanks. His men floundered in marshes and forests of sixty-foot pines. They had few maps, and the Germans had burned signposts between the villages. They milled on sandy tracks, deep and powdery, which German shells threw up into a choking dust. Their own artillery was silent for lack of ammunition. Samsonov tried to ride out of the trap with his chief of staff and a few officers. "The enemy has luck one day, we will have luck another," he said. He fell behind the break-out party in the thick woods. They heard a single shot: he killed himself in shame at losing his army. Only fifty officers and 2,100 men of his Thirteenth and Fifteenth Corps escaped; he had lost 110,000 men in four days.

The Germans named their victory Tannenberg, in revenge for a fifteenth-century defeat the Teutonic Knights had suffered against the Slavs nearby. Then they turned on Rennenkampf. In his Twenty-eighth Division, companies were stretched out in rows with their officers after rapid-firing artillery caught them, "as if they had been frozen into those poses in which they met death"; trenches six feet deep were filled with dead and wounded Russians. Rennenkampf fled back across the border in a car; in contempt his staff called him Rennen ohne Kampf, "running without fighting." He left 145,000 men of the First Army behind him, dead, wounded, or captured.

News of the disaster reached Petrograd, "stilling the music, the cheers, the gay self-confidence." The skies turned leaden with fall. Mobs took vengeance on German bakeries and shops. The music of Beethoven and Bach was banned from concerts. The synod outlawed Christmas trees as a German custom. Alexandra shared the loathing. She said that Germany had become "a country I did not know and had never known" and feared that the "monstrous" kaiser would avenge himself on her by sending her brother to the Russian front, but more than ever the Russians thought of her as German.

The wounded came back in streams. The empress trained as a nurse with her elder daughters and Vyrubova. "We have an amputation in the big hospital," Alexandra wrote on November 20. "My nose is full of hideous smells from those blood-poisoning wounds." She had met gangrene; five days later she saw death. "We were occupied all morning—during an operation a soldier died— the first such time it happened," she wrote. "The girlies were brave—they and Ania [Vyrubova] had never seen such a death. . . . It made us all so sad as you can imagine—how near death always is."

She did not forget to mention Rasputin. "Once more the hour of separation has come—& always equally hard to bear . . . when you are gone . . . a bit of my life gone," she wrote to Nicholas after he left to review troops in the Caucasus. "You always bring revival as our Friend says . . . comforting to know His prayers follow you."

The Friend was making the most of his relations with Goremykin. The premier set up an infirmary for wounded soldiers. Simanovich persuaded the banker Dmitri Rubinstein to make a donation of 250,000 rubles to it. In return Rasputin introduced the financier to the premier. In due course Madame Rubinstein was appointed an honorary president of the infirmary, and her husband was able to boast of his intimate connections with the government. He made a point of telephoning Goremykin when he wished to impress a visitor, asking after his wife's health and having a chat so trivial that his closeness to the premier could not be doubted. Word spread quickly, and Rubinstein used his reputation in share ramping. He bought a majority of stock in the banking house Yunker & Co. He then held a ball—making sure that Goremykin and Rasputin were present—to which he invited a Kiev sugar baron, Lev Brodsky. After he had seen Rubinstein "talking like pals" with the premier and the starets, Brodsky was persuaded to buy several million rubles' worth of overpriced stock. Rubinstein, Simanovich said admiringly, "knew how to put himself forward."

CHAPTER 17

Party Time in Moscow

No balls, no music, no officers in gala uniform greeted the New Year," wrote Meriel Buchanan. "The men we danced with last year had lost their lives in East Prussia or were fighting in the Carpathians." Women with dull, heavy eyes read the casualty lists posted on shop windows. The empress now rose at seven, instead of noon, and busied herself comforting the last hours of "unknown solitary men" from obscure regiments. She strung innumerable icons and knitted comforters, for she wanted each man in the immense armies to have something made with her own hands; "but almost no one knew this."

Rasputin's fall from grace with the tsar was temporary. On the afternoon of January 2, 1915, Vyrubova was traveling from Tsarskoye Selo to see her father in Petrograd when the train jumped the track. Her legs were trapped in wrecked radiator pipes, and a heavy steel cross-beam fell on her face. She was admitted to the hospital unconscious with severe leg and spinal injuries. The doctor told Nicholas and Alexandra not to disturb her. "She is dying," he said. "She cannot live until morning." Occasionally the patient muttered for Rasputin to pray for her.

A telephone call from the palace alerted Rasputin in the late evening. He telephoned Prince Andronnikov for an automobile and was driven to the hospital. He entered the ward, bowed to the tsar, and went over to the bed. "Annushka, do you hear me?" he said. She opened her eyes. "Grigory! Grigory!" she cried. He held her hand and prayed. "She will live, but she will always be a cripple," he said. With that the tsar's head of chancellery, Alexander Mosolov, said, "he tottered from the room and fell outside in a faint, from which he awoke in a strong perspiration, feeling that all his strength had gone from him."

Mosolov was no admirer of the starets and had no reason to exaggerate his powers. It is not possible to judge whether the intervention was lifesaving; but at the least it restored the patient's will to regain consciousness. Vyrubova did live, and she was indeed crippled, though, with the help of crutches, she recovered sufficiently to negotiate the winding stairs up to Rasputin's apartment with agility. The apparent miracle, much to Simanovich's relief, restored the starets to the tsar's favor.

Rasputin came close to death himself four days later. He was almost run down by a troika driven at him at full gallop along the Kamennoostrovsky Prospect. Okhrana security men caught its occupants and found that they came from Tsaritsyn. It was said that they were Iliodor's agents, intent on murder. Although they were expelled from the capital, no charges were preferred against them. From now on the alarmed Okhrana men kept full notes on Rasputin's movements and contacts.

The starets celebrated his escape with gusto, mixing business with large helpings of pleasure. His consumption of wine and Madeira became wilder. His daughter said that he drank more to deaden the continuing pain from his stomach wound. There is an element of truth in this—after one drinking session the Okhrana reported that he was "sick all day"—but his constitution was strong and his recovery rapid. The drinking was part of a general descent into wilder living, a growing sense that indiscretion could no longer harm him. His sexual appetite was always voracious; it fed now on increased opportunity, on power and ready access to cash. It was also better documented in the "staircase notes" taken by his Okhrana minders.

Several visits with prostitutes to his favorite bathhouse on Rozhdestvenskaya Street were recorded. After one of them, feeling exalted, Rasputin cabled Vyrubova: "I could not be with you in body, I send you joy with my spirit. My feeling is a divine feeling. I send an angel to console and comfort you." On January 12 he took 250 rubles from two peasants who wanted pardons. One had been sentenced for belonging to a sect, the other for forging promissory notes. On January 16, while Vyrubova's sister was visiting him, an agent saw him "take the prostitute Tregubova on his knee and murmur something." Maria Sergeyevna Ghil, the wife of a captain in the 145th Regiment, slept with him on the night of January 17–18. In the morning he was given 1,000 rubles by a banker and merchant, Moisey Ginsburg. The bribe was for help in getting a contract to supply coal to the navy.

Simanovich arranged a party in the Gorokhovaya apartment on January 26, paid for by people whose release from prison Rasputin had helped to arrange. Four unknown men and six women attended, the agents reported;

one of them was carrying a guitar. The party was noisy; they sang and danced into the early hours. Two days later Rasputin's wine stocks were replenished by Lev von Bock, a state councillor who owed him favors. On February 12 he visited Prince Andronnikov, returning home at 4:30 A.M. with six men, all drunk. They stayed up singing until 6:00; "in the morning, Rasputin didn't receive anyone for he slept."

Boxes of cigars and pheasants were sent to Goremykin for the premier's seventy-fifth birthday. Rasputin played games with his minders. On February 19 he visited the apartment of Nikolai Solovyov, a senior synod official with a young wife, Elizaveta, with whom he was having an affair. When he left the apartment with two ladies, he outsmarted the Okhrana men by jumping into a motor taxi. The next sighting was at 3:00 A.M. when he returned home alone. Two days later he partied with Evgeniya Terekhova, a twenty-three-year-old gentlewoman, in her rooms in the Severnaya Hotel on Znamenskaya Square. He left the next morning. He visited Vyrubova in her cottage in Tsarskoye Selo, where she was recovering well from her injuries. He was back on February 27, going to the Alexander Palace to bless the tsar on the eve of his departure for a visit to the Austrian front. Nicholas wrote later to Alexandra that he felt a "special peace of mind" after the blessing.

Huge orders for supplies and services were being placed by the military. Simanovich and Andronnikov made sure that Rasputin exploited his royal contacts. On March 10 Evgeniya Ezhova, the wife of a businessman from Klin, near Moscow, visited his apartment. She wanted his help in landing a two million ruble contract for supplying linen to the army. It seems that she obtained it, for shortly afterward she moved from rooms in the medium-rated Severnaya to a suite at the luxury Astoria Hotel. After midnight seven men came and stayed until 3:00 A.M. "They screamed, sang songs, danced, made noise, and, all drunk, together with Rasputin went somewhere," the staircase watchers noted. He was back home at 10:15 the next morning. The agents followed him later to Pushkinskaya Street, where the twenty-six-year-old Vera Tregubova kept an apartment. She was a high-class call girl who claimed to be a music student at the conservatory. The two were seen going into a bathhouse.

———

As they sported in the steam room and cold pool, Austrian officers were raising white flags on the battlements of Przemyśl. The great fortified city, surrounded by concentric rings of trenches and strong points, guarded the approaches to the Carpathian Mountains. Though the Russians were so short of shells that it was a court-martial offense for an artillery officer to fire more than three a day, they had succeeded in encircling it with bayonet charges. Scurvy broke out in the besieged city. After the last horses had been slaughtered for their meat, the

Austrians destroyed their ammunition dumps in an explosion heard fifty miles away. They prepared to surrender.

Nicholas was at army headquarters, the Stavka, at Baranovichi, midway on the railroad from Brest Litovsk to Minsk. Railroad cars were drawn up in a fan shape in pinewoods outside the town, guarded by Cossacks with long Russian bayonets on their rifles. The cars served as offices, map rooms, mess, and dormitories. In his commander in chief's coach, Grand Duke Nicholas Nikolayevich had laid rugs and bearskins. A hundred icons hung on the walls. The headroom was too low for the Romanov giant, and the doors had scraps of paper hung on them to remind him to duck.

A forest clearing was a far from ideal spot to supervise a front that stretched from the Baltic to the Carpathians. The headquarters of the German Oberost, by contrast, were in a palace at Posen, where Ludendorff could relax with his officers over dinner and cigars before returning to his rooms to work into the early hours. The Russians stopped work before an early dinner. Their coaches baked in summer and froze in winter, although the stove in the grand duke's office so overheated it that the tsar could not "endure it above one hour." Strategy was discussed around a sandpit where sections of the front were modeled in clay and sand. Here the grand duke outlined plans for armies by tracing lines with his walking stick. Wireless communication was crude; the field telephone network was little better. The only certain way of sending orders for six million men was to use a messenger.

The grand duke ran panting across the clearing to tell the tsar of the fall of Przemyśl and the capture of 120,000 Austrians. A Te Deum was sung in a little wooden chapel built in the pines. It was packed, Nicholas wrote, "with officers and my splendid Cossacks. What beaming faces!" He presented the grand duke with a viceroy's golden sword, its hilt shining with diamonds, and inscribed *"Pour la libération de Galicie."* It was the high point of Russian fortunes in the war, and of Nicholas's relations with his tall cousin.

—

Later in the month Rasputin went to Moscow to fulfill a vow to pray in the Cathedral of the Assumption in the Kremlin. He had made it while recovering from his wound in the hospital. He left Petrograd on the night train on March 24, shortly before a woman named Varvara Nishchenko visited him. She left a message promising him two thousand rubles if he obtained the discharge of her uncle, a colonel, who had been called up for duty from the reserve. For all his declared, and genuine, patriotism, Rasputin was heavily engaged in the lucrative business of obtaining deferments and soft billets far from the front. Rules, and shame, were for others.

He arrived in Moscow the morning of March 25. He went from the train to have breakfast with an admirer, Maria Arkadyevna. She had promised to introduce him to a friend, Anna-Elena Frantsevna Djanumova. Elena was an attractive woman of thirty-five, the wife of a wealthy Moscow merchant, whose elderly mother had been exiled to Siberia from Kiev. Although Russian born, the mother had remained a German subject and was suffering from the anti-German hysteria. Maria Arkadyevna—Elena discreetly avoided using more than her first name and patronymic in her account—assured Elena that Rasputin would be able to fix her mother's case.

She rang Elena: "Rasputin is here. Come and have breakfast with us." Elena was there by noon. She recognized Rasputin immediately. He wore a white silk embroidered shirt over his trousers. His deep-set gray eyes struck her. "They pierce you as though they want to feel to the very depths of you," she wrote. "They look so shrewdly, so persistently, it makes you feel ill at ease." She noticed that he used the familiar *thou* to everyone, old and young. He leaned toward her with a glass of red wine and said, without any preliminaries, "Drink." Then he said, "Take a pencil and write." Other guests handed her pencils and pieces of paper. "Write," he said. She began to write.

"Be glad at simplicity, woe is frantic and wicked—even the sun is not warm for the woeful," he dictated. "Forgive me, Lord, I'm sinful, I'm earthly and my love is earthly, too. God, do wonders and restrain us. We are Yours. Your love is great, do not be angry at us. Send humility to my soul and the joy of beneficial love. Save me and help me, God." All the guests looked on respectfully. Intelligent people, shrewd and reliable in other respects, suspended judgment on Rasputin's banalities; turning dross to gold through force of mind was one of his characteristics. "You're lucky," an old lady whispered to Elena. "He paid attention to you at once and he loves you."

"Take this and read, read it with your heart," Rasputin told her, pushing the paper back to her. He liked the word *frantic*; it went with Elena's patronymic, Frantsevna. It became his nickname for her, Frantic.

The talk turned to the war. Rasputin was in boastful mood. "If they didn't niggle me, there wouldn't be any war," he said. "I wouldn't allow the tsar. He obeys me and I wouldn't allow him to fight. What do we need the war for? Anything may happen."

After breakfast the guests moved to the drawing room. "Play 'Along the Roadway,' " Rasputin said suddenly. A lady sat at the grand piano and began to play. The starets got up and began to sway to the rhythm and stamp his feet in their soft leather boots. He broke into a dance, moving lightly and easily. He floated about the room "like a feather," approaching the ladies to entice a partner from their circle. One of the ladies could no longer restrain herself and floated to him with her scarf in her hand. Elena saw that nobody was surprised, as if dancing at midday was common. It ended as abruptly as it had begun.

"That's enough," Rasputin said, turning to Elena. "You came here on business. Well, let's go, speak up, what d'you want, sweetie?" They went to an adjacent room. Elena explained her mother's problem. He became thoughtful. "Your affair is difficult," he said. "You can't even mention the Germans these days. But I'll talk to *her*"—he pronounced this word after a pause with particular stress to make it clear he meant the empress—"and she'll talk to *him*. Perhaps something'll come out of it. And you must come to Peter to me. You'll find out there."

Saying good-bye to Maria Arkadyevna, Elena asked her to visit. "Why don't you ask me?" Rasputin butted in. "I'll come." Elena mumbled that she'd thought he would be too busy but invited him for breakfast. "All right," he said. "We're gonna visit the Moscow lady." Elena noticed that he always stressed his *o*'s—*M-o-O-sc-o-w*—in a melodious drawl. She went home in a confused state. So this was the real sovereign of Russia, in a peasant blouse. The racy melody of "Along the Roadway" sounded in her ears, while, she wrote, a "bearded figure flashed before my eyes and tassels of a blue sash fluttered. . . . Deep-set eyes persistently pierced me and I did not know what to think."

———

The following morning, March 26, 1915, Elena was woken by the telephone. It was Maria Arkadyevna with her buoyant laugh. "Rasputin spent the night in my apartment, and he's been agitated since early morning, getting ready to come to your place," she told Elena. "He came to me to ask for perfumed pomatum, *p-O-matum*, you know, with an *o*. And scissors for his nails. When I ask him what for, he says, 'We're going to the dark beauty.' Now you ask him for whatever you want. He'll do anything. Use the situation."

Elena rang up her closest friends to ask them over. She explained, "Like myself, they all wanted to have a look at this weird celebrity."

Rasputin came at 1:00 P.M. in a crimson silk Russian blouse, "merry and complacent." He talked a lot, skipping from one topic to another. An episode from his life would be followed by a totally unconnected dictum, topped off with a sudden question to someone present. Sometimes he seemed not to be paying any attention. Then he would stare and say abruptly, "I know what you're thinking about, my dear." He always seemed to guess right.

He spoke about Siberia and his family. "See my hands," he said. "Because of hard labor. A peasant's labor is not easy." He stretched out his callused hands, the veins swollen. Self-satisfaction inflected in his voice. It seemed strange to talk of peasant life at a table set with crystal and silver. The telephone started ringing. Someone asked him to come for a dinner party with Gypsy entertainers that a group of rich Siberian merchants had arranged for him.

Maria Arkadyevna was worried. "You promised to go," she said. "They're waiting for us."

"I'm not going anywhere," Rasputin replied. "I'm OK here, with the little ladies. Tell 'em I won't come."

Arkadyevna was so upset that red flushes appeared on her face. "It won't do," she said. "People have organized a feast for you. Everyone is there waiting for you, and you aren't going. You promised. You've got to go."

"Tell 'em I won't come," he repeated. "I've got to leave a word here for everyone to remember me by. Give me some paper."

Arkadyevna asked Elena to go into a different room and implored her to help change Rasputin's mind because she had promised to bring him with her. Finally, they succeeded. "All right, I'll go, though I'm OK here," he said. "Well, ladies, take these."

He handed out scraps of paper. He wrote on Elena's: "Don't avoid love—it's a mother for you." To another lady, he scrawled: "God loves those with a pure heart." Elena's maid Grusha had been looking at Rasputin with avid curiosity. She was rewarded with her own note: "God loves those who labor and everyone knows of your honesty."

He walked to the hall and was handed a rich fur coat with a beaver collar and beaver hat. One of the ladies remarked how splendid his coat was. "The dentists gave it to me," he said, referring to recent and successful influence peddling. A group of Jewish dentists had been convicted of forging professional diplomas that gave them the right to live in Petrograd, where Jews were normally denied residence permits. The convictions were quashed after Rasputin appealed to the tsar.

He kissed all the ladies when he left: "it was his usual manner when greeting or saying good-bye."

—

It would have been better if Rasputin had stayed with the ladies. Instead, he went to the Yar, the smartest nightclub in Moscow. He arrived, already drunk, at 11:00 P.M., with a merry widow, Anisia Reshetnikova; a Moscow journalist, Nikolai Soedov; and a young woman the police could not identify. The party had a private room and were joined by the publisher of the *Moscow News of the Season*. Rasputin ordered a Gypsy chorus to sing to them, and he danced the russkaya. As the British secret agent Robert Bruce Lockhart watched the cabaret in the main hall, he heard a fracas coming from the private room. "Wild shrieks of a woman, a man's curses, broken glass and the banging of doors," he wrote. "Headwaiters rushed upstairs. The manager sent for the police. . . . The cause of the disturbance was Rasputin—drunk and lecherous."

Rasputin had tried to seduce one of the women in the party. Frustrated, he smashed the mirrors in the room. He pointed at his embroidered blouse and told the singers, "It's a gift from the 'old woman,' " adding that she had sewn it for him and that "I do with her what I want." The journalists present knew full well that the "old woman" was the empress. Challenged to prove he was

Rasputin, he unbuttoned his trousers and waved his penis at the waiters and onlookers. When the police arrived he told them that he was protected by the tsar. They reported that his behavior was "sexually psychopathic; he was baring his sexual organs and carrying on a conversation with the singers, giving them handwritten notes, such as 'Love unselfishly.' " When the police dragged him away, Bruce Lockhart reports that he was "snarling and vowing vengeance."

———

Rasputin was unrepentant when Elena saw him off on the Moscow-Petrograd express on March 29. He was standing by a first-class carriage surrounded by women. Elena elbowed through the crowd, "under the cross-fire of curious and derisive eyes." He embraced her. "Come to Peter with me, Frantic," he said. "I'll do everything for you, only come. Remember, if you don't come nothing will be done." He kissed everyone who had come to see him off and was gone.

As news of the Yar scandal got out, it was assumed that Rasputin was finished. Russians are tolerant of public drunkenness, but they expected the reference to the "old woman" and the penis waving to inflict terminal damage. He continued, unabashed, in his old ways. He had crossed the line, and he did not care. The first thing he did on his return to Petrograd on the morning of March 31 was send a telegram to Elena: "Gratifying treasure spiritually with you kisses," it read.

Then he set about gratifying himself, the Okhrana log recording that, on April 3, he "brought a woman to his apartment at 1:00 A.M. who spent the night with him." As the couple slept the German troops were loaded on trains that would take them from France to the Russian front. At Easter, Rasputin prayed ostentatiously at the Alexander Nevsky Monastery in Petrograd. At the front Russian troops flew great banners above their trenches proclaiming that "Christ is Risen." Each man was given ten eggs and eight Easter buns.

On April 9 Simanovich arranged for Rasputin to go to a party at the house of Alexis Filippov, editor of the financial newspaper *Stock Exchange Day*. He spoke with businessmen and stockbrokers eager for tips and contracts until he became incoherent with drink. He did not get home until 6:00 A.M. A week later he met his old friend Martian, the father superior of the Tyumen monastery. They went to visit an acquaintance, Vasily Pestrikov, who was not at home. Undaunted, the two holy men went on a spree with Pestrikov's son. They sent for a guitar player and sang with him. Rasputin danced with Pestrikov's housemaid.

At the front of General Radko's Third Army in Galicia, the sheep that normally grazed between the lines were gone. No-man's-land was two thousand yards wide in many places, and shepherds brought their flocks to the grass while

Russian troops from the country swapped jokes with them. Nobody connected the absence of sheep and shepherds with German preparations for attack. The tsar shared the optimism. He was inspecting men sent to Odessa and Sevastopol to prepare the invasion of the Bosporus and Constantinople. They were to be landed on the European side of the Bosporus while thousands of tons of burning oil were dumped in the straits to be carried into the harbor of Constantinople by the current. Nicholas expected to annex the city. The Italians declared war on Austria on April 13, confident that the Russians had broken the Habsburg empire; Rasputin returned to his apartment "dead drunk" at 2:00 A.M. The French and British had by now noted that a number of German divisions had disappeared from their front. They warned the Stavka of a "sledgehammer blow" that the Germans were preparing in Galicia. Russian reconnaissance parties reported that German troops were now stiffening the Austro-Hungarians on the southern front.

At 3:00 A.M. on April 19, the sledgehammer struck. For four hours, 1,500 guns poured 700,000 shells onto Third Army. It was the greatest artillery barrage of the war to date. Ten shells fell on each pace and a half of front. The few Russian guns had not been moved for so long that the German gunners destroyed them in the predawn darkness. A British military observer, Bernard Pares, was on a hill behind the Russian line. He watched an uninterrupted, ten-mile line of enemy fire. "The Russian artillery was practically silent," he wrote. "The elementary Russian trenches were completely wiped out and so, to all intents and purposes, was human life in that area."

German officers watched the barrage without taking cover; there was almost no return fire. At 1:00 P.M. their shock troops advanced in waves; they need not have bothered to fix their bayonets. One Russian division was reduced from 16,000 men to 500. "Here and there," the German war diary reported, "loam-gray figures jumped up and ran back, weaponless, in gray fur caps and fluttering, unbuttoned greatcoats, until there was not one remaining." By nightfall the Germans had taken Third Army's second trench line and were in open country, "sweeping the unwieldy enemy before them in the exuberant joy of the attack."

Reserves, thrown in by Grand Duke Nicholas Nikolayevich, were hurried into gaps in the line without rifles with orders to collect weapons from the dead and wounded. They had no training in taking cover and lay exposed to German shell fire until they were killed or wounded. Companies of 250 men that Pares visited were reduced to 40 survivors. "You know, sir, we have no weapon except the soldier's breast," they told him. "This is not war, sir, it is slaughter." When they fell back to the San River, they found they could not dig trenches or build bunkers because corrupt officers had sold the spades, barbed wire, and entrenching timbers to civilians. With bayonets fixed to empty rifles, they fell back and prepared to defend Russian soil against the first invaders to penetrate it since Napoleon.

—

Rasputin's malice was added to the commander in chief's other problems. Many Russian Germans had been exiled to Siberia in the spy frenzy of the war. Simanovich was running a profitable sideline getting permission from the Stavka for them to return. The fixer petitioned Nicholas Nikolayevich once too often. The grand duke cabled him from headquarters: "Satisfied for the last time. If new petitions are sent you to be exiled to Siberia." Simanovich went immediately to Gorokhovaya ulitsa. Rasputin cabled the grand duke suggesting that he visit the Stavka to see him. He got a definitive answer by telegraph three hours later. "If you come I'll have you hanged."

The starets was furious. "From that time he bore the thought of revenging himself on Nicholas Nikolayevich at the first opportunity," Simanovich said. He rebuked the starets for making an enemy of the grand duke, "threatening our position," and stirring up hatred against himself. "People like me are born once in a century," Rasputin snapped back proudly. "My power cannot spread everywhere, but I achieve all I need."

Over the next days, Simanovich noticed Rasputin's "strange behavior." He ate nothing and drank Madeira heavily. He was silent and often jumped up as if trying to catch someone with jerky movements of his hands, threatening with his fists: "I'll show him! . . . I'll get him!" It was clear to Simanovich that he was going to "revenge someone." He would spend a whole day like this, going out in the evening to the bathhouse with an Okhrana agent, coming back at 10:00 P.M., looking very tired. Without saying anything he went into his study and wrote something on a piece of paper, which he carefully folded. He then went into his bedroom, put the paper under the pillow, and got into bed, falling asleep immediately. It seemed like sorcery to Simanovich, who had seen him do it before and asked what was on the bits of paper. "I put down my wishes," Rasputin replied, "and they come true while I sleep." He added that he had notched his wishes on a stick before he had learned to write and that thus he had prevented many misfortunes.

The next morning he woke relaxed and amiable. He grated the note in his fingers until it crumbled and threw it away. Then he said, smiling, "You can rejoice, Simanovich. My strength won." Simanovich said he did not understand. "Well, you'll see what will happen in five or six days," Rasputin replied. "I'll go to Papa and I will tell him all the truth." He picked up the telephone, and Simanovich listened to him place a call to the palace. He got through to the tsar's office right away; the palace switchboard had standing orders to connect him immediately.

"What is Papa doing?" he asked the aide-de-camp.

"He's busy with his ministers," the young officer replied.

"Tell him that I have a divine message for him." The aide's response to this modest claim was not recorded, but the tsar duly came through on the line. "What's happened, Father Grigory?" he asked.

"I can't tell you over the phone," he said. "May I come over?"

"Please do. I also want to talk to you."

Rasputin was driven to the palace and was received at once. He recounted what had happened to Simanovich and told the tsar that he had had a "divine appearance" during the night. This had informed him that in three days Nicholas would receive a telegram from the commander in chief to say that the army had rations enough only for three days. He sat at the tsar's desk, filled two glasses with Madeira, and insisted that the tsar drink from his glass while he drank from the tsar's. When they had taken sips, he mixed the wine in one glass and told the tsar to drink it. Having completed these mystical preparations, Rasputin said that the tsar should not believe the grand duke's telegram. The army had sufficient food. Nicholas Nikolayevich wanted to sow panic and disorder in the army and the country so that he could retreat under the pretext of food shortages. He would then occupy Petrograd and force Nicholas to abdicate. The tsar was shocked, or so Rasputin reported to Simanovich. "What am I to do?" Nicholas asked. Rasputin replied: "He wants to exile me to Siberia, but I'll send him to the Caucasus."

Three days later the cable advising of bread shortages in the field arrived from the grand duke at Stavka. The shortages were real enough, caused by transport bottlenecks; there was not a scrap of evidence that Nicholas Nikolayevich was plotting a coup. However, Simanovich wrote, "It was enough to seal his fate. Nobody could dissuade the tsar that the grand duke was contemplating a march on the capital to overthrow him from his throne." It would take a little longer, but Rasputin was fertilizing the ground for his vengeance.

CHAPTER 18

Vengeance

Rasputin met the empress frequently at Tsarskoye Selo, traveling to Vyrubova's cottage by train or in a chauffeur-driven car from an army motor pool provided by Sukhomlinov at the war ministry. He was a regular sight in the town. He often looked the worse for wear, a workingman's cap pulled down over his eyes, "dirty and unkempt." He had the trick, however, of sobering up rapidly. On April 26 Dmitri Rubinstein rewarded him for his help in stock ramping by throwing a party for a dozen people. Guitar playing and dancing were heard from the staircase until the early hours. Rasputin was summoned by the empress in the morning. He had hardly slept and was badly hungover. Baroness Vera Kusova urged him not to go in such a state. She was the wife of a cavalry officer, who the Okhrana reported "wanted to get a better position for her husband and struck up an intimate acquaintance with Rasputin into the bargain." "He'll spoil the whole thing," an agent reported her as saying. "Our elder has become spoiled." After an hour's catnap he set off fresh enough.

His confidence in his hold on the empress became strong enough for him to wedge his visits tightly between carousals. On May 9, drunk and horny, he sent the caretaker's wife from his apartment block to fetch him his favorite masseuse, Utina. She failed, and Rasputin staggered to the rooms of a dressmaker who lived on the staircase. "Why don't you come to me, Katya?" he pleaded. When she refused he told her, "Come to me in a week and I'll give you fifty rubles." He saw the empress the next morning. The tsar was proving uncooperative on some plan, possibly the replacement of the commander in chief;

on his return Rasputin cabled Sabler at the synod: "My dear, we talked to Mama there and agreed that it is not simple to disturb our ruler." Then he brought a prostitute to his apartment and locked her in a room until, as the Okhrana men noted, "the servants released her."

He worried for his safety. Word came from his wife that a stranger had arrived in Pokrovskoye. On May 12 he sent a telegram to the governor of Tobolsk, saying: "A suspicious man has been living in Pokrovskoye for three weeks now one time he says he's from Moscow then—from someplace else." He made sure that the governor took the matter seriously by telling him to reply to Vyrubova in Tsarskoye Selo. He narrowly avoided a beating two days later. He went to an apartment on Malaya Dvoryanskaya at 5:00 P.M. At 10:00 an agent across the street saw a woman enter an unlit room in the apartment. She soon ran into a lit room where two men were sitting. The agent then saw Rasputin dash out of the darkened room into the hall, apparently alarmed; he snatched his hat and coat and fled into the street without putting them on. The two men ran after him. Rasputin jumped into a horse-drawn cab while it was still moving. He stood up in it all the way to the Liteiny Prospect, turning every now and then to make sure that nobody was after him. Then he got out of the cab, calmed down, and walked home.

Simanovich, who had good access to intrigues through his gambling clubs, feared another assassination attempt. Maria Rasputin had become engaged to a young Georgian cavalry officer, Simeon Pkhakadze, who asked his prospective father-in-law to a party at the house of Count Tolstoy on Troitskaya Street. Most of the people present were drunk. Suddenly Rasputin saw Pkhakadze draw out his revolver and point it at him. He stared at him and said, "You want to kill me, but your hand won't obey you." Pkhakadze was stunned and fled as the guests panicked. Rasputin turned, left the room, took his fur coat, and went home. The young captain went to his rooms and shot himself but survived. Rasputin was jumping up and down, as he always did when in high spirits, when he next met Simanovich. "Well, the danger is over now," he said. "The attempt has been made. Pkhakadze, of course, is no longer my daughter's fiancé. He'll go home now." Simanovich, convinced that the captain had been given leave from his unit as part of a military plot to kill the starets, told him that the danger was greater than ever.

Later in the month Rasputin accepted a trio of commissions. Ignati Manus, a corrupt Petrograd banker who the French ambassador thought was a leading German agent, was supplying Rasputin with the services of Vera Tregubova. On May 26 Rasputin, drunk, was seen getting out of Manus's automobile with the prostitute. He kissed and stroked her before retiring to his bedroom. Still unsatisfied, he went again to the seamstress Katya's rooms. An engineer, Mendel-Emmanuel Neiman, asked him to arrange a pardon for an eight-month prison sentence he was facing for having attempted to bribe his way out of military service. Rasputin assured him that his petition had been handed to "himself," meaning the tsar. Dolina Mikhailovna asked for Russian citizenship to be arranged for a ready-to-wear clothing magnate from Moscow called Mandl, whose stores had suffered badly during anti-German riots.

———

A vast catastrophe was engulfing Russian Poland. The Germans were forcing their way toward Warsaw, inflicting such terrible casualties that corps were reduced to "miniature regiments." Almost half a million troops had been lost since the start of the enemy offensive. "The Germans expend metal, we expend life," a Russian corps commander said. "They go forward . . . we only beat them off with heavy losses and our blood, and are retreating." Nicholas was briefed on the crumbling fronts on a visit to the Stavka. "His hands trembled," the industrialist Putilov, who was with him, recalled. "He seemed particularly impressed when, myself deeply affected and scarcely able to restrain my tears, I spoke to him of the troops' unswerving devotion and love for their tsar and motherland."

There were worrying signs that this devotion did not extend to the empress. Muscovites rose to protest the slaughter. For three days they roamed the city setting fires while the police stood by. They hurled Bechsteins and Bluthners, grand pianos and uprights, from the windows of the city's finest music store. Crowds in Red Square yelled that the war and interior ministers should be hanged. More ominously, they demanded that Alexandra should be sent to a convent for the duration of the war and that Nicholas should abdicate in favor of Grand Duke Nicholas Nikolayevich. They moved on to the Convent of Mary and Martha, which Grand Duchess Elizabeth had founded after the assassination of her husband. She had once been popular in Moscow; now they described her in the same terms as her sister Alexandra, Ona Nemka—"She is German."

A story about her had made the rounds earlier in May. She visited a hospital after the arrival of a fresh contingent of wounded Russians and German prisoners. Some of the prisoners were lying on the floor because the wards were full. The grand duchess ordered the matron to put the Russian soldiers on the floor while the Germans took their beds. "The Germans are used to culture and comfort," she said. "The Russians won't feel the difference." It was untrue; the grand duchess was a notably humane woman who denied that she had so much as seen a prisoner. But the crowd believed the story; they shouted, too, that she was harboring German spies and her brother, Grand Duke Ernest of Hesse, in the convent. She met them at the convent gate and invited them to search. The first stone had been hurled at her—"Down with the German woman!"—when troops arrived to drive them off. As they went, they shouted Alexandra's name and chanted, "*Niemetzkaya bliad,*" "German whore."

When police opened fire on looters, they screamed, "You have no ammunition to fight Germans, but you have lots to kill Russians." It was a telling insult. General Brusilov still held Przemyśl, taken at such cost on the Galician front; but he pointed out that it was no longer a fortress in the technical sense, since its guns lacked any ammunition. At most 6 prewar regulars were left alive in companies of 250 men; five or six original officers were left in his regiments. "In a year of war, the regular army had vanished," he wrote. "It was replaced by an army of ignoramuses."

—

Rasputin was aware that a full report of the incident at the Yar—indecent exposure, brawling, threatening police officers—had been made by the Moscow police prefect. He was safe only while the compromised Nikolai Maklakov remained as interior minister, and there were signs that Maklakov's hold on his office was slipping. It was time for another tactical retreat to Siberia. "Grieved long to get home," he cabled his wife on June 1. "Annushka is in trouble will be operated on they don't let her out." The reference was to Vyrubova, who was waiting for an operation on her crushed foot. In the evening he got drunk with Manus and went to the seamstress's room again. On his way back he pestered the caretaker's wife on the staircase, asking her to kiss him. She freed herself and rang his doorbell to have his maid lead him back into the apartment.

He left for Siberia the following day, shadowed by two Okhrana agents. The Russians abandoned the Przemyśl fortress. The defeat was a further blow to Grand Duke Nicholas Nikolayevich, already weakened by Rasputin and by the Moscow rioters' calls for him to be made tsar. The empress was envious of his height, his popularity, his image as the only strong Romanov; the comparison with her "little hubby" was hard for her pride to bear. Given her outrage at his threat to hang her Friend, Rasputin and Vyrubova easily persuaded her that the commander in chief was already speaking of himself as Nicholas III. As Rasputin changed trains in Moscow, she wrote to the tsar of her loathing of "N," for Nikolasha, the grand duke. She was not inhibited by the fact that her husband was his cousin's guest at the Stavka. "I have absolutely no faith in N.," she said. "Know him to be far from clever and having gone against a Man of God, his work can't be blessed or his advice good. . . . Russia will not be blessed if her sovereign lets a Man of God sent to help him be persecuted, I am sure." She rarely used Rasputin's name in letters, preferring "Friend," but she did so now. "You know N.'s hatred for Grigory is intense," she added.

She returned to the fray two days later. "N's fault and Witte's that the Duma exists, and it has caused you more worry than joy," she began. "Oh, I do not like

N having anything to do with these sittings which concern interior questions, he understands our country so little and imposes upon the ministers with his loud voice and gesticulations. I can go wild sometimes at his fat position. . . . Nobody knows who is Emperor now. . . . It is as though N settles all, makes the choices and changes. It makes me utterly wretched." The letter dripped with thoughtful malice. It invoked her husband's nightmare memories of Witte and 1905; it damned the grand duke with arrogance and lèse-majesté; it ridiculed—"his fat position"—and it mercilessly exploited her position as the "wretched" wife. And it was all manifestly untrue. The grand duke was touchingly loyal to his diminutive cousin. His knowledge of "our country" was infinitely broader than her own; he was a soldier surrounded by ordinary Russians, she an Anglo-German isolated from all but one, Rasputin. That, indeed, was the rub. He was the only Romanov whom Russians liked and respected. With Rasputin's eager endorsement the empress set out to undermine the commander in chief at the climax of the German assault.

Nicholas was in no state to resist her. "I am beginning to feel my old heart," he complained to her. "The first time it was in August of last year, after the Samsonov catastrophe, and again now—it feels so heavy on the left side when I breathe. But what can I do!" What he did do was take cocaine, which he said cleared his stuffy nose and restored his energy. Alexandra wrote back that she hoped that "the cocain [*sic*] helped well." She said that she was finding it difficult to sleep because of stomachache but that a hot water bottle and opium helped. At the front Russian artillery was firing on its own men. A battalion had been ordered to attack a German position with uncut wire and machine guns at Opatow. The survivors lay in shell holes in no-man's-land. When they began to wave white flags, Russian gunners were ordered to open fire on them.

———

The Trans-Siberian Railroad dropped Rasputin in Tyumen on June 6. He stayed for a night at the Tyumen monastery with his friend Martian, the father superior, who gave a dinner party for him, inviting local worthies and their wives. The Okhrana agents reported that Rasputin was perceptibly drunk after dinner, and that Martian was complaining that he was drinking the monastery dry. The following day Rasputin went with Martian and his maid-mistress Dunia to a scenic spot for a picnic. They rode monastery horses—Rasputin had been a good horseman since he was a small child—and took a parcel of fresh cucumbers and half a pail of wine. Then he left for Pokrovskoye.

On June 11 Rasputin held a party for villagers at his house. "He had a few drinks," the agents reported, "wound up the gramophone, danced, and incoherently joined in singing." He started bragging about his influence peddling. He said that he had gotten three hundred Baptists released from punishment for sectarianism; he was meant to get a thousand rubles from each of them but had collected only five thousand rubles in total. He also said that "when I was at the tsar's last time," he had persuaded Nicholas to defer the next draft of new troops until the autumn, after the harvest was in.

It was an empty boast. The losses in June were so great that the government was proposing to call up even the second category or *ban* of men aged over thirty-five: the second *ban* had only been called up twice in Russian history, in Napoleon's 1812 invasion and the Crimean war in 1854. Thousands of conscripts were arriving at the front in a state of shock. Those with rifles often did not know how to reload them. "Many had never seen a railroad car before, and the long ride down seemed to have unbalanced them in some peculiar way," an officer wrote, "for when they arrived they were little short of demented." Their officers hardly knew what to do with them. "Keep a heavy guard over them until we go into action," an officer advised a colleague. "They will be the first meat."

The man most responsible for the shell shortage, the war minister, Vladimir Sukhomlinov, fell at last. One of his protégés, Col. Sergei Myasoyedov, had been hanged in secret for treason in February. When the news was leaked in March, the war minister's reputation was savaged. Myasoyedov had been dismissed twice from the army before the war, when his extravagance, loose-living friends, and visits to the Second Reich—he had stayed several times with the kaiser at his hunting lodge—led to accusations that he was in German pay. Sukhomlinov had intervened to have him returned to duty. The yellow press revived the charges at the beginning of 1915, and the colonel was arrested on a double charge of pillage and espionage. While serving on the Prussian front, he had sent a relative a lamp and a picture. This constituted the "pillage," though he maintained that he had bought them. As to espionage, he was said to have received ten thousand rubles from the Germans. The money was never traced, but the colonel was shot. The war minister's pretty and promiscuous young wife had been linked with the dead colonel; she was now "coupled in none too pleasant a way with certain well-known German agents."

When it was discovered that Sukhomlinov had turned down a French offer to supply shells, with the airy assurance that "there is nothing to worry about," the tsar could no longer protect him. He was dismissed in June, though Nicholas at first allowed him to keep his apartment in Tsarskoye Selo and to remain at court. This caused such an outburst of public fury that he was arrested and convicted of espionage. The examining magistrate showed the secret police general Vassilyev the "convincing proof" of his guilt. It was a postcard addressed to Sukhomlinov's wife. It was sent from Carlsbad by a prewar acquaintance called Altshiller. The message read: "It's raining in Carlsbad, the roads are bad, so long walks are out of the question." Vassilyev said that this was hardly overwhelming evidence.

The magistrate retorted that the reference to bad roads and no walks obviously covered up something else—"the devil knows what the man meant!" At the trial the prosecutor failed to establish that the war minister had received any large sum of money. Nevertheless, Sukhomlinov, the man who had mobilized the Russian armies less than twelve months before, was found guilty and imprisoned. His replacement was Gen. Alexis Polivanov, able and respected but no admirer of Rasputin. "Forgive me," Alexandra wrote to her husband, "but I don't like the choice of Minister of War Polivanov. Is he not our Friend's enemy?" His card was marked before he was behind his desk.

The casualties were felt deep into Russia. "Getting empty in the villages," a peasant told Bernard Pares with a kind of cheery objectiveness. The man said his three brothers had all been killed at the front. The first two were there long enough to distinguish themselves. He said of the third, "Him they put up like a sheep!" Another British observer, Gen. Alfred Knox, visited a village where twenty-four of the twenty-six men called up had been killed. Nicholas Nikolayevich admitted that "training is beneath criticism"; that, in Alexandra's eyes, was a characterization he shared. Her letters became near-hysterical. "I loathe your being at headquarters," she wrote the tsar on June 12, "listening to N's advice which is not good and cannot be—he has no right to act as he does, mixing in your concerns. All are shocked that the ministers go with reports to him, as though he were now the sovereign. Ah, my Nicky, things are not as they ought to be and therefore N keeps you near to have a hold over you with his ideas and bad counsels."

———

If Rasputin could not defer the draft, his importance was underlined to his fellow peasants when a steamer with the governor of Tobolsk arrived on its regular run. The starets went aboard and persuaded the governor to drop a fine of fifty rubles imposed on a Pokrovskoye peasant for building a house without a permit. Strolling through the village, he told the secret police agents that three ministers "adored" him—Prime Minister Goremykin and Prince V. Shakhovskoy, the trade minister; he did not name the third—and that he knew Nicholas Nickolayevich very well. He said that the grand duke would have given Russia a constitution in 1905 had he been able to, and that he would soon get his just deserts.

The starets was in a poor state on June 13. Memories of the near-fatal stabbing came back to him. A lady had gone to his neighbor Natalya the evening before. She had asked about Rasputin and then added that she would like to stay in Natalya's house. When this was refused she left the village. Natalya told Rasputin of this mysterious woman the next morning. He at once sent a man to find her. She could not be found. The agents noticed that Rasputin became very nervous and described the ladies he knew in Alexandra's circle, apparently frightened that she was checking up on his behavior. In Tsarskoye Selo, Vyrubova was also out of sorts. She wired Rasputin: "Got a feeling like something terrible is about to happen miss you wrote to you bless me. Anna."

In fact, it was the tsar who had ordered an investigation. As Rasputin had feared, Maklakov had been dismissed. His successor was Prince Nikolai Shcherbatov, an able man who said he found the interior ministry in "such a muddle as I could not reconcile myself to." Rasputin had no hold over him; although the empress would start agitating for his removal within six weeks, for the moment the starets was vulnerable. One of the prince's first acts was to order General Dzhunkovsky, his assistant and the Okhrana chief, to produce a complete report on Rasputin and the incident at the Yar in Moscow. Dzhunkovsky was exposed to the full Andronnikov treatment—a flattering letter, gifts of an icon and a Bukhara cloak—but in vain. He took advantage of an audience with Nicholas over the Moscow riots to brief him on the starets. "I reported to the emperor about Rasputin, about his behavior at the Yar, and offered a paper concerning the pernicious nature of his influence that was drawing Russia to destruction," he later testified "I asked the emperor's permission to continue my investigations. He said, 'I not only give you permission but I also ask you to do it. These reports should be made only to us—let us keep it between us.' "

The tsar had left on June 10 for the Stavka, where he was exposed to more criticism of Rasputin. Grand Duke Nicholas Nikolayevich first let fly at Rasputin for his debauchos. As he became angrier he moved on to more sinister ground—German agents had access to Rasputin; the peasant knew everything that was being done at the Stavka through the empress. "I never knew about any of this," the tsar said. "I could never have imagined." The grand duke then suggested that Alexandra come to the Stavka to be shown the Okhrana file. "Put an end to him," he urged. "Resolve the matter within the family." The tsar agreed.

Rasputin was keeping in close touch with the empress. She wrote to Nicholas on June 13, telling him to write at once "if you have any questions for our Fr[iend]." Two days later she indicated that Rasputin felt trouble was being stirred behind his back—"he regrets you did not tell him more"—and forwarded a direct message from him: "Pay less attention to people; use your own instinct." The Dzhunkovsky report was an ill-guarded secret, and Rasputin had gotten wind of it from his numerous contacts in the secret police. The empress was alerted. She read a copy of it, at first weeping, then in a fury when she found that her favorite nephew had seen it. "My enemy Dzhunkovsky," she wrote to Nicholas, "has shown that vile, filthy paper to Dmitri. . . . Such a sin; & as tho you had said to him, that you have had enough of these dirty stories & wished him to be severely punished—ah, it's so vile. . . . If we let Our Friend be persecuted we and our country shall suffer for it. . . . I am so weary, such heartaches and pain from all this—the idea of dirt being spread about one we venerate is more than terrible. Ah, my love, when at *last* will you thump with your hand on the table & scream at Dzhunkovsky & others when they act wrongly—one does not fear you—and one must—they must be frightened of you. . . . If Dzhunkovsky is with you, call him, tell him you know he has shown that paper in town & that you order him to tear it up & not to dare speak of Grigory as he does & that he acts as a traitor. . . . Oh my Boy, make one tremble before you. . . . You are always too kind & all profit. It cannot go on like that."

Rasputin knew what was up. "Well, your Dzhunkovsky's had it," he told the agents in Pokrovskoye. He was correct. Prince Shcherbatov soon received a note from the tsar: "I insist on General Dzhunkovsky's immediate dismissal." In everyone's view it was Rasputin and Alexandra who had done the insisting; the general testified later that Nicholas "did it under the influence of the tsarina." His replacement, Vassilyev, was in no doubt that it was a poor career move to take on the starets. "To tell the truth," he wrote of his predecessor, "he appears to have been rather tactless in his behavior." The new man, who had full access to Rasputin's daily movements from his agents' notebooks, was committed to staying dumb.

Rasputin's mood lifted. On June 17 Father Martian and Rasputin's protégé Varnava, the bishop of Tobolsk, came to visit him in a carriage. Varnava had proved as unpleasant as the synod had feared when Rasputin had forced through his appointment. He had developed into a pogrom lover, baring his teeth through his beard when he hissed the word *Jew* in his strident sermons. His insults were so crude, so tasteless that they excited his audience; he called his many enemies—liberals, fellow churchmen, the intelligentsia, foreigners— "bloodsucking kikes." He had, the synod complained, "soon turned his diocese into a private domain of Rasputin." He was "rude with clergymen subordinate to him," moving them from parish to parish at Rasputin's whim. His sister, the wife of a petty clerk at the synod, was well informed on church politics; "simple but dexterous, clever and highly devoted to her brother"; both were classified by the commission as "tentacles devoted to Rasputin." Varnava had taken a leaf out of Rasputin's book; Stankevich, the Tobolsk governor, complained that the bishop was helping people evade military service by selling them exempt positions in the church.

The clerics brought two kegs of wine with them. They got merry with Rasputin. The steamer from Tyumen called at Pokrovskoye the next morning. A Jew unknown to the agents, but thought to be a businessman from Perm, was aboard. He spent the forty-minute stop at the village talking with Rasputin about obtaining army contracts. Rasputin's wife and Dunia took the steamer for a shopping expedition to the city. While they were away he sent a brief telegram to keep in touch with Vyrubova: "How's health, kisses." The women returned with Elizaveta Solovyova, whose intimacy with Rasputin had been noted in Petrograd in February. The new parish priest, Father Sergei, whom Rasputin had had Varnava appoint, came to pay his compliments and kiss his hand. At 8:00 P.M. the agents saw Rasputin come out of his house with a red face, "apparently drunk," with the pretty Madame Solovyova. "They took a carriage and drove deep into the forest," the agents noted. "They returned after one hour, he was very pale."

The starets had more fun on June 28. Patushinskaya, an officer's wife from Yalutorovsk, came to see him. When he staggered out of the house, she held him under one arm while Solovyova supported him under the other. He was fondling Patushinskaya "over the lower part of her body," the agents said. "During the day the gramophone played and he was very cheerful, drank wine and beer." The ménage à trois came to an end the next morning, when Solovyova got a telegram from her irate husband ordering her to return to Petrograd. Rasputin consoled himself with Patushinskaya, walking around the yard holding her and singing.

On June 30 he took a morning swim in the river and went to the wife of a neighbor, Deacon Ermolai, who read the psalms in the village church. His mind was not on clerical matters. She was waiting for him at the open window of her house and spent half an hour with him. "He visits her almost daily with intimate purposes," the agents noted. In the afternoon Patushinskaya received a telegram from her husband commanding her to return to Yalutorovsk. Before she left on the steamer the agents saw her "voluptuously kiss Rasputin on the lips, nose, cheeks, beard, and hands."

The ability to remain on good terms with husbands he was cuckolding sometimes deserted the holy man. When Elena Patushinskaya's husband objected to the affair, Rasputin had him transferred to Odessa, where he shot himself. In general, though, the husbands accepted their lot, and the phenomenon was well enough known—Rasputin made no attempt to conceal it—to add credence to the rumors of his liaison with the empress.

After a short trip to Tobolsk to see Varnava—the agents did not travel with him and there is no record of the conversations between the two—Rasputin welcomed Ivan Ivanovich Dobrovolsky and his wife, Maria Semyonovna, to the village. Dobrovolsky was approaching fifty, a corrupt and obese state councillor with a sinecure as an inspector of colleges. His wife was twenty years younger. The morning after her arrival on the steamer, she played the piano while Rasputin applauded and stamped his feet. Then he began embracing her—"not being ashamed of his daughters' presence," the agents wrote. They did not bother to mention the patient Dobrovolsky. After that Rasputin with Dobrovolskaya and the children "went out into the fields, sang songs, ran about, and Rasputin played ball games with them."

Deacon Ermolai was equally long-suffering. On July 7 Rasputin and Dobro-volsky were invited to lunch by the villager Arapov. The agents watched as Rasputin "left the house drunk and visited the wife of the psalm reader Ermolai." He returned home but would have gone to her again had the maid Dunia not asked him not to. He told her "to go to hell" and took a walk in the rain with the agents. He started to talk about the war and how his objections to it had been seen by some as treason. "Last year, when I was in the hospital and rumor had it that the war was about to begin, I asked the tsar not to fight," he told them. "I sent him about twenty telegrams. . . . They even wanted to hand me over for trial. The tsar was informed, and he said that 'these are our personal affairs and can't be tried.' "

He visited Patushinskaya later in July, taking his two daughters and the Dobrovolskys and Ermolais with him. They settled down around Dobrovolskaya as she played the piano in the steamer lounge. At Tyumen they took a train for Yalutorovsk. Patushinskaya was at the station to meet them in a carriage with two horses. She let Rasputin into her carriage while the others took cabs. At her house they were welcomed by her husband. Three husbands were now present—the deacon Ermolai, the fat state councillor Dobrovolsky, and the army officer Patushinsky—and Rasputin was fucking all their wives. They must have known; the Okhrana agents certainly did. At 10:00 on the evening of his arrival, they saw Rasputin jump out of a window onto the terrace of the house. Patushinskaya slipped through another window into the courtyard, "made a gesture to Rasputin, and they both disappeared into the dark."

At noon the next day, Rasputin took a carriage ride in the forests with Patushinskaya and his daughters. When they came back the daughters went into the house while Rasputin and Patushinskaya went to an empty summerhouse in the gardens. It was a charming little place; the servants told the agents that it had housed exiled Decembrist revolutionaries almost a century before. Perhaps it reminded Rasputin of his pseudo-rape by the general's wife. The couple spent twenty minutes there. Rasputin left the next morning with his daughters for the train and steamer trip back to Pokrovskoye.

———

On July 23 Warsaw, the hub of Russian power in Poland for a century, fell to the Germans. Nicholas was overcome with grief and humiliation when he broke the news to the empress and Vyrubova. "It cannot go on like this," he said. The Russian retreat turned into a rout. "Creeping like some huge beast," a Russian general wrote, the Germans had turned their heavy guns onto his positions until they had obliterated them. "Then the beast would cautiously stretch out its paws, the infantry units, which would seize the demolished trenches." The poet Vladimir Mayakovsky howled with anger at the fate of the infantryman:

You can't
Simply cannot
Bury him alive
In trenches and dugouts—
Murderers!

As they fell back the Russians torched the towns and villages and forced their miserable inhabitants to flee east with them into Russia.

The scorched earth policy suited the Germans. They found shelter enough among the ruins; they had no civilians to provide for, and the Russians often ran about setting fire to haystacks but left the growing crops intact. Senior officers loaded their mistresses, furniture, even "cages filled with canaries," onto trains while more than a million refugees stumbled beside the track and through the fields. They were emaciated. When they came across an army field kitchen, the men tore basins of food from each other while women with starving children at their breasts trampled each other to snatch at gray hunks of stewed pork. In these shambling columns, twenty miles and more in length, a British military observer glimpsed vignettes—"two carts tied together and drawn by a single miserable horse, one family driving a cow, a poor man and his wife each with a huge bundle of rubbish tied up in a sheet." When he asked them where they were headed, they did not know.

With them the refugees brought epidemics and panic. "Unburied corpses are strewn along the road," the cabinet was told. "Everywhere there is carrion and an unbearable stench. This human mass is spreading over Russia like a vast wave." Spy fever and pogroms intensified. Jews were hanged on trumped-up charges; their shops, synagogues, and houses were looted. Black Hundred newspapers accused them of "sending their gold to the Germans; this tainted gold has been found in airplanes, coffins, barrels of vodka, and breasts of duck and mutton." It was, a Jewish deputy complained, "naught but an ignoble lie, invented by men who are trying to cover their own crimes." The French ambassador warned that the Jews should be treated well, because "there is in the United States a very large, influential, and wealthy Jewish community who are very indignant at your treatment of their co-religionists." It was, he said, "to no avail." As to politics, Wilton wrote to the London *Times* on July 31 that "we may have a situation too serious for anything less than a dictatorship, if not worse." The bureaucracy was "on the verge of complete breakdown. . . . The authority of the government is fast slipping out of its hands."

———

Rasputin arrived at Petrograd at 10:10 A.M. on the same day, summoned by the tsar. He was met by Nikolai Solovyov, the synod member whose wife the starets had fucked in the forests of Pokrovskoye earlier in the month. He saw Nicholas at the Alexander Palace on August 4. He realized that an interrogation over the Yar incident and an immediate return to Siberia were in the cards; he had already sent two identical telegrams to his wife and to Patushinskaya: "See you very soon, we kiss you." The audience was not recorded, of course, but Vassilyev, who owed his promotion to his predecessor's ill-judged handling of the affair, was naturally curious. He asked Rasputin about it the next time they met.

"He confessed, without any more ado, the sin he had committed in Moscow," the secret policeman wrote. He used his standard line, that to sin was human, and that God understood and forgave. "What would you have, my dear man?" he asked Vassilyev. "Who is innocent before God is also innocent before the tsar." Nicholas was angry that Rasputin had referred to the empress—"the old woman"—during his drunken ramblings at the Yar. Rasputin lied, denying that he had made any reference to the imperial family. They also discussed the commander in chief. Rasputin urged that the grand duke be dismissed and that the tsar himself replace him. He later boasted that he had "sunk Nikolasha" at this interview.

He had, nevertheless, come close to a fall, and he knew it. He left Petrograd on the first train the next morning. Vyrubova and her sister Alexandra Alexandrovna von Pistolkors picked him up at his apartment in a limousine from the imperial motor pool and dropped him off at the station. They stayed in the car rather than risk being spotted on the platform. The agents noted other less discreet admirers who were there to wave him off: Tatyana Fyodorovna Shakhovskaya, a twenty-six-year-old princess; the infatuated Baroness Kusova; a swindler, Miller; the cuckold Dobrovolsky and his wife.

The contrition Rasputin had expressed to the tsar the evening before lasted long enough for the train to pull out of the station. The agents watched him chatting with three unknown ladies in the carriage. When they left the train at Kamyshlov, he got down onto the platform to say good-bye to them. They introduced him to the army officers who were meeting them. They talked about the Guseva stabbing and something about a hospital. The agents heard one of the officers, a lieutenant colonel, mutter to another: "It's quite clear that the fellow has hypnosis in his eyes."

Rasputin was in a petulant mood with the Okhrana men when the train moved on. Solovyov had been seen meeting him when he had arrived in Petrograd. The new synod procurator, Alexander Samarin, a well-respected Moscow nobleman, told Solovyov that such conduct was unfitting for a member of the synod. "Solovyov had a bit of trouble from Samarin for meeting me at the station in Petrograd," Rasputin said. "But Samarin isn't going to be procurator of the synod for long." He glared at the agents and said, "Wasn't it you who reported my meeting with Solovyov?"

"It's none of your business," the agents told him.

"Who else can it have been?" Rasputin said. "The emperor asked about this report and said—perhaps the agents informed on Solovyov. So I said to the tsar—I dunno, maybe it's them. Well, I'm going home, and I don't know myself how long I'll stay there—a week, perhaps longer, it depends how matters stand." He said that the tsar had offered him his own carriage to go to Siberia, but he had refused the offer. "Once I was coming back from Tsarskoye Selo to Petrograd, and around midnight I saw one of you agents hiding behind an elevator," he said menacingly. "If I find out who he is, he's gonna have a bad time."

On August 6, as the train crawled toward the Urals, the Germans overran the last Russian strong point in Poland, the fortress of Novogeorgievsk. It had a garrison of 100,000 men with 1,600 guns, but a German patrol had captured the chief engineer and found accurate plans of the fortifications among his papers. "We are being wiped out," the defenders radioed as the Germans systematically destroyed them. "Everything is being swept away, everyone is in panic." A solitary pilot flew out of the ruins to announce that it had fallen. Polivanov told the cabinet that "the army is no longer retreating—it is simply running away." Worse followed. "No matter how badly things are going at the front," the war minister said, "there is another still more terrible situation that now looms before Russia. I feel obliged to inform the government that, when I presented my report this morning, His Majesty told me that he had decided to relieve the grand duke and take over the supreme command of the army himself." Rasputin's vengeance was closing in on Nikolasha.

Rasputin arrived at Tyumen on August 8 and stayed overnight with Father Martian at the monastery. He took a single first-class cabin on the 11:00 A.M. steamer for Pokrovskoye the next morning. He was out to celebrate. Two hours upriver he came out of his cabin drunk. He started talking with ten soldiers who were aboard and gave them twenty-five rubles to sing to him. After a few minutes he went to his cabin and returned with a hundred rubles. He asked them to sing louder and started joining in the choruses. The singing had been going on for an hour when he took the men to the second-class dining room to treat them to a meal. Russian soldiers were beneath society, forbidden to enter first- and second-class compartments on trains, barred from theater stalls, not allowed to enter restaurants and cafés. Civilians addressed them in the familiar, *thou*, as they would a child or pet. On steamers they were restricted to the lower decks. The steamer captain ordered them out of the dining room.

Angry, Rasputin went with them. He made them form a circle, placed himself in the middle, and conducted their singing. His high spirits returned. He gave them another twenty-five rubles and paid fifteen rubles for them to have the third-class dinner. He went back to his cabin, emerging from it to complain that he had lost three thousand rubles. He then returned to his cabin, reappearing twenty minutes later drunker than ever. The agents became alarmed. "He visited third class and had a quarrel with a passenger called Raszumovsky," they noted. "The latter was about to give Rasputin a thrashing, but it passed off peacefully. Then Rasputin quarreled with another merchant from Tyumen—Mikhalev. The deeds of the Tobolsk bishop Varnava were mentioned, at which Mikhalev spat and left." After that Rasputin lurched around the ship until he came across a waiter, whom he called a "swindler" and accused of stealing his three thousand rubles. The waiter asked some passengers to be eyewitnesses on his behalf and complained to the captain, who said he would report the incident to the police in Tobolsk. Rasputin went back to his cabin, opened the window, and slumped with his head on the table, muttering while the curious passengers "feasted their eyes on him."

"Why not take off his hair and shave his beard with some clippers?" one of them suggested. Another laughed. "Rasputin, may your reputation as a holy man last forever." The agents hurried into the cabin and shut the window. At 6:00 P.M., as the ship steamed past the unchanging riverbanks in the yellow heat, Rasputin fell to the floor. He was still there when the ship arrived at Pokrovskoye at 8:00. The agents asked the captain to send two crewmen to help them with Rasputin; the four of them dragged him off. Rasputin's daughters and his brother-in-law Raspopov turned up at the landing stage with a cart and carried him home.

He was up at 10:00 the next morning. He asked the agents what had happened on the steamer trip, "gasping constantly and wondering how he could have gotten drunk on only three bottles of wine." He was worried that word might get out to the tsar. "See, fellow," he told an agent, "it's not good the way it happened." He referred back to the Yar incident. "Dzhunkovsky was dismissed, and now he probably will think it's because of me and I don't even know who he is," he said. "Your guv'nor will be sacked soon, as well." The agents asked, "Which one?" "No, I dunno what his name is," Rasputin said, and changed the subject.

———

Fury over Rasputin's influence, the headlong dismissals that followed his threats, spilled over into the press. Maklakov had used wartime censorship to slash out any reference to him. Shcherbatov, knowing that his own time was short, allowed several attacks to be printed. On August 15 the liberal paper *Birzhevye Vedomosti* ran this headline: HOW COULD IT HAPPEN? Signing himself Lukian, the writer asked how a "dark parvenu" had mocked Russia for so long. He said that those who tolerated him made up a "core of evil . . . whose treachery and vacillation have become common gossip. . . . It is a style of 'all things are possible, all things permitted.' . . . In such a world not even Rasputin seemed unusual. . . . We have reached the point where nothing surprises us anymore, not even Rasputin. No one even realized the disgrace. Simply an effort was made to silence the press. . . . Yet what was there to exaggerate when the naked truth was worse than any lie?" Two days later *Vechernee Vremya* ran a piece suggesting that Rasputin was opposed to the war and working for a "German party."

On August 19 Varnava sent warning from Tobolsk via a priest, Father Nikolai, that the episode on the steamer had been reported to the police and was by no means forgotten. Rasputin spent most of the day with Ermolai's wife, having packed the deacon off to church. The unwelcome news was given to him in the evening. The Tobolsk governor was about to have Rasputin arrested by administrative order to serve three months in prison for drunkenness and dissolute conduct. Only Varnava's intervention was preventing the arrest from being carried out. Rasputin spat and asked, "What do I care about the governor?"

Indeed, he had little reason to. The press campaign merely strengthened him. Alexandra used the articles as a whip with which to beat Shcherbatov, and to convince her husband that he must at once declare himself commander in chief if his authority was to survive. On August 20 Nicholas and Alexandra made a rare visit to their capital. They knelt at his father's tomb in the Peter and Paul Cathedral and then drove to the Cathedral of Our Lady of Kazan, where they prayed for guidance before the icon of the Virgin. They dined with Vyrubova at the Alexander Palace; the tsar was to meet his council of ministers later in the evening. He was nervous, and Vyrubova took a small icon from around her neck and pressed it into his hand. As the meeting dragged on the two women peered in through the French windows from the balcony, watching the foreign minister, Serge Sazonov, argue passionately against the tsar's decision. All the ministers present were in agreement. The administration would be paralyzed if Nicholas removed himself to the Stavka, two days' railroad ride from the seat of government. The blame for fresh military defeats would fall on his head. It was no moment for the autocrat to play soldiers.

The ministers did not mention that the influence of Rasputin and the empress would increase greatly in the tsar's absence; it was understood by both sides. "I did not dot the *i*'s or mention any names, and indeed there was no need to," Sazonov said of his pleadings with Nicholas. "The tsar easily grasped the unsaid meaning, and I saw how distasteful my words were to him. It was painful to me to refer to the dangerous part that the empress had begun to play since Rasputin gained possession of her will and intellect." Nicholas did not contradict him, but, he wrote, "as I spoke he seemed to recede farther away from me till at last I felt that a deep gulf lay between us." Nicholas heard them out, sitting bolt upright. He gave his fatalism full rein. "He replied that he felt it to be his mission and his duty to assume this responsibility," the agriculture minister Alexander Krivoshein told the London *Times* correspondent Robert Wilton. "If it was written that he and his dynasty should perish . . . well, it was written, and he could not alter it." In two days he would leave for the Stavka. He clutched her icon in his hand, Vyrubova said; when he returned he was sweating.

The following morning eight of the thirteen cabinet members met in Sazonov's rooms at the foreign ministry. They signed a joint letter of resignation to the tsar. "Yesterday at the meeting of the council, we unanimously begged you not to remove Grand Duke Nicholas from the High Command of the Army," it said. "We venture once more to tell you that to the best of our judgment your decision threatens with serious consequences Russia, your dynasty, and your person." The irreconcilable differences within the government, it said, were "inadmissible at all times, and at the present moment fatal." The letter was handed to Nicholas on August 21. He left for the Stavka the same evening. He refused to accept the resignations, but Alexandra would drive all those who signed the letter out of office.

She wrote her husband a triumphant letter to read on the train. "I cannot find words to express all I want to—my heart is far too full," she began. "Never have they seen such firmness in you before, proving yourself the Autocrat without wh. Russia cannot exist. Forgive me, I beseech you, my Angel, for having left you no peace but I too well know yr marvellously gentle character. . . . I have suffered so terribly, & phisically [*sic*] overtired myself these 2 days, & morally worried (& worry still till all is done at the Headquarters & Nikolasha goes) only then shall I feel calm. . . . You see they are afraid of me & so come to you when alone—they know I have a will of my own when I feel I am in the right—& you are now—we know this, so you make them tremble before your courage & will. God is with you & our Friend for you. . . . His holy angels guard & guide you. . . . Sleep well, my sunshine, Russia's Saviour."

Sensing catastrophe, Sir George Buchanan sought the empress out in a last-ditch effort to persuade her that no man could run both an empire and a modern war. "You will win not laurels, but a crown of thorns," the court chamberlain warned the ambassador. Alexandra told Buchanan that the tsar's place was with his army in the field. "I have no patience with ministers who try to prevent him doing his duty," she said. "The emperor is unfortunately weak, but I am not, and I intend to be firm." Her face was set and cold, and she dismissed him with "haughty displeasure, barely giving him her hand to kiss."

The Romanov clan was beside itself with fear. Grand Duke Andrei Vladimirovich visited the dowager empress, his aunt. "I found Aunt Minnie terribly despondent," he wrote in his diary. "She believes that the removal of NN [Nicholas Nikolayevich] will lead to N's [Nicholas's] inevitable ruin. She kept asking, 'Where are we going? Where are we going? It isn't Nicky he is sweet, and honest, and good—it's all her doing. . . . She alone is responsible for all that is going on. It was not my dear boy who did this!' " She was reminded of the times of Paul I, "who in his last year began removing everyone loyal, and our great-great-great-grandfather's sad end haunts her in all its horror." Paul was strangled in a palace coup.

The tsar confirmed that the deed was done on his arrival at the Stavka. "Thank God it is all over, and here I am with this new responsibility on my shoulders!" he wrote to Alexandra, telling her that he had read and reread her letter and that it had put him at peace. "Nikolasha came in with a kind, brave smile, and asked simply when I would order him to go. I answered in the same manner that he could remain for two days." The empress knew her man; she feared that backsliding would follow any delay in getting the grand duke safely posted away to a consolation command in the distant Caucasus. "Get Niko-lasha's nomination quicker done," she fired back. "No dawdling, it's bad for the cause." The tsar complied. The grand duke was dispatched immediately, not even allowed leave in Petrograd on his way.

Thus, a tsar, who had led no more than a company as a young man, and whose knowledge of weapons systems was limited to the horse and saber, took responsibility for the six million men of a whipped and bleeding army. From the rear his imperceptive and unbalanced wife reassured him that she and her friend were in control. "Do not fear for what remains behind," she wrote, "Don't laugh at silly old wify, but she has 'trousers' on unseen. . . . God will give me the strength to help you . . . & you have Grigory's St. Nicholas to guard & guide you." The spectacle, a British observer wrote, was "amazing, extravagant and pitiful . . . and one without parallel in the history of civilized nations."

Who was to blame? "The loathsome Rasputin," Robert Wilton wrote privately to London, "played no small part in suggesting the tsar's mystical motives for taking up the High Command. Rasputin always works in the same way. He tells the empress that he has had a vision that certain things must be done. . . . The empress then retails this stuff to her husband and the trick is done. It reminds one of . . . the Byzantine court."

CHAPTER 19

"God Opens
Everything to Him"

Alexandra now careered into politics with manic energy. She dominated her husband in letters, the cajoling and bullying stream of words and dashes and underlinings filling the black leather suitcase in which he kept them. Her views were simple, and ruthless. The autocracy must be preserved at any cost, "for Baby's sake." She despised constitutions, "parliamentarists," the "rotten people" who demanded a government responsible to the Duma, and the cities that bred them. She wanted them hanged or otherwise disposed of—a "strong railway accident" would do. She had cut herself off from other Romanovs. She believed in God, the dynasty, and "the people," of whom Rasputin was the divine manifestation.

She was proud of the power her husband's absence gave her. "I am the first Russian empress since Catherine the Great to receive the Ministers," she boasted to him. Women in Russia were stronger in character, decisiveness, and temper than their menfolk, Ivan Turgenev thought. Another writer, Somerset Maugham, was struck by "the aggressive way in which [Russian] women treat men. They seem to take a sensual pleasure in humiliating them in front of others." Maugham found Russian men "femininely passive, they cry easily." It was a phenomenon that all applied to Alexandra and her husband.

The empress's relation with Rasputin became one of partnership. She provided policy, and he supplied her with politicians, and justification. She had an acute eye for the slightest liberal tendency; when she saw it she was pitiless in destroying it. Her quarry included those who had begged her husband not to leave for the Stavka, some of the most able and respected men in Russia—the foreign minister, the synod procurator, and the ministers of the interior, finance, education, and agriculture. Her contempt for politicians included monarchists. Alexander Guchkov was the leader of the Octobrists, the most right-wing of the major parties, the son of a Moscow tycoon, vigorous, with alert gray eyes, a man who had fought with the Boers in South Africa. He was a royalist and a natural ally, a conservative who stood for landed and industrial interests, but he was a Duma man. "My own beloved darling," Alexandra wrote as Nicholas traveled to the Stavka. "Guchkov ought to be got rid of, only how is the question, war-time—is there nothing one can hook on to have him shut up? He hunts after anarchy & against our dynasty, wh our Friend said God would protect."

She needed a reason for such wholesale changes, and a list of replacements. Rasputin gave her both. His enmity—though she always expressed it in reverse, as the hatred of the intended victim for her Friend—was ground enough for dismissal. "God opens everything to Him," she wrote. Likewise, to enjoy the blessing of the starets was sufficient recommendation for the newcomer. Did Rasputin not have "a wonderful brain—ready to understand everything"? Her campaigns could take several months, scores of letters, but she was, utterly, persistent.

Rasputin was vulnerable to the holders of three key posts. The synod procurator was responsible for church discipline, and the chief of police presided over a network of agents and informers. The interior minister was in many ways the most powerful figure in the cabinet, with broad control over the police and censorship. The three incumbents were hostile, they, or their predecessors, had reported harshly on his conduct. Dzhunkovsky, the errant policeman, went first. Alexandra had the others targeted within a week of Nicholas's departure. She began with the procurator. "Samarin seems to be continuing to speak against me," she wrote on August 25. "We shall hunt for a successor." He was dismissed within days, a fate shared by his successor, Volzhin, when he showed reluctance to meet Rasputin.

Next she turned on the interior minister. Prince Shcherbatov's tolerance of press criticism of her Friend was intolerable. She wrote to Nicholas on August 29 to urge him to replace the prince with someone who knew what was expected of him. "Have a strong & firm talk with him," she said. "Put the position of our Friend clear to him from the outset, he dare not act like Shcherb[atov] and Sam[arin], make him understand that he acts straight against us in persecuting & allowing Him [Rasputin] to be evil written about or spoken of." The new man must "listen to our Friend's councils."

Such a person, she suggested, was Alexis Nikolayevich Khvostov, the Nizhni Novgorod governor whom Rasputin had looked over four years before and thought too young to be prime minister. He was now forty-three, his frock coat stuffed with flesh, his gluttony matched by his venality. He had matured into an extreme reactionary, a Black Hundred supporter who had taken the precaution of cultivating Prince Andronnikov, and through him Vyrubova and Rasputin. Alexandra thought him a "man without petticoats," a strong figure who she assured the tsar "is very energetic, fears no one & is colossally devoted to you." She found "his body colossal . . . but the soul light and clear." For good measure he had promised to "do all in his power to stop the attacks upon our Friend."

That was the empress's opinion. The tsar checked him out with his uncle, the decent and competent justice minister A. A. Khvostov. "This is a person absolutely inexperienced in this work, one who by character is absolutely unsuitable," the elder Khvostov wrote of his nephew in a confidential note to the tsar. "This is a man who is very far from stupid, but who cannot be critical of his own instincts and judgments. He is inclined to intrigue . . . and in all probability will try to become Premier; in any case all his activities in the office of minister will not be devoted to work, but to considerations which have nothing to do with it." Nothing positive could come from appointing him interior minister; indeed, the justice minister wrote, "I expect harm." The character reference was wholly accurate; it was ignored. Alexandra insisted that Khvostov be appointed—the name means "tail" in Russian, and she called him "my Tail" or "my honest Tail" in her letters in English to Nicholas. The tsar gave way before September was out.

The new minister's first decision was to appoint Stefan Beletsky as his deputy and director of the police department. Beletsky struck Bernard Pares, who knew him personally, as a typical professional police official, resourceful, a man of the world, but "not an honest man." Neither he nor Khvostov suffered any illusions about Rasputin, whom Beletsky thought a "scandalous personage." From now on a great number of Rasputin's notes asking for favors were addressed to him. Beletsky testified later that many of them were for exemptions from military service or for subsidies, and he agreed that they were illegal. He was also well aware that Rasputin demanded sex as the price of his favors. He testified that he saved one respectable petitioner after the starets had forced his way into her bedroom, and that another, reduced to hysterics when Rasputin refused to help her unless she submitted to him, was raped when she did not.

Both men later plotted to murder the starets, but for the present they needed him as the Friend at court. Tired old Goremykin, the premier, was no obstacle to them. They drew up a political program—well spiced with invective against Jews, Masons, liberals, and socialists—that they knew would win Alexandra's approval. Prince Andronnikov pointed out that Rasputin's assistance would be essential. Beletsky arranged to pay him a retainer of eighteen thousand rubles from the secret police funds to which he had access. Vyrubova was enlisted to help. The prince told her that he would be acting, after a fashion, as Rasputin's business manager. She arranged an audience for Khvostov at the Alexander Palace. The empress was impressed by his flattery and devotion to autocracy. "I yearned to see a real man at last," she wrote to Nicholas, "and here I see and hear him." Khvostov thought her "clever and brilliant."

———

In Siberia, Rasputin was involved in an affair of blessed bones. He had never tolerated personal slights; he now extended this intolerance to his protégés. Bishop Varnava was not content with the status Rasputin had won for him; he had set his heart on becoming a metropolitan. An outstanding event in his diocese would help him achieve it. The means was Ioann Maximovich, a priest forcibly sent to Tobolsk two centuries before by Peter the Great to baptize Siberian Tartars; his remains were preserved in the crypt of the cathedral. Varnava wanted his predecessor beatified. He had sent a box of petitions to the tsar calling for Ioann to be ranked among the saints; on examination it was found that most of the signatures were in his own handwriting. The tsar passed the request to the synod. Aware that Varnava was more concerned with self-promotion than sainthood, it did nothing.

Varnava had taken the preliminary step of opening the coffin the year before. He did not, however, unwrap the body to see whether God had seen fit to preserve it and thus qualify it for beatification. The synod ordered him "not to open the face and parts of the body of Ioann." Rasputin's presence gave Varnava the confidence to flout the synod in August. The bishop, aping Rasputin, sent a series of flattering telegrams to the tsar. "Thank you, Right Reverend, for the prayers for me and my soldiers who love Christ," Nicholas replied. In another cable, to Alexandra, Varnava said that he had seen a cross appear in the sky. "I congratulate you on this vision and believe that God has sent you this sign to uphold visibly with love his devoted ones," she responded. She was not certain that it was a good sign—"crosses are not always," she wrote—but the essential of involving the rulers was achieved.

On August 27 Varnava proceeded with the glorification of Ioann Maximovich in the Tobolsk cathedral, in open defiance of the synod. Rasputin was present. The following day they met the inevitable outrage by claiming the support of the tsar. Rasputin sent a cable to Stankevich, the Tobolsk governor who was investigating the drunken incident on the steamer. "The tsar's heart will be comforted in the hands of God in front of the Saint Ioann Maximovich who responds to the prayers of the doleful Grigory Novy," it read. Varnava wired the synod that, in response to the tsar's permission to honor the saint locally, "I together with clergy of the parish sang glorification to the metropolitan Ioann of which I humbly inform your holiness and await further instructions." He signed it "sinful bishop Varnava." A ciphered telegram from Stankevich to the synod confirmed: "First glorification sung. . . . Not only the people but most informed people see this as apotheosis."

Support from the empress was swift. She cabled Varnava on August 29: "Let there be glorification of the saint to assist the tsar in his hard tasks. Alexandra." With this telegram as insurance, Varnava and Rasputin left Tobolsk for Pokrovskoye to wait for the synod's fury to break. On August 31 a cable arrived from the synod summoning the bishop to Petrograd to explain himself. He and Rasputin composed a rambling telegram to send to Nicholas. "Stavka, The Emperor," it began. "Glorification sung the people rejoiced wept the right reverend informed him demand him immediately I ordered now we go to pray . . . God with us over the whole orthodox army. Your hand is paradise. Bishop Varnava. Grigory Novy."

The defiance infuriated churchmen and laity alike. "The whole of Russia is talking about it," Grand Duke Andrei Vladimirovich wrote. "Priests everywhere are preaching to the people the kind of thing I would not dare whisper in my sleep." The hostility and the threat of a court case preyed on the starets. On September 6 he took a walk with his two agents. "You know, fellows, the soul mourns, it even makes me deaf," he told them. "Sometimes there's peace in my heart for a couple of hours, and then it's no good again."

"Why's it like that for you?"

"Because, guys, bad things are happening in this country," he replied, "and the darned papers write about me, make me very nervous. I'll have to defend myself in court."

He remained edgy. A family row broke out in Pokrovskoye on September 9. Efim Rasputin appeared and started bawling his son out. Rasputin jumped up from the table and "like a madman pushed his father into the yard, threw him down to the ground, and started to hit him with his fists." Efim cried out, "Don't hit me, you scoundrel." The agents intervened to part them by force. The father's eye was badly bruised and swollen shut. On his feet again the old man scolded his son in even fiercer terms. He dragged up his continuing affair with the maid Dunia. He threatened to tell the world that the only thing his son was good for was "feeling Dunia's soft parts." After that the agents had to pinion Rasputin to stop him from attacking his father a second time. He pulled himself together enough to send two telegrams, one to Tsarskoye Selo and the other to the Stavka. He was becoming bored in Pokrovskoye and wanted Nicholas to allow him back to Petrograd.

His son Dmitry had been called up for military service. Rasputin could not ask Nicholas or Alexandra to arrange a deferment; it was a service he provided for others, at a price, but he could not do it for his son without appearing unpatriotic. He told the empress that his son would serve, referring to himself as "Abraham sacrificing Isaac." In practice, he had his own means of ensuring that Dmitry remained a thousand miles from the front. He took the boy to Tyumen on September 10. His wife went with them. They met up with Patushinskaya, who placed Dmitry in the Seventh Company of her husband's regiment at Yalutorovsk, safely tucked away from the Germans in Siberia. They spent the night at Father Martian's monastery. Rasputin stayed put while the others went into town. "I know lots of people in Tyumen, but I don't have the time to see them," he explained to Terekhov, one of the agents. Terekhov thought the real reason was that he was frightened something could happen to him in the street. "Rasputin sidles," Terekhov noted of his awkward gait. "It looks as though he injured his side during the fight with his father."

Varnava had gone to Petrograd and made a heated appearance in front of the synod. He was ordered to attend a further session on September 10. He failed to turn up and was missing from the apartment where he was registered as staying. The following day he sent a messenger to explain that his mother was seriously ill and that he had left for the provinces to be with her. This was a lie. He remained in Petrograd, hiding in Prince Andronnikov's apartment. From here he wrote a rambling, hysterical letter to the tsar, describing synod members as "bloodsucking Beilises"—a reference to a Jew falsely accused of murdering Christian babies and drinking their blood—who mocked Rasputin. "It was a torture over me I could not stand it," he scribbled. "I said why do you want to muddle me and scoff at me for I am a Bishop of the Orthodox Church and the procurator adds that I am friendly with Rasputin and all these bishops burst out laughing and I, excuse me, Great Tsar, said that I am not afraid of you traitors so long as the Great Tsar Nicholas II reigns so he will defend me and will not allow you bloodsuckers to offend me I wept and left. . . . The poor saint Ioann Maximovich his glorification met suffocating gases of malice from the spiteful synod anarchists he was not spared. Religious feeling of the people violated so as to torment the Tsar and Tsarina." Many would have read the letter as evidence of insanity; to Nicholas it revealed a religious soul.

Varnava also cabled Rasputin asking for help. Rasputin responded with a flattering cable to the tsar from Pokrovskoye on September 17. "Ioann Maximovich glorified himself with wonders," it rambled. "It is no good our fathers objecting—they delay too long—God blessed your intention your word is peace and goodwill for everybody and your hand thunder and lightning will conquer all. Grigory Novy."

It worked. The synod prepared a critical report on the absent bishop. Nicholas split hairs to defend him, saying that the bishop's "local glorification" of Ioann Maximovich was permissible even if the saint did not meet the requirements demanded by the synod for "all-Russia glorification." In a note in the margin of the report, the tsar concluded that the synod, recognizing the bishop's "passionate fervency," should judge his actions "with pardon and love for the sake of the church."

———

It would have been bizarre at any time for Rasputin to pursue the tsar over a two-hundred-year-old corpse, on behalf of a semi-literate bishop with a fetish for being photographed in coffins. To do so when Nicholas had the high command of armies that were daily suffering thousands of fresh casualties was grotesque. A new call-up of two million men was under way. "We have lost something like five million men (I am not exaggerating)," Robert Wilton was writing to London. The war committee of the Duma was complaining that artillery, machine guns, and ammunition were short, that trenches were inadequate, that "neither bravery, nor competence, nor military worth" influenced the choice of commanders.

Nicholas enjoyed himself at the Stavka. "Thank God it is all over," he wrote to Alexandra when he assumed command. "I feel so calm—a sort of feeling like after the Holy Communion." With the German advance the headquarters had been pulled back to Mogilev. The city was set on hills above the east bank of the Dnieper River, almost five hundred miles south of Petrograd. It had a pretty cathedral, a governor's mansion once used by Napoleon's marshals, four horse-drawn tramlines, and a shabby hotel, the Bristol. The petty routines of military life comforted the tsar, and he ignored the larger picture of the war. He enjoyed the absence of politics. "I do not read the newspapers here," he said. "My brain is resting here—no ministers, no troublesome questions demanding thought." He liked to hold parades, at times within range of German guns, for he was not a physical coward; he awarded St. George Crosses by the thousand, and once solemnly promoted all those present at a ceremonial dinner.

He did not know that one of his best generals, Brusilov, found him unsuited to command "by reason of his ignorance, inability, utterly flaccid will, and lack of stern inner character" and that Brusilov thought those who had urged him to come to the Stavka—the empress and the starets—"are not better than criminals." He did not sense that he was awkward with the men, that "he did not know what to say, where to go, or what to do." He believed that he was loved. "The proof—the numbers of telegrams which I receive from all sides, with the most touching expressions," he wrote to Alexandra on September 9. "The ministers, always living in town, know terribly little of what is happening in the country as a whole. Here I can judge correctly the real mood." The only places where he admitted he was unpopular were Petrograd and Moscow, and he mocked them as "two minute points on the map of the fatherland."

The enemy relied on the restless, probing minds of Ludendorff and Hindenburg. As to the Russian supreme commander, he said of himself that "the heart

A devoted father: Grigory Rasputin in Pokrovskoye with his children, Maria, Varya, and Dmitry.

In peasant dress, Rasputin with fishermen on the banks of the Tura River in Siberia. He helped them bring in their nets and taught them psalms; other accounts had him "holding strange ceremonies with girls in forest deeps, weaving crosses from boughs."

Rasputin (left, wearing peasant boots beneath his robes) with two powerful allies acquired in St. Petersburg in 1903: Bishop Hermogen (center) and the fiery, charismatic monk Iliodor (right). As evidence of his sexual excesses mounted, though, they turned on him.

Rasputin, photographed shortly after he first arrived in St. Petersburg. He was already a full-fledged—if strikingly young—holy man, or *starets*.

Father Ioann of Kronstadt, a mystic close to the ruling Romanovs. "My son," he told Rasputin, "I can feel your presence in God's house. The divine spark is within you."

Dubbed "the crows" for their striking black hair and raucous chatter, the grand duchesses Militsa (left) and Anastasia (right) were instantly infatuated with Rasputin. Seeking to extend their influence at court, they performed the fateful introduction of Rasputin to the tsar and empress.

Anna Vyrubova, "completely enslaved" by Rasputin and the empress's most intimate friend, was the key link between them.

Vyrubova's little house in Tsarskoye Selo, five minutes' walk from the imperial palace. It was here that Alexandra most often met with Rasputin.

The tsar and empress with their children, 1913. From left: Olga, Marie, Tsar Nicholas, Empress Alexandra, Anastasia, Alexis, and Tatiana. The children wrote of Rasputin as their "dear, sweet, unforgettable friend."

Alexis, the hemophiliac heir to the throne, with his sailor bodyguard Nagorny, assigned to protect him from falls and carry him when he tired.

A study in sorrow: Empress Alexandra. Proud and unbending—"a will of iron linked to not much brain and no knowledge," the court grand marshal said of her—she despised society, and it her. When a letter she wrote to Rasputin was stolen and published—"I wish only one thing . . . to fall asleep forever . . . in your arms"—her many enemies seized it as proof that she was having an affair with the Siberian peasant.

Agents of the Okhrana, the Russian secret police, in Paris at the time of the investigation into Dr. Philippe. The French pseudo-doctor was the first "holy man" to influence the empress. General Rachovsky, the Russian counterterrorist chief in Paris, described Philippe as a charlatan; the tsar had Rachovsky dismissed for his pains.

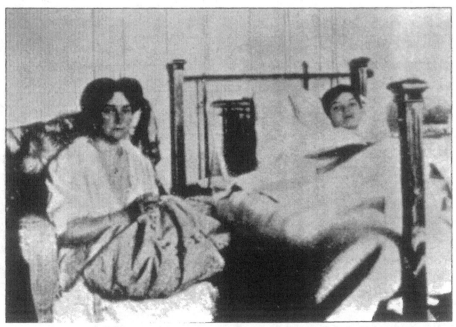

Alexandra never left her son's bedside when he suffered a bout of hemophilia. Rasputin's intercessions for the child—in person, by telephone and telegram—were followed by swift recovery. Coincidence, perhaps; the empress ascribed it to God.

The only picture of Rasputin with the empress, apparently taken over tea at Anna Vyrubova's cottage, may well be a fake. Nicholas and Alexandra were at pains to prevent any record being made of Rasputin's visits.

Rasputin poses in St. Petersburg shortly before the war. He still wears a peasant tunic, but the material is silk.

After an attempt on his life in 1914, Rasputin was sketched recovering in his hospital bed. He has written: "What will tomorrow bring? Thou art our leader, O God, how many thorny paths there are in life!"

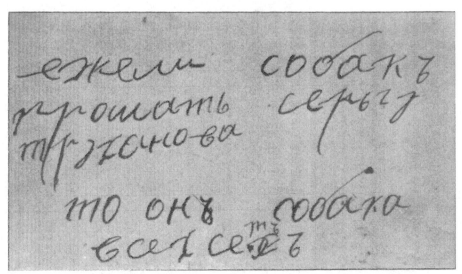

"If dogs are forgiven like Sergei Trufanov," Rasputin scrawled in this note, "he, the dog, will eat everyone up." Sergei Trufanov is the monk Iliodor, Rasputin's ex-friend and would-be murderer. When he was defrocked, he resumed his original name.

The tsar and his giant cousin Grand Duke Nicholas Nikolayevich (right), commander in chief of the Russian army at the start of World War I. When Rasputin asked if he could visit headquarters, the grand duke wired back: "Come and I'll hang you."

Infantrymen kneel at the front as the tsar blesses them with an icon. At the urging of Rasputin and Alexandra, Nicholas dismissed his cousin and made himself commander in chief in 1915. The troops mocked him as a cuckold when he handed out Georgiy Cross medals. "Tsar with Georgiy," they said. "Tsarina with Grigory."

"Utterly false, two-faced," a cabinet colleague said of Boris Stürmer, whom Rasputin and Alexandra maneuvered into office as prime minister in 1916.

The most powerful post in Russia, that of interior minister, was filled in 1916 by Alexander Protopopov. He resembled "an excitable seal," showed symptoms of syphilis, and was "certainly not quite sane." Alexandra championed him; Rasputin remarked approvingly that the new minister's honor "stretches like a piece of elastic."

The corrupt metropolitan of Petrograd, Pitirim, owed to Rasputin his elevation to the most influential position in Russian Orthodoxy. "I begat him," Rasputin boasted. Pitirim's appointment by the tsar outraged the faithful and further sapped the prestige of the throne.

"A stool pigeon, spy, sharper, swindler, chiseler, forger, and ruffian": thus the French ambassador described Ivan Manasevich-Manuilov, who cultivated Rasputin and introduced Boris Stürmer to him as a possible prime minister. When faced with prosecution for fraud, he threatened to expose Rasputin's dealings with Stürmer. The charges were dropped.

A note Rasputin wrote on behalf of a petitioner, in this case to Alexis Khvostov at the interior ministry. "My dear, dear fellow," he scribbled, "I am sending you a beautiful girl. She is poor—she is in need, speak with her, Grigory." It is typical of scores of kindly acts.

Rasputin in 1915, nearing the height of his career. He regained the tsar's confidence after Anna Vyrubova had been given up for dead in a railroad accident and he "miraculously" restored her to consciousness.

A playing card in illegal circulation in 1916 shows Rasputin, bottle in hand, as tsar with Nicholas beneath him. Thousands of copies were run off on underground presses.

The tsar dances to Rasputin's tune in a mocking cartoon. Newspapers were forbidden to mention Rasputin's name or to print his picture. Of course, this merely increased the public appetite for scandal. "Rasputin, Rasputin, Rasputin," a Petrograd lady complained. "It was like a refrain. It became a dusk enveloping our world, eclipsing the sun."

A caricature headed "Russia's Ruling House" shows Nicholas and Alexandra in Rasputin's grasp. The special-sections archive of the secret police had boxes of such cartoons, many of them showing the empress and Rasputin in lewd poses.

Marionette man: Rasputin uses puppets of the tsar and Metropolitan Pitirim to beat weeping Russia about the head.

Admirers surround Rasputin in his Gorokhovaya apartment in Petrograd, 1915. Anna Vyrubova is the third standing woman from the left. Mikhail Rodzianko, a leading politician, was horrified to find that he "recognized many of these worshipers from high society."

Felix Yusupov, Rasputin's murderer, is seen here with his wife, Irina, and their daughter in 1915. He is wearing his military cadet uniform; in his death throes, Rasputin ripped off one of the epaulets.

The Yusupov palace on the Moika Canal in Petrograd, to which Rasputin was lured for his murder.

The basement room in the Moika Palace in which the murder began. Yusupov fitted it out with a bear rug, cozy curtains, and a fire, to put Rasputin at ease.

So reactionary that "the only thing further Right was the wall," Vladimir Purishkevich gave the Duma speech condemning Rasputin as a "filthy, depraved, corrupt peasant" that inspired Yusupov to plan the killing. Purishkevich joined the plot.

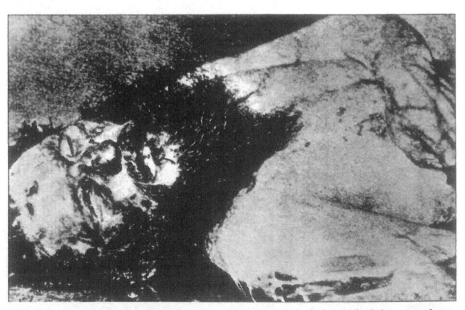

The police photograph of Rasputin's body. An autopsy found alcohol in the body but no evidence of poison. The three bullet wounds were consistent with the killers' own accounts; the bruising to the head was caused by blows from Purishkevich and Yusupov. A small amount of water was found in the lungs, suggesting that Rasputin may not have been clinically dead when his body was dumped into the Neva River.

of the tsar is in the hands of God." He liked the view from his rooms in the governor's mansion over the Dnieper to the water meadows and stands of beech and chestnut. He rose at nine, had a morning briefing from his chief of staff, Gen. Mikhail Alexeev, and examined the neat flags on the maps in the map room. At three he went out for a drive along the river in his Rolls-Royce. After dinner he played dominoes and watched films, romances and American detective serials. It was a pleasant, gentlemanly existence with the occasional echo of war—he slept on a hard camp bed and reminded himself that he must not complain, for "how many sleep on damp grass and mud!"

Alexis was with him, the boy wearing the uniform of a private soldier and sharing his father's bedroom. "It is very cosy to sleep side by side," Nicholas wrote to Alexandra. "I say prayers with him every night. . . . he says his prayers too fast, and it is difficult to stop him." The boy was sleeping well—"as I do"—in spite of the bright light of his icon lamp. He woke early, sat up in bed, and talked softly with his father. "I answer him drowsily, he settles down and lies quietly until I am called." Nicholas thought that the pale boy "gives light and life to all of us"; his lunchtime prattling to visiting generals and diplomats "is pleasant for them and it makes them smile." The smiles covered astonishment at the presence of a boy in this place of war; a sickly boy at that, who caused a Guards offensive in Bukovina to be delayed for a fortnight because he was ill but insisted that he review the guardsmen before the attack. Nicholas was proud of the eleven-year-old's conduct. "I shall never forget this review," he wrote to Alexandra. "The weather was excellent and the general impression astounding." She was proud, too. "Minds will be purified & they will carry the picture of you & yr Son in their hearts with them."

It was touching, loving, but it was not war. Neither could Alexandra's interference qualify as government. It was so frantic that she complained that she could not get a response quickly enough by letter. "Why won't we have a telephone run from your room to mine?" she wrote. "It would be fantastic & you could tell me good news or discuss a question. . . . We would try not to pester you, since I know you do not like to talk—but this would be our exclusive, private conversation, & we would be able to speak without concern that someone was listening in." As the summer heat drained away and the leaves outside her boudoir turned gold and red, she hammered on at the accursed "parliamentarists," hinting that she wanted Guchkov murdered. "A railway accident in wh he alone wld suffer wld be a real punishment fr[om] God," she wrote. "Show yr fist . . . be the master and lord; you are the Autocrat & they dare not forget it, when they do, as now, woe unto them."

She said that she had enemies everywhere—spitefully, she warned that Nikolasha and his "clique" in Caucasian exile "will try to continue making messes"—and reminded her husband of the need for their Friend. She sent a photograph of Rasputin and one of his combs to Mogilev on September 15. "Remember to keep the Image in yr hand again & try several times to comb yr hair with this comb before the sitting of the ministers," she wrote. A stuffed fish on a stick followed. "He used it first and now sends it to you as a blessing," she said.

———

Rasputin complained to an agent in Pokrovskoye that he wanted to return to Petrograd, but "Vyrubova is not allowed to invite me." He received an anonymous letter on September 19 that frightened him. Whoever had written it knew that he was in contact with the tsar in Mogilev. "Grigory, our motherland collapses, they want to sign a disgraceful peace," it read. "As you receive ciphered telegrams from the Stavka, it means that you have great influence. Therefore we ask you to make ministers responsible to the people so that the state Duma meeting on September 23 can save the motherland. If you do not do this, we will kill you without mercy—we will not hesitate like Guseva did. It will be carried out, wherever you are. The lot to kill you fell on us and there are ten of us." It was unsigned.

His renewed pleas to Vyrubova succeeded. Rasputin left Pokrovskoye on September 24 for the four-day steamer and train ride to Petrograd. Elena Djanumova was waiting for him there to see if her mother's exile could be lifted. Over the summer he had urged her in telegrams to go to the capital— "Bringing joy with the light of love and I live with this Grigory"—which otherwise made no sense. Her friend Maria Arkadyevna assured her that they were indeed meaningless, except to admirers, who kept them in expensive caskets like sacred texts and for whom "the darker is their meaning, the better."

A voice with the familiar drawling *o*'s telephoned her at the Severnaya Hotel: "Well, is that you, Frantic? You're in Peter, but didn't visit me? Why so-o? Come at once." A man friend at the hotel, a Monsieur Ch, offered to drive her over in his car. He much wanted to meet the "almighty starets," the local slang for Rasputin. Elena told him to wait in the car while she asked if he could come up. Rasputin flew into uncontrolled fury when she mentioned him. "You've come from Moscow with a man," he bellowed, his pupils dilating. "Nice one. Came to ask me about a petition and brought a man with you. Couldn't part with him. So that's what you are. I won't do anything for you. I've got little ladies of my own who love me and indulge me. Go, go."

He ran to the telephone and spoke in a nervous, shaky voice: "Dusenka, darling, are you free now? I'm coming to you. Are you glad? Well, wait for me, I'll be right there." He hung up and gave Elena a smirk. "I don't need Moscow women, don't need them," he said. "Peter women are better than Moscow women." She rushed from the apartment in tears, vowing never to see the "crude muzhik" again.

She was back the following day with Ch; Rasputin had called her to apologize, meek, gentle. He asked Ch to come up from the car. "Let me take a look at this one," he said, "the spark that set the forest on fire." He kissed the man when he came up the stairs and sat him down for breakfast. Then he drew Elena's maid aside, to complain in tears that Elena was surrounded by "hawks," his expression for men: "I want to help her, but let her be with me, not with others."

It was a bravura performance. "By God, Madam, it was so curious," the maid told Elena. "He speaks so plaintively and the tears keep dropping. Why are you so upset? I ask him—I felt so sorry for him. And he says: 'Pity, my dear, such pity'—and beats his chest. I felt so sorry for him, Madam, so sorry." Elena found something so primitive in Rasputin, so alien to polite understanding, that it was impossible to be angry with him. He asked her to come back on Sunday.

He was holding court for women admirers in the dining room. Elena was meeting almost the full harem. The room was hot and heavy with scent, and she had an impression of silks, dark broadcloths, sables, diamonds, and aigrettes in coiffured hair, counterpointed against the white scarf of a Sister of Charity and the threadbare clothes of an old woman. The nursing sister was Akulina Laptinskaya. The elderly woman was A. G. Gushchina, a lonely person to whom Rasputin showed real kindness.

"This is my most beloved, from Moscow—Frantic," he said. He sat her next to Akulina Nikitishna, called Kilina by all, the pretty and frivolous daughter of the commander of the Peter and Paul Fortress. Tea was poured. Elena was about to help herself to sugar when Kilina took her glass and said to Rasputin, "Bless, Father." She explained to Elena: "When the Father puts in sugar with his own hands, it's God's blessing." Everyone held their glasses out to him Dunia came into the room; Elena described her as an "elderly maid" and thought that she was a distant relative of Rasputin. The ladies told her to take a rest, they would do the work.

A "striking brunette, a baroness," began to collect the dishes. This was probably Vera Kusova, the officer's wife eager to advance her husband's career. Another lady, in a violet velvet dress and sable tippet, washed the tea things. A plump young blonde, simply dressed, jumped up to open the door when the bell rang. She was introduced as Munya Golovina; her mother, an important-looking old lady, was also in the room. Munya acted as a maid in the hall, taking fur coats and helping visitors off with their galoshes. "The samovar has boiled away," Dunia said to her. "You should add water and put on some more coal." Munya grabbed the samovar and darted off to the kitchen. A corpulent lady in a gris de perle dress, her stoutness concealed by soft folds of crepe de chine, went with her; this was probably L. V. Miller, the wife of a rich merchant, whom the agents described as "middle-aged and lopsided, still with pretensions to be attractive."

Kilina began to sing "Wanderer," a haunting folk song. Others caught the air of melancholy and began to sing psalms, Kilina catching the high notes above Rasputin's light bass. The doorbell rang. A messenger brought in a basket of roses and a dozen embroidered silk shirts, the gift of a lady. The singing stopped for a moment, and Rasputin gave a little homily. "One's got to subdue oneself," he instructed. "One's got to be simpler, simpler, nearer to God. All these ruses of yours aren't needed. You're all so cunning, my little ladies, I know you all. I read your souls. Too much cunning."

Then he began to sing again, the folk song "Russian"; he danced. A woman came in, in a white linen dress of strange monastic cut, with a white cowl pulled almost over her eyes. The twelve gospels, with crosses on the binding, hung from her dress. Someone whispered to Elena that it was Olga Lokhtina.

"At the father's, one has to behave as in church, with grandeur," she said sharply.

"Leave them alone," said Rasputin. "Let them have a good time."

Guests were beginning to leave. They kissed Rasputin's hand; he embraced them and kissed them on the lips. "Dried crusts, Father," they asked. He handed out bits of stale bread, which they wrapped in perfumed handkerchiefs. After whispering with some of them, Dunia came back with two parcels wrapped in newspaper. It was Rasputin's dirty linen. The ladies asked for it. "The dirtier the better," they said. "It's got to have sweat." Munya Golovina helped them on with their galoshes. One of them protested. "Father teaches us to be meek," she said and, taking a foot in her hand, put on the overshoes.

On the staircase Elena asked about Lokhtina, the woman in white. "She is the wife of a general and a former admirer of Iliodor," she was told. "Now she worships Father as if he were a saint. Lives the life of a hermit. Sleeps on boards, puts a log under her head. Her relatives beseeched Father to send her his pillow so she wouldn't torture herself like that. Well, she consented to sleep on his pillow. A saint-woman." As she walked into the dark street, Elena felt she had escaped from an insane asylum.

———

She was back, nevertheless, the next lunchtime in a final effort to have her mother's exile quashed. Princess Shakhovskaya, a striking, raven-haired beauty in a nurse's uniform, was in the dining room. She was twenty-six and was married to Prince V. Shakhovskoy, whom Rasputin had recommended as trade minister; she had followed the starets for four years. The police were aware that Rasputin had been sleeping with her—"he calls her 'my duck' and she kisses his hands and feet," they reported—and so were the capital's writers of satirical verse. The prince, aware that his position depended on the starets, ignored both the affair and the lampoons.

Rasputin was eating fish while the princess peeled potatoes with the most exquisite fingers Elena had ever seen, long and delicate with mother-of-pearl nails. He took the potatoes carelessly, without looking at her or thanking her. She kissed his fingers, sticky with the fish he piled on his plate. He brought Elena a copy of his book of meditations on his journey to the Holy Land; the preface had a photograph of him lying disheveled in bed after Guseva's attack. He scribbled on the front page: "To my dear simpleton Frantic to remember me by, Grigory."

The princess wanted him to go to his study, to give her some confidential advice. He did so with ill grace. They were back in a few minutes. He was angry; she had tears in her eyes. She kissed his hand and left. Elena asked him why he was so unkind to the princess. "I loved her so much once, but I don't love her anymore," he said. Elena asked him if he could make men ministers. "No big deal, why not?" he replied, and took her into his study to discuss her mother's petition. "I'll do everything for you, my dear one, but you also have to humor me and obey me," he said. "A promise is a promise. If you do things my way, the affair will be settled. If not, nothing will be done."

She said she had to return to Moscow. "All right, then, the affair will wait too. You come back and you'll be with me. We'll do everything." His eyes burned; something fettered her movements, and she could not flee. She was saved by the maid, who shouted through the door, "Telephone from Tsarskoye." Elena left and went straight to the station. That evening the agents saw Rasputin bringing back an unnamed woman to his apartment; she left in the early hours.

———

The starets was careful to give the empress a different account of his nights— sleepless, filled with somber insights into the fate of Russia. Alexandra faithfully passed them on to Nicholas. She wrote on October 10 that the starets foresaw a food crisis and had dreamed of its solution. "He says that you must give the order that wagons with flour, butter and sugar should be allowed to pass: there are to be no other trains for 3 days. He saw the whole thing in a night vision."

All passenger traffic was held up, causing such chaos that it did not return to normal for six days. The food supply was indeed in a critical state. Peasants were hoarding their grain because they had no reason to sell it. The goods they had bought before the war—plows, stoves, harnesses, water pumps, clothing—were no longer being made by factories, which had converted to war supplies. The army was taking the lion's share of freight traffic; locomotives were scarce, for they had been built and repaired in Warsaw, and Warsaw was lost. The railroad minister, Rukhlov, was a Black Hundred reactionary who drove out senior staff who did not share his politics. Inflation arrived at a gallop; by August 1915 the cost of a basket of thirteen basic foodstuffs was up 150 percent over its prewar level. The poor were hungry. Rasputin's instincts were sound, but his vision did not include preparation. No food stocks were moved to the railheads, and the freight trains ran fast but empty. The minister, "appalled by the frightful disorganization of the railways," fled to a spa in the Caucasus to take the waters.

Unabashed, Alexandra continued to bombard the tsar with Rasputin's advice. Much of it was personal and vindictive. The empress reported that he was "very grieved" at Trepov, the transport minister, "as He knows he is against Him." The starets criticized a new stamp duty scheme by the finance minister on the same ground. He recommended the dismissal of Goremykin as premier, adding that the tsar should wait until he had seen if the elder Khvostov, the justice minister, measured up as a successor. Khvostov did not; Alexandra wrote that when Rasputin saw him, he treated him "as if he was a petitioner." After a ninety-minute meeting she said that the starets recommended the tsar delay a decision on the premier "according to God."

Though he remained against the war—"Our Friend was always against the War," the empress wrote, "saying that the Balkans were not worth fighting about"—he had visions on military strategy. He demanded an advance on the front near Riga, "prompted by what He saw in the night. . . . He says it is necessary, begs you seriously, says we can and we must." He told the empress that he had seen Russian troops enter Constantinople in another vision; "He dictated to me," she wrote to the tsar, "walking about, praying and crossing Himself, and about Rumania and Greece and our troops passing through." In politics he suggested that the tsar pay a surprise visit to the Duma. The empress reassured her husband that this involved no softening toward the parliamentarists. "He loathes their existence, as I do, for Russia," she added. Rasputin was shrewd enough to know that some contact had to be maintained with Duma members; with cruel insight he thought of them as "dogs collected to keep other dogs quiet." The visit duly took place.

Sometimes Rasputin was so overwhelmed by his own thoughts, Alexandra said, that "He cannot exactly remember one of them . . . but He says we must always do what He says."

CHAPTER 20

The Idealists

R asputin escaped standing trial for the drunken outburst on the steamer, though Beletsky and Khvostov pressed him for an explanation. "He maintained to us that he was not drunk, that he did not annoy women and passengers, but they provoked him to a scandal," Beletsky later testified, "that the captain of the steamer took their side for reasons of principle because he was a liberal, knowing that he was Rasputin, and that it was entirely under the influence of the captain that the steward made his official complaint against him, which the police did not want to report." He claimed that he had joined up with the soldiers because they were going out to shed their blood for the country, and that he felt it was his patriotic duty to entertain them.

It was ingenious—the slur that the report was a liberal plot to discredit the government and the throne, the bathos of doomed soldiers on their way to the front—and Beletsky noted that it had convinced the palace. Beletsky himself did not believe a word of it. He checked with Father Martian, who confirmed that Rasputin was "very drunk and annoyed the public." Rasputin and Vyrubova were clamoring for Stankevich, the Tobolsk governor, to be sacked for wishing to prosecute. As the price for the affair being dropped, Beletsky insisted that Stankevich be promoted to governor of a more important province. Rasputin agreed, on condition that he could name his own governor in his native Tobolsk, where "he must have his own man."

He was not frightened into discretion. Returning to Gorokhovaya ulitsa "absolutely drunk" at 1:00 A.M. on October 14, he shouted at the woman doorkeeper that she had taken a twenty-five-ruble bribe from an unnamed government minister. "He wanted to bury me," he yelled, "but he's buried himself instead." The wife of an ensign lying wounded in a Petrograd military hospital visited him on November 3. She wanted Rasputin to make sure that her husband would not be returned to the front line when he recovered. On her way out she told the doorkeeper what a weird person he was and described how she had been welcomed. "A girl let me in and led me to his room," she said. "I saw him for the first time. He said: 'Undress and go in here.' I undressed and went with him to a room, the first from the front door on the left. He hardly listened to my request but started to paw my face and then my breasts and he said: 'Kiss me, I got to like you.'

"He scribbled a note for me and started to pester me over again: 'Kiss me, kiss me, I like you.' He wouldn't give me the note. He said: 'You make me angry, come back tomorrow.' "

Agent Terekhov asked her if she would come back the next day.

"No, to come to him means to bribe him the way he wants," she replied. "I can't do that, so I won't come."

Khvostov knew that the imperial favor he enjoyed depended on keeping such stories out of the newspapers. "The interior minister has done everything to charm his enemies and disarm them," Robert Wilton reported privately to London. "He has been 'hail fellow, well met!' with all members of the Russian press. He went round to call on all the editors." He planned to muzzle them by floating a media company on the stock exchange. The shares would be offered to the public, but Okhrana secret agents supplied with special funds would acquire majority control. The company would buy up newspapers, printing plants, newsstands, advertising agencies, cinemas, and even telephone companies. The new owners would then suppress all mention of Rasputin. The scheme collapsed because it was too complex. That it was also illegal was of no consequence to a minister who Witte said "took the prize for rascality, being a man for whom the law does not exist."

An easier way of keeping the starets out of the press was to remove him from the capital. Khvostov and Beletsky drew up an itinerary for a tour of provincial monasteries. They arranged for a large supply of Madeira and a number of priests to accompany him. The priests demanded so many promotions and perks for escorting Rasputin that Beletsky said he "blushed for them." Rasputin refused to go.

He needed a minder. Beletsky found an ideal spy-bodyguard in a general of gendarmes, M. S. Komissarov. The general's career had foundered after he had openly incited pogroms in 1906; his sin was not Jew-baiting, which was government policy, but lack of discretion. Since then, as he later testified, he had been used by the interior ministry for all manner of espionage and dirty tricks. He had, for example, stolen and deciphered correspondence from foreign embassies; he boasted that the interior ministry knew what was happening in foreign policy before the foreign ministry did. He had also supplied bodyguards for senior officials.

Beletsky gave him a squad of Okhrana men and briefed him carefully. The general was to prevent Rasputin from becoming involved in public scandals; if he failed, witnesses were to be bought off. He was to stop the starets from making unexpected trips by citing the danger of assassination. Before Rasputin made his regular morning telephone call to Vyrubova, the general was to pass him details of favors requested by Beletsky and Khvostov for forwarding to the empress; in return, all Rasputin's petitions to the interior ministry would be granted where possible. Finally, the general was to keep Rasputin alive, and to collect any evidence that would strengthen their hold over him.

Komissarov's men came from the Okhrana's external service. The secret police maintained two agencies to spy on revolutionaries. The Internal Agency relied on informers within the groups, what Vassilyev called "secret cooperators or assistants drawn from the ranks of the enemy." As well as workers, prostitutes, and students, the secret police chief boasted, they included "respected party leaders and even members of the Duma." These informers were acquired through fear, greed, or malice. The threat of punishment—the noose, forced labor shackled to a cart in an east Siberian mine, imprisonment in the Fortress of Peter and Paul, in a cell with iron-bound doors and double sentries—loosened lips.

Some collapsed as soon as they were arrested, Vassilyev noted, while others needed the secret police "to use their most skillful persuasive powers" before they could be induced to cooperate. Others volunteered to inform, either "in a fit of rage or spite . . . if they felt insulted, slighted, or betrayed" by their fellows or "answered bluntly that they were doing it for money's sake." The general said that the Internal Agency had a system of "inner supervision" of Rasputin, developed by Komissarov, which "penetrated as far as the tsarina's alcove." Spying on the tsarina ran well beyond the purview of the secret police. "I couldn't stay in the dark when such a mysterious and enigmatic trump card as Rasputin loomed on the political and court horizon," Komissarov said to justify his lèse-majesté. "He had to be deciphered clean." The inner supervision came across "the most fantastic suppositions of cynicism and pornography" but little concrete fact.

The real effort was made by the agents of the External Agency. Their official duties were to provide discreet security for Rasputin at street level—they were armed—and to report immediately if they got wind of any plot to assassinate him. In practice they treated him exactly as they had been taught to treat a terrorist. They shadowed and noted his movements and contacts. They were an elite. Only a thousand existed to cover all the Russian empire; of these a hundred were on duty in Petrograd. Six of those were on regular daily assignment to Rasputin, an indication of the Okhrana's intense interest in him. They were full-time professionals, trained at a special school run by Eustraty Myednikov, the chief of the Moscow Okhrana. He liked to recruit former army sergeants and corporals. They had the necessary discipline and courage for work in which days of boredom could suddenly, if their quarry turned on them, be transformed into moments of extreme danger. The agents had to be "politically and morally reliable," Vassilyev wrote, "honest, sober, bold, adroit, patient, prudent, obedient, and of good health." Recruits from minorities with potential revolutionary leanings were barred. "Individuals of Polish or Hebrew descent," he added, "were, on principle, excluded from any kind of employment in the External Agency."

Vassilyev described their duties this way: to "keep an eye on suspicious characters in the street, theaters, hotels, railway trains, and similar places of public resort" and to "discover all possible detail concerning the mode of life of such persons and the company frequented by them." The agents had to be familiar with the city they were posted in, particularly with its "drinking saloons, beer gardens, taverns, and houses with an access to two or more streets." The last included Gorokhovaya ulitsa 64, with its front and rear entrances. They disguised themselves as porters, doormen, caretakers, newspaper sellers, soldiers, cabmen, and railroad officials. They had to know the taxi stands and fares for droshkys and motorcars, the railroad timetables, the uniforms of garrison regiments. During his training period the rookie agent had to hand in a daily report to show that he had grasped these essentials. His political reliability was tested by other agents, who sought his confidence and made provocative remarks to see if they could draw a response. He belonged to the agency; though he might be married, it was "always regarded as rather an unfavorable circumstance if he showed any excessive devotion to his family."

Rasputin's minders allowed themselves only a professional interest in the stream of women who called at his apartment. They interviewed the prostitutes and maids; ladies were recorded only by name and length of visit. They never referred to Rasputin other than by his code name. Agents were instructed to give their subject a "nickname . . . short and characteristic, suggested, if possible, by some striking peculiarity in the exterior of the suspect." In deference to Rasputin's long black hair and beard, they nicknamed him the Dark One. The external service had its own store of uniforms and clothing. The transport section ran a pool of horses, cabs, and motorcars. Agents were trained to handle horses and cabs like born droshky drivers and to acquire "a perfect mastery of the droshky man's mode of speech" so that they did not stand out at a cab stand. The daily reports on Rasputin were rarely short of detail on his droshky rides; the drivers were either agents or informers. Money was kept on deposit at all railroad stations "for the purpose of allowing agents of the Okhrana to undertake journeys at short notice or no notice at all." When Rasputin set off for Moscow or Tyumen, an agent went too.

Four agents were always on duty at Gorokhovaya ulitsa, three at the front door and one by the gates. There was also a concierge at the doorway, a yard keeper and a doorkeeper by the gates. "Because they have nothing else to do, the agents play cards all the time," Rasputin's neighbor Blagoveshchensky, a clerk in the synod office, wrote. "Sometimes they go up to the second floor, where one of them stays, and sometimes one of them climbs to the third floor, where there is a bench next to apartment 20. He stays there on duty." The agents were well known both to their subject and to others in the house; according to their moods, both Rasputin and another neighbor, Neistein, joshed or sneered at them. Rasputin was aware that his conduct outside the apartment might be recorded. Vassilyev said that he was "frankly nervous" whenever he was summoned to Tsarskoye Selo by Vyrubova; the agents "testif[ied] that whenever he knew he was about to meet the tsarina he became extraordinarily excitable and ill at ease." This jittery state, the secret police chief said, was doubtless caused by fear that word of his excesses had reached the palace.

It is unlikely, though, that Rasputin realized the full extent of the surveillance. Vassilyev's men were skilled in streetcraft. They knew how to use side streets to hurry ahead of their quarry. If a direct confrontation was unavoidable, they avoided any eye contact; it was through their eyes that they would be recognized again. To see which apartment Rasputin entered in a block, an agent would race up the attic stairs and count footsteps to see which floor he visited. His mail and telegrams were intercepted; a list of people whose correspondence interested the agency was supplied to the post and telegraph office. The Okhrana had "black cabinets" whose job was to steam open envelopes and copy or photograph the contents before returning them to the mail. These agents, Vassilyev said proudly, "acquired such a flair that they would open letters not written by people on the list and discover things."

———

Rasputin had silenced prying clerics in Siberia with Varnava's appointment to Tobolsk. The death of the metropolitan of Kiev created the opportunity to extend this protection to Petrograd. He first had the Petrograd metropolitan transferred to Kiev. On November 12 Alexandra told the tsar that he insisted that Pitirim, the bishop of Georgia, was the "only suitable person" to fill the vacancy in Petrograd. Pitirim was as gross as Varnava; he was suspected of being a homosexual and a thief. As bishop of Tula and later Kursk, he left the administration of the diocese to a deacon, Mitrofanych, with whom he had "relations disapproved of by both the church and the law." The two stole and sold the plate and other treasures from the bishop's palace and vestry; Sabler later testified that Mitrofanych had bought a country estate for ten thousand rubles with his share of the booty. Pitirim patronized suspected Podgornovs, followers of the khlyst pilot Stefan Podgorny, who had established arks in Kursk and Kharkov. He "became so popular among them that they claimed that they saw aureola around his head and almost ranked him among the saints." The scandal forced his transfer to another diocese, where he took up with a young priest named Osipenko. Pitirim had met Rasputin before the war and shown himself to be subservient and useful.

Such was the man whom the starets wished to become the most powerful figure in Russian Orthodoxy. The new synod procurator, Volzhin, whose predecessor, Samarin, had only recently run afoul of Rasputin, warned the tsar that the appointment would outrage the church. Pitirim's name did not appear on the list of suitable candidates prepared by the synod; Nicholas crossed out the name of the bishop of Riga, the front-runner, with his own hand and wrote in Pitirim. Volzhin resigned; he was replaced by Rayev, another of Rasputin's creatures, whom Simanovich described as "old and completely insignificant, with a wig, and very comical."

It took little time to put the new metropolitan to work. Pitirim visited the fixer Ivan Manasevich-Manuilov as soon as he arrived in the capital; the two discussed a mutual contact, a mediocre provincial governor called Stürmer, as a possible new prime minister. Pitirim also arranged the rehabilitation of a close friend of Rasputin and Vyrubova, Isidor Kokolov, a bishop who had been stripped of his see and banished to a monastery as a simple monk for homosexuality. With Rayev's help Kokolov became father superior of a monastery in Tobolsk, close to the like-minded Bishop Varnava. Pitirim's "secretary," Osipenko, proved equally malleable. Beletsky soon realized that he could be bribed, giving him three hundred rubles from police department secret funds.

———

At the front, the Russians were striving to hold the Germans west of Riga. The *Times* correspondent Robert Wilton saw the aftermath of a counterattack. The fighting took place in a wet swamp that had frozen. The marks where the Russian infantry had lain formed ice-crusted pools; around them were craters twenty feet in diameter, where German eleven-inch shells had fallen. Company commanders were ensigns who had left school in the summer; battalions were led by captains. Wilton found Russian losses to be "more terrible than anything we knew or even suspected." One regiment, the 130th, had attacked with 2,400 men. Some of the 225 survivors were badly frostbitten. The young soldiers conscripted in August found conditions "very trying. There is no warm clothing and very little straw. They have to sleep on the bare ground in the trenches."

The supply problem was easing as industrial production picked up. Wilton reported that the real crisis was in morale, and that was worse in Petrograd than at the front. "Internal politics," he wrote wearily, "have sunk into a slough of reaction." Nobody knew why the "fossilized premier" Goremykin survived; the foreign minister, Sazonov, described his boss to Wilton as a "medieval survivor organically incapable of comprehending modern conditions." The only decisions seemed to be made by "the female head of the Court and Rasputin. . . . The censorship is becoming daily more oppressive, and every minister seems to be a law unto himself. Things could not be worse, alas!"

By now Rasputin had what Simanovich called "his own council of ministers . . . more practical and positive than the tsar's." It consisted exclusively of women. Old Madame Golovina was the president, supporting Rasputin by her name and authority in society. Her daughter Munya was his intermediary with the higher clergy. Vyrubova helped nominate ministers. The lady of court Nikhitina was in touch with the prime minister. The pretty Lili von Dehn provided contacts in the palace, where she was a maid of honor; she never spoke to Rasputin when he was in the palace, but they often met in the apartment of Kushina, another of his mistresses, who held "merry, intimate parties" for him. Akulina Laptinskaya was Rasputin's intelligence service, supplying him with the latest gossip and rumors; unknown to him, she also supplied news of his movements to his enemies for a fee.

Nominating ministers involved finding them. This was not easy, for Rasputin's knowledge of bureaucracy was limited to despising it. "So he constantly turned to me with requests to name suitable persons for this or that ministerial post," Simanovich said. It was an onerous task. Sackings followed appointments so rapidly that "many of our candidates, knowing the unstable character of the tsar, declined the offers." The pressure was intense, since the tsar "often telephoned Rasputin demanding that he immediately name a candidate." Rasputin would ask him to hold the line, then turn to Simanovich. "We need a minister," he would cry. Everyone in the apartment threw in suggestions while the tsar "was waiting holding the telephone at the other end." Once, while the tsar was on the phone, Rasputin said, "We need a general." Simanovich's son Semyon, who was in the room, suggested a contact called Volkonsky, not a general but a Duma functionary. Rasputin passed on the name, and the astonished Volkonsky became a deputy interior minister. Rayev's only qualification to head the synod was his chairmanship of the "Scientific-Commercial Unit," which, despite its high-sounding title, was a front for one of Simanovich's gambling clubs.

If a choice was particularly difficult, Rasputin turned to Manasevich-Manuilov, the journalist who had interviewed him in 1912 after the Iliodor scandal. He was a small man, elegant, suit impeccably cut, head erect over stiff collar and bow tie, with a bold, oval face, stern and perceptive eyes, and a chill but sensual set to the mouth. Although Rasputin would always make time to see him, he did not appear to exploit the intimacy. He was calm, he did not brag. He smiled often, and kept a distance. There was good reason for the reserve. Beneath the elegance, wrote the French ambassador, who knew him well, was "a stool pigeon, spy, sharper, swindler, chiseler, forger, and ruffian."

Manuilov was the son of a provincial Jewish merchant—at various times he practiced Judaism, Lutheranism, and Orthodoxy—and he owed his advancement to the patronage of Prince Meshchersky. When he took up with Manuilov, the prince had introduced the provincial boy to the best tailors, and to the secret police. Informing and spying came easily to him, and he had taken over in the Okhrana's Paris bureau after General Rachovsky had been dismissed for criticizing Dr. Philippe. He betrayed intelligence secrets to revolutionaries, stealing documents from the office safe with a counterfeit key, and betrayed revolutionaries to the Okhrana. In 1904 he photographed the Japanese cipher at the Japanese Legation in The Hague and was rewarded with an Order of Vladimir. Returning to Russia in 1905, he collected thirty thousand rubles from the industry ministry to reopen workingmen's libraries, which had closed during the risings. He embezzled all but seven thousand rubles of it. Stolypin threw him out of government service. "I am a vicious man," he said. "I love money and I love life." The war suited him. He specialized in extorting money from banks, and in helping and then blackmailing men trying to evade military service.

Manuilov was a natural partner for the nomination machine. He dined regularly with Rasputin, Manus, and Beletsky, and attended Prince Andronnikov's salon. "Of course, he would offer his own people," Simanovich said, but neither he nor Rasputin resented it. Business was business. There was enough to go around, and the tsar appeared to be happy. Simanovich claimed that Nicholas told each new minister that "Rasputin is a messenger of God. . . . Never in my life did I have such love and confidence in anyone as in Rasputin." The notes Rasputin scrawled to ministers often contained the phrase "I will tell the loving one." This implied that he would talk to the tsar on the subject. "A minister on such occasions regarded Rasputin's request as an order of the tsar," Simanovich claimed, "and put a corresponding resolution on the note."

If there was exaggeration in this, and there is ample evidence that the tsar did not share his wife's total trust in the starets, it was nevertheless taken seriously by the diplomatic corps. Petrograd was a top-caliber posting for ambassadors and foreign correspondents. None had the slightest doubt of Rasputin's importance. Maurice Paléologue, the shrewd French ambassador, thought it critical to meet the starets and sound out his views on the war. Keeping Russia in the war was a mortal matter for the French and British, for if the Russians sued for peace, more than a hundred German divisions would be freed to fight on the Western front. Paléologue dismissed the more lurid accounts that Alexandra and Rasputin headed a "peace party" that was in secret negotiations with Germany. He remained deeply suspicious of the embezzlers and cardsharps in Rasputin's entourage. "He is the distributor of German subsidies," he said flatly of Manus. "He secures the relationship with Berlin, and it is through him that Germany hatches and maintains her intrigues in Russian society."

The ambassador made a careful note of his meeting with the starets. "Brown hair, long and ill-combed," he wrote, "a black, stiff beard; a high forehead; a large, jutting nose; a powerful mouth." He found the whole expression of the face to be concentrated in eyes of a strange brilliance, depth, and fascination. Their gaze was at once "piercing and caressing, ingenuous and astute, direct and remote." Those eyes. People disagreed on their color—Paléologue thought them flax blue, others steel gray, emerald, yellow, viper green, red—but all sensed their strength. They talked about the war. At first Rasputin condemned it for the sufferings it piled on the Russian people. "There are too many killed, too many wounded, too many orphans, too many ruins, too many tears!" he cried. "I know villages, large villages, where everyone is in mourning. . . . And those who come back from the war, in what a state, dear Lord! Crippled, maimed, blind! . . . For a space of more than twenty years only pain will be harvested on Russian soil."

It was not the talk that Paléologue wanted. He argued back that it was terrible, yes, but an indecisive peace, a peace of exhaustion, would be a crime against the dead. It would risk internal catastrophe. To his surprise, Rasputin agreed. "You are right," he said. "We must fight until we are victorious." The ambassador was intensely relieved. He said that he knew people in high positions who had told him Rasputin was trying to persuade the tsar to end the war. The starets gave him a suspicious look, scratched his head, and said, "There are fools everywhere." He went on to say that Kaiser Wilhelm was inspired by the devil, but that God would abandon him one day and "he'll crumple up like an old shirt that's thrown on the dung heap."

Rasputin had reversed his views to please the ambassador. In fact, he was opposed to the war—"in his opinion," Simanovich said, "any kind of peace was better for Russia than war"—and he admired the Germans. But it was beyond his powers to influence war and peace. He had no official post, no staff, no direct control of policy, and none of its implementation. He did not govern Russia; what he was doing, with the empress and their appointees, was so rotting the country's morale that it was becoming ungovernable. The distinction was acute, and it was one that his intelligence fully recognized. Rasputin rarely became involved in political arguments; when he did, as with the ambassador, he retreated. Instead of confronting him, it was easier to ruin a man by dropping a word to the empress.

Rasputin had his ideas, though, and they had a rugged honesty. Above all, as Simanovich said, he "always remained a peasant stressing his muzhik, uncouth nature in front of people who regarded themselves as mighty and superior to all, and he never forgot the millions in the Russian villages." He had as little time for the Allies as he had for the war. At a party a guest asked him why he sympathized with the Germans and hated Englishmen and Frenchmen. He was drunk, Simanovich says, and answered unexpectedly: "I cannot like the French, because I know they don't like me," he said. "They are republicans and revolutionaries, and they think I'm funny. I can only work with monarchists. Monarchists should never fight with each other. They can always get on well. Therefore Russia should reconcile with Germany as soon as possible."

When he was warned that it was dangerous to talk of peace, he exploded. "I'm not afraid of anything!" he yelled. "No one has the right to kill people. There are people who are agents in money dealings and the sale of land. I want to be such a go-between in peace. Even Papa says I'm right and we should remain neutral." He was not impressed when he was told that "Papa" had vowed to fight until the last German had left Russian soil. "The tsar can say that," he said. "He owns his own word. He can give it, and he can take it back. He's the tsar and he can do anything." He praised the German colonists who had settled in Russia under Catherine the Great. He was impressed that they drank coffee as well as tea, a sign of wealth. "A Russian likes German goods," he said. "German merchants have good products, and they look after the customer in every way. Germans know how to work. If a German war prisoner gets to a Russian village, women try to have him in their house because he's a good worker."

He was pro-American, too; a fair number of peasants had relatives in the States and received money from them. "Many poor immigrants have become rich farmers in America and were happy with their big wages," Simanovich commented. "America seemed a fairy land for a poor Russian peasant. Rasputin therefore liked America, and he advised living with America in friendship and peace."

A deep-dyed reactionary when it came to the autocracy, Rasputin was liberal elsewhere. He backed land reform and wanted manor houses turned into schools. He complained that serfs had lived better than modern country folk. "They got food and clothing," he said. "Nowadays a peasant gets nothing and he has to pay taxes. His only cow gets taken by the bailiff and sold at auction.

Peasant kids run around naked until they're ten. They get wooden clogs instead of boots. There's not enough land. . . . Life stops in the villages." His passion for railroads went further than making love on them. "They're afraid that railroads will spoil the peasants," he complained of landowners. "That's shit. With railroads a man can look for a better living. Without railroads a Siberian peasant has to stay home because he can't walk all through Siberia." He despised noblemen, if not their wives. "Noblemen have too much," he said with socialist fire. "They don't do anything themselves, and they stop others from doing anything. If an educated person appears, they cry that he's a revolutionary and mutineer and get him locked up. A peasant isn't allowed to have an education. This master's policy won't lead to anything good."

Rasputin was also sympathetic to minorities. Simanovich said that he favored Polish independence—"they are the same Slavs as Russians and they must feel themselves right"—and civil liberties for Jews. Simanovich was a Zionist and owned a small strip of land in Palestine, where he dreamed of retiring. Rasputin shared his attraction to the Holy Land. At moments in 1915 when they tired of "our unhealthy and dangerous life" in Petrograd, they discussed moving there. All that detained them, Simanovich claimed, were "the goals we had set for ourselves. Rasputin wished to conclude peace, and I thought about equalizing Jews' rights." Simanovich insisted that the Jewish question must come first. "If we could solve it," he said, "I might get so much money from American Jews that we would have enough for the rest of our lives." Ingeniously, he suggested that Rasputin's departure for Palestine would be such a relief to the establishment that he could use it to win concessions. "I presume that the palace circle and the nobility will agree to equal rights for Jews if thus they can be freed from you," he said. "I'll take the money and share it with you. It'll be enough for the two of us and our families."

Rasputin was more realistic. "Papa doesn't want peace," he said. "He doesn't even want to hear about the Jews. His relatives won't allow him to grant a constitution. More than once I said to him: 'If you grant a constitution, you'll be called Nicholas the Great.' . . . He's afraid of everyone. When he talks to me in his study, he looks around to see if anyone is eavesdropping. I insisted that my peasants be granted a constitution. But the rich don't want it. . . . The fact that Papa won't allow himself to be persuaded is a great trouble. As soon as I'm away he forgets his promises. That's our misfortune."

———

Were these, as it suited Simanovich to suggest, really two idealists set on helping their fellow men? Certainly Rasputin had few of the prejudices that marked the Russian stereotype. He was fond of Simanovich, giving him pet names, Simochka and Simoniki, and a ring inscribed "To the best of Jews."

The treatment of Jews, "against whom everything was permitted, everything was possible," was indeed a moral disgrace; it was, Witte wrote, transforming them "from timorous creatures into bomb throwers, assassins, brigands—revolutionaries—willing to sacrifice their lives for the cause." Eight hundred thousand Jews had been driven from the combat zones, their shops and synagogues looted, hanged on false charges of espionage.

The two would-be idealists had unpromising material to work with. The tsar was almost casually anti-Semitic, so natural was his inherited contempt. The war was used as an excuse to increase restrictions; all publications in Hebrew characters were banned and correspondence in Yiddish prohibited. Alexandra shared her husband's views. When she was in Germany in 1910 seeking treatment for her heart, her brother recommended that she see a leading specialist from Frankfurt. In the atmosphere of *zhidoedstvo*—kike-eating—she did not want to be treated by a doctor who, however well known, was a Jew. She went instead to a local gentile doctor, who did her no good. Rasputin himself associated with Black Hundred pogromists.

Yet there is evidence that he tried—and sometimes tried hard—to fight bigotry. The Siberian had a strong streak of compassion, and, for all his venality, Simanovich was sincere in his Zionism. The two often acted in concert to help individual Jews. They arranged residence permits, helped petitioners to practice legally in the law and medicine, and had fines and exile orders quashed. They put much effort into sidestepping the numerus clausus that restricted the number of Jewish students in colleges and universities. Simanovich said he was besieged every day by "trains of young Jews" seeking entry to Petrograd University. Rasputin wrote standard notes for them to take to ministers and professors. "Dearest minister," they ran. "Mama wishes that these Jewish students learn in their motherland and that they should not be forced to go abroad, where they become revolutionaries. They have to stay at home. Grigory." The reference to the empress—Mama—usually meant that the students were admitted despite the quota. Simanovich used his expertise in setting up gambling dens under academic-sounding titles to establish the "Agricultural and Hydrotechnical Institute," a front that enabled hundreds of Jews and Christians to have their military service postponed until they had finished their nonexistent studies.

The pair also fielded many requests by Jews who wanted to travel outside their domicile or settle in Petrograd and Moscow. Simanovich exploited a loophole that gave rights of domicile to craftsmen and apprentices. He used Rasputin's reputation to get a foothold in the Petrograd Craft Bureau, which handled such cases. As a jeweler, he also appointed his own "apprentices"—in reality "actors, writers, teachers, et cetera"—and kept a few unused worktables in his apartment to maintain the fiction. In other cases Rasputin arranged for petitioners to register as members of the Petrograd governor's staff, which gave the right of domicile in the capital.

The starets invariably made his peasant supplicants "doubly welcome, thinking nothing of keeping much more fashionable people waiting," seldom refusing them money. He was equally generous with Jews and Poles, insisting that "the blood of the minorities is precious." Even if he had not slept after a night's drinking, he would appear at ten, bow low, look at the crowd, and say, "You've all come to ask me for help. I'll help you all." He "never thought twice" about whether a petitioner was worthy of his help. He said to those sentenced by courts, "The conviction and the fear experienced are punishment enough." He liked to humble the powerful. "Dear generals," he told senior officers waiting to see him. "You are used to getting priority. But there are Jews without any rights here, and I must deal with them first. Come on in, Jews, I want to do everything for you."

There is evidence that the empress's anti-Semitism softened during the war. In one letter to Nicholas, she complained of the treatment of a Russian Jew in her hospital who had returned from America the moment war broke out to enlist in Russia. He had lost his right arm at the front and had been awarded the St. George's Cross. "He longs to remain here & have the right to live wherever he pleases in Russia, a right the Jews don't possess. . . . One sees the bitterness & I grasp it . . . one ought not to let him become more bitter & feel the cruelty of his old country." Nicholas replied that "I have made a note on the petition of the wounded Jew from America: 'to be granted universal domicile in Russia.' " But the success was limited to individual cases. There were no legal reforms. "The tsar is afraid to give Jews equal rights," Simanovich quoted Rasputin. "He's sure he'd be killed if he did."

CHAPTER 21

Two Weeks in the Life of
Grigory Efimovich

The satyr and the saint mingled with each other by the moment in the fall of 1915. Elena Djanumova returned from Moscow on November 24 to plead with Rasputin for her mother. He had bombarded her with telegrams in her absence: "Bringing joy with greetings honoring with calmness," "Indulging my treasure firmly spirit with you kisses Grigory." Some of them were such apparent nonsense that she thought the telegraph office had jumbled the words; when they were retelegraphed, they were just as incomprehensible. Djanumova came with a friend, whom she called simply Lyolya. The Okhrana agents identified her as Galina Fyodorovna Filippova, age twenty-nine, the wife of a hereditary honorable citizen. She risked losing her fortune in a complicated family lawsuit. Her lawyer had advised her that Rasputin was the best bet to help her; she was a striking blonde with sly blue eyes.

The women put up at the Russia Hotel and phoned Rasputin at Petrograd 646-46. He asked them to come over right away. He liked Lyolya; he sat on a sofa with her and put his hand on her knee. He took them out to dinner in a private room at the Donon Restaurant on the Moika. He wore a beautifully tailored peasant's cloth coat with a brocade lining. His eyes wandered over Lyolya, but he was restrained and well behaved. He spoke about Siberia and its grandeur and invited them to visit him there in the summer. "We'll be fishing," he said. "I'll treat you to honey like you've never eaten before. Flowers in Siberia smell so sweet." He got the car to drop them back at their hotel and went on somewhere else.

Elena noticed the Okhrana men trailing them. Komissarov's agents were remorseless appendages, but Rasputin did not resent them. He got on well with the gendarmerie general, a beefy, coarse man with a sharp eye for humbug and a hard drinker. At first the starets had tried to mount a pious smoke screen during their regular chats. "Stop the holiness, talk sense, and have a drink," Komissarov said. Rasputin was delighted and began taking his minder with him to nightclubs and the Gypsies. The general amused him, and he picked up the bills. As to the agents, they gave him protection, and he knew he needed it.

"It's no surprise," he explained when Elena asked why he was followed. "I've got a lot of enemies. I'm sort of an eyesore to people. Would be glad to have me done in. But—try and do it!"

"They love you very much in Tsarskoye, and they protect you?"

"Yes, they do, both he and she," he replied. "He loves me even more. How can they not love me? If I'm not there, there won't be them, there won't be Russia. . . . You think I'm giving myself airs, Frantic? No, my dear one, I know what I'm saying. Everything will be as I say."

———

Rasputin had a hard day with petitioners on November 26; he asked Elena and Lyolya to join them. Some sat in the dining room, while others milled in the hall—priests, students, ladies of the world, monks, officers from crack regiments, all seeking favors. The starets invited individuals into his study, darting out from time to time to embrace a lady, pat a man on the head, or make a telephone call. The ladies sighed with ohs and ahs and said how sorry they were for him.

"How Father works, he gives so much to people."

"And everybody reaches out for him, he makes everyone warm, he's like a sun to everyone," Laptinskaya said, pacing the dining room.

"They tear him to pieces, they don't give him rest, they torture the father," the ladies wailed.

Vyrubova came at 1:00 P.M. with a big portfolio. She was treated unceremoniously; everyone called her Annushka. She headed straight for the study and came back with a pack of petitions. She glanced through them and put them in the portfolio. Rasputin came out of his study and threw himself on a chair, wiping the sweat from his brow.

"Can't stand it anymore," he complained. "So many folks have come. Received them since morning and still they keep coming."

Vyrubova comforted him. "I'll help you, Father. I'll see some of them. With some of them I can solve their problems without you." She took over in the study.

Elena had received a telegram that her niece Alisa was seriously ill in Kiev with scarlet fever and diphtheria. "What's the matter with you, Frantic?" Rasputin asked. "You're so sad, what's on your heart?" He led her into his bedroom. She made a sign to Lyolya to follow her. "Comfort Lenochka, Father," Lyolya said. "Think how unhappy she is, her niece is dying." There followed "something strange," which Elena could not explain.

Rasputin took her by the hand. His face changed; it became like a dead man's, yellow, waxen, immobile. He showed the whites of his eyes and jerked her hand. He said hoarsely: "She won't die, she won't die, she won't die." He let go of her hand, and color flushed back into his face. He carried on talking as if nothing had happened. The telephone kept ringing. New petitioners arrived with flowers and cakes.

When Elena returned to her rooms, a telegram from Kiev was waiting for her: "Alisa is better her temperature has fallen." Rasputin called at the hotel later; he had turned down an invitation to a dinner party, he said. Elena thought that he was drawn like a magnet by Lyolya. She showed him the telegram. "Was it really you who helped?" He answered firmly: "But I told you she would be better."

"Well then, do what you did last time and perhaps she'll recover entirely," Elena said.

"Silly one, do you really think I can do it?" he said. "It's not me. It was from above. And it can't be done again. But I said she'd recover, so why do you worry?" Indeed, letters kept coming for Elena from Kiev. Alisa was making a perfect recovery. As with the tsarevich's illness at Spala, Rasputin was many hundreds of miles away from the patient when he predicted a recovery that followed at once. Alisa's doctors, like the tsarevich's, were astonished; her mother, like Alexandra, thought it a miracle.

—

Rasputin had recovered from the strains of healing and was in a lusty mood two days later. He spent the night with Princess Stefaniya Semenovna Dolgorukaya in her suite at the Astoria Hotel on the Morskaya. This was risky; the princess was the wife of a gentleman of the emperor's bedchamber. He was equally free with the mistresses of politicians. The following evening he was visited by a Madame Leikart, who wanted him to intervene in a business affair on her husband's behalf. He asked her to kiss him; she refused and left. He was not frustrated for long; that night he enjoyed Nadezhda Ivanovna Voskoboinikova, a young widow and the kept woman of Sen. Vasily Nikolayevich Mamontov.

No word of these activities appeared in the press. Alexandra was delighted with Khvostov's efforts, as well she might have been, for the fat young interior minister had much to conceal. Rasputin was drunk for most of December 1915. He was also working at a gallop. *Proizvil*, arbitrary and high-handed actions by the bureaucracy and the police, were the greatest grievance in Russia. Few were immune; many petitioners—government officials in frock coats, officers in spurs, Polish refugees, nuns, bankers, messengers, peasants, fine ladies in dresses by the couturiers Paquen and Ducet—filled Rasputin's hall and anteroom, straining to catch a glimpse of him when the door into the dining room opened. A large sideboard, with a bronze lamp under a large glass shade, stood against the wall, stocked with wine bottles, plates of fried fish, jams, and tea, and baskets of flowers. A rocking chair was by the window.

A clerk from the banker Manus tried to push to the front, but Rasputin stopped him and turned to two young girls. "Well, my doves." He smiled at them. They asked for help in their education. He peeled off some ruble notes and handed them to the girls. He ignored the banker's clerk—the man was pushing a receipt book in front of him—and wrote a clumsy note to Vladimir Voyeikov, the palace commandant at Tsarskoye Selo. He scratched a cross beneath the name and the letters *Kh V,* for "Christ is Risen." Then he scrawled: "My dear and valued friend, do it for me. Grigory." He folded the note carefully, handed it to the girls, and gave them his hand to kiss.

He chose an old peasant from Saratov province next. He had come on behalf of a man called Gavrilo Shishkin, who had been sentenced to prison for fraud, and begged Rasputin to use his influence with the tsar to get a pardon. The peasant undid his shirt and extracted a bit of newspaper, unfolded it, and took out 250 rubles. He handed them to Rasputin with a petition. Rasputin pocketed both, made the sign of the cross over the peasant, and told him he would deal with the matter. Evgeniya Terekhova, a rich businesswoman, followed the peasant; she held a petition in her elegant gloved hand, asking for a contract to supply underclothing for the war ministry. "Yes, yes, my dear, I will do it," he said, stroking her breast and smiling at her while she kissed his hands, then left with a look of triumph. A bald officer with gold pince-nez introduced himself as Sublieutenant Makasov, but a shabby civilian with a greasy hat elbowed him aside and told the starets urgently that he was a village teacher, that he had suffered an injustice at the hands of his director, that he—Rasputin cut him short but promised to write him a letter of introduction to the education minister.

A pretty brunette waited timidly, her eyes red with tears, holding a letter from a Moscow friend of Rasputin's in her cheap gloved hand. She was called Maria Alexeevna, and she wanted help in getting her husband's sentence of administrative banishment lifted. Many men—leftists, anarchists, Jews—were being exiled beyond the Urals. Rasputin asked her to wait in a little room off the kitchen. He returned and talked to the officer. An old widow in a poor coat and round hat said that she was destitute and at her wit's end. Rasputin dipped into his pocket and gave her the 250 rubles he had just received on behalf of the fraud Shishkin.

A young man gave him a sheaf of banknotes; he handed them out to the peasants among his petitioners. An influence peddler named Pogan, a frequent visitor, introduced an engineer, Mendel Neumann, who wanted a pardon from the tsar from an eight-month sentence. Rasputin confirmed that he would bring the case to the tsar's attention. He greeted a bathhouse attendant whom he knew, a wizened man with thinning gray hair, went into his study, and reappeared with a note. It was addressed to the local prefect of police. "My dearest friend, please excuse me," it ran. "Help the poor bath attendant. Grigory." The telephone rang constantly—Vyrubova, Sister Akulina, or Rasputin himself answered it—and messengers with presents of fruit and flowers and wine kept the doorbell jingling. Dunia reminded him that Maria Alexeevna, the girl with the exiled husband in Siberia, was waiting alone for him. He smiled and went to her.

—

The women whispered to each other as he went to the room; a "peculiar smile" played on their lips. It was a narrow room with an iron bed with a foxskin cover, a gift from Vyrubova, icons hung with ribbons, pictures of the tsar and empress, and biblical quotations on the walls. It was the place where he initiated novices in redemption from sin. Some women had left happy; some stormed out, their dresses awry, to complain bitterly of insults to the agents on the staircase. After a short time Maria Alexeevna came out of the room; eyes scanned her minutely for clues and found her "more sad and frightened than before." When Rasputin reappeared his "hair clung untidy and rumpled to his temples," and he was breathing heavily, evidence to the onlookers of payment in kind.

The interlude was brief—as usual a few minutes sufficed him—and Rasputin returned to the waiting petitioners. He blessed two nuns from Verkhoturye, where he had learned his trade from Makari, and promised to help some peasants who complained of a rapacious landlord. A fat banker from Kiev, accompanied by a servant carrying his fur cape, requested a private audience; a messenger from Baron Ginsburg gave him money and asked him to sign a receipt. The sculptor Aronson sat in the dining room; he had been commissioned to do a bust of the starets and was waiting to arrange a sitting.

When Elena and Lyolya appeared, Rasputin's women became agitated and angry. The starets had ranted about the irritation these "haughty devils" had caused him by their resistance. He took a phone call, from Tsarskoye Selo, and laid siege to Lyolya again. He demanded that they have a tête-à-tête. "Don't let your soul dry up without love," he told her. "The soul darkens without the light of love and the sun won't bring you joy and God will avert his face. Love is paradise. . . . I want you—and this comes from God and it is sinful to turn Him down. I am deprived of my strength without love. . . . Give me a moment of love and my strength will grow and"—here he grew crafty—"it will be better for your petition." The two Moscow women found, they said, that, although "we don't believe him and regard him critically," he paralyzed their will and gave everything around them an aura that was "so unusual and it attracts." They returned to their hotel.

———

Rasputin sent a colonel's wife and singer, Madame B, to visit the hotel the following morning. She reproached Lyolya for torturing Father. "We are all indignant at seeing his sufferings. Why don't you consent to belong to him? Is it possible to turn down such a saint?"

"Does this saint need sinful love?"

"He makes everything holy, and whatever you do with him is holy," the colonel's lady said without a second thought.

"Would you consent?"

"Of course," she said matter-of-factly. "I've belonged to him, and I regard it as the greatest bliss."

"But you're married, aren't you? How about your husband?"

"He knows about it, and he regards it as a great happiness," she said. "If Father wants somebody, we regard it as a great bliss—both we and our husbands, those of us who have husbands. We all see now how tormented he is about you. I made up my mind to tell you everything and to ask you on behalf of all the admirers not to torture the holy Father anymore, not to turn down the bliss."

The Muscovites answered her sharply; she left offended and perplexed.

Rasputin came himself in the evening. He sat with Lyolya on the sofa, not letting her go.

"What a shame," Elena said. "They think you're a saint, but you incline her to fornication. It is sin, isn't it?"

"Am I a saint?" Rasputin answered. "I'm more sinful than anyone. But there's no sin in that. In fact, there is no sin. Man invented it. Look at the animals. Do they know what sin is?"

"Animals don't know what sin is because they don't know God."

"Don't speak like that," Rasputin snapped. "There is wisdom in simplicity but not in knowledge."

Lyolya changed the subject to her petition: "All you do, Father, is promise, but you don't do anything."

"You don't do anything for me," he replied. "All you do is use cunning. Give me a moment of love and your affair will go along smoothly. If there's no love, there's no strength in me and no luck. Just like with Frantic. I love her too much, would like to help her with all my heart, but nothing comes out without love."

Lyolya left the room. Rasputin paced nervously. His face became rapacious; the eyes burned. He wanted an excuse to get Elena out of the suite. "You've got wine?" he asked her. "What have you got?"

"We have some white wine."

"No, you know I drink only Madeira," he said. "Listen, Frantic, slip out to my place. Tell Dunia, she'll give you some."

It was midnight, and there was a strong frost. Elena refused. "But I'm telling you that you will go," he said. "If I send you, you must go." He looked at her steadily; "sparkles of fury burned and skipped in his eyes." Perhaps it was the look he had used on Stolypin and Rodzianko, the attempt at hypnosis. Elena looked away and cried out: "Don't forget yourself. I'm not your servant, and I won't run your errands."

Lyolya ran back into the room. Rasputin slowly composed himself and, suddenly, embraced Elena. "Don't be cross, Frantic," he said. "I did it on purpose. I wanted to test whether you love me. If you loved me, you would obey me. You'd go in snow and at midnight. My Peter[sburg] ladies wouldn't have turned me down. Each would have gone with joy. But you, perhaps, don't love me." Soon he left.

———

On December 3 Nicholas set out with Alexis on the imperial train from the Stavka to inspect the southern front. The boy had a heavy cold, sneezing so violently that he started to bleed from the nose, a most dangerous condition for a hemophiliac. His tutor, Pierre Gilliard, fetched Dr. Fedorov, who was aboard the train, but the bleeding was difficult to control and the boy's temperature began to rise.

Rasputin rang the Muscovites to invite them to a dinner party, boasting that ministers would be present. They refused and were glad to spend an evening in peace. They were dozing off at around 1:00 A.M. when there was a pounding on the door. "Open it, hurry up, my sweet ones," Rasputin roared. "We're waiting. I've brought a minister with me." Eventually the knocking stopped. Elena learned that the officer in the room opposite had saved them. He had come to investigate the noise and recognized Rasputin and "Minister Kh." He stared at them; the minister became embarrassed and persuaded Rasputin to leave. "Minister Kh" was Khvostov.

At 3:00 A.M. Dr. Fedorov woke the tsar and asked him to order the train to steam directly to Tsarskoye Selo. The boy's condition had deteriorated. The train had to be stopped several times the following day to allow Fedorov to change the plugs he had inserted in the heir's nose. The boy was cradled in his berth by the giant sailor, Nagorny; it was too dangerous to allow him to lie full length.

In Petrograd, Rasputin was on a spree. The Muscovites avoided him by getting the hotel doorman to say that they had gone to the theater; the doorman said Rasputin was angry and swore at them. He consoled himself by visiting

Elizaveta Evgenyevna Svechina, the young wife of an army officer. This was a potentially dangerous rendezvous, since Svechina's husband was a colonel at the Stavka and thus uncomfortably close to the tsar. Rasputin left at 2:00 A.M. with Maria Markovna Yasininskaya, a twenty-eight-year-old married to a man rich enough to afford an apartment at 104 Moika, a close neighbor of the Yusupovs. The couple took a motorcar to the Villa Rhode, in the Novaya Derevnya district.

They were refused entry because of the late hour. The Okhrana had arranged for Rasputin to have the use of a private dining room, well away from prying eyes in the public areas. Rasputin was furious that—as the restaurant's single most important client—he should be treated without respect. He kicked the door and tugged at the bell cord. It came away in his hand. When a policeman intervened he gave him five rubles to keep quiet. The couple then moved on to Masalsky's Gypsy Choir, a block away. They stayed with the Gypsies until ten the next morning. After that, "heavily drunk," they went to Yasininskaya's apartment on the Moika.

—

His admirers were worried about Rasputin's disappearance. Kulina Laptinskaya rang the Russia Hotel to see if he had slept with the Muscovites. She was surprised at Elena's indignant denial. "Were it so, it would be happiness for you," Laptinskaya said. "He left yesterday said he was going to you, didn't come back, so we're thinking: the Moscow lady consented to accept the bliss. But you take offense. Where is he? Petitioners are waiting for him."

Kulina rang back at midday to report that Rasputin was back from the Gypsies. He had a bad hangover. His admirers sat silent in the anteroom—Elena had joined them—while the sound of breaking glass came from the dining room. He came in with a bottle of wine in his hand, pale, his hair stuck to his forehead, eyes gloomy. He poured some wine into a tea glass and told the colonel's wife to drink it. She reminded him that she was singing in a concert that evening, and that he had promised her that ministers would be in the audience. He told her to drink it anyway. Then he telephoned Beletsky. "My good little lady gives a concert tonight," he told the police director. "Look out, don't refuse and make sure you come." Then he rang Khvostov, employing the same peremptory tone: "Look out you don't miss my little lady's concert."

A priest was sitting by the wall. He listened to the telephone calls with surprise and respect: a starets who ordered ministers about was a power indeed. "What a good night I've had, Priest," Rasputin said. "A pretty Gypsy was singing, and she sang so good—'I'm coming, coming, coming to my dearest one.' "

"Those were cherubs who sang to you. Angels in the skies," the priest said. Elena thought he was mocking the starets but realized he was serious. "Angels in the skies. Angels sang in their glory."

"I'm telling you, Priest, a pretty Gypsy she was, a young one."

"Cherubs, cherubs are singing to you with their heavenly voices," the priest kept saying.

Rasputin grinned and went out to the petitioners. He came back with a pretty young girl, a refugee from the lost Polish provinces. "I'm looking at you, and you are so pretty," he said. "The little nose, and the teeth—but I don't love you, I love these Moscow women. They've tortured me to death. Had to drink all night long because of them." He became maudlin. He went to the kitchen and began smashing plates again. Even Dunia, who normally treated him with robust good sense, was silent. Munya Golovina was frozen. They did not see a drunken peasant, Elena realized, but "an infuriated God."

The telephone rang. Rasputin was asked to come to Tsarskoye Selo immediately. The heir had "swooned away" twice during his journey, and Gilliard thought the end had come. Alexandra was crying and praying as the boy was driven slowly from the railroad station to the palace. His little, pointed face had a "waxen, gravelike pallor," Vyrubova wrote, as he was carried with infinite gentleness to his room and laid on his small white bed. His blue eyes looked out from his blood-soaked bandages with "pathos unbearable." Blood poured down his face each time the doctors unwrapped his nose. Science could do nothing; "in despair," Vyrubova said, "the empress sent for Rasputin."

His women urged him to go to a bathhouse to sober up before he went to the palace. "You know my horses, they'll carry you like birds," one of them said. "First we'll drive in the sleigh, and you'll feel better in the frost. And then I'll take you to a bathhouse. You know it always helps." Rasputin consented. The women brought clean clothes. He dropped his trousers and changed in front of them; they helped him into fresh boots. Munya Golovina helped him stand upright as they put a fur coat on him. He started to sing merrily and snapped his fingers, "I'm coming, coming, coming to my dearest one," the Gypsy song of the night before.

The sleigh ride and the bath had sobered him by the time he caught the train for Tsarskoye Selo. "He came into the room," Vyrubova wrote, "made the sign of the cross over the bed, and, looking intently at the almost moribund child, said quietly to the kneeling parents: 'Don't be alarmed. Nothing will happen.' Then he walked out of the room and out of the palace. That was all." The boy, who had been whimpering with pain, fell asleep. He was well enough to sit up in bed the next morning.

On his return to Petrograd, Rasputin rang Elena to invite her to dine with the Gypsies. "The intoxication was gone," she noted. "He was cheerful and lively." She turned him down, and instead he met up with a lieutenant colonel, Nikolai Semyonovich Ezersky, and a Gypsy singer, Varvara. He had arranged for charges brought against Varvara by a Kiev court to be dropped, and in return she "sang songs during his orgies and entertained him in other fashions." Ignoring the scene he had made two days before, he insisted on returning to the Villa Rhode. His party was asked to leave when the restaurant closed at 2:00 A.M. He slept with Varvara.

Elena was with him when the palace telephoned again. "Alyosha [Alexis] is not sleeping? His ear aches? Call him to the phone," Rasputin said, gesturing for silence. The tsarevich was put on the line. "Why, Aloyshenka, are you burning the midnight oil? Hurts? Nothing hurts you. Go and sleep. Your ear doesn't hurt. It doesn't, I'm telling you. Sleep. Sleep right now. You hear me? Sleep." Fifteen minutes later the palace rang back. The boy's ear no longer hurt, and he was sleeping.

"He fell asleep just like that?" Elena asked.

"Why not?" Rasputin said. "I told him to."

"But his ear hurt."

"I told him it didn't." He spoke with a calm confidence, as if nothing else could have happened.

———

Elena left for Moscow, her honor intact and her petition unanswered. Lyolya stayed on in the hope that Rasputin would intervene in her lawsuit. He sent Ivan Osipenko, the bribable secretary to Metropolitan Pitirim, to collect her from her hotel and take her to a dinner party. She did not know where she was going, but the Okhrana agents reported it as the apartment of a financier, Andrey Knirsche, on Pesochnaya ulitsa. It was a smart affair, with Gypsy singers and a Russian choir. Rasputin was lively, drank heavily, and danced. He took Lyolya to a corner every now and then, talking to her about a "moment of love."

After dinner a young man asked her to accompany him on the piano. Rasputin followed her with gloomy eyes. When she finished she sat with the singer on a sofa. She heard Rasputin's voice: "So that's what you are!" He demanded pen and paper. "I'll write everything about you to Frantic," he said angrily. "She'll understand, and she'll be sorry for me." A politician called Alexander Protopopov, who was standing nearby, brought him a sheet of paper.

He sat in an armchair and scribbled a letter. "Here, take that to Frantic, to my simpleton," he said. "She's not the kind you are, she's not a tart." It read: "Sweet dear my Frantic angry at you don't send me sly ones my sweet one don't send them she's for others give me someone simpler. Come to me I feel like I'm with you. Tears drop. Heart moans. In joy with you. Grigory." With that he told Lyolya that she could leave. At 2:00 A.M. an Okhrana agent reported that he could see Rasputin dancing through a window. Rasputin returned to his apartment at seven, supported by two unknown men, "dead drunk."

He returned to the Villa Rhode for a gala Gypsy evening a few days later. Some young civilians and officers at a table took offense when he asked a lady in their party to dance. The officers jumped to their feet, so Simanovich reported, and unsheathed their swords. Rasputin jumped away and fixed them with his "awful stare." He cried: "You want to have done with me!" They were silent. "You've been my enemies, but you're not anymore," he said quietly. "You've seen that my power won. . . . You don't have any power anymore that you can turn against me. Go home." They did so. There were other occasions on which people set on attacking Rasputin apparently lost their nerve when he confronted them; the incident with his daughter's fiancé was one. His powers were not magical—they did not save him from Hermogen's fists and Guseva's knife, nor would they prevent his eventual murder—but his force of character was an effective deterrent to some who wished him harm.

He had avoided a beating, or worse; he had drunk several cases of Madeira; he had slept with at least six women, and failed to sleep with two; he had received and helped several hundred petitioners; the tsarevich and the little girl in Kiev had pulled through. Rasputin's fortnight was busy.

CHAPTER 22

"They Are Certainly
Going to Kill Me, My Dear"

R asputin welcomed 1916 by singing in his apartment until four in the morning. At Tsarskoye Selo the empress was sick and stayed in bed. "Mama doesn't feel good so she lied all day," the tsarevich confided in his diary. Rasputin came home drunk at 1:00 A.M. on January 2. Later in the day he went to Tsarskoye Selo, where Vyrubova had opened a convalescent home for wounded soldiers. Khvostov and Beletsky, she testified later, "each sent me a sealed envelope by courier with 1,000 rubles." The catering was provided free by Adolph Rhode, the owner of Villa Rhode, who had grown rich on Rasputin's carousals. Prince Andronnikov sent flowers and candles. The financier Manus gave her 200,000 rubles in all; the banker Rubinstein's wife sent 50,000, and Simanovich presented her with exquisite silver vases. It was unclear whether the gifts were for the infirmary or for Vyrubova herself; she said later that her friends wanted to secure her future after the railroad accident.

The partying and drinking—the agents described Rasputin's various states as "drunk," "dead drunk," and "absolutely drunk"—continued at a reckless pace. Maria said that her father deteriorated after the mistress-maid Dunia left for Siberia to tend her ill mother; with nobody to restrain him, he "began seeking relief from his torment in the sort of wine, women, and dancing found in the less inhibited cabarets." He complained to an elderly petitioner, bent with arthritis, that his capacity to heal had dimmed. "I am sorry, babushka, I cannot do it," he told her. "The Lord has taken my power from me." He crisscrossed the city in carriages, cabs, sleds, and a variety of motorcars, hired, borrowed from the court, lent by automobile importers. The agents planted informers among the drivers on the Gorokhovaya rank and kept a car themselves, but the starets sometimes gave them the slip.

Rasputin's name day, January 10, began with a brilliant morning. "Why, there is sun for our Friend," the empress wrote. "That is lovely, indeed it had to be for him." Maria Sergeyevna Ghil, the wife of a captain in the 145th Regiment, had spent the night with him and did not leave his bed until eleven. He followed peasant tradition with a name-day visit to bathhouse and church. Presents from businessmen and from Beletsky's secret funds arrived by cab and messenger. The agents logged pictures, carpets, sofas, chairs, and gold and silver ornaments that he later took to Pokrovskoye. Vyrubova lunched with him and passed on greetings from the imperial family. His drinking began in earnest when she left, helped by the state councillor Daniel Kornilovich Klionovsky, who brought ten bottles of wine. "They played the harmonica, guitar, and balalaika," the Okhrana men reported. "They danced and sang songs and then, later, prayers. The guests left at 2:00 A.M." When the agents checked the apartment, they found the visiting cards of their superiors Generals Komissarov and Globichev attached to some of the presents.

Rasputin was taken by car to a party hosted by Count Tatishchev, a leading banker, at the Hotel de l'Europe on the evening of January 13. The agents loitered outside until the cold drove them away at 2:00 A.M. Rasputin staggered home at seven, "absolutely drunk," supported by Metropolitan Pitirim's secretary, Osipenko. He was much the worse for wear—"he broke a large pane of glass in the gates of the house, and his nose was swollen for he must have fallen somewhere"—but he pulled himself together enough to visit Vyrubova with the financier Rubinstein at Tsarskoye Selo in the afternoon. A change of prime minister was looming, and he was warned that the palace had received a report that he had been misbehaving. They had a long conversation. He was in a difficult mood when he returned home in the evening. "One of you said to somebody that a lady sat on my knee," he complained to Okhrana agents. "It's bad saying things like that. You are here for my safety, but you inform on quite different things."

———

The business of the new premier was difficult. Goremykin was now so senile that his foreign minister, Sazonov, complained, "*Il est fou, ce vieillard.*" Rasputin was hard-pressed to name a successor and discussed it with Simanovich, who in turn approached Manuilov for advice. From a starets to a gambling den operator to a former catamite who lived off the spoils of betrayal—such had the selection process for high office in a mighty empire become.

The choice fell on Boris Vladimirovich Stürmer, whom Manuilov had discussed with Metropolitan Pitirim in the fall, a corrupt reactionary in his mid-sixties whose white beard, pink cheeks, and watery blue eyes gave him the "jovial appearance of a false Father Christmas" but whose oily manners, moist red lips, and crafty smile the French ambassador found were "curiously repellent and filled one with an instinctive and profound mistrust." Simanovich made no bones about why he had been chosen. "Manuilov recommended us Stürmer as 'an old thief and crook,' " he wrote, "and guaranteed that Stürmer would satisfy all our wishes. We bargained with him for a long time. His nomination took place only after it seemed to us that he was prepared enough."

Rasputin prepared the ground with the empress. "Sweety, are you seriously now thinking about Stürmer?" she wrote to Nicholas. "I do believe it's worth risking as one knows what a right man he is." She followed up by stressing that "his head is plenty fresh enough and he very much values Grigory wh [*sic*] is a great thing." He was "excellent and honest" and a true believer in "our Friend's God-sent wisdom." The appointment was agreed on while the tsar was at Tsarskoye Selo. "How glad I am that you have got Stürmer now to rest upon," Alexandra wrote to him on January 16 as the train was taking him back to the Stavka. Nicholas agreed: "I am going away this time with greater peace of mind."

They had "unlimited confidence" in their new premier. Rasputin naturally shared it, though his was based on the expectation that Stürmer would prove "an old man on a string," as he put it. Almost every other Russian regarded the appointment as proof that their country had taken the decisive step into the madhouse. Stürmer had been in public life for forty years. He had the reputation of being easily bribed and the nickname Bully of Tver, after the unfortunate province where he had been governor. He had no experience of central government beyond a brief spell in an interior ministry department with a staff of less than a hundred. His own justice minister now described him as "utterly false, two-faced, and not particularly intelligent." Another colleague said that he debased the language, for "the word *liar* is inadequate to describe him." A third said that "Stürmer was about as suitable as the last person I could think of." Manuilov himself agreed, saying contemptuously that his protégé was "finished at fifty, constantly dozing."

Stürmer's true colors were soon on display. He slipped a resolution establishing a secret fund of five million rubles for his private use into the pile of papers that his cabinet colleagues routinely signed at the end of meetings. The education minister, Count Pavel Ignatev, noticed it by chance. "What's this?" he asked. Since the five million were charged to the war ministry, Ignatev pointed the paper out to Polivanov. "Look at this," he said. "Do you need this?" The war minister denied any hand in it and asked the new prime minister for an explanation. Stürmer mumbled that it was for "espionage expenses," at the tsar's special request. Polivanov insisted that the fund was "utterly impossible." The scowl he earned made him feel that his future was bleak. "After that," he said accurately, "I had the distinct feeling that my days in office were numbered."

Rasputin lost no time in playing with his puppet's strings. Agents followed him on January 21 as he headed alone for 36 Basseinaya ulitsa, the apartment of a twenty-five-year-old actress, Ekaterina Fyodorovna Orlova. She was one of Manuilov's kept women—he pimped for powerful contacts—who was having an affair with Stürmer. "According to information gathered in a secret way," the agents reported, "there were present Manasevich-Manuilov and the chairman of the council of ministers B. Stürmer." Manuilov now described himself as Stürmer's "secretary." His apartment had an imposing reception room, from which he pretended to telephone direct to ministers to impress those he was blackmailing, always careful to call his payoffs "loans." He visited Paléologue, scenting a French subsidy to keep Russia in the war. The ambassador found that he had been indicted on multiple counts of fraud and blackmail in 1911; the charges had been dropped as a "question of expediency" since they revealed his links with the secret police. Grandly, Manuilov introduced himself to the ambassador as the premier's private secretary with special responsibility for the security of Rasputin. "What a title to our respect!" Paléologue hissed as he left.

———

Rasputin celebrated Stürmer's appointment in style, returning home at 7:30 A.M. singing songs in the street. The number of his petitioners increased with the fresh evidence of his power. "Three to four hundred people would call on Rasputin daily," an agent wrote. "I saw uniformed generals, students, schoolgirls asking for financial support." He tried not to turn them away empty-handed, and they added to his soaring expenses. To his lavish entertaining, his use of prostitutes and expensive Gypsy singers and musicians, were added more mundane bills, for the rent on his apartment, school fees and clothes for his daughters, remittances to his wife in Siberia, the constant use of the telephone and cabs. He often had trouble with the telephone—he complained that people would ring him up and curse him—but thought it more confidential than the telegraph, not realizing that Komissarov was tapping it. He dined out every day, and a night's amusement at the Villa Rhode cost the better part of 1,000 rubles. He was drinking several bottles of wine and Madeira a day, and he had acquired a taste for fresh fruit and sturgeon.

Though the interior ministry was giving him a monthly remittance of 5,000 rubles, some $2,000 at a time when factory hands were making $25 a month, and many of his bills were picked up by others, Simanovich complained that Rasputin's "grand living and carousals" meant that this was never enough. He relied on Simanovich to top it up whenever necessary with the cash he procured for influence peddling. Rasputin showed no interest in where the money came from; "he accepted my favors," the fixer wrote, "but never asked about the motives." Many of these rubles he gave away; had he not, Simanovich said, "he could have saved serious money." When the banker Ginsburg called, Rasputin made him turn out his pockets and hand around the contents. He would send petitioners on to other millionaires with a note to give this or that sum. "By nature," Simanovich said, "he had a kind heart."

On Ash Wednesday the empress invited Rasputin to join the family for the service in the imperial chapel. "How happy I am that we took communion with Him!" she wrote. It was a singular honor, which the gossips soon transformed into a khlyst orgy where the pilot Rasputin indulged in "fervors" with Alexandra and her daughters. The surveillance teams, concerned at the increase in public malice, were finding it difficult to keep up with their quarry on his nighttime expeditions; he was sometimes driven in an automobile so fast that they could not shadow it. The car was supplied on Stürmer's orders from the war ministry motor pool.

Vassilyev made sure that he received a report at police headquarters each morning with a detailed list of "all persons who had appeared at Rasputin's quarters the day before and of all the people he had visited." Visits to ministers and to Vyrubova in Tsarskoye Selo were often omitted as too sensitive to commit to paper. As to the palace itself, as noted earlier, only three entries in the *Kammerfurier* journals, the official court record, bore Rasputin's name. One records "Their Majesties" receiving "Grigory Efimovich Rasputin" in the evening of October 17, 1914. The other two, on April 23 and September 5, 1916, state that "Her Majesty" received him at 9:20 P.M. and 9:45 P.M. respectively. These were oversights—the tsar had given instructions that Rasputin's visits were not to be recorded—and give no indication of the true number. The journal, however, confirms that Rasputin's protégés had ready access to the empress: Varnava and Metropolitan Pitirim, Madame Pistolkors, the admirer Baroness V. I. Iskul, Golovina, Laptinskaya all had a string of audiences with her. The visits, Vassilyev said, "rare in 1914, take place more often in 1915 and, finally, reach a peak in 1916." Twice a month Vassilyev himself prepared a special Okhrana report in a single copy for the tsar's eyes only; it contained minute detail on the discovery of secret printing presses, safe houses, arms, and the like, but Vassilyev was too canny to compromise himself with references to Rasputin.

Some raw reports by the surveillance team survive. Each is prefaced by the date, the address, Gorokhovaya ulitsa 64, and the subject's police code name, the Dark One. Name, age, marital status, and address of fresh contacts were noted whenever possible.

They indicate the frenetic scale of the comings and goings in Rasputin's daily life. The report for February 8 is exhausting simply to read:

Knirsche left Rasputin at 1:00 A.M. Two unknown gentlemen drew up in a motorcar at the same time. Knirsche went back into the apartment with them, and they left at 2:00 A.M. Solovyova came at 10:00 in the morning; soon she left. At 10:10 Munya Golovina came, left after one hour. At 11:50 Tatyana Shakhovskaya [wife of the trade minister] came, left after fifty minutes. Simanovich came at 12:00, left after ten minutes. Sandetskaya came at 12:10, left after ten minutes [Klavdia Amvrosievna Sandetskaya, age twenty-six, wife of a captain, Rasputin's admirer, Zakharyevskaya 9]. At 12:15 came a chorister from Afonsky Monastery, Derevensky, who said that the previous year a scribe of Alexandro-Nevskaya Monastery had read in the newspaper *Kopeika* about Varnava and Grischa. The passport clerk at the monastery listened to him reading out the passage and asked, "When will there be a revolution in Russia?" Derevensky asked what the revolution would be about. To which the passport clerk replied: "The Romanovs would not reign anymore and then they would throw down this filth, Varnava and Grischa."

The agents noted that the scribe was now a priest, and that the passport clerk's name was not known; otherwise he would have been identified as a potential dissident.

"At 12:40 an unknown clerk in military uniform came in a motorcar number 3," the raw report continued. "At 12:50 he left with the Dark One. In the yard two volunteers were waiting for them. The Dark One said that he would join them later. The Dark One left with the clerk, and supervision missed them." The war ministry car was too fast for them. They had made sure that the driver was an informer, however. "According to the chauffeur," the report went on, "they went to the Nikolayevskoye cavalry school and to the Polish church on Torgovaya ulitsa. At 1:50 P.M. the Dark One returned home with the clerk, who left after ten minutes. Senator Mamontov came at 1:35 P.M., left after thirty minutes [Vasily Nikolayevich Mamontov, sixty-five, councillor and senator; Voskoboinikova, Rasputin's admirer, was his kept woman, Furshtadskaya 12]. At 1:40 P.M. Gaar and Bazilevskaya came, left after one hour and twenty minutes [Lydia Platonovna Bazilevskaya, twenty-eight, daughter of a major general, divorced from Maltinovsky, an engineer, Rasputin's admirer]."

As usual Simanovich put in several appearances. "At 2:00 P.M. a man in military uniform came for the second time with Simanovich in a motorcar No. 5064, left after twenty minutes. At 2:15 a lady came, wife of an officer of the Izmailovsky Regiment, lives at Izmailovsky Prospect in a government house, left after one hour, forty-five minutes." The agents never reported whether a woman had sex with Rasputin, confining their observations to whether there was laughter or singing. Simanovich was soon back: "At 3:40 P.M. Simanovich came for the third time, left after thirty minutes. At 4:10 P.M. Knirsche came, brought what looked like several bottles of wine, left after forty minutes. At five in the evening came Chervinskaya, stayed for thirty minutes [Natalia Il-larionovna Chervinskaya, forty-eight, wife of a nobleman, sponger in the family of Prince Andronnikov]. At 5:10 came Solovyova. At 6:20 Simanovich came for the fourth time, stayed for one hour. At 6:45 Reshetnikov came, stayed for thirty-five minutes [Nikolai Ivanovich Reshetnikov, fifty-seven, hereditary honorable citizen, Morskaya 39/12 Astoria Hotel]. At 7:20 in the evening came an unknown lady. At 9:20 in the evening Turivich came for the second time, left after twenty minutes. Dobrovolskaya came at 9:30 in the evening. Turivich with husband came at 10:10. Knirsche came at 11:20, stayed for twenty minutes."

The agents appended a note to the report: "At 8:15 in the evening five women arrived—according to the cabman, from the Ofitserskaya ulitsa," it ran. "At ten in the evening they sang songs, played the piano, and danced. There were about twenty-five visitors but the Dark One would not receive them." The report was signed by two agents, Terekhov and Svistunov.

The following morning, Rasputin received ten separate visitors—the agents carefully logged their names and license plate numbers—before taking his customary steam bath in the early afternoon. As he did so Nicholas was paying the unprecedented visit to the state Duma that Rasputin had suggested two months before. He was nervous, he "could scarcely force his voice out of his throat" as he spoke, but he was rewarded with spontaneous hurrahs. It was the last moment that his people, or at least their elected representatives, accorded the tsar such respect; when Stürmer, his premier, rose to address the Duma, he was met with contemptuous silence. Another seven individuals called at Gorokhovaya ulitsa in the evening.

On February 10 Rasputin saw fifteen people in addition to the usual crowd of petitioners; they included "stock exchange sharks and swindlers," a general's wife, the corrupt Manuilov, a messenger from Beletsky, and Lydia Vladimirovna Nikitina, the daughter of the commander of the Peter and Paul Fortress and a maid of honor to the empress.

Six Okhrana men—Terekhov, Svistunov, Popov, Vasily, Ivanov, and Grigory, the cream of the service—kept a twenty-four-hour vigil over this period, but the sheer volume of Rasputin's contacts was threatening to swamp them. There were disturbing references to visits by "unknown men" whom they did not have the time to identify. Rasputin shared their uneasiness; he was overheard muttering about "an attempt on my life" as he walked to the bathhouse.

———

His placemen now headed the church and the government—"I begat Pitirim and Pitirim begat Stürmer," he boasted—but Rasputin feared for his life. So did Alexandra. She no longer trusted the interior minister she had so lavishly praised. "As long as Khvostov is in power & has money and police in hands—I honestly am not quiet for Grigory and Ania [Vyrubova]," she wrote to Nicholas. Rasputin's relations with Khvostov and Beletsky were soured by their attempts to keep their association with him secret. Rasputin knew why—the relationship would further tatter their reputations—and he resented it. He took to telephoning their wives when he was drunk, calling them by their first names, and sending messengers to their apartments when they were entertaining to announce that they carried important messages from him. He nicknamed the plump Khvostov Tolstopuz, "Fat Belly." For his part the interior minister blamed Rasputin for having had Stürmer made premier, a position he wanted for himself.

Obliquely, Khvostov hinted to Beletsky that it was time to do away with "all the filth." By that he meant killing Rasputin. Beletsky discussed it with Komissarov, who warned the police chief against getting entangled in a deed from which the interior minister would run as soon as it was done, leaving the blame to fall on him. Komissarov suggested humoring the minister by proposing fictitious murder plans with obvious flaws, which Beletsky could then point out. A pseudo-plot evolved in which a car would be sent for Rasputin, inviting him to the house of an anonymous woman admirer—the flattery would surely work—with the car breaking down in a dark alley. Okhrana agents, dressed as vagabonds, would jump into the car, strangle Rasputin, and dump his body in the Neva. Beletsky told Khvostov of the plot but warned that the police agents might be traced back to the conspirators. The minister agreed but said the murder must take place—he waved a Browning pistol and said he had a mind to do it himself—and without delay. Beletsky next claimed that Komissarov had arranged to have Rasputin waylaid and severely beaten when he left a dinner party. He neglected to tell the minister that he had informed the intended victim of this; on the evening in question Rasputin stayed at home and told a journalist that a "minister who has kissed my hand" wanted him dead.

Frustrated, Khvostov went directly to Komissarov. He offered him 200,000 rubles from the government's secret funds to dispose of the Siberian. He suggested that the police officer use poison, to be put into a crate of Madeira, which would be sent to Rasputin as a gift from Rubinstein. This would involve the financier, whom Khvostov also wished to harm. Komissarov went to Saratov, where he had been police prefect, to get poison from a friendly chemist. He returned—Khvostov sent him a telegram when he dallied—with a variety of bottles supposedly containing a range of poisons. Khvostov was delighted, Beletsky unnerved. Komissarov reassured the police chief that most of the "poisons" were no more than medicines from his wife's bathroom; he had glued the labels on himself after looking up names in a book on dangerous drugs. One poison was real, however, and Komissarov proved its effectiveness by putting some into a saucer of milk used by Rasputin's cat. The cat died in agony, much to Rasputin's distress. He blamed the poisoning on Prince Andronnikov.

The cat, however, was the only victim. Khvostov despaired of the police duo and contacted Boris Rzhevsky, a yellow journalist "incapable of keeping faith with anyone," whose soiled services he had used as provincial governor. Rzhevsky was a regular guest at the influence-peddling salon of Baroness Evgeniya Rozen, a woman of expensive tastes and "no visible means of support whatsoever." Her salon was renowned for its "never-ending orgies and drunkenness." In the afternoon she entertained grand dukes and duchesses, generals, admirals, and ministers. After dark came courtesans, publicists, actresses, and Rzhevsky. Through the baroness Rzhevsky had maintained contact with Iliodor; he had obtained further letters between the empress and Rasputin and was threatening to publish them in the hope of being paid off. Khvostov suggested that he use Iliodor to organize a fresh plot and that he visit the ex-monk in Norway. Iliodor was continuing to rant against Rasputin from exile. He had written a pamphlet called "Rasputin the Holy Devil" and dreamed of dropping copies over the Russian front lines from an aircraft.

Beletsky had Rzhevsky followed to the Finnish frontier, where a gendarmerie officer deliberately barged into him. The journalist lost his temper, and while he shouted at officials—he told them that he was on a secret mission for Khvostov—his papers were searched. He was allowed to continue to Norway, where Iliodor assured him that his surviving disciples in Tsaritsyn would kill the starets. Beletsky meanwhile unearthed evidence that the journalist was stealing Red Cross donations and passing them to his mistress. Telegrams from Iliodor were intercepted, demanding cash to help his men get from Tsaritsyn to Petrograd. Confronted with this on his return to the capital, Rzhevsky gave Beletsky details of the murder plan.

Thoroughly alarmed, Khvostov had Beletsky appointed governor of Irkutsk, deep in Siberia. Beletsky, a lachrymose man, wept bitterly when Khvostov told him of his unwanted "promotion"; the minister laughed heartily and said that he should have made sure of killing Rasputin. Beletsky retaliated, giving Rasputin and Vyrubova details of the plot, which were passed to the empress; he also outlined Khvostov's murderous intent in an off-the-record interview with the editor of the *Stock Exchange Gazette.*

Rasputin was rattled. On March 1 he visited Spiridovich at Manuilov's suggestion to beg for protection. He dressed himself up in a blue blouse, wide velvet trousers, and high boots, scrubbed his hands and washed his hair. He needed to make a good impression. He told the head of palace security that he was surrounded by murderers and that Khvostov was out to kill him. He begged for palace security men to guard him in place of the Okhrana agents. The general said that he had none to spare. The starets also complained that Stürmer was pressing him to return to Pokrovskoye. "I won't go, not for him or anyone," he said. "They'll kill me on the way, my dear. That's for sure. And even if they don't murder me, they'll exile me so deep that even the tsar won't be able to find me."

Then he cheered up. "It's all right. He's finished!" he said of Khvostov. "The tsar has already asked the old man [Stürmer] to give him four suggestions for interior minister. . . . I telephoned Papa today. . . . To make sure he doesn't see Fat Belly. . . . He's an intriguer. . . . This murderer must be chased out. Murderer. Murderer." He gave Spiridovich a fixed look. "They are certainly going to kill me, my dear," he said. "And you're all going to die too. And they will kill Papa and Mama as well. You understand, old chap, all, all, you'll *all* be killed."

Rasputin's intelligence was accurate. Khvostov, desperate at the turn of events, prepared a dossier of agents' reports highlighting Rasputin's womanizing and drinking. He also gave a press interview claiming that the starets was close to the "pro-German party" and that he was an agent of "world espionage." As interior minister he was able to relax his own censorship orders and permit his remarks to be published. They did immense damage, for they seemed to confirm salon rumors that the empress and the starets were stabbing the Russian army in the back by leaking military secrets to the enemy. Khvostov then submitted his compromising material on Rasputin to the tsar, who was briefly in Tsarskoye Selo. "The emperor listened to the report grudgingly," he testified later. "He walked over to the window pretending that he found the view interesting."

Far from saving the interior minister, this act finished him. Nicholas invited Rasputin to the palace to fast and take communion with him. "The tsar embraced him," Khvostov testified he was told by Father Vassilyev, the tsar's confessor. "He said: 'We shall never part.' Rasputin replied: 'I've got to leave and I came to say good-bye.' The emperor answered: 'We shall never, never part,' and drew out a paper—my resignation." Khvostov's resignation was announced on March 3. The tsar left for the Stavka the next day. "I'm desperate that we recommended Khv[ostov] to you," the empress wrote to him that afternoon. "This thought leaves me no rest. . . . The devil has got into him, there's no other explanation!"

His portfolio was given to Stürmer, who now combined the offices of premier and interior minister. On paper he was the most powerful figure in Russia since Stolypin; in practice he was the creature of those who had made him. As to Beletsky, the confidential interview he had given the *Stock Exchange Gazette* was published in full. The murder plot was laid out for all to read; Beletsky wrote a letter to the editor confirming that the account was accurate. The scandal—the interior minister plotting with a defrocked monk to kill the royal fa-vorite—seemed a throwback to the intrigues and court stranglings of the dim past. Beletsky was dismissed, and the offer of the Siberian governorship was withdrawn. He and Khvostov were to meet again, in a Bolshevik prison cell as they awaited execution.

For once the vileness the affair had dredged up from the heart of govern-ment left Alexandra at one with the country. She felt fouled. On March 5 she wrote to Nicholas that she could find nothing to stimulate her: "No great au-thors already since a long time & in no other country either," she said, "nor cel-ebrated artist, nor composer—a strange lack. Machinery & money rule the world & crush all art; & those who think themselves gifted have ill minds." Her depression was matched by the poet Mayakovsky, who was writing:

> *When all are distributed through heaven and hell*
> *Conclusions will be drawn about this earth—remember well*
> *In 1916*
> *the beautiful people disappeared from Petrograd.*

A "hideous and dirty tangle of gossip" was rolling around the starets. The Okhrana special sections archive had boxes of newspaper clippings, lewd car-toons, obscene pamphlets, and intercepted letters. The stories writhed their way to the front and the Stavka. The senior military chaplain, Georgiy Chavel-sky, was so concerned that he sought an audience with Nicholas. "I spoke about the rumors of Rasputin's closeness to the tsar's family," he later testified, putting as delicately as he could the street stories that Rasputin was fucking Alexandra nightly and selling the secrets he gleaned from their pillow talk to the Germans. "I spoke about his great influence in nominating people to high government positions, in arranging contracts and deliveries for the army. I said the army was rife with rumors that he was giving away military secrets, which he might have known because of his closeness to the tsar's family. I said agita-tors were using it to undermine tsarist prestige."

Nicholas listened attentively without interrupting, Chavelsky testified. Then he said simply: "I've heard all about it."

Simanovich was equally disturbed at the "filthy rumors," which "even the tsar's relatives and high dignitaries were engaged in spreading." Alexandra was aware of them; she received a "vile anon. letter," reading the first four lines of it before ripping it up. Simanovich warned Rasputin that he would be a "lost man" if he did not put a stop to them. His warning had little effect.

"What do you want from me?" Rasputin shouted at him. "What can I do? Is it my fault I'm slandered like this?"

"It's intolerable that rumors are spread about the grand duchesses because of you," Simanovich replied. "You ought to realize that everyone pities the poor girls and that even the tsarina is being drawn into the dirt."

"Go to hell," Rasputin said. "I've done nothing. People should realize that nobody fouls the place where he eats. I'm at the tsar's service, and I'd never dare do anything of the sort. What do you think the tsar would do to me if I had?"

"It's all because you're forever chasing women. Leave them alone. You can't let a single one pass you by."

"Is it my fault?" Rasputin objected. "I don't rape them. They come to me of their own free will so that I'll put a word in for them with the tsar. What am I supposed to do? I'm a healthy man, and I can't resist it when a pretty woman comes to me. Why shouldn't I take them? I don't go looking for them. They come to me."

Vera Zhukovskaya noticed that Rasputin was drunker than ever when he invited her to a party on her return to Petrograd. He was talking to four Caucasians and a lady when she was shown into the apartment. She heard the words "concession" and "stock exchange" several times, together with "putting pressure" on people. Rasputin said he would deal with the business the next day, took her arm, and led her down the stairs. An official car was waiting for them; the driver saluted Rasputin.

They were greeted by a fat little woman at a house not far away and led into a dining room. Their host, an old man in a coarse pilgrim's coat, hurried up to them with bottles of port and asked Rasputin to drink it before his Madeira arrived. He drank glass after glass until the hostess brought in a steaming dish of bream. He ate the fish with his hands and put big lumps on Zhukovskaya's plate. His host began to discuss church politics with him and asked about Pitirim. "He's a good fellow who will find his way about," Rasputin said. "Pitirim belongs to us." Then he demanded music and champagne. Two balalaika players came into the room. Rasputin danced and sang:

Drink to the last drop,
Only lose not your head.

He insisted that Zhukovskaya keep up with him—"drink, my little bee"—as he danced and drank, feet flying in polished boots, torso rocking in a mauve silk blouse.

At length he sank onto a sofa, breathing heavily. He spoke of revels in Siberia. "All day we fell trees, such trees," he boasted. "Three men could not get their arms around them. And when evening comes we make a fire in the snow and sing and dance till midnight. That's the life, I tell you." He was too drunk to prevent Zhukovskaya from slipping away. On March 11 he consoled himself for her escape by visiting the apartment of the prostitute Tregubova. From there he went to a bathhouse.

—

Spurred on by Rasputin and Stürmer, Alexandra was set on bringing down Alexis Polivanov, the war minister. She was interfering freely in military affairs, Polivanov complained, dashing off advice from Rasputin on food supply, transport, fuel, and other "subjects of which she has no idea." She begged for the exact dates of operations so that Rasputin could pray for their success. She pushed for naval appointments, drawing a rare rebuke from her husband; "an excellent man," Nicholas agreed of a naval officer she recommended for an important seagoing command, but one who "has not been on a ship for many years." Her letters quoted Rasputin's approval for being rid of the "revolutionist" war minister; the Friend wanted Polivanov removed because he stood for a responsible ministry, which would be "the utter ruin of everything."

On March 13 she wrote: "Lovy mine, don't dawdle, make up yr mind, it's far too serious, & changing him at once, you cut the wings of that revolutionary party; only be quicker about it . . . hurry up Sweetheart, you need Wify to be behind pushing you. . . . Promise me that you will at once change the M of War, for your sake, your Sons & Russia." The letter crossed with one from Nicholas in which he announced: "I have at last found a successor for Polivanov." Alexandra added a postscript to her letter: "O! the relief! Now I shall sleep well."

"All the ministers will feel relieved," Nicholas echoed her. Stürmer, perhaps, and the empress and Rasputin; others were appalled. The British observer General Knox thought Polivanov "undoubtedly the ablest military organizer in Russia." Equipment supply had improved greatly during his tenure. All frontline units had their full complement of rifles, Knox noted, machine guns were up to a dozen per regiment, and most infantry divisions had three dozen field guns with adequate shells. His successor was Gen. Dmitri Shuvaev, who admitted tearfully to Knox that he was not up to the job. He was "a nice old man," Knox found, with "no knowledge of his work, but his devotion to the emperor was such that if . . . His Majesty were to ask him to throw himself out of the window, he would do so at once." Polivanov— honest, hardworking—did not even rate the normal compliments tossed to dismissed ministers; Nicholas wrote snidely that he found him "insufficiently authoritative."

—

Despite his fears Rasputin did leave for Pokrovskoye, on March 14. He was in Siberia for Easter. "During the evening Bible I thought so much of our Friend and how the bookworms and pharisees persecute Christ," Alexandra wrote to

Nicholas. "It was thus that the Pharisees persecuted Christ. . . . How true it is that a prophet is always without honor in his own country. But what reasons to recognise it: how often His prayers have been answered. . . . He lives for his Sovereign and for Russia and it is for us that He suffers such persecution." She had a letter from Siberia the next day. "Our Friend writes with great sadness of how, because He is far from Petrograd, many will go hungry this Easter. He gives so much to the poor. He gives them the last kopeck he gets and He brings divine benediction to those to Whom he gives."

Pornographic letters between herself and Rasputin were now in free circulation. They were fakes, but these genuine letters, with their capitalized pronouns—normally used only for God, Christ, and the tsar himself—might have caused greater outrage if they had leaked. This was not lust; it was blasphemy.

The poet Alexander Blok, watching the celebrations outside St. Isaac's Cathedral in Petrograd, was overcome with the feeling that old Russia—all of it—was doomed. There was no Easter solemnity in the air. He watched a pack of little urchins swarming unchecked over Falconet's magnificent equestrian statue of Peter the Great, the symbol of the city. They hung on to the horse's tail, lit cigarettes under its belly, and sat on the serpent it was crushing under its hoof. "Total demoralization," he wrote. "Petersburg finis."

On Easter Sunday, Russian troops were attacking the Germans in Lithuania to relieve pressure on the French at Verdun. The enemy found the Russian assaults "conducted, as usual, with the utmost bravery and determination and with complete disregard of loss of life." Fog shrouded the battlefield during the day, and at night the frosts were so severe that the men had to hack themselves from the frozen mud at dawn. The Stavka had deprived them of heavy artillery support and aircraft. The Germans counterattacked. Lying in the marshy ground with a few flooded trenches for shelter, the Russians were shelled and gassed from a range of four hundred yards. After five hours no battalion had more than a hundred survivors. Seven officers of the Smolensk Regiment were left from the thirty-five who had opened the assault. Yet they fell back no more than a mile and a half, bivouacking in the mud and blood. Each night the Germans could hear them singing the Easter hymn "Christ is risen from the dead, conquering death by death." In the Alexander Palace the empress wrote: "Christ has risen! My own sweet Nicky love, On this our engagement day, all my tenderest thoughts are with you." She was wearing his favorite brooch.

She begged Nicholas to send a telegram of Easter greetings to Pokrovskoye. The tsar complied. Even from Siberia, Spiridovich reflected, Rasputin remained in a "communion of ideas" with the rulers; indeed, absence seemed to give his influence on them "a mystical and more powerful character." When Alexis had a painful hemorrhage in his ear, Alexandra asked Vyrubova to telegraph the starets. "Christ is risen," he replied. "In the most radiant joy, know that the Church is invincible and we its family have joy in the Resurrection of Christ."

The empress sent the cable on to Nicholas at the Stavka with her own note: "Yesterday hearing the gospels I was struck so vividly of Grigory and the persecution He endures for Christ and our own sakes. Everything had a double significance and I was so sad you were not beside me."

———

In mid-April, Meriel Buchanan was waiting to cross the street near the Nicholas Bridge. The winter of 1915–16 had been the most persistent for years. The ambassador's daughter was working as a nurse in a British-sponsored clinic, and wounded soldiers were still shivering under piles of blankets in the unheated wards. The street was blocked by carts and trams, their bells shrilling, while horses skidded in the yellow, half-melting snow. Her nurse's flannel kerchief blew across her face in the bitter wind, and she put a hand up to pull it down. An izvoshchik, drawn by a shaggy white horse, stopped in front of her. A black-bearded man sat in it, a fur cap pulled down over his long, unkempt hair, a bright blue blouse and high boots showing under his fur-trimmed greatcoat. His eyes, "pale grey, deep-set but amazingly brilliant," stared at her.

She stood motionless under his gaze, her veil flapping about her face, "held by a sensation of helplessness so intense that the hand I had lifted dropped to my side." The policeman on the bridge waved the traffic on, and he was gone. She gave a little sigh of relief, shaking herself "as if with that movement I could rid myself of something disturbing and repellent." She heard two women on the sidewalk confirm what she already knew—"Did you not see the two men in the other izvoshchik just behind? They were following him to see that no harm came to him; they say he has a special guard now when he goes out, and well may he need it, if all the tales about him are true." Rasputin had returned to Petrograd.

Between revels—"Rasputin was driven to the Hotel Nord and spent two hours in the apartments of the courtesan Evgeniya Terekhova"—he continued to help individual Jews. Simanovich handed him the case of Madame Lippert, the wife of a Jewish doctor who had been captured by the Germans. She was highly excited when she arrived at Gorokhovaya ulitsa; "being received by the tsar did not excite people as much as calling on Rasputin." When Simanovich asked him to take the case up with Sazonov, the foreign minister, Rasputin was visibly embarrassed. "He'll chuck us out," he said. "He's for the war and I'm against it." The foreign minister was hostile; Simanovich said that Rasputin rarely asked favors of his enemies. He agreed, however, to make an exception.

He seated himself at a table to write a note and screwed his face up with effort. "Dearest," the scribble read. "Help the one who is pining in German captivity. Demand one Russian against two Germans. God will help in salvation of our people. Novykh-Rasputin." Madame Lippert saw the foreign minister the next day. He read the note and handed it back to her. "Keep it," he said, not wishing to be compromised. "Tell Rasputin that I would have satisfied your request without it." She was told that six wounded Russians were already waiting for an exchange, and her husband would have to take his turn. She said that he was too old and weak to wait. Sazonov said he would try to go through the Red Cross.

A week later nothing had happened. Rasputin was acutely aware of his importance, Simanovich said; "he did not like it if his prestige began to sway." He dashed angrily to his desk and wrote to Sazonov: "Listen, Minister. I sent a woman to you. God knows what you told her. Cut it out! Have things settled, then everything will be fine. If not, I'll beat your ribs. I'll tell the loving one about you and you'll go flying. Rasputin."

Sazonov was not amused when Madame Lippert returned. "What!" he yelled as he read the note. "Am I to allow an old fox like Rasputin to write me letters like this? If you were not a lady, I'd have you thrown out." She asked to have the note back. The foreign minister refused. She threatened to go directly to Rasputin and noticed a change in Sazonov's attitude. "Let's forget it," he said. "I was beside myself. Pay no attention to it. Tell Father Grigory that it was only a joke." She was upset. "You'd better tell him yourself," she said, picking up Sazonov's telephone. "You know pretty well that he changes ministers like gloves." She rang 646-46, got Rasputin on the line, and handed the receiver to Sazonov. "You've sent me a strange letter, Grigory Efimovich," he said. "Are you angry with me?" "What do you mean?" Rasputin said. "I'm not to blame. You offended me. I advise you not to play dirty tricks. We'd better be friends." Sazonov took the advice. A fortnight later Dr. Lippert arrived in Petrograd, but the foreign minister would not last much longer.

—

Rasputin went to Moscow on May 23. He stayed with the Reshetnikovs in Devichye Pole, where Bishop Varnava was also staying. Madame Reshetnikova admired religious celebrities, and her houseguests had included Ioann of Kronstadt and Iliodor. Elena Djanumova was there. She found Rasputin had grown thinner since she had last seen him. His face was longer and more lined, though his eyes were the same. Varnava followed Elena and Rasputin to a corner. "Oh, Grigory Efimovich," he said with a sly smile. "I'll tell your Fedorovna how you're paying court here to your ladies." It was an unsubtle double entendre; the empress was Alexandra Fedorovna, Rasputin's wife was Praskovya Fedorovna. Rasputin told him to "cut out the twaddle."

Varnava asked her name. "Elena?" he said. "That means your name day is in three days. You should donate something to God's church. Perhaps you've got a carpet you could give to the church."

Rasputin took Elena into the dining room. Varnava followed. "Show you a pretty lady and you're gone," the bishop said. Rasputin scowled at him. "Hear what Varnava just stuck in?" he asked Elena. "He envies me. He's artful, I don't like him." She invited the starets to dinner. She bought Madeira and hors d'oeuvres from Eliseyev's delicatessen and ordered fish soup to be sent to her apartment. Rasputin came at 7:00 P.M. with a Georgian officer who had been assigned to guard him.

Rasputin was sarcastic about Varnava during dinner: "He doesn't like me, that one. His eyes are so shifty." After the meal he said he wanted to listen to the Gypsies. They went to the Yar. Everyone recognized Rasputin from the scandal the year before. The party were shown to a private room; several fresh Okhrana agents arrived to shadow them. A Gypsy choir with the famous singer Nastya Polyakova appeared. Rasputin ordered fruit, coffee, cakes, and champagne. He drank heavily; the only visible sign was that his eyes reddened, his face paled, and the wrinkles showed more clearly. Polyakova sang:

> *Oh once, and once again*
> *And many times more . . .*

"Well, my dear ones, let's be alive," the starets said, jumping up and singing along in a loud voice. "Now, Nastenka, let's have a drink, I love Gypsy songs. My heart leaps with joy when I hear them." Polyakova glared at him, and the choir was unfriendly. Elena was told that the Gypsies had suffered as a result of last year's episode—police investigations, unpleasantness—and they wanted no repeat. Rasputin was indifferent to the hostile looks. "Now, my favorite song," he said. "Hey, 'Troika, Fluffy Snow.' " He began conducting the orchestra, head thrown back, pale, eyes half-closed. He sang: "I'm coming, coming, coming to her . . ." Other people, Moscow industrialists, some Englishwomen from a military mission whose eyes were bulging, begged to join the party. Thirty people had crammed into the room when someone suggested going on to the Strelna nightclub. There was no bill to pay; a waiter explained that the tab had been picked up by a municipal official.

They were given a large room at the Strelna with windows overlooking the winter gardens. People began climbing the palm trees to see Rasputin. He ordered champagne for the choir. The singers got noticeably tipsy; they cried and laughed and sang: "We shall drink for Grischa, dear Grischa." Rasputin began to dance wildly when they played "The Russian." The tassels of his crimson belt, locks of black hair, his soft and shining boots, all flew. Gypsy women danced with him.

The Okhrana agents, their eyes on Rasputin, failed to notice two army officers who came into the room. One of them sat next to Elena. "What do they find in this man?" he asked with a sneer. "It's shameful—a drunken muzhik is dancing, and everyone likes it. Why do women stick to him?" Dawn came. The municipality of Moscow settled the Strelna bill too. The party drove out to a restaurant in the country to watch the sun come up. It had a big garden with lilacs in blossom and a summerhouse. The birds sang; the spring air was clean after the smoky nightclub. "What paradise, what beauty from God," Rasputin said. He ordered coffee, tea, liqueurs.

The army officers had come along; they were whispering to each other. An Okhrana agent asked them to leave. There was noise and a scuffle. Shots, screams, and whistles followed. Elena was pushed into an automobile. Rasputin was shoved in next to her, protesting. He was gloomy as they were driven back into Moscow. "My foes don't like me," he said and fell into a sour silence. The agents told them later that the army officers had been arrested. They had said that they did not intend to kill Rasputin, only to beat him up. His face went yellow when he was told this; his nerves were on edge, and he looked old.

Later in the day he went missing. The Georgian officer told Elena that most of the Moscow Okhrana was out looking for him. He reappeared at her apartment. "I've got a new lady with me," he said through her bedroom door. "Want you to meet her. She's good." Elena was resting and refused to receive them. Rasputin went on to a reception given by a general's wife. One of the guests was a countess, a refugee from the lost Polish provinces who suffered a hysterical fit. Rasputin patted her on the back, but she was immune to his normal calming influence. "Can't stand these eyes," she cried. "They see everything. Can't stand them." She was left in a bedroom. Several of the ladies said that they wanted to be photographed with the starets. They went off to a studio, and pictures were taken. He refused to ride back in the car. He took a horse and carriage, his hair blowing in the spring wind. The agents followed in another carriage. They were relieved when he took the train back to Petrograd; he had not slept for two days.

———

Rasputin saw the empress straight off the train. She passed on four questions that he wanted to be put to the tsar, on the Duma, a new governor for Petrograd, the food shortage, and the Union of Towns, a municipal body that was agitating for a responsible government. There had been a fifth, Alexandra wrote, but she had forgotten it. Rasputin met her again at Vyrubova's cottage on June 11. Again he listed his requests. He wanted the ex–war minister Sukhomlinov to be released from jail and Vyrubova to accompany the empress on a visit to the Stavka; he did not want streetcar fares to be raised, or the synod to approve a potentially hostile federation of municipal dioceses.

Rasputin's neighbor on the Gorokhovaya staircase, the synod clerk Blagoveshchensky, took some notes on "GER" over the summer. Between June 7 and 14 he wrote of many visitors arriving from morning until late evening. Most were ladies, girls, and Sisters of Charity; the men were fewer but still numerous. Whenever the apartment door opened Blagoveshchensky saw a line of people sitting in the hall; "when there is not enough room some of them sit on the bench at the door on the landing." Most of the women "are very elegantly dressed, the last word in fashion, not quite young, of Balzac age." There was a large number of "fresh pretty girls, very young" too, who always impressed the clerk "by their seriousness when they walk along the yard to see 'him' or climb the stairs—they think something over and are very concentrated, as if they're up to something serious." Some of the men were "non-Russian types"—he meant Jews—but there were also "reliable gentlemen of Russian origin, apparently of some position."

Rasputin ate in the kitchen. " 'He' sits in the middle, one side—a dark gentleman in the role of 'his' secretary"—Rubinstein—"on the other, a simple woman, village type, in black dress with white kerchief on the head, Ioannite-style." This was Dunia. They all ate soup from the same bowl with wooden spoons. While he was receiving guests Rasputin often went to the kitchen to take fruit—oranges, apples, strawberries—and other food into his study. " 'His' kitchen is right opposite mine," the clerk noted in his diary, "so that I can see everything clearly, but in the evening they put down the blind."

On June 15 Blagoveshchensky was writing up his diary in his study and listening to "a sort of bacchanalia" next door. The sounds came clearly through the wall. Rasputin was having "a drinking bout on the eve of his departure to his native land." Many guests had come during the day. They were very cheerful, and their number swelled in the evening. "They dance and sing," the clerk noted. Musicians arrived at midnight—"a string orchestra, ten to twelve persons from some pleasure garden, like Villa Rhode or Bouff"—and played tunes from operettas accompanied at the end by "wild dancing." A baritone sang Georgian songs. After noisy applause the "Song of Prophetic Oleg" was repeated three times, with ad-libs to the verses, in the style of a comic theater, and cries of "Wishing you health."

The kitchen window was left open, and the blind was not drawn. Blagoveshchensky could see the guests going into the kitchen to get food, fruit, wine—"mostly these were ladies and girls, all in high spirits, red faced, unduly cheerful." The clerk noticed that the servant, the "Ioannite girl," sat while the ladies did the washing up and cleaning. The carousal went on into the early hours. At the end the clerk made out separate drunken voices, a person dancing, and applause. "Apparently, 'he' let himself go and danced solo," he noted disapprovingly.

CHAPTER 23

"For Their Sakes, Go"

While Rasputin was in Siberia the empress took a trip with her daughters and Vyrubova to Mogilev. Rasputin had wanted to go with her— he was worried that the tsar was drifting out of orbit—but General Alexeev, the senior Stavka officer, declined. Alexandra brought the general an icon as a gift from Rasputin, and took up his refusal as she walked with him after dinner. She asked him what he had against the starets. "Nothing, Majesty, personally I have never met him," Alexeev replied. "Then why do you prevent his coming here? He gives the tsar such comfort. We owe him so much. Twice his prayers have saved Alexis from death." "Majesty, the voice of the people is the voice of God," he said. "It is not possible for me to allow the presence here of a man whom the people and the army think ill fated."

The empress bade him a cold adieu. She hated with the same furious totality that she loved. She loved few, and Alexeev now joined the many she hated. When she heard a few weeks later that he had cancer, she reveled in his sickness. "God sent this illness to save you fr[om] a man who was lossing [sic] his way & doing harm by listening to bad letters & people," she wrote to the tsar.

It was at best eccentric to entertain four beautiful young women and their mother at a high command in wartime. Nicholas, however, was happy to have the diversion—he thanked Alexandra for "bringing me life and sun in spite of the rainy weather"; tender and loyal after so many years, he said that "when I meet you, having been parted for long, I become stupidly shy, and only sit and gaze at you"—for doing so took his mind away from the disintegration of his government. The agriculture minister found it impossible to get the tsar to concentrate on real problems such as the food crisis. "He kept interrupting me with the everyday trivia that interested him . . . how the weather was, whether the flowers were out," Alexander Naumov said shortly before resigning. "Like the neurotic who preserves his equanimity only until some vulnerable point is touched upon, the emperor, clearly exhausted . . . preferred to think about lighter and happier things."

Strikes escalated, transport was in chaos. The prices of flour and fat were up 260 percent over prewar levels; the cost of meat had more than tripled, salt sextupled. Internal dictatorship, General Alexeev wrote in a top-secret report, was the sole means of preventing anarchy. He suggested that all civil power be placed in the hands of one man, a supreme minister for state defense. This man would "unite, lead, and direct by his will alone the activities of all ministries and all government and civic organizations." The idea attracted Nicholas. He would retain military power as supreme commander, while the "dictator" would rule behind the front on his behalf. The man he had in mind was— Stürmer; Stürmer, friend of the empress and the empress's Friend, Stürmer, the five-million-ruble swindler, "low, intriguing, and treacherous," "a man on whose word no reliance can be placed." That was what the Allied ambassadors thought of him. Russians despised him far, far more.

Secrets were no longer kept. The Duma president Mikhail Rodzianko got hold of a copy of the report. He had already warned Nicholas that Rasputin was a direct threat to the dynasty. He now turned on Stürmer, the protégé, over coffee at a private dinner for ministers and Duma men. "You spend your time trying to discover an imaginary revolution," he accused the prime minister. "You organize monarchist congresses, persecute public organizations, provoke endless intrigues which paralyze administration, and deliver the country into the hands of self-seekers. . . . Bribery, extortion, plunder are growing on all sides." Then, without using a name, he moved on to Rasputin. "Persons who deserve the gallows continue to remain in high favor." The other ministers were restless with embarrassment, but Rodzianko was not done with Stürmer yet. "You should realize that you are neither beloved nor trusted by the nation," he boomed on. "In your senseless search for a bogey revolution, you are murdering the living soul of the people and creating unrest which sooner or later may breed an actual revolution."

Rodzianko hastened to the Stavka to warn the tsar against any thought of a dictator, least of all Stürmer. "What measures would you propose for setting affairs in the rear in order?" Nicholas asked him. "Grant a responsible ministry," he replied. The tsar said he would think it over. He did not. "It goes without saying that Rodzianko talked a lot of nonsense," he wrote to Alexandra. "Of all the foolish things which he said, the most foolish was . . . replacing Stürmer." Far from sacking him, the tsar had a stunning promotion in mind.

Intelligent, cultivated, and able, Sergei Sazonov had been foreign minister since 1910. Trusted by the public and the Allies, he suffered the fatal flaw of loathing Rasputin. The empress also suspected—rightly—that he favored a responsible ministry and Polish autonomy. Both of these, she said, would compromise "Baby's future rights." She campaigned relentlessly against him. "Long-nosed Sazonov . . . is such a pancake," she wrote to Nicholas. "Wish you cld think of a good successor to Sazonov—need not be a diplomat. . . . Stürmer always disapproved of him as he is such a coward towards Europe and a parliamentarist—and would be Russia's ruin." Nicholas gave way in characteristic style. He saw Sazonov at the Stavka and appeared to agree with him over Poland. Sazonov was taking a short holiday in Finland at the end of June when he learned that he had been dismissed. His deputy minister was in tears when he begged the British ambassador to persuade the tsar to reverse the decision. "I cannot exaggerate the services which Sazonov has rendered the cause of the Allies," Buchanan cabled Nicholas. There was no reply.

Sazonov was replaced by Stürmer. In the five months since Manuilov and Rasputin had brought him to Alexandra's eye, the "honeyed and furtive" nonentity had acquired the great offices of prime, interior, and foreign minister. Although he now dropped the interior portfolio, he combined the other two. He fancied himself in his new diplomatic role. He hung three paintings in his office, of the great European congresses of Vienna, Paris, and Berlin, with space for a fourth, which he told visitors was reserved for the great postwar Congress of Moscow, over which he would preside. "How fine it will be at Moscow! How fine it will be!" he congratulated himself, repeating his sentences by nervous habit. "God grant it! God grant it!"

———

On his return from Siberia, Rasputin was pleased enough to see Sazonov gone. He was not so happy that Stürmer had acquired another office without his help. He disliked the distance that Stürmer kept from him. "I'll do for him," he threatened. Manuilov, who used them both, tried to maintain friendly relations between the two. He secretly arranged meetings at night in the Peter and Paul Fortress through Lydia Nikitina, Rasputin's admirer and the daughter of the fortress governor, for Stürmer was terrified of any public association with the starets. Stürmer even denied to Klimovich, the director of the police department, that he knew Manuilov. When Klimovich gave the premier a copy of Manuilov's police record, Stürmer shook his head and said, "Yes, yes, what a scoundrel! A fine gentleman!" Yet Klimovich testified later that he had seen the two chatting and smoking cigarettes together, and that he was paying Manuilov a salary of eighteen thousand rubles a year on Stürmer's direct orders.

Rasputin was also angry that the justice minister, Alexander Alexeivich Khvostov, had replaced his fat nephew as interior minister. The uncle was ill and tired. He did not want interior, the most exhausting post in the cabinet. "How did you dare to do me this dirty trick?" he asked Stürmer when he was pushed into it. Khvostov disliked Rasputin and was honest, a combination that troubled the starets.

It did not, though, dampen his spirits. On August 3 his neighbor Blagoveshchensky was kept awake by an all-night drinking bout. He estimated that it involved forty people and a Gypsy choir. "They all sang and danced from nine in the evening until 3:00 A.M.," he wrote in his diary. "In the end, everyone was drunk, particularly 'him.' " He drank all day from August 6 to 9—he "pestered the servants in the yard, thrust himself kissing on them"—until, to his neighbor's relief, he returned to Siberia. Alexandra had hoped to go to Tobolsk to visit the shrine to St. Ioann of Tobolsk, illegally beatified the previous summer by Bishop Varnava. Instead she sent Vyrubova and Lili von Dehn, and asked Rasputin to go with them.

Public feeling against the starets was now so strong that Dehn thought it dangerous to advertise the trip. They left Petrograd, however, in a blaze of publicity. "Wires were sent in advance all along the line to announce our advent, and crowds thronged the stations to catch a glimpse of us," she wrote. They traveled in style in a special saloon carriage attached to a Trans-Siberian train. At Tyumen they took a steamer for Tobolsk, arriving at dusk to find its churches and houses sharply silhouetted on the hills above the black river. The governor and Varnava met them, and they were quartered in the governor's mansion. They visited the new saint's tomb the next day and attended a special service in the cathedral.

On the way back Rasputin insisted they stop at Pokrovskoye and meet his wife, whom Dehn found a "charming, sensible woman." He said that he wanted the tsar and tsarina to stay with him in his house. "But it's too far," Dehn said, shocked. "They must," Rasputin said, and added, "Willingly or unwillingly, they will come to Tobolsk and they will see my village before they die." After his murder, as prisoners of the revolution, they did. The little party moved on to Ekaterinburg; it was to be the death place of the imperial family, and Dehn said that, as soon as she got off the train, "I felt a sense of calamity. We were all affected: Rasputin was ill at ease, Anna perceptibly nervous." They visited Rasputin's old mentor, Makari, at his fowl-infested hermitage in the woods of Verkhoturye. He fed them bread and cold water, and they slept miserably on the mud floor of his hut. The ladies were glad to return to Petrograd. Rasputin followed them on September 7.

———

Rasputin returned to unpleasant news. Manuilov had been arrested by Klimovich on Alexander Khvostov's orders. He was charged with extorting a large amount from a Moscow bank and with selling exemptions from military service. A honey trap, using ten thousand rubles in marked notes, had been laid for him. When the bait was taken, Khvostov told Stürmer that he had "an interesting piece of news which at first will probably frighten you, but later will please you." Stürmer threw his arms around his interior minister and denounced Manuilov, his self-styled secretary, as "a blackguard and a blackmailer." But he was not pleased; he was terrified. Manuilov made it clear that he would implicate both Rasputin and the premier at his trial. Stürmer had Klimovich dismissed without reference to Khvostov, who was then relieved of his own post. When he bade good-bye to Stürmer, Khvostov said, "It is the first time that I leave you with a feeling of sincere pleasure." Russia had no interior minister.

Another of Rasputin's circle was in deep trouble. Dmitri Rubinstein was accused of spying for the Germans. The financier had bought up all the stock in the Anchor Insurance Company, which specialized in factory insurance, and sold the company to a Swedish firm at a large profit. As part of the deal he sent plans of all the factories insured by the company to Stockholm. Many were plants engaged in the war effort. All mail and couriers were searched at the Swedish border with Russian Finland. When the plans were discovered Russian military intelligence believed it had stumbled on a giant espionage ring. Rubinstein, the Friend's friend, was imprisoned and faced probable execution. The affair was headline news across the country.

Worse, Simanovich and Rasputin had introduced Rubinstein to Alexandra as a confidential banker. She had used him to transfer money, via Sweden, to needy friends and relatives in Germany. Rubinstein's role, Simanovich said, was "very ticklish and dangerous and he carried out the tsarina's commission with great craftiness and won her gratitude." It was indeed sensitive, for transferring funds to enemy nationals was a hanging offense. Rubinstein's connection to Rasputin and the empress was common knowledge. He had assiduously used Rasputin's name, and the claim that he was banker to the royal house, to impress investors on his stock-ramping schemes. Rasputin did not charge Rubinstein for his help in influence peddling. Instead, with typical generosity and disdain for cash, he sent a stream of petitioners on to Rubinstein's offices and the financier rewarded them with salaried but fictional posts in his bank.

The empress, Simanovich said, was "very much afraid that her relations with Rubinstein might become known, which would have set off an unheard-of scandal." She tried to get the military to drop the prosecution, but the senior officer responsible, General Ruzsky, a "great enemy of the Jews," refused. Afraid that she would be able to get his release from prison in Petrograd, the general had the banker transferred to the Pskov penitentiary. Rasputin took Rubinstein's wife to Tsarskoye Selo to visit the empress in her infirmary. "Calm down and go home," Alexandra told the hysterical woman, promising to intervene with the tsar. Rubinstein, however, had set up his bank with capital from the Voyeikov brothers, one of whom, Maj. Gen. V. N. Voyeikov, was palace commandant. The bank had run up huge losses, and the brothers were 800,000 rubles out of pocket. For this they blamed Rubinstein, and they connived with the military in Pskov to keep him locked up.

Scandal had almost lost its power to shock; by the late summer of 1916, the country was close to catatonia. The self-seeking adventurers in high office, the *Times* correspondent Robert Wilton thought, were now copied in all walks of life. The whole of Russia "seems to be engaged in a whirl of plunder," he wrote. "Every man is trying to rob his neighbour to the utmost of his capacity. . . . Never was there a time when money could be earned so easily by nefarious methods." The collapse in vital areas such as food supply, he wrote, "has, I fear, gone beyond all remedy." A friend who had just traveled through Siberia told Wilton that it was overflowing with food. In Petrograd, in one of the greatest wheat-growing countries on earth, white bread had disappeared. There was no sugar, little milk or butter, and no meat beyond scrawny chickens.

—

Pogroms were in the air, and spy mania was universal. Vassilyev met senior government officials who told him that two aides of Kaiser Wilhelm had been seen walking down the Nevsky Prospect with their coat collars turned up; they wanted to know what sort of an Okhrana he was running that allowed such men to stroll unmolested through Petrograd. Radio stations were scented out everywhere. The Germans were said to run regular flights by Zeppelin airship to a forest clearing near Petrograd to land fresh agents and to carry others back to Berlin for debriefing. "It was such idle gossip," Vassilyev wrote wearily, "that gave rise to the parrot cry, soon in everybody's mouth, 'Things cannot go on like this!' "

Anyone with a German name, or who had worked for the Germans, was suspect. Russian journalists who had been correspondents for German newspapers were banished to Siberia, though Vassilyev agreed that there was not a shred of evidence against them. He noted that life was intolerable for unfortunates with the surname Kaiser. The privileges of German Baltic barons at court had long been an issue; when Prince Menshikov, known for his wit as well as his catamites, was once asked what favor he would like, he replied, "I'd like to be promoted to be a German." The war, and the stories of enemy atrocities, added fresh venom to attacks on leading court figures—the German-born empress herself, Count Fredericks, the head of the imperial household, and others with German names: the chief court marshal, the adjutant general, the master of horse. On the Baltic coast the towers of country houses belonging to Baltic barons were reported to be signal stations for the German fleet; the observatory of an amateur astronomer near Riga was ransacked separately by the police, army, and navy.

Inevitably, Prince Andronnikov was the next of Rasputin's circle to be suspected of spying. The prince was spending immense sums on high living and his lovers. "I cannot even approximately define the amount of his expenses," his valet Kilter later testified. "My wife used to bring almost every other day 1,000 rubles to him from the Russian-Asian Bank. She received the money by check. He paid 600 rubles a month for his apartment. Not a single day passed without guests coming for breakfast, lunch, and dinner. People used to come in groups, not caring whether the host was at home or not." The Okhrana received reports that all this was paid for with German money. When Andronnikov was investigated by the Rasputin inquiry commission the following year, no proof of treason was found. The commission was satisfied that he was too flighty and self-obsessed to be a thoroughgoing traitor. He had no political ideals; like Rasputin's, his opinions of politicians were based on his personal relations with them. "If they ignored him or he quarreled with them, he discredited them in every possible way," the industrialist Alexis Putilov testified. "If they were good and kind to him, he praised them left and right."

Nevertheless, the pro-German myths surrounding the empress and Rasputin and his circle were widely accepted and immensely damaging. It was even suggested that Rasputin had engineered the loss of the Royal Navy warship *Hampshire*, which struck a mine in the North Sea while bringing General Kitchener, the British war minister, on a secret visit to Russia. It is true that Rasputin was pleased—"our Friend says it is good for us that Kitchener died, as later he might have done Russia harm," the empress wrote to Nicholas—and true that the Germans were grateful to him for the demoralization and scandal he bred. There was no evidence at all that he was in their pay, or of the existence of a "German camarilla" at court. But hard fact in the sullen cities was in yet shorter supply than food.

The drifting scum of gossip was unnerving the empress. "Why does Grigory stay in Petrograd?" she asked Lili von Dehn. She half-wished he would return to Siberia; though, she said, "we can't possibly discard him, he has done no wrong." At Alexandra's suggestion Dehn visited Rasputin at his apartment. He was having tea, and she asked him for a private word. He took her into his room. To her irritation, Laptinskaya went with them. "Grigory, you must leave Petrograd at once," she told him. "You can pray for Their Majesties just as well in Siberia. You know what is being said. For their sakes, go."

He seemed ready to take the hint—"I'm sick and tired of it all, I'll go"—but Laptinskaya raged: "How dare you try to control Father's spirit! I say that he must stay. Who are you?" Rasputin then said, "Perhaps you're right. I will stay."

———

Rasputin was thus in Petrograd to welcome the new interior minister. Alexander Protopopov came from Simbirsk, a city that sat quietly above the mile-wide Volga, its courtyards and cherry orchards overgrown with grass, a place where "here and there someone sticks his head out of a window, looks around, gaping in both directions, spits, and disappears." It had produced the revolutionaries Kerensky and Lenin, and Oblomov, the symbol of Russian lethargy in Ivan Goncharov's eponymous novel. Protopopov had little in common with any of them. He was the "typical noble in debt who is always prepared to do anything that is wanted," a compulsive busybody with "a finger in every pie," and his opinions veered at will between the liberal and the reactionary. He came from the gentry—his father owned a large cloth factory in Simbirsk—and had trained as a lawyer. He was small and neurotic; his "wild bright eyes shifted all the time"; with his sleek hair he was said to resemble "an excitable seal."

His behavior hovered between eccentricity and lunacy. Although the charitable attributed his obvious ill health to a progressive spinal disease, he was almost certainly syphilitic. He had first met Rasputin the previous winter through Peter Badmaev, a practitioner in Tibetan herbalism who was treating him for leg ulcers, hallucinations, partial paralysis, and other symptoms of advanced syphilis. Badmaev was quite as extraordinary as his patient. He was a Russified Buryat Mongol who had gone to St. Petersburg in his youth to study orthodox medicine before abandoning it for Tibetan cures. Tibetans used plant extracts and animal secretions as medicines and were skilled at osteopathy, massage, and hypnotism. Badmaev developed a thriving practice; when he converted to Orthodoxy he was well enough known at court for Alexander III to stand as his godfather. He prescribed powders as specifics against cholera. His popular "herbal infusions"—with names like French perfumes, Elixir du Tibet and Lotus Noir—were probably laced with heroin. Rasputin said they made the deepest concerns "seem like petty trifles. . . . You'll become happy, so-o ha-appy, and s-illy that you won't worry about anything."

Badmaev suggested to Rasputin that his patient—then a deputy president of the Duma—would make an excellent minister. Rasputin assured Protopopov, with "much giggling and simpering," that he would find him a portfolio. Simanovich approved; "we had his promise to do something for the Jews," he claimed. Alexandra duly took up the cause at the beginning of September. "My own Sweetheart," she wrote Nicholas on September 7. "Grigory begs you earnestly to name Protopopov. . . . You know him & had such a good impression of him—happens to be of the Duma (is not left) & so will know how to be with them. . . . He likes our Friend since at least 4 years & that says much for a man." In the same letter she showed mounting irritation with Stürmer, who was failing to see Rasputin and was thus "a big act" who had "lost his footing." She had not changed her views on the Duma—it was still full of "rotten people"—but she thought Protopopov's appointment as interior minister would "make a great effect among them & shut their mouths."

At first Nicholas hesitated. "Our Friend's opinions of people are sometimes very strange," he replied on September 9. "All these changes make my head go round. In my opinion they are too frequent. In any case, they are not good for the internal situation of the country, as each new man brings with him alterations." He knew his wife's meddling was dangerous—he apologized nervously: "I am very sorry that my letter has turned out to be so dull"—but he gave way the next day. "It shall be done," he wrote.

Alexandra was delighted with her Friend's new find. Far from thinking Rasputin erratic, she felt that his worldliness compensated for the protocol-induced limitations of her own and her husband's existence. "He will be less mistaken in people than we are—experience in life blessed by God," she assured the tsar. Rasputin and Simanovich took Protopopov to Vyrubova's cottage and introduced him to the empress on September 21. She spent ninety minutes with him and found him "very clever, coaxing, beautiful manners, speaks also very good French & English." She was frank with him; she told him that she found it difficult to trust people, and that she expected him to obey. "I am no longer the slightest bit shy or afraid of the ministers and speak like a waterfall in Russian!!!!" she boasted to Nicholas. "And they kindly don't laugh at my faults. They see I am energetic & tell all to you I hear & see & that I am yr wall in the rear . . . eyes & ears." She reveled in her power, her vigor restored, in command; had not her grandmother stamped her name, Victorian, on an epoch? Nicholas acknowledged her role in his reply on September 23. "It rests with you to keep peace and harmony among the ministers," he wrote. "Thereby you do a great service to me and our country." In Protopopov she served catastrophe.

The new minister was hopelessly compromised. As Rasputin remarked, his "honor stretches like a piece of elastic." He was heavily in debt. Simanovich bought out his promissory notes for 150,000 rubles to prevent his being declared bankrupt. "Protopopov promised to give me back this sum after his nomination out of the secret funds of his ministry," Simanovich said. Some of the promissory notes, together with others from grand dukes and ministers, were found in Simanovich's apartment after the revolution.

Protopopov met Rasputin regularly if clandestinely at Gorokhovaya ulitsa, coming late at night, wearing false spectacles, "stealing through a back door, with raised collar so as not to be recognized by his own detectives." His "lascivious girlfriend," Madame Lunts, an attorney's wife, was also a frequent visitor.

Rasputin deeply impressed him. "Confidential interpreter of events, judge of the people," Protopopov testified later. "Great influence upon the tsar. Upon the tsarina—enormous. . . . Anyone else approaching the tsar would have been confronted by the will of the tsarina, while Rasputin not only had her support—but obedience, Vyrubova's worship, and the love of the tsar's children." Vain himself—although he was a civilian, he wore the uniform of a gendarmerie general, with high boots and a dress belt he had designed—he was awed by the "care and attention" the empress paid to Rasputin's appearance. "His silken shirts were embroidered by her," he testified. "She gave him the golden cross on a gold chain he wore around his neck, and the clasp had the tsar's letter, N. He talked to them firmly and with confidence."

The new interior minister was put to work at once to free the Friend's friends. He dined with the empress at Vyrubova's cottage on September 25. Madame Sukhomlinova, the voluptuous young wife of the ex-war minister, had visited Rasputin several times to plead for her husband's release from prison. The starets had agreed to help; whether she paid him in kind is not known. Alexandra now took a large sheet of paper and wrote to the tsar asking him to order the release of Sukhomlinov and her banker Rubinstein. "Protopopov quite agrees with the way our F[riend] looks upon this question," she wrote. "Write this down to remember when you see him and also speak to him about Rubinstein to have him sent quietly to Siberia. . . . Prot[opopov] thinks it was Guchkov, who must have egged on the military to catch the man, hoping to find evidence against our Friend. Certainly he had ugly money affairs— but not he alone."

The two were released. Graffiti was daubed on walls in the cities: "Traitors defend Traitors." For good measure Protopopov also had the charges against Manuilov dropped and banned all private meetings of civic organizations. The hopes liberals had in him were dashed within days of his appointment. "A man who works with Stürmer, frees Sukhomlinov, whom the entire country considers a traitor, liberates Manuilov, and persecutes the press," cried Pavel Miliukov, leader of the Constitutional Democrats, a renowned historian who had taught at the University of Chicago, "cannot be our friend!"

A Tragedy Played
in a Brothel

At Donon's smart restaurant, the former premier Vladimir Kokovtsov dined with the industrialist Alexis Putilov and said that revolution was in the wings. Putilov disagreed; it was much worse than that. "We're heading for anarchy," he said. "There's a vast difference. Revolutionaries reconstruct. Anarchists destroy." The owner of another top restaurant, Alvin Juin, was arrested for spying. "The regime is finished," an observer wrote. "If the spy hunt has been taken into the kitchens of the Maxim's of Russia and an innocent French patriot taken for a German spy, then anything is possible."

The journalist Konstantin Paustovsky went to the backwoods town of Yefremov to find out what provincial Russia was thinking. The stands of spruce were slashed scarlet by the autumnal sunsets, and the air crackled with early ice crystals. Idiot beggars sat on the church steps, and "white ticket men" exempted from army service idled in the streets. Paustovsky's hotel had two other guests, a fortune-teller, Madame Troma, her fingers metallic with cheap rings, and "Princess Greza," in fact a man who wrote an agony column for cheap magazines. An enormity of hopelessness lay over the land like the smoke from the villages. "It was as if no one, anywhere, expected any happiness," he wrote. "Everyone, languishing, was waiting for the drama's denouement."

On his estates the writer Ivan Bunin was surrounded by peasants who "grow more furious every day." He sat on his bed and waited for them to burn down the house. They had already stolen his horses. The editor of the magazine *Kolokol*, returning from the villages, reported that everyone was "hawking around the prophecy which Grigory had often uttered to Their Majesties: 'If I die or you desert me, you will lose your son and your crown within six months.' " The governor of Tula province warned Protopopov's interior ministry that "such terrible times have set in that I don't know how to cope. . . . I am sitting on a powder keg."

Visitors to the Stavka observed the tsar's sunken cheeks. "He can't continue this way much longer," the grand marshal, Paul Benckendorff, told the tsar's physician. "He is no longer seriously interested in anything. . . . He goes through his daily routine like an automaton, paying more attention to the hour set for his meals or his walk in the garden than to affairs of state." Alexandra, who spent a few days at the headquarters, sensed the tsar's isolation among the professional military men. "You are so lonely among this crowd— so little warmth around," she wrote on her return on October 12. She was sure that Rasputin could lift his gloom. "A touch of His on your chest would have soothed much pain," she went on, "and given you new wisdom & energy from Above—these are no idle words—but my firm conviction. . . . I know too well & believe in the peace our Friend can give & you are tired, morally, you cannot deceive old wify!"

The average tenure of a minister was less than six months; in a year there had been five interior ministers, three war ministers, four agriculture ministers, three justice ministers. The changes came so fast that a right-wing Duma man, Vladimir Purishkevich, wrote a doggerel on "ministerial leapfrog":

> You'll see your minister uncrowned
> Within a month—or rarely two.
> By minutes now we count their term.
> They go and leave a sulfurous smell;
> Only Rasputin still holds firm.

Purishkevich noted in his diary that new appointees no longer bothered to move into the government apartments their positions entitled them to. They were unlikely to survive long enough to make the furniture transfer worthwhile.

Protopopov recklessly insisted on meeting the Duma leaders. "We do not want to talk to you," they told him, "a man who received his appointment through Rasputin and freed the traitor Sukhomlinov." He retorted that he was the tsar's creature and proud of it. "I am the personal candidate of the sovereign, whom I now have come to know better and to love. All of you have titles, good positions, connections. . . . I have nothing besides the personal support of the sovereign." But his colleagues thought him mad; he kept an icon in his office and held long conversations with it. Peter Bark, the finance minister, thought him a "pitiful figure" but allowed him one talent—"he can talk without end." His offices were full of people with "appointments he did not keep, and urgent current business fell into chaos."

———

Rasputin was at the center of the whirlwind—"the most talked-about man in Russia"—and it was blowing him off his feet. He was degenerating with drink and exhaustion. "He would repeat certain words in a fever," the journalist N. A. Teffi wrote. " 'God, prayer, wine,' mixing everything up, confusing things, could not understand himself, tortured himself, had convulsions, threw himself into the dance despairingly, with a cry on his lips." It was as though he were "plunging into a burning house"—the house of Romanov. He did not care; he seemed to have written himself off. "The fools don't understand who I am," Teffi quoted him. "A sorcerer, perhaps. . . . They burn sorcerers, and let them burn me also. One thing they do not realize. If they do burn me Russia is finished. They'll bury us together."

Rasputin was afraid not of death, Simanovich thought, but of his fall from power. He was insecure and uneasy and "tried to comfort himself with belief in his 'power.' . . . Tortured by doubts and troubled about the future, he turned to me for friendly advice and support." Simanovich kept the starets busy with a million-ruble sugar scandal. A Kiev sugar plant owner, Ziv, had been arrested with two other businessmen for selling a large amount of sugar to the Germans, which had been shipped via Persia. The military authorities wanted the men charged with treason and hanged.

Rasputin agreed to help. Ziv said he would pay whatever was necessary and made a down payment of fifteen thousand rubles to cover Rasputin's carousals at the Villa Rhode. Simanovich contacted Nikolai Dobrovolsky, a lawyer and the synod procurator, who was heavily in debt to him. He was thickset, narrow-minded, corrupt, and influential, a perfect choice. "He liked money very much and did favors for gifts," Simanovich recalled. "For me, therefore, he was very valuable. Petrograd in general was full of such people." When the army refused to drop the charges, Rasputin and Simanovich promised Dobrovolsky the post of justice minister. They appealed to Alexandra for a pardon and arranged an audience with her for Dobrovolsky. The lawyer claimed that the sugar had been delivered to German buyers in Persia before the war and that the businessmen had no idea of how it had gotten to Germany. It was a thin story—why should a German buyer have wanted sugar delivered via Persia before the war when it could have gone direct from Kiev to Germany by freight train?—but Alexandra forwarded the appeal to the tsar. It was effective. The treason charge was dropped, and the businessmen pleaded guilty to a technical charge of speculating in sugar. Dobrovolsky duly became justice minister, but Rasputin's reward to him was posthumous. By then the starets was dead.

Despite the success Rasputin was right to feel vulnerable. His enemies—a host, "Rights and Lefts, churchmen and revolutionists"—were gathering. A new Duma session opened on November 1. Pavel Miliukov led the debate. On his arrest Manuilov had claimed that the large amount of cash found on him had come not from the Germans but from Stürmer. He said it had been given to him from secret funds for buying off various journalists and for "swelling the personal income of the prime minister." Miliukov read out this testimony, adding that, according to Manuilov's figures, "a sum of 400,000 rubles has found its way into Stürmer's pockets from mysterious sources."

He then produced a bundle of German newspapers, quoting their crows of delight at the dismissal of Sazonov and his replacement by Stürmer. The same newspapers, he said, were delighted at the appointment of the "idiot" Shuvaev as war minister. It was a standing joke that Shuvaev, after a stormy cabinet meeting, had said, "I may be accused of stupidity, but not dishonesty." Miliukov now bellowed, "Is this stupidity, or is this treason?" He then, as *The Times*'s man Robert Wilton put it, "belled the principal cats." He said that Russia was effectively being ruled by Rasputin, Stürmer, and—he quoted for effect in German from an enemy newspaper, the Viennese *Neue Freie Presse*—"die junge Kaiserin," Alexandra. He asked of each name if this resulted from "stupidity, accident or treason." In each case, Wilton said, "the whole assembly howled its answer, 'Treason!' "

Wilton learned that most of the cable he sent to London was "burked by the censor." The verb meant "to murder by smothering," after the modus operandi of the nineteenth-century Edinburgh serial killer William Burke. It was impossible to burke all Russia; the inflammatory speech, with its illegal mention of Rasputin, circulated in millions of duplicated sheets, selling for a ruble each.

The Romanov clan converged on Kiev for the wedding of the tsar's sister Olga to a cavalry captain; as Rasputin had predicted when he first met her in 1907, her earlier marriage had ended in divorce. The dynasty was in peril; it was the sole topic of conversation. The family agreed to send Grand Duke Nikolai Mikhailovich to see the tsar at the Stavka. The grand duke was liberal enough for the family to call him Monsieur Egalité; he had spent much of his life alone in his palace writing an enormous biography of his ancestor Alexander I. He was a mystic who had already foreseen his own death—"on a dark, warm night, a few paces from the ponderous graves of my ancestors"—and felt it his duty while he was still alive to urge the tsar to grant a responsible government and so to remove the influence of the empress and Rasputin.

The tsar wrote to Alexandra on November 2: "My precious Nikolai M has come for one day; we had a long talk together last night, of which I will tell you in my next letter—I am too busy today. God preserve you, my dearly beloved Sunny, and children. . . . Eternally your old Nicky." He was being deceitful. He was badly rattled by the family message. He did not know what to say to Alexandra about his talk, so instead he sent her the letter the grand duke had brought with him.

"You have told me many times that you can trust no one, that you are being deceived," it read. "If this is so, the same phenomenon must also hold true for your spouse, who loves you ardently but has been led astray thanks to the malicious and utter deception of the people who surround her. You trust Alexandra Fedorovna, which is understandable, but what comes out of her mouth is the result of clever juggling and not the actual truth." It warned against her "constant interferences and whisperings," predicted an imminent "era of assassination attempts," and concluded by calling for "the much desired ministry responsible to the Duma."

Alexandra's counterattack was furious. She replied on November 4: "I read Nikolai's & am utterly disgusted. Had you stopped him in the middle of his talk & told him that, if he only once more touched that subject or me, you will send him to Siberia—as it becomes next to high treason. He has always hated & spoken badly of me since 22 years . . . during war & at such a time to crawl behind yr Mama & Sisters & not stick up bravely . . . for his Emperor's wife—is loathesome [sic] and treachery. . . . Wife is your staunch One & stands as a rock behind you." He replied the next day, shamefaced and again deceitful. "I am so sorry that I have upset you and made you angry," he wrote, claiming that he had been too busy to read Nilokai's letter and that the grand duke had never mentioned her in their talk. "Had he said anything about you, you do not really doubt that your dear hubby would have taken your part!" The tsar's family could threaten him with renewed revolution; it was his wife who excited in him true terror.

—

The country was cracking rapidly now. "If there is trouble the troops I am told will refuse to fire," Sir George Buchanan cabled London. The ruined economy would bring revolt, the ambassador said, and "it will begin not with the workmen in the factories but with the crowds waiting in the cold and snow outside the provision shops." The lines started in the freezing predawn. It was said that in each one there was a German agent, a woman like all the others, with a brown or gray or black shawl clasped to her chin, who whispered through blue lips to her neighbor: "Why should we put up with this? Why does Russia not make peace? Germany is ready to end the war. . . . The Little Father [the tsar] is so far away from us, what does he care? And the empress is German at heart and has betrayed our armies again and again. . . . Let us get rid of the Romanovs."

Rumors of coups "blew in on every breeze and floated out on every tide." An Okhrana report said that "the industrial proletariat of the capital is on the verge of despair." The agency warned that inadequate diet and unsanitary lodgings, cold and damp, and a soaring death rate had already prepared the ground for "the wildest excesses of a hunger riot." It predicted "thousands and tens of thousands of victims." Workers in the Vyborg and Narva districts shouted, "Down with the war! Give us bread!" Cossack patrols were out in force in the city, with whips, sabers, and carbines, carrying trusses of hay on their saddles so that they could ride their wiry horses for twelve hours at a stretch. In isolated incidents the horsemen were stoned. A rumor spread that they had responded by opening fire on the mobs; "there was a tremendous panic among the stockbroking public." Machine-gun sections were posted the next day, and the uneasy calm was restored. Wilton added a handwritten postscript to a letter he sent to London on November 7: "I hear that banners inscribed 'Down with the Romanovs' have been found in workmen's houses."

The price of bread was now increasing by 8 percent a month and that of meat by 28 percent. Few workers still ate eggs, meat, sugar, or fruit; they made do with watery gruel and bits of bread. Firewood and coal were so dear that families had to choose between warmth and near starvation. The city had been largely lit and heated by Cardiff coal, German warships had cut off supplies. A trickle came through from the Donets mines, far to the south. Thieves raided the coal cellars of the rich. "The sharks are working their gigantic jaws," the *Stock Exchange Gazette* wrote of the speculators, Rasputin and Simanovich's clients. They held huge stocks of wheat, sugar, cotton. They had cornered the market in drugs, forcing the price of aspirin from 1.5 rubles per kilo before the war to 200. Quinine was up from 4 rubles to 400.

———

Something had to give. Stürmer was the obvious target, universally despised and now without the backing of the empress and Rasputin. He was dismissed on November 9. He was replaced by Alexander Trepov as premier, with N. N. Pokrovsky as foreign minister. Both were honest conservatives; neither liked Rasputin. Worse news followed. Trepov asked the tsar to get rid of Protopopov. "I am sorry for Prot[opopov]," Nicholas wrote to the empress on November 10. "He is a good honest man, but he jumps from one idea to another, and cannot make up his mind on anything. . . . They say that a few years ago he was not quite normal after a certain illness." Rasputin could survive a hostile premier—had he not seen off the great Stolypin? The interior minister, with his control of the police and the press, was another matter.

Alexandra was not well. Her heart condition recurred, and she sometimes took to her wheelchair—with Rasputin gaunt and exhausted, and Vyrubova on crutches, the principal actors around the throne were a battle-worn trio— but she came to Protopopov's defense with fierce energy. "Don't go and change

Protopopov now," she replied on November 11, claiming that the minister was "quite as sane" as anybody. "Remember"—this on November 12—"that it does not lie in the man Protopopov or xyz, but it's the question of the monarchy & yr prestige. . . . Don't think they will stop at him, but they will make all the others leave who are devoted to you one by one—then ourselves." It would be a hard fight—the Duma "are impertinent brutes . . . it is war with them"—but "a man of God is near to guard you safely through the reefs."

Protopopov survived. He gave up on the food crisis. Sixty thousand railroad wagons filled with fuel and food lay under snowdrifts, waiting for locomotives that never came. The drafts had emptied the villages. Prisoners of war and contract laborers from Persia and China were brought in. "Their distribution was accidental," Protopopov admitted later, "without plan and with no particular accounting." The Supreme Power, he said, "ceased to be a source of life and light. It became the prisoner of stupid influences and stupid forces." The army was worn out, the cities starved. "No one was happy," he testified.

The men at the front were "colorless, expressionless, endless." Under "the mask of servile submissiveness," a trooper warned, "lies a terrible anger. . . . Just strike a little match and everything will go up in flames." Individuals had responded with desertion and self-mutilation, the severing of a trigger finger with a bayonet, the shot into the foot. Now came the first mutinies of regiments. Some demanded boots and warm clothing before they would move; others said that they would hold the front but not attack. "Take us and have us shot, but we just aren't going to fight anymore," one company cabled the Stavka. Wild rumors circulated at the front. Fresh cemeteries were being opened in which to dump the bodies of hunger victims in the cities; bread now cost a ruble a loaf; the empress and Rasputin spoke to Berlin each night by radio; the government had paid the Germans a billion rubles to kill every peasant in Russia.

There were stories—persistent, believed—that Grand Duke Nicholas Nikolayevich was plotting to advance from his Crimean semi-exile to Tsarskoye Selo with four Guards regiments. Nicholas would be forced to abdicate, and the empress confined to a convent. Alexis would be proclaimed tsar, with either Nikolasha or the tsar's brother Grand Duke Mikhail Alexandrovich as regent. In both versions the coup would begin with the murder of Rasputin. The Romanovs, the writer Dmitri Merezhkovsky thought, had reduced Russia to "the fifth act of a tragedy played in a brothel." His wife, Zinaida Gippius, wrote in her diary: "People are dying like flies. . . . Young, old, children, all the same. Stupid ones, clever ones—all are stupid. Honest men, thieves, all are thieves—or else they are mad." The atmosphere was charged, neurotic; "the most frightening and crude rumors are disturbing the masses." At the Stray Dog, the cellar bar for the capital's artists and writers, the poet Anna Akhmatova, in a black dress with a yellow scarf on her shoulders, lamented through the smells of vodka, tobacco, and sweat:

> *We are all sinners, we are all whores*
> *How sad we are together.*

"Those evil fumes of Petrograd!" Nicholas railed at the Stavka. "One can smell them even at the front. And it is from drawing rooms and palaces that the worst emanations come. What a misfortune! What a disgrace!"

———

Alexandra alone showed confidence. It was the result, the court marshal Benckendorff thought, of "a will of iron linked to not much brain and no knowledge." Rasputin acted as her "amulet," he thought. He tranquilized her. She knew that she was hated, but that was only by "the corrupt and godless society" of Petrograd, which "thinks of nothing but dancing and dining." They were jealous of her, she rationalized, "because they know I have a strong will and when [I] am convinced of a thing being right (when besides blessed by Grigory) do not change my mind & that they can't bear." The Russia that mattered, village Russia, loved her. She was quite convinced of that. Her mailbag proved it.

Scores of letters and telegrams arrived in her mauve boudoir each day. The writers were apparently simple folk who loved her and who blamed the country's ills on the grand dukes, the errant politicians, the godless intellectuals. She asked her rare visitors—mostly, now, intimates of Rasputin, Vyrubova, Lili von Dehn, Pitirim, Simanovich—to leaf through them. She was consoled daily, she wrote, by knowing from her mail that the "whole of Russia—the real Russia, poor, humble, peasant Russia—is with me." She felt herself truly a Russian, as if, mystically, Rasputin had made her one. "I stand up for yr cause, Baby's and Russia," she wrote to Nicholas. "Yes, I am more Russian than many another and I won't keep quiet. . . . All my trust lies in our Friend, who only thinks of you, Baby, and Russia." All that was needed was strength and God, and she had both. "I have no fear," she said. "Let they [sic] scream."

But the loyal letters were fakes. They were being forged by an Okhrana department on Protopopov's orders. The same department was paying men to demonstrate with banners praising the autocracy. The British correspondent Arthur Ransome watched a band of "scallywags" emerge from a police station with flags rolled up around sticks. The men unfurled them, marched around the city for an hour, and returned to the police station to hand in the banners and collect their pay. The Okhrana intercepted genuine correspondence from the provinces and kept it locked in a "black room." It showed none of the happy patriotism the empress was receiving. "Horses and livestock have been taken, there's no one to plow and nothing to plow with," a writer from Irkutsk complained.

The Duma deputy Vassily Alexeyevich Maklakov thought that a psychiatrist was needed more than a politician. A disease was loose, wasting the dispositions of centuries, destroying belief in the tsar, in his power, in its divine basis. This catastrophe in the innermost depths of the Russian soul, he said, was being carried out not by evil revolutionaries but by the Supreme Power itself, "maddened, drawn by ill fate, condemning itself to absolute emptiness, depriving itself of its last foothold." The dynasty was no longer a mighty historical force but a "hollow trunk of oak, eaten by mice, dried-up inside," waiting for a final tremor to fell it.

"Mystical and sexual perversions" ran to the top of Petrograd society. Even Alexandra's beloved village Russia was now infected. "God knows how it found out so soon what every cook or yard keeper in Petrograd knows," Maklakov said. But it knew, and it did not torment itself with intellectual talk about pathology and psychosis. "It appreciates events with one word," he said. " 'Treason.' The betrayal of Russian people to the Germans. This is the horror of the imminent revolution. It won't be a political revolution but a revolution of wrath and revenge of the dark lower classes, and it will be spontaneous, convulsive, chaotic."

—

On November 19 Vladimir Purishkevich rose to his feet in the Duma. He was a Jew-baiter, a prime mover of the Black Hundreds, a believer in autocracy and the divine right of the tsar, founder of the Union of the Archangel Michael, so reactionary that "the only thing further right was the wall." He was short, bald, and energetic, a wit and satirist who circulated his doggerel on opponents—as well as photographs of Rasputin and his admirers—in thousands of copies. He sometimes wore a red carnation jutting from his fly buttons. In 1905 he had paid thugs to rampage against Jews and democrats. In the war he had become a one-man patriotic center, organizing hospital trains, canteens, and delousing units. He named his good works for himself, emblazoning one TEAROOM OF STATE COUNCILLOR PURISHKEVICH in letters eight feet high.

Purishkevich had dined with the tsar at the Stavka a fortnight before. The generals and staff officers had begged him to speak to Nicholas: "Point out the pernicious role of Rasputin. Don't spare the colors." He was sickened that they were too cowardly to tackle the monarch themselves. He told the Duma that only public pressure could save the dynasty. He said, "There burns in me an endless love for my country and . . . a deeply loyal love for my sovereign." But a tocsin had to be rung, a warning given, not the lowly tolling of a provincial belfry but the peal of the Ivan the Great bell in the Kremlin. He savaged the stupidity of the censors, the "marauder-profiteers," the "ministerial leapfrog." He mocked Protopopov and Prince Andronnikov "and others who make infamy of Russian life." Then he spoke of the "filthy, depraved, corrupt peasant" on whose every word the empress hung. "All these evils stem from those dark forces, from those influences," he cried, "which are headed by Grischa Rasputin." He urged the ministers to "go over there, go to the tsar's Stavka, fall at his feet," and assure him that the "crisis at home cannot continue, the multitude is muttering in its wrath, revolution threatens, and an obscure muzhik shall govern Russia no more!"

Watching from the gallery, deeply impressed, was Prince Felix Yusupov.

≡

CHAPTER 25

"Vanya Has Arrived"

Prince Yusupov had been thinking of killing Rasputin for more than a year. He was an unlikely assassin, but the times were unlikely; a golden boy, heir to the greatest fortune in Russia, one of the best-looking men in Europe, married to a niece of the tsar, whose own beauty and breeding made her a natural snare for Rasputin. The prince wore the olive uniform and white belt of the Corps of Pages, an elite officer training school. Most of his fellow cadets were still in their teens; Felix was twenty-nine, and had no intention of going near the front. He was playing at soldiers, as he had played all his sweet life. In murdering Rasputin, a friend said, he was "acting out a scenario worthy of his favorite author, Oscar Wilde." He was a fop, an idler, a salon decadent, but the observant noticed a quality of menace in him. "You have God in one eye," the ballerina Anna Pavlova told him, "and the devil in the other."

His great-great-grandfather Prince Nicholas Yusupov, a favorite of Catherine the Great and an acquaintance of Voltaire and Pushkin, had founded the family's colossal wealth. His mother's prewar annual income was 1.3 million rubles, equivalent to a ton of gold. There were thirty-eight Yusupov houses and estates scattered across Russia, few of which he had seen. The main Moscow palace, one of three, had been built by Ivan the Terrible, and Felix got a thrill of horror from imagining the ghosts of the chained wretches who had died in the subterranean passages that linked it to the Kremlin. In the Crimea the family owned 125 miles of Black Sea coastline so rich in oil that peasants used the surface deposits to grease the axles of their wagons. The highest mountain on the coast had been given to his mother as birthday present. The family had two private railroad trains, one for use in Russia and the other, kept at the frontier, for the narrow-gauge railways of western Europe.

Felix had little interest in visiting these possessions. He was happiest in Petrograd, in the family's 1760s palace, which fronted the limpid waters and stone and iron bridges of the Moika Canal. Its ocher and white facade was faultlessly classical and restrained. The interior was exquisite. The main ballroom—there were three—was large enough to accommodate an orchestra; the colonnaded picture gallery had paintings by Tiepolo, Rembrandt, Rubens, Velázquez, Fragonard, and Watteau. The furniture in the petit salon had once belonged to Marie Antoinette, the crystal chandelier above the sweep of the main staircase to Madame de Pompadour. A superb Moorish room, with mosaic and a fountain, was inspired by the Alhambra. A Louis XV theater in miniature had gilded boxes and tapestries. It was here that Felix had started dressing up, pretending to be his ancestor Prince Nicholas, a famous debauchee who kept three hundred portraits of his mistresses and traveled with a menagerie of monkeys, dogs, and parrots.

The Yusupovs were eccentrics. Felix's grandmother devoted her life to collecting stamps and snails, which she stomped on, convinced that crushed snail made a perfect fertilizer for her rose gardens. His father found a dirty, foul-smelling dwarf on a fishing trip and made him Felix's tutor. On Sundays the dwarf wore a dinner jacket and yellow shoes. Arabs, Tartars, and Kalmyks in traditional dress added to the color of the servants' hall at the Moika Palace. One servant was employed solely as a lamplighter. When the palace was electrified Felix watched with glee as the man drank himself to death with boredom.

Felix cultivated his own oddities, primarily transvestism. When he was twelve he dressed up in his mother's clothes, borrowed a wig from her hairdresser, and amused himself standing with the prostitutes on the Nevsky Prospect. He told the men who accosted him that he was already spoken for. He did so in French. At home he liked to irritate his mother's friends by speaking to them in Russian, a language the older generation of aristocrats hardly knew. From the Nevsky he progressed to the fashionable Bear restaurant, where he enjoyed trying to lasso the heads of his admirers with a string of his mother's pearls. Visiting a theater in Paris in drag, he was amused to be ogled by the lecherous Edward VII of England. In 1908 his elder brother was killed in a duel and he became sole heir.

Felix had flirted briefly with the left; it gave him the chance to dress up as a beggar and visit the slums. On close inspection, however, the dark people did not please him. "All around us the dregs of humanity, both men and women, lay half-naked, drunk, and filthy," he wrote with patrician disgust. "The unfortunate wretches quarreled, copulated, used the filthiest language, and vomited all over each other." He took a valet, chauffeur, housekeeper, and macaw with him to Oxford. His skill with disguise enabled him to pass off his bulldog as a baby to evade British quarantine laws. In 1914 he married the tsar's niece Irina. The empress disliked him; she had heard of his transvestite escapades and thought him depraved. She was particularly unhappy that he was very close to her favorite Romanov, the young Grand Duke Dmitri Pavlovich, whom she thought of almost as a son. Felix was inseparable from him, and she felt he was a bad influence.

Felix's interest in politics was trivial. He had, however, an aristocrat's disdain for the peasant in Rasputin, and a monarchist's contempt for the damage Alexandra was causing to the throne. These traits combined with his love of self-drama to make him, beneath his spoiled and languid charm, a very dangerous young man. His hostility was encouraged by his parents. His father had had to resign as governor-general of Moscow after the excesses of the anti-German riots. The tsar was warned that Yusupov senior had become a "megalomaniac of the worst kind," who was turning Moscow into his own satrapy; the dismissal was one of Nicholas's better decisions. The Yusupovs, however, blamed it on the "pro-German camarilla"—that favorite, foggy, and hate-filled phrase of 1915 and 1916—of Rasputin and the empress. The family anger deepened when, after Felix's mother, Princess Zinaida, criticized the empress during an audience, Alexandra dismissed her from court with this icy farewell: "I hope never to see you again." Through the hot summer of 1916, Zinaida sent her son letters from her Crimean estates with coded messages in which Rasputin was "the book" and the empress was Valide, a mocking use of the Crimean Tartar word for "great mother." "Nothing can be done unless the book be destroyed and Valide tamed," she wrote him. Yusupov took on a fresh disguise, savior of the motherland.

———

He had easy access to Rasputin through Munya Golovina, who had originally introduced them before Felix went to Oxford. Munya had invited Felix to her mother's house in the early fall; she said that Rasputin very much wanted to meet him. Felix was struck by the change in the starets. He had become fat; his face was puffy, and he was wearing an embroidered silk blouse and velvet breeches. His "offensive familiarity and insolent assurance" made him still more repellent to the prince than he had been seven years before.

Felix complained about his health, saying that he was suffering from an intense fatigue, which doctors could not treat. "Doctors don't know anything," Rasputin told him. "My dear fellow, I can cure anyone, for I work in God's own way. . . . You'll see for yourself." They met several times, both at Gorokhovaya ulitsa and at the Golovinas' house. Once, Rasputin attempted to hypnotize him as part of the cure. The prince felt heat was pouring into him "like a warm current" as his body became numb. "All I could see was Rasputin's glittering eyes," he said. "Two phosphorescent beams of light melting into a great luminous ring." A "merciless struggle" was being fought between Rasputin's personality and his own. Though the prince prevented Rasputin from getting complete mastery over him, he could not move until the starets ordered him to get up.

Or so Yusupov claimed; the murderer had good reason to demonize his victim. The prince also alleged that he met "seven shady-looking men" in Rasputin's apartment, four of them "distinctly Jewish," the other three "fair and curiously alike"—implying Germans—whom he was certain were "a gang of spies." The spy story has no credible basis. It was later established that several Russians, most notably the exiled Lenin, had dealings with wartime Berlin; nothing has emerged to link Rasputin, or the empress, with German agents. Nor, although there are claims of hypnotic attempts by Rasputin from Rodzianko and others, and many accounts of his troubling stare, is there conclusive evidence that Rasputin hypnotized anyone, successfully or not. The only reliable reference is from Spiridovich, who wrote that Rasputin paid a few visits to a teacher of hypnosis in St. Petersburg in 1913; the motive appears to have been the professional curiosity of a starets, and he soon lost interest in the subject.

Though he said that he felt "polluted each time I met him," Yusupov continued to visit Rasputin. The starets's daughters met him—"an exquisitely tailored young man . . . faintly repellent, a languid manner not usual in young males"—when they came back from a shopping expedition. They laughed when Felix picked up a wineglass and drained it from the spot on the rim where their father's lips had touched it. "He's got ice in his eyes," young Varya said. Maria asked why he had come. "He has a problem and he needs me," Rasputin said, nodding when she asked if he would come again.

The prince, inspired by the Duma speech, telephoned Purishkevich and arranged to meet him in his apartment at 9:00 A.M. on November 21. He said that he wanted to talk about Rasputin, who had become an "embarrassment"; the peasant's disappearance would end the "satanic power which envelops our sovereigns." They spoke for two hours, the politician noting the conversation in his diary.

Yusupov warned Purishkevich that speeches would accomplish nothing; the tsar had an intense dislike of any attempt to put pressure on him. There was only one answer: "Eliminate Rasputin." Purishkevich thought that easier said than done. There were no resolute men left in Russia. The government, he said, which might do such a thing, and even do it skillfully, "is controlled by Rasputin himself." Yusupov agreed that the government could not be counted on. But there were men in Russia, still, who could be relied on.

"D'you really think so?" Purishkevich asked.

"I'm certain of it," Yusupov replied. "One of them stands before you at this very moment."

The politician was about to tell his visitor to stop making jokes when he realized that Yusupov was in earnest; he was prepared to kill. He offered his hand; the prince shook it and told him that he had two others in the plot. "Come to visit me if you happen to be free this evening," he said. "Then you can meet them both." In such a well-bred, carefree way, the two men, who had not met before, became conspirators.

Purishkevich went to the Yusupov palace that evening. He was astonished to meet Grand Duke Dmitri Pavlovich, Alexandra's favorite nephew, whom she was thinking of marrying to her eldest daughter, Olga, a good-looking boy of twenty-six, with a weakness for drink but beautifully mannered, sympathetic, kind. With him was a Captain Sukhotkin, a convalescing officer of the elite Preobrazhensky Regiment, which had just suffered terrible casualties on the central front. They talked eagerly over dinner. They planned to lure Rasputin to the Moika Palace, using Yusupov's beautiful young wife as bait. They would poison him—there was a police station opposite the palace, and they were worried that shots would alarm the police. Purishkevich agreed to get the poison from his close friend and physician Dr. Lazovert. They discussed disposing of the corpse by taking it to the front by train and dumping it as a battle casualty. When that seemed too complicated, they decided to carry it out of the palace to an automobile, weight it, and sink it under the frozen Neva. They gave themselves four weeks. Rasputin was to die on December 16, a Friday.

—

The tsar made a brief trip from the Stavka to Tsarskoye Selo. Rasputin met him at Vyrubova's cottage; she found Nicholas "depressed and pessimistic." Heavy storms were cutting food deliveries to Petrograd, and some battalions at the front were reporting shortages. As Rasputin left the cottage the tsar asked him for his usual blessing. "This time it is for you to bless me, not I you," Rasputin replied. It was natural for Vyrubova to suggest that her idol prophesied his own death in this manner, but other evidence from his daughter and Simanovich suggests that he was in a particularly nervous and uneasy state.

On November 27 Purishkevich bought heavy lead weights in a street market. With Dr. Lazovert he toured the city's bridges, looking for a convenient place to dump the body. They found an area under the Petrovsky Bridge linking Krestinsky and Petrovsky islands where the flow of the river around an arch was preventing the water from freezing. Lazovert bought a chauffeur's heavy coat. The conspirators met again on Purishkevich's hospital train on December 1. Yusupov reported that he had mentioned a meeting with Princess Irina to Rasputin, who seemed eager. They thought of a cover-up. After the killing they would telephone the Villa Rhode and say that they had been expecting Rasputin to come to the Moika Palace but that he had not arrived and would he please come now. They also agreed on a secret sentence to summon each other by telephone on the night of the murder: "Vanya has arrived."

The enterprise was amateur; the alibi was flimsy, the reconnaissance perfunctory. Purishkevich, the wild man of the far right, had one of the best-known faces in Russia. Leading politicians did not make a habit of buying lead weights in the market; he might have been—he was—remembered. He also talked too much. At the beginning of December he spoke with Vasily Shulgin, a proudly whiskered and patriotic Duma deputy.

"Remember December sixteenth," he said.

"What for?" Shulgin asked.

"I will tell you . . . I may tell you this. . . . We'll kill him on the sixteenth."

"Who?"

"Grischa!"

"You will kill him—nothing will change," Shulgin said. "Everything will remain the same. . . . By killing him, you won't do any good. It's too late!"

Yusupov was also indiscreet. He wrote a coded letter to his wife and his mother, who were in the Crimea, speaking of a mighty blow he was about to deliver for Russia. "Thank you for your insane letter," Irina replied. "I could not understand the half of it. I realize that you are about to do something wild. Please take care and do not get mixed up in any shady business." He also discussed the plan with the Duma deputy Maklakov, who refused to join the plot because he was due to make a speech to the Moscow Society of Jurisprudence on December 16 and did not want to let the lawyers down. He suggested beating Rasputin over the head with a club and running an automobile over the body. He lent his own blackjack to Yusupov.

———

Alexandra remained confident that firmness would avert any crisis. "Show to all that you are Master & your will shall be obeyed—the time of great indulgence & gentleness is over—now comes your reign of will & power, & obedience they must be taught," she wrote to Nicholas on December 4. The tsar, in fact, was so withdrawn and robotic that it was widely believed he was taking herbal concoctions supplied by Rasputin to sap his will. Yusupov claimed that Rasputin told him he was using Badmaev's medicines to treat the tsar, lacing his tea with them so that "his heart is filled with peace, everything looks good and cheerful to him."

In family desperation Alexandra's sister Ella went to Tsarskoye Selo from her Moscow convent to convince the empress of the "horror" of the situation, but they parted for the last time at the railroad station in silence. Rasputin was aware of her visit. He was nervous—he knew that Ella wanted him exiled and the empress locked up in a convent—and he scribbled notes and put them under his pillow for "vengeance" before going to sleep. He put her hatred of him down to his opposition to the war. "The tsar dodges and weaves and is ready for neither peace nor war," he complained to Simanovich. "Mama wants peace, but all she does is weep. Ella wants war, although she's German she sets everyone against Germans." He was greatly relieved when Alexandra sent her sister packing.

Violence was in the air. There was a run on books about the strangling of Emperor Paul and a sudden increase in the number of people visiting the room in the Michael Palace where the killing had taken place. In the Yusupovs' Moika Palace, workmen were whitewashing the walls of a basement room, carrying oak chairs and tables down the narrow, winding staircase, and laying a great rug of white bearskin to make it a cozy and relaxed place for Felix to entertain his guests. Red vases were placed in the wall niches, and a fine Oriental armoire of inlaid ebony stood in a corner, with a silver and crystal cross upon it. Purishkevich was delighted when he saw the cellar magically transformed into "an elegant bonbonnière." The prince had exquisite taste.

—

The first rumors of approaching murder reached Simanovich at the Fire Club, a gambling club he ran in Countess Ignateva's house on the Champs de Mars. The chairman of the club board had been Tomilin, the city governor of Pskov; Simanovich paid people with prominent names "huge salaries" to act as figureheads. Tomilin had transferred himself—the pay was huger—to the nearby National Club, taking two clerks called Ivan and Alexis with him. Simanovich had not objected because they would enable him to find out what was happening at the rival club.

Ivan came to him to say that there were mysterious meetings at the National, where a lot was said about Rasputin. Alexis sometimes worked in the room where the meetings were held. Simanovich gave him 500 rubles and told him to ask Alexis to find out as much as he could. Alexis reported back that the meetings were chaired by Purishkevich and were attended by Grand Duke Dmitri Pavlovich, Prince Felix Yusupov, and some young officers. "They spoke a lot about Rasputin in these meetings," Simanovich said; the name of the English ambassador, Buchanan, and those of the tsar and tsarina were also mentioned.

Simanovich took Alexis to see Rasputin, who confirmed—not surprisingly, after the Duma speech—that Purishkevich was his enemy. One of Simanovich's assistants, Evsey Bukhshtab, was friendly with a doctor who had a venereal disease clinic on the Nevsky Prospect and was treating Purishkevich. Bukhshtab offered the doctor a large sum to find out Purishkevich's plans; his patient was known to be talkative. After an injection of salvarsan, a compound of arsenic used in the treatment of syphilis, Purishkevich lay on his couch. The doctor casually mentioned that Rasputin was a great misfortune for Russia and that it would be better to annihilate him. Purishkevich assured him that Rasputin would soon be done for. "You'll see what'll happen in the next three days," he told the doctor. Alarmed, Simanovich passed the information on to the empress.

———

On December 10 the tsar wrote to Alexandra about a planned offensive in the Danube region and his plans to prorogue the Duma on December 17 and reconvene it on January 19. Reopening the body would prove that the government and the country could work together. He had discussed the plan with Trepov, the new premier, who, he said, was "quiet and submissive and did not touch upon the name of Protopopov. . . . I went to pray before the icon of the Mother of God before this conversation, and felt comforted after it."

On December 12 Rasputin had dinner with Vyrubova and the empress, who wrote to Nicholas to reassure him that he could rely on Rasputin's "wonderful brain—ready to understand everything." The following day Rasputin asked Simanovich to deposit several thousand rubles in a bank account in his daughter Maria's name. He was depressed; he said his soul was in torment.

Alexandra was furious when the tsar's letter about the Duma arrived on December 14. She wanted the Duma prorogued, period. To recall them in January, she replied, meant "nobody goes home & all will remain, fomenting, boiling in Petrograd. . . . Love, our Friend begged you to shut it . . . & you see, they have time to make trouble. . . . Be Peter the Great, John [Ivan] the Terrible, Emperor Paul—crush them all under you—now don't laugh, naughty one—but I long to see you with all those men." Nicholas wrote back—he signed himself "Your poor, weak-willed little hubby"—that the date for reassembling the Duma had been proclaimed and thus could not be altered.

The same day, December 14, Rasputin took a walk through Petrograd with Munya Golovina and visited St. Isaac's and Kazan cathedrals. He went on to Tsarskoye Selo, where he met the empress at Vyrubova's cottage. The empress thought it odd that he had taken a walk. "He never goes out since ages, except to come here," she wrote to Nicholas, but she was pleased to report that on his stroll the starets had received "not one disagreeable look, people all quiet." He seemed to have recovered his spirits. "Says in 3 or 4 days things will go better in Roumania & all will go better," she said. In the evening he wrote a long letter, sealed it in an envelope, and put in Maria's desk. "Don't open it until after I am dead," he told his daughter. Simanovich was not alone in urging Rasputin to leave the capital. Trepov offered him 200,000 rubles and a monthly remittance to return to Siberia. Rasputin reported this colossal bribery attempt to the empress, neatly claiming incorruptibility for himself and undermining the premier in her eyes.

Simanovich told Rasputin on Thursday, December 15, that the situation was so grave—conspirators were about to kill him, and "then it will be the turn of the tsar and tsarina"—that drastic steps had to be taken. The tsar "must give you up," he said. "Only with this offering can the impending revolution be stopped. When you are not there anymore, everybody will calm down. You set the nobility and all the people against you." He made a suggestion to soften the blow: "Tell Papa and Mama to give you one million English pounds. Then we can both leave Russia and move to Palestine." Simanovich said that they would be able to live peacefully there. "Also, I'm afraid that something may happen to me," he went on. "I now have many enemies because of you. But I want to live."

Rasputin paced the room. He called for wine; it appeared that he wanted to drink himself into a state of clairvoyance. He drank two bottles of Madeira. "What you say I'll keep to myself," he said, speaking quickly, his eyes shining. "I won't tell the tsar of your talk. It's too early." He thought further. "Noblemen are against me," he said suddenly. "But noblemen don't have Russian blood. Their blood is mixed. Noblemen want to kill me because they don't like a Russian muzhik standing near the Russian throne. I'll show them who's stronger. . . . I'll send my muzhiks home from the front. Noblemen can bite as much as they like."

"Grigory, you may be killed today or tomorrow," Simanovich said. "Better listen to my advice and make yourself scarce. Otherwise there's no salvation for you." The telephone rang. Rasputin took the call. An unknown woman's voice asked, "Can you tell me when the funeral service for Rasputin will take place?" He had complained of anonymous calls. "You'll be buried first," he answered viciously, and hung up.

"See, they're burying you already," Simanovich told him. "Listen to me. Forget your fantasies. I don't want to argue with you anymore. I'll tell the tsar, tsarina, and Vyrubova everything. Maybe they'll teach you what to do."

"Listen," Rasputin said. "I'll drink twenty bottles of Madeira tonight. Then I'll go to a bathhouse, and then I'll go to bed. When I fall asleep, divine instructions will come down on me. God will teach me what to do, and then nobody'll be dangerous to me. And you go to hell." After he had drunk a "pretty portion" of a case of wine, he went to the bathhouse; he came back later and went to sleep without saying a word.

———

The following morning, Friday, December 16, Simanovich found Rasputin in the "strange condition" that "marked crucial moments in his life"; others might have thought it a hangover. A large kitchen basin with Madeira stood in front of him, and he polished it off in a single go. Simanovich asked him whether he felt his "strength" coming on. "My strength will win, not yours," he snarled.

Simanovich visited Protopopov to confide his fears. The interior minister thought them groundless. "I'll take care of the affair myself," he said. "The tsarina ordered me to see to it that Rasputin doesn't leave home today. All the measures have been taken. Rasputin has promised me on his word of honor not to leave his apartment tonight. There's nothing to worry about." Simanovich was reassured and returned to Rasputin's apartment. Vyrubova was there, with Nikitina and others, limping about on her stick, remonstrating with him about the strains of late nights and heavy drinking. "I'm like a horse," Rasputin told her.

The guests began to leave. Simanovich locked Rasputin's boots, fur coat, and hat in a cupboard. Osipenko, Pitirim's secretary, promised to stay in the apartment. The Okhrana agents outside the house were under orders not to let Rasputin into the street, Simanovich said, but the starets "outwitted us all." He gave the agents money and persuaded them that he was going to sleep. They believed him and went to a restaurant. He dined on fish and black bread with honey. After dinner he took Maria into his bedroom and showed her a bundle of banknotes, about three thousand rubles, which he had set aside as her dowry. Before the girls went to bed, Maria read aloud from the Gospel of St. John: "In the beginning was the Word, and the Word was with God, and the Word was God." Protopopov visited the apartment at 10:00 P.M. to make sure his orders had been carried out. Rasputin was already in bed. He asked the minister to tell Osipenko to go because his presence was unnecessary; the minister did so. When he said good-bye to Protopopov, Rasputin said, "Listen, dear. I am master of my word. I gave it, but I can take it back."

At midnight Rasputin telephoned Simanovich and said: "The 'Little One' has come, I'll go with him." He liked giving people pet names; he would not tell Simanovich to whom this one referred.

"For God's sake," Simanovich exclaimed. "Stay at home, or they'll kill you."

"Don't worry," Rasputin replied. "We'll be drinking tea, and at two o'clock I'll telephone you." He hung up.

The Dead Dog

The police were first alerted to the possibility of a crime by a uniformed policeman, Vlassiyev, who was on duty close to the Yusupov palace. Vlassiyev later made a statement to a gendarmerie lieutenant colonel, Poppel. "On the night of December 16 I was standing at my post at the corner of Moika Street and Maximilian Lane," the policeman declared. "At 4:00 A.M. I heard three or four shots in quick succession. Judging by the sound, they appeared to have come from the right side of the German church on Moika Street." He went to Post Bridge and shouted across the canal to Constable Yefimov, who was on duty outside 61 Morskaya Street, to find out which side of the canal the shots had come from. Yefimov yelled back to say they had come from the Moika Street side.

Vlassiyev went to Number 94, the Yusupov palace, and asked the gateman what was going on. The man called out that he had heard nothing. Vlassiyev, craning to see through the railings, made out two men, "bareheaded and in loose smocks," crossing the courtyard toward the gates. He recognized Prince Yusupov and his steward Bushinsky. The policeman asked Bushinsky about the shots; the steward replied that he had not heard any but that perhaps someone in high spirits had been shooting in the air to amuse himself. Vlassiyev said he thought Yusupov also said that he had heard nothing. Both men disappeared inside the palace; Vlassiyev took a good look at the courtyard, could find nothing suspicious, and went back to his post.

About a quarter of an hour later, around 4:20 A.M., Bushinsky asked Vlassiyev to come into the palace because his master wished to speak to him. He led the policeman through the marbled entrance and across to the prince's study. Yusupov was accompanied by a man Vlassiyev did not recognize, with "close-cropped reddish whiskers and a mustache of the same hue." He was wearing a green cloak with the epaulets of a councillor of state.

The stranger asked the policeman if he was an Orthodox Christian and a patriot who loved tsar and country. Vlassiyev nodded agreement. When the stranger asked him if he knew him, he said no.

"Have you ever heard of Purishkevich?" the stranger asked.

"Yes," the policeman replied. "I've heard of him."

"I am he. And Rasputin, you've certainly heard of him, haven't you? Do you know him?"

Vlassiyev said that he did not know the starets, although like everyone else he naturally had heard of him.

"This Rasputin has just been dispatched," Purishkevich told him. "If you love the tsar and your country, you must keep silent about the matter and not say a word to anyone."

"I understand, sir!" Having given that assurance, Vlassiyev was allowed to return to his post. It took him twenty minutes to break his word. At about 4:40 A.M. the district police commander, Superintendent Kalyaditsh, passed by on his rounds. "I reported exactly all that had taken place," Vlassiyev declared. The two policemen returned to the Yusupov palace.

At the entrance they found an automobile with its engine running. They asked the chauffeur whom it was waiting for. "For the prince," he replied.

The superintendent told Vlassiyev to note who used the car and resumed his tour of inspection. "Before very long Prince Yusupov left the main entrance and drove off in the direction of the Potseluyev Bridge," Vlassiyev declared. "I waited for some time longer in front of the house, and, as I saw nobody else, I went back again to my post."

At 6:00 A.M. the superintendent returned and took the constable to Colonel Rogov, the divisional superintendent. They gave the colonel a full report. Vlassiyev then went home. Since he had seen no evidence of anything amiss, he thought that the conversation with the "strange gentleman" in the prince's study was "an attempt to put me to the test," to see if he knew what was expected of a policeman. He noted that neither the prince nor the other gentleman showed any trace of excitement or confusion, other than that Purishkevich spoke "very rapidly." He could not say for sure whether either of them was drunk.

The evidence of the second policeman, Yefimov, differs concerning the automobile. Vlassiyev mentions one car leaving the palace with Prince Yusupov in it shortly after 4:40 A.M. Yefimov also heard only one car, but he timed it much earlier, at shortly after 4:00 A.M. In his deposition Yefimov said that he heard a shot at 4:00 A.M., with three more shots in quick succession three or four seconds later. He thought that they had been fired on Moika Street, somewhere around Number 92. "After the first shot," Yefimov declared, "there was audible a half-suppressed cry, as if uttered by a woman." He heard no other noise.

A "short time after" a car came down Moika Street in the direction of the Potseluyev Bridge; he did not see it stop anywhere. He reported the shots by telephone to the headquarters of the Third Kazan Police District. Then he headed off to where the shots had come from, meeting Vlassiyev on the Post Bridge. He told Vlassiyev that the shots had probably come from 92 Moika Street and returned to his post. He had nothing further to report. "Apart from the motorcar already mentioned," he said, "no motor vehicle of any kind passed along Moika Street till between five and six in the morning."

———

A policeman on the beat might accept Purishkevich's remark that Rasputin had been "dispatched" as merely bizarre; higher up the ranks alarm bells were ringing furiously. Colonel Rogov at divisional headquarters was worried enough to place an early morning call to Gen. Alexander Balk, the Petrograd city police chief. Balk, realizing it was a matter for the secret police, immediately telephoned Vassilyev, who lost no time in calling Protopopov.

The interior minister and the secret police chief agreed to set up an urgent investigation under Gen. P. K. Popov, the commander of the gendarmerie corps. Vassilyev personally ordered Popov to make a careful search of Rasputin's apartment and "to confiscate at once all compromising documents" that might be found there. By this he meant intimate correspondence between the empress and the starets. Vassilyev said that none was found.

The police were soon at Gorokhovaya ulitsa. Maria Rasputin made a statement that she had left the apartment at 7:00 the evening before, returning at about 11:00 P.M. As she was going to bed, she told the police, "my father said to me that he was going to pay a visit that night to the 'Little One's.' " She explained that her father always referred to Prince Yusupov by that nickname. "Soon after I went to bed," she concluded, "and therefore I do not know whether Father really went to Yusupov's."

No car tires crunching on the snow, no glimpse of a tall and slender man in evening clothes, no premonition of death, no "Farewell, Papa." Maria's bald statement to the police on the morning of December 17—that she had been in bed asleep when, if, the car came calling for her father—clashes with the intimate and detailed recollection she published years later. Simanovich is no more reliable. He claimed that he spent a sleepless night waiting for Rasputin's telephone call, and that it was he who woke Maria to tell her that the "Little One" had murdered her father.

Maria could give the police no further leads. They did better with the care-taker at the Gorokhovaya apartment house, a man called Korshunov. His state-ment was detailed and polished. It suggested that he was an experienced police informer, which was normal for staff in blocks where important people lived. He told them that he had been on duty the previous night, standing in the street in front of the gate. Toward 12:30 A.M. a big automobile had driven up. The body was painted military gray; it was a convertible with a waterproof hood and mica windows. It came down Gorokhovaya ulitsa from Fontanka Street and stopped outside Number 64. The driver looked rather older than his passenger, with a normal-size black mustache, a black coat with a lambskin collar, a fur cap, and long tan gloves. The passenger was a gentleman Kor-shunov had not seen before. He stepped out, and Korshunov asked him whom he wished to see. "Rasputin," he replied.

The caretaker opened the gate and showed the man to the main staircase, but he said he would take the back stairs. Korshunov could tell by the confident way he moved that the man had been in the house before. After about half an hour the man left the house with Rasputin. Korshunov described him as about thirty years old, of average height, well built, with a little black mustache. His description of the man's winter clothes tallies with Maria Rasputin's recollec-tion; Korshunov described "a long reindeer coat with the fur outside, a black cap, and long boots."

It was a fair description of Yusupov. A much better one —everything but confirmation of the name—came from Rasputin's maid Yekaterina Ivanovna Potyomkina. Her police deposition said that very few visitors had called on her master the day before, and that all of them were known to her. At 11:00 P.M. the children—Maria, Varya, and Rasputin's niece Anna—went to bed while Rasputin himself sprawled on his bed with his clothes and boots on. When Po-tyomkina asked the starets why he had not undressed, he said, "I've got an-other visit to pay yet." She asked to whom. "The Little One, he's going to call for me," Rasputin replied. She did not know the Little One's name, but she did know that he was married to the Grand Duchess Irina Alexandrovna. She had seen him in the apartment twice before, on about November 20 and about a week earlier. He had used the back stairs both times.

Rasputin told Potyomkina to go to bed, but she went first into the kitchen. He came in to ask her to help him do up the buttons on his blue shirt, "the one embroidered with cornflowers." The bell at the door leading to the back stairs rang. She heard the visitor ask if there was anyone around. "Nobody is up," she heard Rasputin reply. "The children are asleep. Step in, my dear." As they walked past to the drawing room, Potyomkina pushed the kitchen curtain aside. She caught a clear glimpse of the visitor's face. It was "no other than the Little One—that is, the husband of Grand Duchess Irina." She described him as "tall and lanky, with a thin face, straight nose, dark hair, no beard, dark rings under the eyes."

She was already in bed when Rasputin left with his visitor. He whispered to her that he had bolted the front door and would use the side entrance.

—

While Potyomkina was being interviewed, Munya Golovina contacted the police. Rumors that something had happened to Rasputin were already circulating; the ballerina Tamara Karsavina had been woken early in her apartment by her maid, who said that the milkman was claiming that Rasputin had been "done in" at the Yusupov palace, a block away. Golovina had called Yusupov to ask if he had seen the starets. The prince told her that he had not set eyes on him. This denial, in flat contradiction of the Potyomkina statement, convinced Vassilyev that he was dealing with murder.

Maria Rasputin telephoned Vyrubova during the morning to say that her father had not returned after leaving late with Felix Yusupov. Vyrubova walked from her cottage to the Alexander Palace. The empress was writing a letter to Nicholas. She was concerned about both her own and Alexis's health; he had been suffering an upset stomach. "Heart is not famous & don't feel well," she wrote. "The moral strain of these last trying months on a weak heart of course had to tell . . . the old machine broke down. . . . Has Baby's 'worm' quite been got rid of? Then he will get fatter & less transparent—the precious Boy!" She was "puzzled" when Vyrubova told her that Rasputin had gone to Yusupov's to meet his wife; she knew her niece was still in the Crimea. Protopopov telephoned the palace soon after. He reported that the duty policeman outside the Moika Palace had rung the bell after hearing shots and was told by a drunken Purishkevich that Rasputin had been killed. The same policeman had seen a military automobile without lights driving away from the house soon after the shots. This was all the interior minister knew. It left Alexandra deeply anxious.

Protopopov also telephoned Vassilyev several times during the morning. He reported that the empress was in touch with him, desperate to know what was going on. The secret police chief convinced Vassilyev that Rasputin was almost certainly dead, and that the Yusupov palace should be searched in an effort to find the corpse as speedily as possible.

A police detachment soon discovered large bloodstains on the steps leading from the courtyard to the palace basement. Yusupov explained that the blood had come from a dog, which one of his guests had shot during the night after becoming fuddled with drink. He showed the police the dead body of a dog that had been shot with a revolver; they thought it too small to account for the blood. The palace caretaker could add nothing to the information already given by the two beat policemen. He had heard some shots in the night, and the prince had spoken with the constable; that was all.

Yusupov's servant Nefedov struck the police as shifty and concerned to cover up for his employer. He said that the prince had told him to prepare the dining room for two or three guests. He and the butler Bushinsky kept watch at the front door by turns. When Nefedov came back on watch at 11:00 P.M., Bushinsky told him that Grand Duke Dmitri Pavlovich had arrived and had gone to the dining room. The two stayed on duty in the small anteroom by the front door until about 4:00 A.M. The prince had told them that they should not go into the dining room, since there would be ladies present; the two heard doors opening and closing, and a gramophone playing. That was all. It was not unusual; the prince had given parties before at which no servants were present.

Around 4:00 A.M. the bell rang and Nefedov went to the prince's study. No guests were present. Yusupov ordered him to go down to the courtyard and see if anything was amiss. Nefedov found the courtyard quite normal. A few minutes later the prince rang again and told him to look more carefully, because a shot dog was lying in the courtyard. Nefedov went into the yard of Number 92 and found the body of a dog near the railings. He picked it up and brought it into the prince's garden. "It is lying there now," he told the police.

He had cleared up the dining room that morning, Nefedov said, and "everything was just as it should be." He noted that there were enough empty wine bottles to assume that all the guests had been drunk; "the prince himself was rather tipsy." He said that the dead dog had been one of the prince's ordinary watchdogs.

It was time now for Yusupov to be interviewed by the officers on the scene. The prince told them that he had first met Rasputin at Munya Golovina's house five years before. He did not like him. Then he had met him again, in November, and gotten on better with him. Yusupov told the policemen that he was suffering from chest pains, and that Golovina had advised him to go to Rasputin, who had many cures to his credit. He had gone with her to see the starets at the end of November.

Some of Rasputin's suggestions—that he should go to the Gypsies and have a pretty girl cure his pains—struck Yusupov as lewd and unpleasant. However, simply by circling his hands around the patient, Rasputin did seem to bring the prince relief from the chest pains. When the starets began discussing the prince's beautiful wife, and asking if he could meet her, Yusupov said that he gave an evasive answer while resolving never to let Rasputin into his house.

In the meantime, Yusupov continued, he had decorated new rooms at 94 Moika Street. Grand Duke Dmitri Pavlovich suggested that he give a small party there. The two decided to invite Vladimir Mitrofanovich Purishkevich and some officers and society women; Yusupov would not give their names to the police, he said, for fear of embarrassing them. The grand duke arrived for the party around 11:30 P.M., with the rest of the guests coming soon after. "We drank tea, played the piano, danced, and finally we dined," Yusupov said.

The meal was interrupted about 1:00 A.M. by the telephone ringing in Yusupov's study. "It was Rasputin," the prince said in his statement, "insisting that I go with him to the Gypsies." Yusupov told him that he already had company and asked him where he was calling from. He could hear women's voices in the background and thought that Rasputin was either in a restaurant or with the Gypsies. Rasputin did not reply and hung up.

Yusupov said that he returned to the dining room and had a good laugh with his guests about Rasputin's call. They thought about all going on to the Gypsies, then thought better of it. The party broke up at about 3:00 A.M. The guests left by the side gate. Suddenly, the prince said, he heard a shot fired in the courtyard. He rang for Nefedov and asked him to investigate. The servant found nothing, but when the prince went down to the yard himself, he saw the body of a dog lying by the railings.

He heard footsteps in the street and saw a man in a gray uniform overcoat speeding away. He was tall and slim; more than that Yusupov could not see because the light was dim. When he came back into the palace, Yusupov asked Nefedov to remove the dog and telephoned Grand Duke Dmitri Pavlovich to tell him about the dog. The grand duke said that he had killed the dog; "he said it was just a silly prank," Yusupov said, "and that I was not to think any more about it." Yusupov sent out into the street for a constable and told him that a friend had just shot a dog. Purishkevich was present and also spoke to the constable. Yusupov could not hear all he said, but he remembered that Purishkevich was "all the time gesticulating wildly."

At about 4:00 A.M., Yusupov said, he had left the house and was driven in his motorcar to the palace of the Grand Duchess Xenia Alexandrovna, his mother-in-law and the tsar's sister, where he was currently living. "This morning I spoke on the telephone to Munya Golovina, who asked me where Rasputin was," his statement continued. "I replied that I did not know anything of his whereabouts, for I had not seen him, but had merely spoken to him by telephone." Golovina said that Rasputin's servants were saying that he had called for Rasputin at his apartment at about 1:00 A.M. "This, however, is a mistake," Yusupov asserted, "for neither by day nor by night was I there."

He had been told that Purishkevich had said something about Rasputin's death. Perhaps he had; "but during the night Purishkevich was very drunk." Yusupov concluded by saying that the people who had planned the murder—if murder it was—had intentionally arranged it so that there was a spurious link between the killing and Yusupov and his party.

—

Vassilyev was "on tenterhooks" waiting for a copy of Yusupov's statement. But this was not the expected confession; it was "an involved and highly improbable story, which was in glaring contradiction of all that we already knew." Although news of Rasputin's disappearance was all over Petrograd long before noon on December 17, there was still no body. Vassilyev was sure that it was murder, and that Yusupov was involved, but without a corpse some of the many people who telephoned him thought it might be an abduction. At 5:00 P.M. a supposedly secret telegram—it was soon leaked to the press, including the *Times* correspondent Robert Wilton—was sent to all police stations to discover the movements of the automobiles that had come up to the prince's palace during the night and the one that had removed Rasputin's body in the early hours. At the same time numerous police patrols were dispatched to the islands and the suburban districts.

The empress scribbled a note to Nicholas in pencil during the afternoon. She lay on the couch in her mauve boudoir. The room was full of flowers and the scent of the log fire. Vyrubova and her four daughters were with her. "We are sitting all together—you can imagine our feelings, thoughts—our Friend has disappeared," she began and then referred to Vyrubova's meeting with Rasputin the day before. "Yesterday A. saw Him and he told her that Felix asked Him to come to him at night, that a motor would collect Him so as He could see Irina. A motor, a military one, came to take Him with two civilians, and He left. This night a great scandal at Yusupov's house great gathering, Dmitry, Purishkevich, etc—all drunk. Police heard shots. Purishkevich ran screaming to the police that our Friend was killed. . . . Felix pretends that He never came to the house he never invited him. It was, apparently, a trap. I shall still trust in God's mercy that one has only driven Him away somewhere. Protopopov is doing all he can. . . . I can't and won't believe that He was killed. God have mercy. . . . Felix came often to him lately. Come quickly. Kisses, Sunny."

That night Grand Duchess Olga wrote in her diary, "Father Grigory has been missing since last night. They are looking everywhere. It is terribly hard. The four of us slept together. God help us!"

———

At 1:00 P.M. the following day, Sunday, December 18, some workmen crossing the Petrovsky Bridge saw bloodstains on the parapet. A policeman was called; he reported to his station that he could see blood on the parapet and pier of the bridge. A superintendent sped to the bridge and spotted a lone brown boot on a ledge on the bloodstained pier. A man was lowered on a rope and brought it up. It was rushed to Gorokhovaya ulitsa. Maria Rasputin recognized it at once; so did the Okhrana agents who shadowed the starets.

The murderers telephoned the empress during the afternoon. Grand Duke Dmitri Pavlovich asked for permission to come to tea at 5:00 P.M. Pale and thoughtful, the empress refused him. Yusupov then rang the palace switchboard to ask permission to come to the palace with "an explanation" for the empress. Alexandra refused to speak to him. He tried several times to get through to Vyrubova. The empress would not let her speak with him either. She told the switchboard to tell him that he should send his explanation in written form. "In your name I order Dmitri forbidden to leave his house till yr return," she wrote to the tsar. "Dmitri wanted to see me today, but I refused. Mainly he is implicated. The body is still not found. When will you come?" Nicholas cabled from the Stavka: "Am horrified and shaken. In prayers and thoughts I am with you. Am arriving tomorrow at 5 o'clock."

When Vassilyev was told of the discovery of the snow boot by General Popov, he wondered what had gone through the minds of the murderers as they sped to the bridge in their elegant motorcar with a corpse in the back. Were their thoughts patriotic, of saving their country, or merely of how to escape justice by disposing of the evidence? Strange nightmares hung over the frozen capital, a reporter on the newspaper *Birzhevye Vedomosti* wrote, for "bloodshed is always horrible and smoking blood is always poisonous"; in the depths of night "shots ring out in a dead garden, secret cars hurry across the city carrying corpses and live men."

The river was dangerous to search, because it had only fully frozen over in the past few hours and the ice was thin. Vassilyev contacted the harbor board to get divers. They searched the bottle green waters for an hour without success, until an old riverman who knew how corpses traveled with the currents told them where to look. They investigated a pool in the ice 250 yards downstream from the bridge. "They first saw a fur coat, hairs coming through the ice," the reporter wrote. "There was a lot of blood." The arms and legs of the corpse were tied with cords, and it showed evidence of multiple wounds.

It was the Siberian.

—

"Ania [Vyrubova] is staying with us, since Mama is afraid for her," Olga wrote in her diary that night. "We have finally learned that Father Grigorii [*sic*] was killed, probably by Dmitri, and thrown from the bridge by the Krestinsky [island]. He was found in the water. No words can say how hard it is. We sat and drank tea, and the whole time we felt Father Grigorii was with us."

The corpse was taken in a military ambulance three miles out of the city to a veterans' home on the Tsarskoye Selo Road. It was frozen and had to be thawed before an autopsy could be carried out by Professor Kosorotov. He found three bullet wounds. One bullet had entered the left side of the chest and traversed the stomach and the liver. A second had struck the right side of the back and entered the kidneys. The third was fired into the head and penetrated the brain. The first two shots had been fired while the victim was upright, the third when he was on the ground. The third shot appeared to have been the cause of death, although there were traces of water in the lungs, suggesting that Rasputin may not have been clinically dead when he entered the water. There were multiple contusions on the body, mainly on the head. The brain matter smelled of alcohol. The professor found twenty soupspoonfuls of grayish brown liquid in the stomach, which also smelled of alcohol. There was no evidence of poisoning. The corpse was dressed in a blue blouse with a cornflower motif. A small gold cross inscribed "Save and Protect," and a platinum and gold bracelet, with the tsar's monogram N and a double-headed eagle, were also found on the body. These were later reclaimed by the empress.

The body was laid out by Akulina Laptinskaya, the Sister of Charity, with the sideline in selling Rasputin's secrets, at the orders of the empress. She spent much of the night washing the corpse and its wounds and dressing it in fresh clothes before it was placed in a casket. A crucifix was put on the breast, and Akulina placed a note in Rasputin's hands. "My dear martyr," it read, "give me Thy blessing that it may follow me always on the sad and dreary path I have yet to traverse here below, and remember us from on high in Your holy prayers! Alexandra."

CHAPTER 27

Confessional

T he police investigation was swift and competent. They knew, almost immediately, the identity of the guilty; but they were prevented from in-
terrogating them in depth or from charging them. Alexandra's orders
for Yusupov and Dmitri to be placed under house arrest were illegal—she had
no such powers—and bitterly resented by the rest of the Romanov clan. "This
means open revolt," Grand Duke Andrei Vladimirovich exclaimed. "Here we
have the war, with the enemy threatening us from all sides, and we have to deal
with this sort of nonsense. How can they not be ashamed to stir up all this fuss
over the murder of such a filthy good-for-nothing!" The scandal was already
prodigious. The tsar did not contemplate adding to it with the arrest of men
closely related to him by blood and marriage.

There was to be no trial. In its absence the accounts of the murderers have
been accepted as filling in the detail missing from police evidence. They were little inhibited by guilt, for they felt their deed had served their country, but both
Yusupov and Purishkevich had high opinions of themselves and were open to
exaggeration. They also felt it their duty, as a prince and a gentleman, to deflect
attention from others involved in or supporting their deed.

Yusupov wrote that he spent the greater part of December 16 completing
the furnishings of the cellar. It was built of dark granite, with two small windows and a vaulted ceiling that gave full headroom only in the center. After
dark, red plush curtains and a fire gave it warmth. A samovar bubbled cheer-
fully on the table. Rose cakes and wineglasses were laid out on a sideboard. He
told the staff that they were to remain in the servants' hall unless he rang for
them. Lazovert worked on the automobile they were to use. He painted out the

red emblem *Semper Idem* that identified it as belonging to Purishkevich's medical services. Purishkevich passed the day at the Duma, writing letters and chatting on the telephone. Lazovert collected him in the car at about 11:00 P.M. Purishkevich brought a heavy Sauvage pistol with him. Dmitri came separately to the Moika Palace at the same hour.

The doctor put on rubber gloves and carefully ground crystals of potassium cyanide into powder. He sprinkled this liberally into the cakes. He also dissolved three decigrams of cyanide into a few drops of water and poured it into two of the wineglasses. Four centigrams was a lethal dose. When he had finished Lazovert tossed the gloves into the fire. That was a mistake, for the room filled with the acrid stench of burning rubber. Lazovert then put on the chauffeur's coat Purishkevich had bought earlier and drove Yusupov to Gorokhovaya ulitsa. The prince went up the back staircase. Rasputin answered the door himself, saying, "No one is up, the children are asleep, enter, Little One." The prince was struck by how good he looked, the preparation he had put into meeting Princess Irina, his hair and beard freshly washed and combed, the blue blouse immaculate. He felt a pang at the "despicable deceit" of inviting a guest to his own murder. "What had become of his second sight?" he thought. "What use was his facility for reading the thoughts of others if he was blind to the dreadful trap that was laid for him?" Like a lamb, then, a lamb in fur coat and beaver hat and size sixteen snow boots, Rasputin followed Yusupov down to the automobile.

At the palace Yusupov took Rasputin across the marble entrance hall and down the steps to the cellar. "You know how I am being slandered," Rasputin said. "Remember how Christ was persecuted. He too suffered for the sake of truth." Or so Yusupov said that he said, conveniently, for it branded his guest as a blasphemer; admirers, not Rasputin himself, compared him with Christ. Rasputin heard a gramophone upstairs playing the hit song "Yankee Doodle Dandy." "What's this?" he asked. "Someone giving a party?" The prince replied that his wife was entertaining a few girlfriends. She would soon be down.

He gave the starets an unpoisoned biscuit. At first Rasputin refused the offer of the poisoned cakes. When Yusupov pressed him he ate two of them. Cyanide has a bitter almond scent, but he made no comment. After a little he said he was thirsty and asked for tea. The prince offered him wine—Yusupov wine from the family estates in the Crimea—but Rasputin said he preferred Madeira. Had Yusupov studied his man, he would have known that. He persuaded him to have a glass of unspiked wine and then, by dropping the glass, gave him one with poison in it. He drank. Nothing happened; Rasputin merely complained of "a tickling in my throat."

Rasputin amused himself by playing with the many drawers in the ebony cabinet. Yusupov, waiting for him to collapse, said he would check on when Irina was coming and excused himself from the cellar. His fellow conspirators were huddled at the top of the stairs, playing and replaying "Yankee Doodle Dandy." They had to be kept out of sight; had Rasputin seen Purishkevich, who had attacked him so savagely in his Duma speech, he would have realized instantly what was afoot. Lazovert was so unnerved by the failure of his poison— so he said—that he fainted and had to be revived in the snowy garden. The secret police chief, Vassilyev, claimed that Lazovert, overcome by conscience, had substituted soda or magnesia for the cyanide. Another explanation for the failure of the autopsy to find poison is that a corrupt drug manufacturer was selling the army medical service placebos instead of genuine pharmaceuticals. A third, and the one favored by Yusupov, was that the Dark One was protected by the forces of evil.

When the prince reappeared in the cellar, Rasputin noticed a guitar case. He asked Yusupov to play to him. "Play something cheerful," he said. "I like listening to your singing." Yusupov sang Gypsy songs. They had been alone together for two hours; the murder was becoming a marathon. The hen party excuse was wearing thin; Felix was embarrassed and frightened. The upstairs crew had become restless and noisy, and Rasputin heard them and asked what was happening. Yusupov left the cellar to investigate. Grand Duke Dmitri said he was tired and wanted to leave. "We can't leave him down there half dead," Purishkevich said. He thought they should "stake their all" and descend together to shoot the starets. The prince said that Rasputin would be alarmed if he saw them all. He took Dmitri's Browning revolver and went back to the cellar.

Rasputin sat at the table with a drooping head. His breathing was labored. "My head is heavy and I've a burning in my stomach," he complained. "Give me another glass of wine. It'll do me good." He swallowed a glass "at a gulp" and revived. Despite his cargo of cyanide, he suggested Yusupov go to the Gypsies with him. "All our thoughts belong to God," he said. "But our bodies belong to ourselves." Yusupov said it was too late. Rasputin played again with the ebony cabinet. "Grigory Efimovich," Yusupov said, "you'd far better look at the crucifix and say a prayer." Rasputin seemed to realize what was to happen; he looked at the prince gently, resigned. Yusupov said later that he feared that the "supernatural powers" protecting Rasputin might render a bullet harmless. But when the starets started making the sign of the cross, the "dark protecting power" dissolved. "My arm grew rigid, I aimed at his heart and pulled the trigger," Yusupov recalled. "Rasputin gave a wild scream and crumpled on the bearskin."

The others now rushed down. They lifted the body from the bearskin to prevent the blood from staining it. Rasputin's face twitched in spasms as the blood soaked into the blue blouse. The body then went still. It was about 3:00 A.M. Lazovert examined him and pronounced him dead. The plan was now for Captain Sukhotkin to put on Rasputin's coat and beaver hat and to be driven by Lazovert with Dmitri in Purishkevich's automobile, to suggest to any watching police agent that they were taking Rasputin home. In fact, they would drive to Purishkevich's train, where Rasputin's clothes would be burned while they returned to the Moika Palace to collect the corpse and dump it in the river.

As they set off Purishkevich and Yusupov relaxed over cigars, confident that they had saved Russia. Yusupov went back to the cellar to reexamine the results of his night's work. The body fascinated him; he was alone with it for perhaps half an hour. Something strange may have happened during this time—the Duma deputy, Maklakov, said that he subsequently had an "unusual conversation" with Yusupov about the murder, adding cryptically, "I imagine he remembers it well, but I will say nothing about it." Maria Rasputin claimed that Yusupov had tried to seduce her father on one of his visits during November and raped him at his death; Simanovich maintained that Yusupov had visited Rasputin to be cured of homosexuality, and that during the therapy Rasputin "made him lie down and then lashed and hypnotized him." There is no independent evidence to support either statement. By his own admission the prince held the body's wrist, could detect no pulse, and began to shake it with rage. The corpse stirred and opened "green viper eyes." With a roar Rasputin rose and rushed at him. "He sank his fingers into my shoulder like steel claws," Yusupov recollected. "His eyes were bursting from their sockets, blood oozed from his lips." As he tried to strangle him Rasputin kept repeating: "Felix, Felix." Yusupov tore himself free, leaving one of the epaulets of his cadet uniform in Rasputin's hand, and ran up the stairs.

Purishkevich described Yusupov as "literally faceless" with terror, his "lovely large blue eyes" bulging, as, "virtually oblivious of me, seemingly out of his mind," he fled into the main part of the palace. Then the politician, too, saw a "terrible reality." Rasputin, who had lain dead in the cellar half an hour before, had climbed the stairs and was running across the snow-covered courtyard to an iron gate that led into the street. "I couldn't believe my eyes," Purishkevich said, "But a hard cry, which broke the silence of the night, persuaded me. 'Felix, Felix, I will tell everything to the empress.' " He took out his Sauvage pistol and fired, the shot echoing in the night. He was a good shot—he practiced regularly on the Semyonovsky Guards' pistol range—but he missed. He fired again as Rasputin closed on the gate. He missed again. "I bit with all my force the end of my left hand to force myself to concentrate and I fired a third time," he said. "The bullet hit him in the shoulders. He stopped. I fired a fourth time and hit him probably in the head." He ran up and kicked Rasputin as hard as he could with his boot. Rasputin fell into the snow and tried to rise but could only grind his teeth. "This time, I was certain that his swan song had been sung and that he would never rise again," Purishkevich wrote in his diary a few hours later. For good measure Yusupov appeared with a rubber club—probably the blackjack he had borrowed from Shulgin—and beat the body.

Both men's accounts of the actual killing are confirmed by the autopsy. The wound found in the left side of the chest corresponds with Yusupov's original shot to the heart, and those in the right side of the back and the head to Purishkevich's shot at the shoulders and his "probable" hit in the head. Professor Kossorotov also found contusions consistent with Purishkevich's kicks and Yusupov's clubbing.

After dealing with Vlassiyev, the policeman who heard the shots, Lazovert and the others drove back to the palace at about 5:30 A.M. The body was wrapped in a shroud—variously linen, a blue curtain, a rug, canvas—and was driven off at high speed north, toward Petrovsky Island. All the conspirators were in the car except Yusupov, who was exhausted. It took them two efforts to hurl the body over the low parapet. They forgot to attach weights to the body, and the telltale boot was left on the ice.

—

"Something has to happen"—it had become an all-Russian saying. Such were the accounts of those who achieved it. There were others; persistently it was said that ladies were present in the palace at the time of the murder. In his police statement, if not in his later books, Yusupov himself said that he had given a small party, with Dmitri and Purishkevich, and some officers and society women whom he refused to name. The conspirators were at pains to clear all others of involvement in the killing. Purishkevich took great care to emphasize that the young Romanov was innocent of murder: "Thank God that the hand of the Grand Duke Dmitri Pavlovich is not stained with this dirty blood. He was only a spectator, that's all. Pure, young, noble, regal youth, so close to the throne, cannot and must not be guilty even in such a highly patriotic deed connected with the spilling of someone's blood, be it even Rasputin."

Policeman Yefimov gave evidence to his superiors within a few hours of the event that he had heard a cry from the palace, "as if uttered by a woman." The servant Nefedov said in his police statement that when he cleared up the dining room the following morning, he found "everything was just as it should be." He confirmed that he had been told ladies would be present at the party, as they had been at previous parties; the debris of mixed company is different from that of a stag party—lipstick on cigarette ends and glasses, a smell of perfume—and it is unlikely that an experienced servant could have mistaken the signs.

Yusupov also referred to the presence of ladies in a letter he wrote to the empress on the day after the murder, which corresponds closely to his police statement recorded by Vassilyev. "Your Majesty," he wrote. "I hasten to fulfill your command and tell you about everything that happened in my house yesterday so as to throw light upon the terrible accusation I was charged with. On the occasion of housewarming on the night of the sixteenth I invited a few friends for dinner, among them some ladies. Grand Duke Dmitri Pavlovich was also there. Around 12:00 Grigory Efimovich telephoned me and invited me to go to the Gypsies. I refused, saying that I have a party myself and asked where he called from. He answered, 'Isn't it a bit too much what you want to know?' and hung up. While he spoke I could hear many voices. That's all that I heard of Grigory Efimovich that evening.

"Returning to my guests, I told them about my conversation on the telephone, which elicited tactless remarks from them. You know, Your Majesty, that the name of Grigory Efimovich is rather unpopular in many circles. Around 3:00 A.M. people started to depart, and, having said good-bye to the grand duke and two ladies, I went to my study with the other guests. Suddenly it seemed to me like a report [gunshot] was heard. I called for the servant and ordered him to find out what it was. He came back and said, 'A report was heard, but nobody knows where it came from.' After that I went out into the yard myself and asked the yard keepers and policeman who had fired the shot. The yard keepers said that they had been drinking tea in the lodge, and the policeman said that he heard the report but did not know who made it. Then I went home, called for the policeman, and telephoned Dmitri Pavlovich to ask whether it was he who fired. He laughed and answered that leaving the house he fired several times at a dog, and one of the ladies fainted. When I told him that the shots had made a sensation, he answered that this could not be so because there was no one around.

"I called for the servant and went out to the yard and saw one of our dogs lying dead near the fence. Then I ordered the servant to bury it in the yard.

"At 4:00 A.M. everybody left and I came back to the palace of Grand Duke Alexander Mikhailovich, where I live. On the following day, that is, this morning, I learned about the disappearance of Grigory Efimovich, which is being connected with my party. Then they told me he was seen with me last night and that he left with me. This is a downright lie, for my guests and myself did not leave my house all through the night. Then they told me that he [Rasputin] said to someone that one of these days he was to go to meet Irina [Irina Alexandrovna, Yusupov's wife]. There is some truth in it for, when I saw him last, he asked me to introduce him to Irina and asked whether she was here. I said to him that my wife was in the Crimea but that she could come [back] on the fifteenth or sixteenth of December. On the night of the fourteenth I received a telegram from Irina in which she wrote that she'd fallen ill and asked me to join her brothers, who leave tonight. I cannot find the words, Your Majesty, to tell you how I've been shocked by what happened and how outrageous are the accusations against me.

"I remain, deeply devoted to Your Majesty, Felix."

The empress was unimpressed, replying in pencil, "No one has the right to indulge in killing. I know conscience gives no rest to many as not only DP

[Grand Duke Dmitri Pavlovich] has been mixed up in it. I am surprised by your communication to me."

Simanovich visited the Moika police station on the morning after the murder with Bishop Isidor, another Rasputin protégé. He claimed that Rasputin was killed during a real party in the palace, at which ladies were present. He was told this by Vera Koralli, a ballerina and a cousin of Yusupov, who claimed she had attended the party with two of Yusupov's brothers-in-law. When Rasputin arrived in a reception room, a brother-in-law, who had been hiding behind the curtain in the hall, fired and hit him in the eye. Rasputin fell, and "everybody fired at him and hit him in the eye, only Vera Koralli refused to do it and she cried, 'I don't want to shoot.' " The body was then taken down to the cellar. Rasputin revived, dragged himself out to the courtyard, and was trying to escape to the street when he was betrayed by a barking guard dog. He was then caught by Grand Duke Dmitri Pavlovich, his arms and legs were tied, and he was taken by automobile to be thrown, still living, into the icebound Neva.

Robert Wilton, the London *Times* man in Petrograd, also mentioned the presence of women—though demimondaines, high-class courtesans, rather than society ladies—in his account of the murder. He obtained his story from police officials and from reporters on *Novoye Vremya*, who had excellent police contacts. His original story was censored, but he kept the notes he had written up on the day after the murder and sent them in a letter to Wickham Steed, the *Times* foreign editor, on December 20.

In Wilton's version Rasputin, his tongue loosened by drink and the prospect of an orgy, revealed government secrets at a party hosted by Yusupov at which courtesans were present. He was invited to commit suicide as a final act of patriotic redemption but turned the proffered revolver on his hosts before himself being shot. The conspirators—Wilton mentioned the sons of the late Grand Duke Constantine as well as Yusupov, Dmitri, and Purishkevich—had "decided to 'remove' Rasputin because they regarded him as the cause of a dangerous scandal affecting the interests of the dynasty and of the Empire. So many persons being in the plot rumours were bound to leak out, and as long ago as Monday last it was reported that Rasputin's death might be expected hourly." Wilton claimed that Yusupov had often invited Rasputin to the Moika Palace to pump him for information on the "doings of 'August Personages,' " the use of initial capitals indicating that this meant the tsar and tsarina.

Rasputin was asked to a party at the palace on December 16, together with a number of courtesans. Under the influence of liquor he "gave away not only his own secrets but also the secrets of all the Ministerial and other political changes that have so much incensed Russian public opinion within recent months, notably the dismissal of Sazonov, the appointment of Stürmer and the successive and persistent failures to introduce a stable Ministry and internal re-

forms." At about 2:30 A.M. Rasputin was told that he would have to die. "A revolver was placed in his hand," Wilton wrote, "but he flatly refused to commit
suicide and discharged the weapon some say in the direction of the Grand Duke
Dmitri. The bullet smashed a pane of glass thereby attracting the attention of
the police outside." The butler told them that a distinguished guest had practiced target shooting.

"Hardly had the police officers left the palace," Wilton continued, "when a
motor car drove up along the Moika canal quay and stopped near a small footbridge almost facing the palace." Four men were seen to alight, their faces covered "by some black substance." As soon as the passengers had left the car, the
chauffeur turned off his lights "and putting on full speed made off along the
canal." This scene was witnessed by an Okhrana agent named Tihomirov, who
had been detailed by the police department to look after Rasputin. Tihomirov
presumed that the "masked or disguised men" were robbers, since they had entered the palace by a side door in the back part of the garden. The agent hurried
across the canal to the police station and telephoned a report to the Okhrana.

A further commotion followed. Two women were carried out of the palace;
"they were offering resistance and were refusing to enter a motor car and were
doing their best to force their way back into the palace." The car whirled off
down the quay with them. An inspector drove off in pursuit. "It was impossible
to overtake the fugitive car on account of its enormous speed; it carried neither
number nor lights," Wilton wrote. "The policemen who came to the palace
were informed that two ladies belonging to the half-world had been miscon-
ducting themselves and had been asked to leave." The affair seemed to be at an
end when four shots were heard from the little garden fronting the wing of the
palace. "Once more the alarm was sounded in both police stations and again
detachments of police appeared at the palace," Wilton wrote. "This time an official wearing a colonel's uniform came out to them (his identity is not yet established) and announced in categorical fashion that within the palace was a
Grand Duke and that H.I.H. [His Imperial Highness] would explain everything
that was necessary in person to the proper quarters. After such a declaration
the police inspector . . . returned to his official duties, leaving a patrol on the
opposite side of the Moika as a measure of precaution. The servants assisted by
the chauffeur, in the presence of an officer who was wearing a long fur cloak,
carried out what looked like a human body and placed it in the car. The chauffeur jumped in and putting on full speed made off along the canal side and also
promptly disappeared."

When the police returned to the palace, they were met by Yusupov. He told
them that they should "draw up a report as to the killing of Rasputin. At first
this announcement was not accepted seriously in view of all the strange oc-
currences of the night, but the police officials were invited to come into a

chamber of the basement and were there shown the spot where the body had been lying. They saw a pool of congealed blood, and traces of blood were also visible on the snow in the garden. In answer to the question as to where the body was, the prince replied that the body was 'where it should be.' He declined to give any further explanation."

Wilton added to his story a day later, this time accounting for the dead dog. During the carousal at the Yusupov palace, he wrote, Rasputin was asked if he would get three new ministers appointed. For this he would receive half a million rubles. He replied, "Why not?" Purishkevich said, "But we want three scoundrels to enter the ministry!" "What of that?" Rasputin replied. "Have I not appointed others?" Then the starets was told, "So you confess that it was your work and that you betrayed Russia. We sentence you to death. Take this revolver and shoot yourself." Rasputin "took the weapon and fired it at the company but missed them and hit a large dog that was in the room. Then Purishkevich and the others shot Rasputin."

—

The lack of a formal investigation, and the absence of a trial with evidence, witnesses, and cross-examination, made it inevitable that the Rasputin rumor mills would grind as furiously after his death as before it. The official statement issued to newspapers after the discovery of the corpse was so brief—sixteen words plus a dateline—that it incited speculation. Wilton cabled it to London, adding thirteen days to the Russian date of December 19 to fit the Western calendar of his British readers: QUOTE PETROGRAD MORNING 1 JANUARY NEAR PETROVSKI BRIDGE WAS FOUND BODY GRIGORY RASPUTIN CLOSE TO BANK STOP JUDICIAL AUTHORITIES CARRYING OUT INVESTIGATION UNQUOTE.

The official background briefing, which the censor passed for transmission, was bizarre. "Body which bore mark [of] several bullet wounds in head [and] chest was very much disfigured," Wilton was allowed to cable. "Feet tied [and] hands had evidently been similarly pinioned but when flung [into] river rope broke and arms outspreading remained frozen [in] that position." The myth was thus encouraged that Rasputin's body had frozen as if it had been crucified. Wilton was also told that "immediately after being extracted from under the ice . . . the body was taken to the mortuary in the Peter and Paul fortress where it remained all day. It is expected that the body will be taken to his native village in Siberia for burial."

These falsifications—the body was taken to the veterans' home outside the city and it was to be buried at Tsarskoye Selo—were probably deliberate. The interior ministry did not want the body to be the focus of any demonstration; hence the canard that it was in the fortress, the best-guarded site in the city. It was also easiest to distance the royal family from the affair by suggesting that the burial would take place in distant Pokrovskoye.

There is a symmetry, a pleasantness, to the idea that Rasputin amused himself with ladies at his last party; as he had lived, so he died. In his death, as in life, Rasputin offers choice and little certainty. Simanovich no doubt felt that this was the way his friend would have chosen. No Okhrana agent reported Rasputin attending any evening or nighttime engagement without women being present. Uniformed policemen, palace staff, and Yusupov all mentioned women. Wilton, who had become a near neighbor of Rasputin after *The Times* moved its offices from Potchtamtykaya to 4 Gorokhovaya ulitsa, had collaborated with experienced Russian journalists.

But certainly the murderers tally over the character of their victim. There, in the accounts of Yusupov and Purishkevich, is the energy, the refusal to submit, the force of a soul that unnerved armed men, the love of good times and Gypsy music, the flash of lust and its philosophy—"our bodies belong to ourselves . . ." There is the knowledge, sober and perceptive in his agony, that the peasant-colossus he had made of himself, in whose presence Russia quivered with awe and malice, depended on another. It was Alexandra who gave his power its flesh and sinew—those last in extremis words, "Felix, Felix, I will tell all to the empress . . ." And there, too, is the rage for life—even as it was being poisoned, shot, and beaten out of him.

CHAPTER 28

Finis

He was buried at 9:00 A.M. on Thursday, December 22, in the grounds of a small chapel Vyrubova was building in the imperial park at Tsarskoye Selo. The weather was frosty and fine, the morning sky a clear, metallic blue, and the snow sparkling. Lili von Dehn attended, bringing her memories of the healing of her son Titi. She stopped her carriage on the road and walked across a frozen field toward the chapel. Planks had been put on the ground as a footpath. A police motor van was waiting near the open grave.

"I heard the sound of sleigh bells, and Anna Vyrubova came slowly across the field," Dehn wrote. "Almost immediately afterward, a closed automobile stopped and the imperial family joined us." They were dressed in black. The empress carried white flowers; she was pale but composed until the oak coffin was taken from the police van and she began to cry. The court archpriest read the service. The tsar and the empress threw earth on the coffin. Alexandra handed around her flowers, and they threw those in too. The imperial limousine left for the Alexander Palace, and Vyrubova got into her sledge for the drive back to her cottage. Dehn spent a moment looking back at the snowy fields and the bare walls of the unfinished chapel as her carriage sped her away.

After Rasputin's death, as before, no witness told the same tale. In his diary, in which for decades he had accurately noted the day's events and weather, Nicholas wrote that Rasputin was already in the ground when the family arrived. Dehn's touching scene—the brave empress weeping only when she saw the coffin emerging from the makeshift police hearse—was invention. "At 9 the whole family went past the photography building," the tsar wrote that evening, "and turned right towards the field, where we assisted at a sad scene: the coffin with the body of the unforgettable Grigory, murdered on the night of December 17 by monsters in the house of F. Yusupov, had already been lowered into the grave. Father Alexander Vasiliev finished the eulogy, after which we returned home. The weather was gray with 12 degrees of frost. . . . In the afternoon took a walk with the children."

Technically, the murder changed nothing; psychologically it changed everything. It did not, as the killers hoped, restore the dignity of the throne; and Alexandra's influence was untouched, for she kept her nerve while the tsar retreated into nervous collapse. Her mauve boudoir and her telephone beneath a picture of Marie Antoinette remained the focal point of government, and, when ministers came to report to the tsar in his study, she listened from his dressing room. In a broader sense, however, the death was what Russians call *perelom*, the great turning point. It left the rulers utterly exposed. To assault Rasputin was to assault the throne, and two of those who had done so were Romanovs by blood or marriage; the chains of loyalty that still bound those of lesser rank were snapped. Centuries of convention had protected the tsar and empress from outright defamation by all but the boldest and most reckless subject. Blame for catastrophe had been heaped on Rasputin; he had been their lightning rod, deflecting hatreds and contempt that now had no target but themselves. Rasputin had been their glue, too; he was "their mainspring, their toy, their fetish." If he could be taken from them, so could their power. And the penalty for lèse-majesté, certain death or torture under previous tsars, was suddenly seen as little more than a slap on the wrist. Although the empress had shouted "Hang them!" the murderers were simply sent away—Yusupov to his estates in the Crimea, Dmitri to join the army staff in Persia. Purishkevich took his hospital train to the front, where the military police kept watch on him.

———

On New Year's Day the tsar received the congratulations of the diplomatic corps in Tsarskoye Selo. A burst of bitter cold greeted 1917. The windows of the carriages taking the ambassadors to the palace were impenetrable with frost, and the horses were smothered in ice. A courtier asked Maurice Paléologue if he did not feel that "now we are on the very brink." The Frenchman thought they were over it. "I am obliged to report," he cabled the Quai d'Orsay in Paris, "that at the present moment the Russian empire is run by lunatics."

The tsar had left unfinished business at the Stavka; with General Alexeev on sick leave, nobody was in effective supreme command of Russia's armies. Nicholas did not return to Mogilev for two months. He closeted himself in the Alexander Palace with Alexandra and the children. He abandoned his mornings to petty projects, replacing German court titles—Kanzler, Ritter—with

Russian ones; he walked in the afternoon, and in the evening he played cards and watched movies, *Madame du Barry*, with the guillotines and blood of revolutionary France, and the spiritualist thriller *Mysterious Hands*. His eyes were flat, his face thin and lined. Alexandra remained defiant, but the tutor Gilliard found that "her shattered face revealed how much she suffered. The pain was tremendous." Vyrubova was with her continuously; the empress insisted that her friend move out of her cottage to the Alexander Palace for fear she too would be murdered. Her other comfort was Rasputin's ghost. "He is still close to us," she wrote.

Tchaikovsky's *Sleeping Beauty* played at the Mariinsky Theater with Smirnova as première danseuse. Her arabesques were no more fantastic than the stories passing from lip to lip in the stalls; Alexandra would be taken to a convent, a famous fighter pilot, Captain Kostenko, would crash his aircraft on the imperial limousine. "We are back in the time of the Borgias!" an Italian embassy counselor whispered in the intermission. Grand dukes, Romanovs, were overheard plotting to force the tsar to abdicate in favor of the tsarevich and a regent. Alexandra conducted her own plots; her sights were set on the too-liberal Trepov. The prime minister was replaced by an ill man of seventy, Prince Nikolai Golitsyn, a "good-natured Russian squire and an old weakling," who protested that he was "utterly incapable" of doing the job. For good measure he warned Nicholas that officers in Moscow regiments were openly threatening to proclaim another tsar. Nicholas ordered him to accept. "The empress and I know that we are in God's hands," he said. "His will be done!" The education minister, Count Pavel Ignatev, loyal to Nicholas for thirty years, begged to resign his post so as to be spared "the unbearable burden of serving against the commands of my conscience." He had no reply for a week. Nicholas then let him go, with no word of thanks.

The dead starets had promised Nikolai Dobrovolsky the justice ministry for his help with the German sugar scandal. Simanovich said he "supposed that he would fulfill all my wishes in gratitude" when the empress steered him into the office, but he supposed wrong. Dobrovolsky refused to have the banker Rubinstein released when he was rearrested. Protopopov was brought in to help and had a furious but fruitless argument with Dobrovolsky over the telephone. The problem was that the new justice minister knew very well "how the tsar values the instructions of the deceased"—Rasputin—and felt immune. "Under such circumstances," Simanovich said, "I decided to resort to my old and tested method—a bribe. Protopopov agreed." The interior minister thus connived in the corruption of the justice minister. Madame Rubinstein drew 100,000 rubles in cash from her bank. Her husband was discharged from prison into a sanatorium.

None of the Rubinstein bribe money made its way to Rasputin's dependents; Simanovich claimed but failed to aid his dead friend's children. Maria

Rasputin said that her father left no more than 3,000 rubles—some £300 or $1,400 at the exchange rate of the day—a pittance compared with the millions he had helped others make. Her dowry, which he had been keeping in his desk, was missing. It was left to the empress to send 30,000 rubles for each of the three children from her private privy purse.

———

The Okhrana was still functioning. It spread rumors—that Rasputin had been buried in an obscure monastery in the Urals—and it collected facts. On January 9, the anniversary of Bloody Sunday, it calculated that 300,000 workers had come out on strike. In Moscow a Red banner was raised in Theater Square for the first time in the war. On January 28 it predicted that "events of extraordinary importance, fraught with exceptional consequences for the Russian statehood, are not beyond the hills." The number of troops in the capital, 170,000, was a record, but many were shell-shock victims from the front, reservists, and agitators drafted into the army from factories for troublemaking. Even the Cossacks were draftees, not volunteers. The Okhrana found them to have "much raw, untrained material, unfit to put down disorders."

The warnings fell on the deaf ears of Protopopov. He busied himself by day replying personally to the torrent of toadies and petitioners who had sent him Christmas and New Year's greetings. By night he communed with the ghost of Rasputin at séances. With Prince Kurakin, a hook-nosed necromancer, he was locked "in secret conclave for hours every evening, listening to the dead man's solemn words" and passing them on to Alexandra. He was to deny later that he had succeeded in raising Rasputin's spirit but agreed under cross-examination that he had told the empress that he had, because it made her happy.

The tsar's childhood friend Sandro—Grand Duke Alexander Mikhailovich—visited him and Alexandra on February 10. He brought a letter he had written to them: "We are living through a most dangerous moment in Russia's history. . . . Everyone senses it: some with their mind, some with their heart, some their soul. . . . Certain forces in Russia are leading you, and consequently Russia as well, to irrevocable ruin. . . . The government today is the organ preparing the revolution. The people do not want it, but the government is taking every possible measure to create as many dissatisfied people as possible and is succeeding completely at it. We are assisting at an unprecedented spectacle of revolution from above, rather than below." The analysis was accurate. He tried to discuss it at Alexandra's bedside—she often took to her bed now. "When you are less excited," she said in a voice hard with anger, "you will admit that I knew better." Nicholas said nothing; he chain-smoked.

On February 14 ninety thousand came out on strike, led by workers from the giant Putilov engineering works. The garrison was restive. "You shouldn't be fighting here," a group of ensigns yelled at policemen. "They ought to send you fatsos to the front." The Duma reconvened that day. Revolution was so tangible that Vasily Shulgin, the monarchist deputy whom Alexandra so hated, felt that the debaters were drained of all emotion by futility in the face of the approaching terror. "Behind the white columns of the hall grinned Hopelessness," he said. "And she whispered: 'Why? What for? What difference does it make?' " A small helping of potatoes, fifteen kopecks prewar, was hard to find at eight times that price. There was panic buying of dry rusks for hoarding. Restaurants laid off their orchestras. The temperature dropped to twenty-two below zero.

In the morning of February 20, Nicholas told Golitsyn that he was preparing to proclaim that he would grant a ministry responsible to the Duma. In the evening the prime minister was recalled to the palace; the tsar said that he was leaving for the Stavka and that no announcement on a new ministry would be made. Nicholas had spoken with the empress during the afternoon; she had not given up on autocracy. Golitsyn sensed that Nicholas was not going to the Stavka. He was running away there.

He did not escape his wife's twin obsessions. "Our dear Friend in another world prays for you too, now even closer to us, but I would so love to hear His consoling & heartening voice," she wrote him on February 22, adding a lecture on autocracy: "Lovy, be firm, because the Russians need you to be—at every turn you show love & kindness—now let them feel your fist, as they themselves ask. So many of late have told, that we need the knout. It's strange, but that is the Slav nature. . . . They must learn to fear you, love is not enough. Tho a child adores his father, he must fear his anger. I embrace you tight and hug your tired head. . . . Feel my arms hold you, my lips press tenderly to yours. Eternally together, always inseparable."

"Be firm, lovy, don't let them cheat you out of what is yours"—it was so close to the first note she had written to him, twenty-two years before, in his diary, at the deathbed of his father. As to his "adoring children," his people—Ambassador Paléologue was told that if the tsar appeared in public, in Moscow at least, they would boo him. The empress they would tear into pieces.

—

The children came down with measles on February 23. "Well now, Olga & Alexis both have measles & Olga's face is all covered with rash. Baby suffers more in the mouth—a bad cough and sore eyes," the empress wrote to her husband. "They lie in the dark." That day, a Thursday, was International Women's Day. In midmorning women in the Neva Thread Mills heard demonstrators outside demanding bread. "Into the street! We've had it!" the mill girls shouted. They walked out and threw snowballs at the windows of the neighboring Nobel machinery works to bring out the men. They linked arms with them and marched off. After the lunch break workers in the giant Arsenal munitions works came out in large numbers when marchers banged on the gates and windows. The afternoon was warm and snow melted. The demonstrators boarded streetcars, forced the motormen to stop, evacuated the passengers, and overturned them. By early evening they were on the Nevsky; mounted police and Cossacks dispersed them with whips and sabers, but they re-formed when the horsemen cantered off. The Okhrana men noticed that the agitators working the crowds did not bother to hide their faces by pulling their caps down over their eyes, as they usually did. They were becoming bold.

At the Duma a young Socialist lawyer called Alexander Kerensky spoke of starving women "for whom hunger is becoming the only tsar." He called for someone to do "what Brutus did in classical times"—an open call to murder the caesar, the tsar. Alexander Protopopov was driven home late at night down the deserted Nevsky, its yellowing snow lit by a brilliant searchlight on the Admiralty spire. He was in a mood of morbid euphoria; he thought the government was winning. "The day of the twenty-third was not all that bad," he wrote in his diary. "Several policemen were injured; but there was no shooting."

On February 24 Alexandra wrote to the tsar: "Strikes now in Petrograd—80,000 workers have struck, lines of the hungry have formed outside the bakeries. Not enough bread in the town." She said she hoped Kedrinsky, as she called the Duma man, would be hanged. Nicholas sent Alexandra and Alexis honors from the king and queen of the Belgians. He thought of his son—"he will be so pleased with a new little cross!" During the morning a crowd of 2,000 was cornered by Cossacks. Many were women. "We have husbands, fathers, brothers at the front!" they cried. "You too have mothers, wives, sisters, children." The horsemen were ordered to charge; they rode by the edges of the crowd, which greeted them with hurrahs. A Duma deputy asked himself what was happening when demonstrators cheered Cossacks. By later afternoon the police estimated that 200,000 were on strike.

Alexandra wrote again in the evening. "There were riots yesterday, on Vasilievsky Island and Nevsky Prospect because some poor people stoned a bakery, tearing Filippov's bakery to pieces & the Cossacks were called in." Filippov's, so famous for its cream tarts and chocolate cakes—sacked. "At 10 went to see Ania [Vyrubova] (she probably has measles too). . . . Am going from room to room, from sick bed to sick bed." Nicholas wrote again, too, more relaxed: "My brain is resting here—no Ministers, no troublesome questions demanding thought. I consider that this is good for me, but only for my brain. My heart is suffering from the separation." He played dominoes in the evening.

On February 25 Mikhail Rodzianko went to see Premier Golitsyn and demanded his resignation. Golitsyn showed him a decree disbanding the Duma, which the tsar had signed before he left for the Stavka for use at any time. "I am keeping this for emergencies," the old man said, but both men realized that the Duma would pay it no attention; it was too late for that. The Cossacks were now fraternizing with the crowds. "It's a movement of hooligans, boys and girls running around shouting about no bread—just to stir up excitement," Alexandra wrote, calmed by Rasputin's spirit. "If the days were very cold, they would probably all be sitting at home, but all this will pass & calm down." They were not boys behaving badly, but soldiers, and from regiments that had saved the dynasty in 1905. During the afternoon the officer commanding a mounted police unit near the Nikolaevsky railroad station was shot dead by a Cossack. A cavalry squadron, still loyal, transferred from Tsarskoye Selo, killed nine demonstrators on the Nevsky. Police snatch squads were still able to make arrests, but the crowds sometimes rescued those arrested. Police were frequently beaten; some changed into civilian clothes or wore army greatcoats for disguise.

———

On February 26 Nicholas suffered excruciating chest pain during morning service. It covered him with sweat. Later it disappeared, "vanishing suddenly when I knelt before the image of the Holy Virgin." He was warned by the war ministry that soldiers were refusing orders to fire on the rioters. Some were going over to the revolutionaries. Nicholas sent a telegram to General Khabalov, the garrison commander. "I command the disorders in the capital end tomorrow," it read. "They are impermissible in the difficult time of war with Germany and Austria. Nicholas." Then he took a walk. Khabalov was not amused. The rising could not be put down by telegram. "When people said, 'Give us bread,' we gave them bread and that was an end to it," he said of happier days. "But when inscriptions on banners read, 'Down with the autocracy,' what kind of bread will calm them?"

Alexandra remained confident. "They say it's not like 1905 because everyone adores you & only wants bread," she wrote to Nicholas. She went to pray at Rasputin's grave in the early afternoon and wrote later, "It seems to me that it will all be all right. The sun is shining brightly—I feel such peace at His dear grave. He died to save us." As she wrote, at 3:30 P.M., ambulances were racing down the Nevsky to the Catherine Bridge to collect the dead and wounded shot by the training unit of the Pavlovsky Guards; through the center of the city, gunfire sounded like "the dry and regular fall of hail." At six in the evening other Pavlovsky Guardsmen set off to persuade their comrades to stop killing demonstrators. They shot dead a policeman who tried to stop them; when their commanding officer, Colonel Eksten, caught up with them and ordered them back to barracks, they slashed off his head with sabers. A detachment of Preobrazhensky Guardsmen disarmed and arrested the mutineers; nineteen of them were sent to the Peter and Paul Fortress to await court-martial and execution.

Princess Leon Radziwill held a glittering party in the evening—her house ablaze with lights, lackeys in powdered wigs. The city governor thought the crisis was over; loyal troops had produced "brilliant results." Others were not so sure. The premiere of Lermontov's *Masquerade*, with its mournful requiem to the poisoned heroine in the last act, was playing to a small audience at the Alexandrevsky Theater. "Are we witnessing the last night of the regime?" Maurice Paléologue's companion asked him as the ambassador drove home. An Okhrana agent, Limonin, thought everything hung on shaky military units; "if the troops turn on the government, then nothing can save the country," he reported.

On February 27 Volynsky Guardsmen formed in full battle order for morning parade. During the night they had held a meeting and decided not to act as "executioners" anymore; they determined to "join the people." They greeted their commander, Captain Lashkevich, with a "Hurrah!" in place of the normal and docile "At your service." They told him that they would not fire on the people and asked him to leave. As he crossed the parade ground a shot rang out, and they watched the captain "suddenly fling his arms wide and crash to the ground facedown into a snowdrift."

To avoid the firing squad, the men needed to spread mutiny far and fast. They moved to the parade ground of the Preobrazhensky Guards and brought out the battalions drilling there. Officers and NCOs were seen "stooping close to the ground, crouching in ditches, past heaps of garbage and behind stacks of wood, running and crawling." They were fleeing from their own men.

A stenographer at Okhrana headquarters, taking down a report of the mutiny, was so amazed that she logged it in the wrong century, as 9:00 A.M. on February 27, 1817. By 10:00 A.M. there were ten thousand mutineers on the streets. At 11:30 the U.S. ambassador, David Francis, called the foreign ministry to ask for a guard to be put on the embassy to protect officers who had fled inside it. An official said he would ring back. He did not do so; this was the last American communication with the imperial foreign ministry. Alexandra ordered an icon to be paraded around the palace corridors during the morning, with prayers chanted for the sick children. Her valet heard a soldier mutter, "You trample on the people and you carry idols about."

At 1:03 P.M. her nerve cracked. All her adult life she had propped up the autocracy; her political philosophy enshrined in the three words, *pas de concessions*. "Concessions essential," she cabled Nicholas at the Stavka. "Uprising continues. Many troops have gone to the side of the revolution." Nicholas did not reply. He took his normal postlunch walk on the highway running along the Dnieper toward Orsha.

The law courts burned; the crowd cut the firemen's hoses. Alexander Kerensky—unhanged despite the empress's wishes—hurried to the Duma. Troops broke into the Kresty and Litovsky prisons and freed the inmates; three dozen women convicts in prison gowns came out of the Litovsky and shuffled off through the snow in their carpet slippers. Policemen were routed out and murdered. "I saw on our street a man white as a sheet, being pulled away," a schoolboy wrote. "He wore a *shinel,* a police greatcoat, and a *papaha,* a gray fur hat. . . . He was taken away and shot just around the corner." The secret police chief, Alexis Vassilyev, who had gotten on so well with Rasputin, telephoned his own headquarters from his apartment and ordered the staff to leave. He and his wife escaped on passports made out in false names. Alexander Protopopov fled from the interior ministry. He took with him a briefcase with memorabilia—letters to and from the empress, police photographs of Rasputin's corpse.

In the early evening the American naval attaché, Captain McCully, reported that he had seen a cavalry regiment riding quietly away and "abandoning the city to the mutineers." In the Catherine Hall of the Tauride Palace, a soviet—the first since 1905—had been formed. Dirty and disheveled mutineers announced themselves before it to cheers: "We're from the Pavlovsky . . . the Litovsky . . . the Sappers . . . the Chasseurs . . . the Finnish." The regiments had gone.

Nicholas dined at Mogilev with his chief of staff. Grand Duke Mikhail telephoned; the tsar refused his brother's call. The chief of staff, Gen. Mikhail Alexeev, took it instead. The grand duke begged for the cabinet to be dismissed. Nicholas refused. He said he would leave for Tsarskoye Selo on the imperial train at 2:30 A.M. The suite train did not get under way until 5:00 A.M. on Tuesday, February 28; the first train, which steamed out an hour earlier, was a decoy. An hour later the diarist Nikolai Sukhanov, sleeping in the Tauride, was woken by soldiers noisily cutting Ilya Repin's famous portrait of Nicholas out of its frame with their bayonets.

———

A unit of loyal bicycle troops held out against the mutineers until midmorning on February 28. When its commanding officer ordered a cease-fire and walked over to the crowds pleading for his men, saying that they had fought only at his orders, he was shot through the heart. Thieves with army trucks looted tons of coal from the mansion of the tsar's ex-mistress, the ballerina Mathilde Kschessinskaya. The Astoria Hotel was sacked. No cabs or streetcars ran. Fashionable ladies who had to travel went in low peasant sledges sitting on straw in the bottom. Alexander Protopopov was rounded up and brought to the Tauride, his face "hopelessly harassed and sunken," his mustaches trembling; though the crowd froze with hatred when it spotted him, he was protected.

Youths climbed the fronts of drugstores and shops that supplied the Romanovs and threw the double-headed wooden imperial eagles and monograms onto bonfires. Maurice Paléologue came across one of the famous "Ethiopians"—one, in fact, was an American black called Jim Hercules who spent his holidays in the States and returned with jars of guava jelly as presents for the children—who had guarded the doors to the tsar's study and the empress's boudoir, in scarlet trousers, curved shoes, and white turbans, shuffling and crying in civilian clothes. A count muttered to the ambassador of the mutineers: "They've seen many things they ought not to have seen. They know too much about Rasputin."

Nicholas woke late aboard his train and breakfasted at 10:00 A.M. In each successive province the governor turned out at the main railroad station to pay his respects as the train passed through. From Vyazma at 3:00 P.M. the tsar sent a telegram to the empress saying that he was "sending many troops from the front" and that the weather was marvelous.

Trucks filled with mutineers reached Tsarskoye Selo during the afternoon. Alexandra had been busying herself with the measled children and Vyrubova. "I kept seeing her beside my bed," Vyrubova recalled, "now preparing a drink, now smoothing the cushions, now talking to the doctor." In the evening the local garrison mutinied and threw open the local prison. There was a skirmish with a palace patrol in the park. Alexandra went out with Maria, cheered the defenders, and brought groups of them in to have tea and get warm. The noise of songs, music, and shots drifted across the park from the town.

After midnight, the tsar's train was halted at the small station of Malaya Vishera, ninety miles from the capital. An officer who had fled on a railroad trolley warned that the next station up the line was in the hands of mutineers. Nicholas was woken and agreed to backtrack to Pskov. He reached there at 7:00 P.M. on March 1.

In the early hours of Thursday, March 2, Alexander Guchkov burst into the Duma committee room. A young landowner had just been shot dead next to him in his automobile, for no better reason than that he was wearing an officer's uniform. It could not continue, Guchkov said. Nicholas must abdicate. Vasily Shulgin agreed to accompany him to Pskov to persuade the tsar to step down. The two got into Guchkov's bloodstained car and drove to his house, where they scribbled out a draft act of abdication. They drove on to the railroad station and ordered the stationmaster to make up a train—a locomotive and a single carriage—for their journey to Pskov.

Alexandra wrote to Nicholas on March 2; she did not know where he was, but she had two Cossacks sew the letter under their trouser stripes and try to find him. She was still fighting a constitution. "I wanted to send an aeroplan [sic]," she wrote, "but all have vanished. . . . My heart breaks from the thought of you living through all these tortures & upsets totally alone—& we know nothing of you, & you know nothing of us. . . . Clearly they don't want to let you see me so above all you must not sign any paper, constitution or other such horror—but you are alone, without your army, caught like a mouse in a trap, what can you do? If you make any concessions, under no circumstances are you obliged to honour them since they were obtained in ignoble fashion." That was what Rasputin had so often said, that the tsar could give his word and take it back, like a little boy who crosses his fingers when he makes a promise. She told him that the children were sleeping peacefully in the darkness, though the elevator no longer worked. She felt that "God will do something. . . . The two movements—the Duma and the revolutionaries—are two snakes & I hope they bite each other's heads off, which would save the situation." They did so, too late.

Then she came back to Rasputin. "PS," she wrote, "wear His cross, even if it is uncomfortable, for my peace of mind."

Nicholas took soundings from his army commanders. Unanimously they recommended that he abdicate. During the late afternoon he had a heart-to-heart talk with Dr. Sergei Fedorov, his personal physician. He said that he would retire to the Crimea and devote himself to educating his son. The doctor doubted that a man who had abdicated would be allowed to bring up his son. The tsar was startled. He raised his son's health. Rasputin had assured him that, if Alexis lived to seventeen, he would be healthy thereafter. Fedorov told him gently that—Rasputin's miracles apart—Alexis could die at any time. "Then I cannot be separated from Alexis," the tsar said. "It is beyond my strength." He began to cry; then he took afternoon tea. Guchkov and Shulgin's train arrived at Pskov at 10:00 P.M. The platform was lit by blue lanterns. They walked over to the drawing room car of the suite train, hung in green silk. They explained why the monarch must abdicate. "Literally no one supported the tsar," Guchkov wrote. "Total emptiness surrounded the throne." A fresh copy of the act of abdication was typed out. Nicholas signed it in pencil, indifferent to it all, "as others are when they scribble notes in pencil to a friend or make a list of dirty laundry." Varnish was coated over the signature.

After the empress was brought the text of the abdication message; after she had said, "No, I do not believe it, these are all rumours, newspaper slander"; after she realized that her pride, her majesty, her life was as murdered as her Friend—then at length she collapsed, and whispered in French: "*Abdique! Abdique!*"

———

It was over. It took only a week for the revolution to obliterate the mortal remains of Grigory Rasputin. His body was exhumed on March 9 by members of an antiaircraft battery stationed in the imperial park at Tsarskoye Selo. The task was overseen by an artillery officer, Klimov. Rasputin's face was found to have turned black, and an icon was found on his chest. It bore the signatures of Vyrubova, Alexandra, and her four daughters. The body was put into a packing case that had once held a piano and was driven in secret to the imperial stables in Petrograd. The next day it was loaded onto a truck and taken out of Petrograd on the Lesnoe Road.

Eight men were aboard the truck. Koupchinsky, a representative of the Duma provisional committee, which was emerging as the revolutionary government; V. Kolotsiev, a captain in the Sixteenth Lancer Regiment; and six student militiamen from the Petrograd Polytechnic. They signed an affidavit saying that they burned the body at the roadside near the forest of Pargolovo, "in the absolute absence of persons other than the signatories."

It was, perhaps, inevitable that even this final accounting for Rasputin was untrue. Koupchinsky later admitted that he had been ordered by Alexander Kerensky, soon to be head of the new provisional government, to rebury the corpse at an unmarked spot in the countryside. But the truck broke down on the Lesnoe Road. A crowd gathered. They forced open the packing case, looking for gold, and discovered the corpse. Koupchinsky decided to burn it on the spot. His men cut down trees for a pyre, doused the corpse in gasoline, and set fire to it by the roadside.

The ashes were lost to the wind and the mud.

After the Deluge

The empress had wanted Alexander Kerensky hanged. But her life and those of Rasputin's circle were safe for the eight postrevolution months in which he and the moderate provisional government remained in power. True, there were arrests and investigations. Nicholas and Alexandra were held in the Alexander Palace. Kerensky visited them and found them far from monsters. The tsar he rated "a pleasant, somewhat awkward Colonel of the Guards, very ordinary except for a pair of wonderful blue eyes." Alexandra was made of sterner stuff, "a born empress, proud and unbending, fully conscious of her right to rule." Vyrubova was held in less pleasant surroundings—a cell in the Peter and Paul Fortress—and was subjected to the medical examination that found her a virgin.

Otherwise the family was untouched; these first revolutionaries had proudly abolished the death penalty. In August 1917 Kerensky transferred them from Tsarskoye Selo to Tobolsk, partly for their own protection, for the Petrograd region was becoming dangerous. The train that took them to Tyumen, on the track Rasputin had so often traveled, carried the flag of the Rising Sun and was marked "Japanese Red Cross Mission." Kerensky did not want the Romanovs freed by monarchists or murdered by extremists; rural Russia was becoming a place of lynch law and arson, "turning into a Texas," the newspaper *Rech* reported, "into a country of the Far West." As the riverboat *Rus* taking them from Tyumen to Tobolsk steamed past Pokrovskoye, the family came on deck to look at the village and Rasputin's unmistakable two-story house, fulfilling his prophecy that they would see his home before they died.

In October the Bolsheviks seized power in a coup d'état. The country slid into civil war. In April 1918, Nicholas and Alexandra were transferred from Tobolsk to Ekaterinburg. The rivers were still frozen, and they were taken in carts along Trakt 4, a journey Rasputin had driven many times. The road, Alexandra wrote, was "perfectly atrocious, frozen ground, mud, snow, water up to the horses' stomachs, fearfully shaken." They stopped for a noon rest in Pokrovskoye; Alexandra noted that they "stood long before our Friend's house, saw His family and friends looking out of the window." The children joined them later by steamer. In the summer of 1918, the Bolsheviks began to execute every Romanov they could lay their hands on. Grand Duke Mikhail, the tsar's brother, was shot in June and his body burned in a smelting furnace. Nicholas and Alexandra were murdered in Ekaterinburg, together with Alexis and their four daughters, Dr. Botkin, three servants, and Anastasia's pet spaniel, in July. The killers found that each girl had an amulet with Rasputin's picture on it. A day later Grand Duchess Elizabeth, Grand Duke Serge Mikhailovich, and the three sons of Grand Duke Constantine were beaten and thrown, still living, down a mine shaft at Alapayevsk; a peasant heard them singing, and when the bodies were recovered by Whites, the injured head of one of the boys was found to have been carefully bandaged with a handkerchief. In January 1919 four more grand dukes, including the liberal historian Nikolai Mikhailovich, were executed in the Peter and Paul Fortress. This confirmed his own prediction that he would die close to the tombs of his ancestors, who lay in the nearby cathedral.

Some Romanovs escaped. Dowager Empress Marie, together with her daughters Grand Duchesses Xenia and Olga, were evacuated to the West aboard a British battleship. The dowager empress returned to her native Denmark. Xenia settled in Britain. Olga died in a room above a barbershop in Toronto, Canada, in 1960. The tsar's first cousin Grand Duke Cyril escaped to France, where he declared himself "tsar of all the Russias" and held court in a Brittany village until his death in the American Hospital in Paris in 1938. Grand Duke Nicholas Nikolayevich, Alexandra's despised Nikolasha, died in Antibes in the south of France in 1929 and was accorded full military honors at his funeral by the Allies.

Rasputin's actual and would-be assassins had mixed fortunes. Khvostov and Beletsky were shot in the Bolshevik Terror after sharing the same condemned cell. Purishkevich died of typhus while fighting for the Whites in southern Russia during the civil war. Felix Yusupov lost his colossal fortune when he fled into exile, but his coffers were replenished by a $375,000 defamation action against MGM for the Hollywood movie *Rasputin and the Empress;* he died in France in 1967. The Moika Palace became a trade union rest home. Grand Duke Dmitri was saved by his exile to Persia. In 1926 he married an

American heiress in Biarritz; he was a champagne salesman in Florida in the 1930s. He died at age fifty of tuberculosis in Davos, Switzerland, in 1941. Iliodor went to New York, became a Baptist, and worked for a time as a janitor in the Metropolitan Life Insurance Building on Madison Square. He died in the United States in 1952. Guseva, the instrument of his attempt, was released from a mental asylum after the revolution; her subsequent fate is unknown.

Rasputin's daughter Maria became a lion tamer, touring the United States before settling in Los Angeles. Anna Vyrubova fled Petrograd for Finland, where she died in 1964 at eighty. The tsar's onetime mistress Mathilde Kschessinskaya ran a ballet school in Paris for thirty years and lived into her nineties. Her St. Petersburg palace, which was used by the Bolsheviks as a headquarters, became a shrine to Lenin. The ballerina Tamara Karsavina, who had recognized Rasputin instantly by his eyes, married a British diplomat and died at age ninety-three in London. Prince Andronnikov was shot by the Reds. The tutor Pierre Gilliard became a professor at Lausanne University.

With poetic justice, the once-disgraced Bishop Hermogen replaced Varnava as bishop of Tobolsk but was arrested by the Bolsheviks in 1918. Although his flock raised 100,000 rubles for his release, a band of Red Guards flung him into the Tura River—not far from Rasputin's Pokrovskoye—and drowned him. Metropolitan Pitirim was replaced in Petrograd by Bishop Veniamin, who was himself shot by the Reds. Rasputin's old adversary Bishop Antony fled to Yugoslavia, where he presided over the Synod of the Russian Church Abroad.

Of the politicians, Boris Stürmer and Alexander Protopopov were shot by the Reds. Old Goremykin was caught by a mob in 1918 and strangled. Sukhomlinov fled to Finland in a sailing boat, showing more initiative than he had in office, and went to Berlin. His pretty wife left him for a Georgian officer, and both were shot in the Red Terror. Alexander Guchkov, Mikhail Rodzianko, and Vasily Shulgin, Alexandra's loathed "parliamentarists," fled into exile—although Shulgin returned to survive years in Soviet prison camps before dying at age ninety-eight.

In his last days—so Simanovich claimed—Rasputin wrote a final and extraordinary document. He titled it "The Spirit of Grigory Efimovich Rasputin-Novykh of the village of Pokrovskoye."

"I write and leave behind me this letter at St. Petersburg," it began.

I feel that I shall leave life before January 1. I wish to make known to the Russian people, to Papa, to the Russian Mother, and to the Children, to the land of Russia, what they must understand. If I am killed by common assassins, and especially by my brothers the Russian peasants, you, Tsar of Russia, have nothing to fear, remain on your throne and govern, and you, Russian Tsar, will have nothing to fear for your children, they will reign for hundreds of years in Russia. But if I am murdered by boyars, nobles, and if they shed my blood, their hands will remain soiled with my blood, for twenty-five years they will not wash their hands from my blood. They will leave Russia. Brothers will kill brothers, and they will kill each other and hate each other, and for twenty-five years there will be no nobles in the country. Tsar of the land of Russia, if you hear the sound of the bell which will tell you that Grigory has been killed, you must know this: if it was your relations who have wrought my death then no one of your family, that is to say none of your children or relations, will remain alive for more than two years. They will be killed by the Russian people. I go and I feel in me the divine command to tell the Russian Tsar how he must live if I have disappeared. You must reflect and act prudently. Think of your safety and tell your relations that I have paid for them with my blood. I shall be killed. I am no longer among the living. Pray, pray, be strong, think of your blessed family. Grigory.

Simanovich says that he passed the letter to the empress, pleading with her not to show it to the tsar. She later returned it to him. He showed a facsimile of the letter to the historian Sir Bernard Pares while living in exile in Paris in 1934. Pares ran the letter verbatim in his classic work, *The Fall of the Russian Monarchy*, which was published in 1939, mentioning how he had come to see it but adding, "I cannot vouch for anything further." The prophecy is pitilessly accurate—Dmitri was a Romanov, Yusupov a great noble, the future held Red Terror—and the letter appeared to confirm Rasputin's powers of precognition. Did he write it? It is measured and properly punctuated, the sentence structure and meaning are clear, it does not race off at tangents—in short, it bears none of the hallmarks of the meandering and staccato style of Rasputin's known scrawlings. "He spoke an almost incomprehensible Siberian dialect," Lili von Dehn remembered, "he could hardly read, he wrote like a child of four." At best, he dictated it.

The investigating commission that sat after the revolution found no hard evidence that Rasputin was a khlyst. It excused his visits to the bathhouse with women on the ground that mixed bathing was common in parts of Siberia. The "night orgies" with harlots and petitioners were established. The affair with the empress was not. The commission looked carefully into the rumors of "intimacies in higher circles, especially those circles through which he had risen to power." It drew a blank.

The run of negatives can be extended. He had no one killed. Those who tried to kill him escaped with their lives; so did those who succeeded. He was not venal. He could have made millions of rubles; he lived in a rented apartment in the capital, and his only real estate, the Pokrovskoye house, was not the lair of a fortune hunter. In a society riddled with prejudice, he was not a bigot. He was not a German spy; he was not—so many nots, but this the most important—he was not a demon. At his worst he was spiteful, self-important, and dissolute. The spite came from the fear that enemies would destroy the power he so loved; the self-importance from the extraordinary journey from the medieval obscurity of the Siberian backwoods to the modern condition of superstardom; the dissolution—dependent on the observer's own moral stance—from inner depravity or love of life.

He was, at his best, humane and perceptive. The throngs who climbed the staircase on Gorokhovaya ulitsa benefited from innumerable acts of kindliness. When he could, he healed. He had immense charisma—"spiritual force," "magnetism," "hypnotic strength" they called it then—and few pretensions. At a time of warmongering he had the insight to realize its dangers. Most of his political preferences—peace, land for the peasants, rights for minorities, slogans successfully used if not practiced by Lenin—were the only realistic alternatives to revolution. The exception was autocracy. It made him; and those who wished to preserve it destroyed him.

They did so because they held that his excesses—the elevation of the corrupt to the highest positions in the state and the church, the drink, the women, the endless surf of scandal—tainted the throne and demoralized the nation. In truth the throne tainted itself. Concessions were torn from it, and slyly reversed. The tsar, his cousin Wilhelm said, was suited "to be a country gentleman growing turnips"; would that he had done so. Privately loyal and decent, in public he was vacillating, petty, treacherous to his best ministers, constant only in his jealous mistrust of men with character. He paid his lip service to Rasputin, the empress obliged it; after the murder his aide General Voykov remarked that "I did not once observe signs of sorrow in His Majesty, but rather gathered the impression that he experienced a sense of relief." It was true to type.

As to the empress—the scarlet woman in mauve, the wellspring of reaction, the hysteric with the will of iron—she and Rasputin locked characters. Without her he was no more than a fashionable starets. Without him she was a creature of the vapors, the weak heart, the hours in bed, the neurasthenia. With him she was the tigress—cancer as divine retribution for opponents, the knout as a political prescription. She needed him, she was devoted to him; it was a love story, without the sex, the empress and the shaman. It helped to prepare Russia for revolution and a further half century of the knout, one wielded by Lenin and his progeny with incomparably more venom than any tsarist.

But Russia, polite Russia, helped, too. It had taken the measure of Alexandra from the moment she arrived in St. Petersburg behind a coffin, proud, distant, and politically deranged. Like Rasputin, it knew that Nicholas "lacked insides." Why did it allow them to ruin themselves, and the country? Because it lacked insides itself? Did it despise Rasputin for himself, or as an impertinent peasant? The fear of Siberian exile, or disgrace, does not wholly explain how the empress and Rasputin were able to defy grand dukes, bureaucrats, nobles, senior army officers, and the other props of the autocracy for so long. The latter knew the country was rotting long before it collapsed; perhaps the truth is that they felt themselves rotten, too, and knew their loyalty had crossed the line that demarcated it from cowardice.

"He has never been bad to me and he did not do anything wrong to other people," Simanovich wrote. "He could not be blamed for Nicholas being a weak tsar. He helped thousands of people with my assistance and thanks to his kindness saved many people from poverty, death, and persecution. . . . In my opinion, Rasputin was more honest than all the people who assembled in his apartment." And, he could have added, than many of those outside it.

Bibliography

Agafonov, V. K. *Zagranichnaya Okhranka.* Petrograd, 1918.

Alexander Mikhailovich. *Once a Grand Duke.* Garden City, N.Y., 1932.

Alexandra Feodorovna. *The Letters of the Tsaritsa to the Tsar.* London, 1923.

Almazov, Boris. *Rasputin.* Prague, 1922.

Argumenty i Fakty [Moscow], no. 23 (June 1993).

Askoldov, S. A. *Religious Meaning of the Russian Revolution.* Moscow, 1918.

Baratinski, V. V. *Une Faute d'histoire.* In *Illioustrirovannaia Rossia* [Paris], no. 16 (1932).

Baring, Maurice. *What I Saw in Russia.* London, 1927.

Beletsky, Stefan. *Grigory Rasputin.* Moscow, 1928.

Benckendorff, Paul. *Last Days at Tsarskoye Selo.* London, 1927.

Bing, E. J., ed. *The Letters of Tsar Nicholas and Empress Marie.* London, 1937.

Bobrick, Benson. *East of the Sun: The Epic Conquest and Tragic History of Siberia.* New York, 1992.

Botkin, Gleb. *The Real Romanovs.* New York, 1931.

Brusilov, Gen. A. A. *A Soldier's Notebook.* London, 1930.

Buchanan, George. *My Mission to Russia and Other Diplomatic Memories.* Boston, 1923.

Buchanan, Meriel. *The City of Trouble.* New York, 1918.

———. *The Dissolution of an Empire.* London, 1932.

Buxhoeveden, Baroness Sophie. *The Life and Tragedy of Alexandra Fedorovna.* London, 1928.

Chas Pik, February 10, 1992.

Crankshaw, Edward. *The Shadow of the Winter Palace: Russia's Drift to Revolution.* New York, 1976.

Dehn, Lili von. *The Real Tsaritsa.* London, 1922.

De Jonge, Alex. *The Life and Times of Grigorii Rasputin.* New York, 1982.

Dostoevsky, Fyodor. *The Brothers Karamazov.* London, 1993.

——. *The Idiot.* London, 1955.

Duma proceedings: *Gosudarstvennaya Duma, stenograficheskie otchoty.* St. Petersburg, 1906–1916.

Ferro, Marc. *Nicholas II: The Last of the Tsars.* New York, 1993.

Francis, David. *Russia from the American Embassy.* New York, 1921.

Fülöp-Miller, René. *Rasputin: The Holy Devil.* New York, 1928.

Gilliard, Pierre. *Le Tragique Destin de Nicholas II et de sa famille.* Paris, 1921.

——. *Thirteen Years at the Russian Court.* New York, 1921.

"Grishka Rasputin." *Almanac Svoboda* [Petrograd], no. 1 (1916).

Gurko, V. I. *Features and Figures of the Past.* Stanford, 1939.

Harcave, Sidney. *Years of the Golden Cockerel: The Last Romanov Tsars, 1814–1917.* New York, 1968.

Harcave, Sidney, ed. *The Memoirs of Count Witte.* New York, 1990.

Iliodor [Trufanov, Sergei]. *The Mad Monk of Russia, Iliodor; Life, Memoirs, and Confessions . . .* New York, 1918.

Karsavina, Tamara. *Theatre Street.* New York, 1931.

Kasvinov, M. K. *Twenty-three Steps Downward.* Moscow, 1979.

Kennan, George. *Siberia and the Exile System.* New York, 1891.

Kerensky, Alexander. *The Crucifixion of Liberty.* New York, 1934.

King, Greg. *The Last Empress: The Life and Times of Alexandra Feodorovna, Tsarina of Russia.* Secaucus, N.J., 1994.

Kleinmikhel, Countess M. *Bilder aus einer versunkten Welt.* Berlin, 1922.

Knox, Alfred William Fortescue. *With the Russian Army, 1914–1917.* 2 vols. London, 1921; reprint, New York, 1971.

Kokovtsov, Vladimir N. *Memoires,* Vol. 2. Paris, 1933.

Kovyl-Bovyl, Ivan. *Rasputin.* Petrograd, 1917.

Krasny Archiv, (1923) vol. 4.

——, (1924) no. 5, pp. 270–288.

——, (1926) vol. 14.

Kurlov, P. G. *The Fall of Imperial Russia.* Berlin, 1923; Moscow, 1992.

Lieven, Dominic. *Nicholas II: Twilight of the Empire.* New York, 1994.

Lincoln, W. Bruce. *In War's Dark Shadow: The Russians before the Great War.* New York, 1983.

——. *Passage through Armageddon: The Russians in War and Revolution, 1914–1918.* New York, 1986.

Lockhart, Robert Hamilton Bruce. *Memoirs of a British Agent.* New York, 1932.

Ludendorff, Erich von. *Meine Kriegserinnerungen.* Berlin, 1919.

Lyubosh, S. *The Last Romanovs.* Moscow, 1924.

Maniguet, Louis. *Un Empirique lyonnais: Philippe.* Annales de l'Institut de Médecine légale de l'Université de Lyon, vol. 2 (1914–1919, 1920).

Manley, Deborah, ed. *The Trans-Siberian Railway.* London, 1988.

Markov, A. N. *Rasputin und die um Ihn.* Konigsberg, 1928.

Massie, Robert K. *Nicholas and Alexandra: An Intimate Account of the Last of the Romanovs . . .* New York, 1967.

Maximov, V. E. *Admiral Kolchak.* Minsk, 1991.

McKean, Robert B. *St. Petersburg Between the Revolutions.* New Haven, 1990.

Minney, R. J. *Rasputin.* New York, 1973.

Mosolov, A. A. *Pri dvore poslednego imperatora.* St. Petersburg, 1992.

———. *Mes Mémoires.* Paris, 1933–34.

———. *Claws of the Bear: The History of the Red Army from the Revolution to the Present.* Boston, 1989.

Moynahan, Brian. *Comrades: 1917—Russia in Revolution.* Boston, 1991.

Nicholas II. *Dnevnik imperatora Nikolaya II.* Berlin, 1923.

———. *Journal intime, 1914–1918.* Paris, 1934.

———. *Letters of the Tsar to the Tsaritsa.* New York, 1929.

———. *The Secret Letters of Tsar Nicholas.* Edinburgh, 1938.

Nikolaya II Materialy alya Khataktevistiki lichnosti i tsarstvovaniya. Moscow, 1917.

Novoye Vremya, no. 12.908, February 18, 1912.

Ogonyok, nos. 47–49 Supplement (November 1992).

Oldenburg, S.S. *Nickolai II.* St. Petersburg, 1991.

Omskaya Pravda. November 13, 1990.

Paléologue, Maurice. *An Ambassador's Memoirs.* 3 vols. New York, 1924–1925.

Paley, Princess Olga. *Souvenirs de Russie.* Paris, 1923.

Pares, Bernard. *The Fall of the Russian Monarchy: A Study of the Evidence.* New York, 1939.

———. Introduction. *Letters of the Tsaritsa to the Tsar.* London, 1923.

Paustovsky, Konstantin. *The Story of a Life.* New York, 1964.

Pipes, Richard. *Russia under the Old Regime.* New York, 1974.

Purishkevich, V. M. *Comment j'ai tué Raspoutine.* Paris, 1923.

Pyman, Avril. *The Life of Aleksandr Blok.* Vol. 2: *The Release of Harmony, 1908–1921.* New York, 1979.

Radzinsky, Edvard. *The Last Tsar: The Life and Death of Nicholas II.* New York, 1992.

Radziwill, Catherine. *Nicholas II: The Last of the Tsars.* London, 1931.

Rasputin, Maria. *My Father.* London, 1934; reprint, New Hyde Park, N.Y., 1970.

Rasputin, Maria, and Patte Barham. *Rasputin, The Man Behind the Myth: A Personal Memoir.* Englewood Cliffs, N.J., 1977.

Rodzianko, Mikhail V. *Krushenie imperii.* Leningrad, 1927; reprint, Valley Cottage, N.Y., 1986.

———. *Memoirs: The Reign of Rasputin.* London, 1927.

Russkoye Slovo [Moscow], no. 294, December 21, 1916.

Rutherford, Ward. *The Tsar's War.* Cambridge, 1992.

Sablinsky, Walter. *The Road to Bloody Sunday: Father Gapon and the St. Petersburg Massacre of 1905.* Princeton, N.J., 1976.

Salisbury, Harrison E. *Black Night, White Snow: Russia's Revolutions, 1905–1917*. Garden City, N.Y., 1977.

Sazonov, Sergei. *Fateful Years, 1909–1916*. New York, 1928.

Schegolev, P. E., ed. *Padenie tsarskogo rezhima; Stenografisheskie otchety doprosov i pokazanii, dannikh v 1917 q.v. Chrezvychaino: Sledstvennoi Komissii Vremennogo Pravitel'stva*. 7 vols. Moscow and Leningrad, 1924–1927.

———. *Otrechenie Nikolaia II: Vospominaniia ochevidtsev, dokumenty*. Leningrad, 1927; reprint, Moscow, 1990.

Shlyapnikov, A. G. *Kanun semnadtsatogo goda*, vol. 1. Moscow, 1920–1922.

Simanovich, Aron. *Rasputin, der Allmächtige Bauer*. Berlin, 1922.

———. *Rasputin i evrei: Vospominaiia lichnago sekretaria Grigorii Rasputin*. Riga, 1928?; reprint, Moscow, 1991.

———. *Rasputin and the Jews*. Moscow, 1991.

Solzhenitsyn, Alexander. *August 1914*. New York, 1972.

Spiridovich, A. I. *Raspoutine*. Paris, 1935.

———. *Les dernières années de la cour de Tsarskoie-Selo*, vols. 1 and 2. Paris, 1928.

Stone, Norman. *The Eastern Front, 1914–1917*. New York, 1975.

Trotsky, Leon. *My Life*. New York, 1970.

Tuchman, Barbara. *The Guns of August*. New York, 1962.

Vassilyev, A. T. *The Ochrana [sic]: The Russian Secret Police*. Philadelphia, 1930; reprint, Westport, Conn., 1981.

Voprosy Istorii, 1964, no. 12. Pp. 90–103.

———, 1964, no. 10. Pp. 117–135.

———, 1965, no. 1. Pp. 98–109.

———, 1965, no. 2. Pp. 103–121.

———, 1965, no. 3. Pp. 211–217.

Vulliamy, C. E., ed. *The Letters of the Tsar to the Tsaritsa, 1914–1917*. New York, 1929.

Vyrubova, Anna. *Memories of the Russian Court*. New York, 1923.

Wilson, Colin. *Rasputin and the Fall of the Romanovs*. New York, 1964.

Yusupov, Felix. *La Fin de Rasputine*. Paris, 1927.

———. *Lost Splendor*. Trans. Ann Green and Nicholas Katkoff. New York, 1953.

Notes on Sources

The Provisional Government investigation into Rasputin, which was opened after the revolution of February 1917 and closed by the Bolshevik coup d'état in October of the same year, is recorded in "Materials of the Extraordinary Investigating Commission of Inquiry of the Provisional Government into the Decay of Autocracy," published in *Padenie tsarskogo rezhima* [*The Fall of the Tsarist Regime*] (7 vols., Moscow, 1924–1927).

Nicholas II's diary, and his correspondence to and from his wife and his mother, was seized and published after the revolution. His diary appeared as *Journal intime, 1914–1918* (Paris, 1925) and as *Dnevnik Nikolaya vtorogo* in *Krasny Archiv* (vols. 20–22 and 27). His letters to Alexandra were published as *The Letters of the Tsar to the Tsaritsa* (New York, 1929) and hers to him as *The Letters of the Tsaritsa to the Tsar* (London, 1923). His correspondence with the dowager empress was published as *The Secret Letters of Tsar Nicholas* (Edinburgh, 1938).

Of the early biographies of Rasputin, René Fülöp-Miller's *Rasputin: The Holy Devil* (New York, 1928) is the most powerful. Alex de Jonge's *Life and Times of Gregorii Rasputin* (New York, 1982) is the most thorough of more recent works. *The Fall of the Russian Monarchy* by Bernard Pares (New York, 1939) remains an excellent general history, benefiting from the author's own experience of Russia. Two more recent books by W. Bruce Lincoln, *In War's Dark Shadow* (New York, 1983) and *Passage through Armageddon* (New York, 1986), place Russia in fine context for the period from 1891 to Rasputin's murder.

Sergei Witte's *Memoirs* provide firsthand insight, sometimes farcical, often snide, but always compelling, into the unstable and dangerous world of Russian political life. Harrison E. Salisbury's *Black Night, White Snow* (Garden City, N.Y.,

1977) gives a graphic account of Russia's descent into political and social chaos between 1905 and 1917. Robert K. Massie's *Nicholas and Alexandra* (New York, 1967) remains the most compelling account of the Romanov tragedy.

The atmosphere in Petrograd in the fall of 1916, described in Chapter 1, " 'Proshchaitye, Papa,' " is drawn from accounts by eyewitnesses of differing perspectives. Most of these were published abroad. The Bolsheviks reintroduced censorship almost immediately after they seized power in the fall of 1918; it did not suit their purposes to permit the publication of non-Marxist interpretations of events, nor to allow that Rasputin had individual importance in the preliminaries to a revolution supposedly caused by the impersonal forces of materialism and class warfare. The only leading Communist to deal with the Rasputin phenomenon at any length was Leon Trotsky, whose vigorous *History of the Russian Revolution* (3 vols., London, 1932–33; reprint, Ann Arbor, Mich., 1957) was itself banned by the Bolsheviks.

The description of refugees "blown away like gossamer" is by Zinaida Gippius, a tall, striking, red-haired poet and philosopher who kept a vivid diary over this period, published in *Sinyaya kniga: Petersburgsky dnevnik 1914–1918* in Belgrade, 1929. With her husband, Dmitri Merezhkovsky, a critic and novelist, and their friend Dmitri Filosofov, she created a "mystic union." They hoped for a religious revival, a "Third Revelation" that would reconcile the Russian intelligentsia with spiritual values. Insight into the writings of this intriguing and sensitive woman is provided by *A Difficult Soul: Zinaida Gippius*, edited by S. Karlinsky with an introduction by V. Zlobin (Berkeley, 1980). The observation that Rasputin had become "a dusk enveloping all our world" was made by the sister of one of his murderers, V. M. Purishkevich, whose own record of the times was published as *Dnevnik* in Riga in 1918.

The ballerina Tamara Karsavina, who found Rasputin's eyes "the eyes of a maniac," was one of the original members of Diaghilev's company and created roles in ballets by Fokine and Nijinsky. She moved to London with her husband, a British diplomat, in 1918 and included her reminiscences of wartime Petrograd in her autobiography *Theatre Street* (New York, 1931). She became vice president of the Royal Academy of Dancing and died in 1978. Meriel Buchanan, who noted the irritations of society hostesses and the talk of "Dark Powers," was at the time the eighteen-year-old daughter of the British ambassador; her fresh and youthful impressions of Petrograd were published as *The City of Trouble* (New York, 1918), and later in *Dissolution of an Empire* (London, 1932). Like Karsavina, Buchanan came across Rasputin by chance in the street and knew instantly who he must be. Tolstoy's description of the "tormented" city is from W. Bruce Lincoln's *Passage through Armageddon* (New York, 1986).

Mihkail Rodzianko, who was horrified to recognize Rasputin's "worshipers from high society," was the Duma chairman, a powerful man of three hundred pounds whose voice could "be heard for a kilometer" on a still day; he was a leading moderate during the revolution. He left Russia and died in Yugoslavia in 1924; his book *Krushenie imperii* was published posthumously in Leningrad in 1927 and *Memoirs: The Reign of Rasputin* appeared in London the same year. Boris Pasternak, later obliged to refuse a Nobel Prize for his novel *Dr. Zhivago*, was twenty-six at the time of Rasputin's death; his account of revolutionary Russia was published as *Safe Conduct* in New York in 1958. Vasily Shulgin, a whiskered and patrician conservative who found people "dancing a 'last tango,' " escaped to Belgrade after the revolution; he published his reminiscence, *Dni*, in 1925; he was arrested by the Red Army when Yugoslavia was liberated from the Germans in 1944, spent twelve years in Soviet prison camps, and was ninety-eight when he died in Russia in 1976.

Robert Hamilton Bruce Lockhart, ashamed of his "puerile and reprehensible" conduct when he visited Petrograd, wrote his account in 1932 in *Memoirs of a British Agent*. Reports by Russian secret police agents are included in A. T. Vassilyev's *The Ochrana* (Philadelphia, 1930), Alexander Spiridovich's *Raspoutine* (Paris, 1935), and Trotsky's *History of the Russian Revolution*. The French ambassador who complained of Jews "wandering over the snows" was Maurice Paléologue in *An Ambassador's Memoirs* (New York, 1924–25), the most vivid of diplomatic memoirs. Paléologue had an inquiring and lively mind and made a point of seeking out Rasputin. He found Stürmer "shallow and dishonest"; his colleague the American David Francis recorded his experiences in *Russia from the American Embassy* (New York, 1921). Shulgin found Stürmer "absolutely unprincipled," while Rodzianko added, "a complete nullity." Alexander Guchkov, the leader of the right-wing Octobrists, told Bernard Pares that Protopopov was thought queer in the head. Gen. Alexei Brusilov, a caustic commander who had driven the Austrians out of Galicia, ridiculed Grand Duke Paul and his fellow corps commander in *Moi vospominaniya*, published in Moscow in 1963 and quoted in W. Bruce Lincoln's *Passage through Armageddon*. The observer who found the troops "just men who were going to die" was the remarkable Marina Yurlova, who masqueraded as a man to enlist and whose book *Cossack Girl* was published in London in 1934. The condition of the Russian army is covered in this author's book *Claws of the Bear* (Boston, 1989).

Alexander Blok, another acute weathervane of Petrograd opinion, was a Symbolist poet and seducer who supported the Bolsheviks but died of exhaustion and venereal disease in 1921, his poems suppressed. His remarkable life is told in Avril Pyman's *Life of Aleksandr Blok* (2 vols., New York, 1979). The letters from Robert Wilton, the *Times* correspondent in Petrograd, to the newspaper's London office are from the archives of *The Times*.

The account of Rasputin's farewell to his daughter is from *Rasputin* by Maria Rasputin and Patte Barham (Englewood Cliffs, N.J., 1977). Some of the accounts that Maria Rasputin gives of her father, including this, clash with other evidence. The Moscow newspaper *Russkoye Slovo*, for which Alexander Yablonsky was an obituarist, suggested that Rasputin shared the peasant dream to "eat fat all day long" in its issue of December 21, 1916, while Petrograd's *Svoboda* (no. 1, 1917) wrote of photographs and claimed that Rasputin had slept with "ladies of the 'best' aristocratic families."

Background material on Siberia during Rasputin's lifetime, used in Chapter 2, "Grischa," is included in two excellent histories of Siberia, Benson Bobrick's *East of the Sun* (New York, 1992) and W. Bruce Lincoln's *Conquest of a Continent* (New York, 1994). Leon Trotsky wrote of his experiences in Siberian exile, and the midge problem, in *My Life* (New York, 1970). The investigation into Rasputin, including the evidence of village witnesses of his childhood, is recorded in "Materials of the Extraordinary Investigating Commission of Inquiry of the Provisional Government into the Decay of Autocracy." The recollections of Anna Egorovna and Efim Aklovlevich Rasputin are recorded by their granddaughter Maria in her book *Rasputin*; the alleged pseudo-rape at the hands of Madame Kubasova and the Stepanova incident come from the same source.

Rasputin claimed to have been "dreaming about God since early childhood" in an interview published in the newspaper *Novoye Vremya* on February 18, 1912. The article was written by Ivan Manasevich-Manuilov, a journalist and bribe taker who became a significant member of the Rasputin clique after the outbreak of the First World War. Yablonsky's references to "drinking and leading a depraved life" were published in *Russkoye Slovo*.

E. I. Kartavtsev gave his evidence on fence poles to the Commission of Inquiry. Pierre Gilliard's reference to Rasputin wishing to "abandon his dark and dissolute life" is made in *Thirteen Years at the Russian Court* (New York, 1921).

Dostoyevsky's great novel *The Brothers Karamazov*, quoted in Chapter 3, "Monastery Man," affords considerable insight into the psychology of the starets, the career chosen by Rasputin, and his clients. Mikhail Rodzianko's perceptive character sketch of Rasputin—"remarkable intelligence . . . in search of some unknown religious path"—is made in his book *Krushenie imperii*. Podshivalov gave his account of Rasputin as "a madman" to the Commission of Inquiry.

Of Rasputin's time as a wanderer, the secret police chief Vassilyev aired his views on stranniky in *The Ochrana*. The monk Iliodor, to whom Rasputin described his feelings on the road and his "comfort in daily readings from the Gospel," later attempted to have Rasputin murdered, was defrocked, and reverted to his original name, Sergei Trufanov. His book *Rasputin: The Holy Devil* was first published in Russian as *Svyatoy chort* in Moscow in 1917. Rasputin's daughter Maria claims that her father found "nothing but dirt, vermin, and moral filth" at Mount Athos and describes the "absent look" with which he told of his adventures.

Villagers complained to the Commission of Inquiry that it was "impossible for a stranger" to take part in the meetings in the "chapel under the floor." The claim of Rasputin urging his devotees to "test your flesh" was made in the first issue of *Svoboda* (Petrograd, 1917). Material on Russian sects was collected by Vassilyev, Paléologue, and Pares, and the chant of "I whip. I whip. I search for Christ" is recorded in Spiridovich's *Raspoutine.*

Rasputin's descriptions in Chapter 4, "Breakthrough," of the Kiev catacombs— "the silence seems to breathe"—were recorded by Aron Simanovich in *Rasputin i evrei,* reprinted in Moscow in 1991 and translated by Igor Bogdanov for this book. Yablonsky's account of Rasputin's meeting with Bashmakova is given in *Russkoye Slovo.* Chavelski, who discovered of Rasputin that "you couldn't not notice him," gave evidence to the Commission of Inquiry. The horror of the Kazan worthy—"I do know of a most respectable lady"—is recorded by Spiridovich. The description of provincial Russia's "torpidity of peace" is from the novelist Ivan Goncharov, creator of the heroically idle character Oblomov. Lively insights into life in the provinces are also offered in Maxim Gorky's *Fragments from My Diary* (1940; reprint, New York, 1972) and, from a Western viewpoint, in Maurice Baring's *What I Saw in Russia* (London, 1927). Bassett Digby's portrait of trains as "stables on wheels" is quoted in an excellent and amusing traveler's anthology, *The Trans-Siberian Railway,* edited by Deborah Manley (London, 1988), which includes details of first-class travel, Rasputin's preferred method of transport.

The facilities of St. Petersburg, together with nostalgic and long-superseded details of restaurant and hotel prices described in Chapter 5, "Peter," are included in Karl Baedeker's *Russia* (Leipzig, 1914). The origins of the great city are covered in Robert K. Massie's *Peter the Great* (New York, 1980). An excellent account of literary life in the city, and much else, is given in W. Bruce Lincoln's *In War's Dark Shadow.* Hugh Walpole's *The Dark Forest* (New York, 1916) provides a Western impression of the city.

The description of Rasputin on his arrival in St. Petersburg is from Iliodor. Fyodor Chaliapin's *Autobiography* (London, 1968) records the singer's impressions of the city. Valery Bryusov was a leader of the Russian Symbolist movement, influenced by the Europeans Verlaine, Mallarmé, and Maeterlinck, whom he translated. He became a Bolshevik after the revolution. Count Alexis Tolstoy was to join the Whites against the Reds in the civil war but returned to Soviet Russia in 1923 after a period as an émigré in Paris, a dangerous move but one that he survived. Siberian exiles—leaving "not only home and country, but life itself"—are the subject of George Kennan's influential *Siberia and the Exile System* (2 vols., New York, 1891), which did much to turn Western opinion against the autocracy.

Rasputin's relations with churchmen are covered in *Voprosy Istorii* [Leningrad], no. 2 (1965) and his introduction to Feofan in Spiridovich and Pares. Maria wrote that Ioann of Kronstadt found "the divine spark" in her father. Iliodor described his meeting with Rasputin and Hermogen. Vassilyev mentions his being apolitical in *The Ochrana.* Kazakova and the Berlandskaya and Manchtet letters were subjects of the Commission of Inquiry. The observation that Berlandskaya was typical of "nervous women with wretched souls" is made in *Voprosy Istorii,* no. 10 (1964). Sergei

Witte excoriates the Montenegrin sisters and their father—"cupidity and lack of scruples"—in his *Memoirs*. Simanovich describes their tea parties with Rasputin in *Rasputin i evrei*.

Alexandra's childhood, described in Chapter 6, "Blood Royal," is covered in great detail in Greg King's *The Last Empress* (Secaucus, N.J., 1994). Nicholas's diaries were published as *Dvevnik imperatora Nikolaya II* (Berlin, 1923) and in *Nikolaya II materialy dlya kharakteristiki lichnosti i tsarstvovaniya* (Moscow, 1917). The autocratic system Alexandra so ferociously upheld is described in many books, of which *Russia under the Old Regime* (New York, 1974) by Richard Pipes is an outstanding example. Social life in Russia is splendidly captured in Henri Troyat's highly readable *La Vie quotidienne en Russie au temps du dernier tsar* (Paris, 1959). The pleasure that Alexandra was leaving Hesse—"how lucky we are"—was recorded by Witte. Sandro, Grand Duke Alexander Mikhailovich, to whom Nicholas admitted that "I know nothing of this business of ruling," wrote his memoirs, *Vospominaniya* (3 vols., Paris, 1932). Rasputin made his remark that Nicholas had "no insides" to Simanovich.

Prince Sergei Volkonsky, who thought of Alexandra that "sociability was not in her nature," wrote *My Reminiscences* (London, 1945). The experiences of Dr. Eugene Botkin, the personal physician to whom Nicholas criticized his ancestor Peter the Great for "too much admiration for European culture," were recorded by his son Gleb Botkin in *The Real Romanovs* (New York, 1931). Constantine Pobedonostsev, who held Alexandra responsible for the tsar hurling a "threat at the head of the entire nation," expressed his anger to Sergei Witte. General Spiridovich examines the relations between the Montenegrin sisters and Dr. Philippe in *Raspoutine*. Philippe's career is related by P. Encausee in *Le Maître Philippe de Lyon* (Paris, 1955). Sergei Witte recorded the machinations to replace the unfortunate General Rachovsky in Paris. Prince Elston Yusupov's bizarre encounter with the sisters and the "doctor" in the Crimea was recorded by his son Felix in *Lost Splendor* (New York, 1953).

An account of the doomed naval expedition in Chapter 7, "A Man of God from Tobolsk," is given by Donald W. Mitchell in *A History of Russian and Soviet Sea Power* (New York, 1974). The reference that God "required some mission" of Rasputin is made by his daughter, who also recorded that her mother thought he had had another vision. Witte recorded the start of Bloody Sunday, while Maxim Gorky includes his experiences of events in *Untimely Thoughts* (New York, 1968). Vladimir Bonch-Bruevich's observations of Rasputin's appearance in St. Petersburg society and the "phosphorescent light" that sparkled in his eyes appear in *Voprosy Istorii* [Leningrad], no. 10 (1964). Bonch-Bruevich was an expert on sectarians who in 1899 went with members of the Dukhobor sect to Canada to study their life and belief at first hand. An early Bolshevik, he wrote for *Pravda* from 1912 on and was arrested several times before the revolution. He was the Bolshevik commander in the Smolny district of Petrograd during Red October in 1917 and, with his wife, was a significant figure in early Soviet farm and health policies. Alexandra's anger at the weight of "my poor Nicky's cross" is recorded by Baroness Sophie Buxhoeveden in *The Life and Tragedy of Alexandra Fedorovna* (London, 1928).

The diary of A. A. Polovtsev, who found the imperial couple to "constantly vacillate, now doing one thing, then another," is included in issues of *Krasny Archiv* [Moscow], vols. 3–4 (1924–25). Sergei Mintslov's diary—"Peter is now cut off from the rest of Russia"—is quoted in W. Bruce Lincoln's *In War's Dark Shadow*, which includes a striking account of 1905. Witte's *Memoirs* give a devastating if perhaps one-sided picture of Nicholas and Alexandra during the crisis. Rasputin's family idyll in Siberia in the fall of 1905 is described by his daughter. Marc Chagall recollected the traumas of the pogroms—"I feel panicky . . . my legs weak"—in *My Life* (New York, 1960). The artist, whose whirling, dreamy paintings with their references to Russian folklore are said to have led Apollinaire to coin the word *Surrealist*, left Russia after the revolution to settle in France. The British ambassador so concerned over the tsar's lack of activity, Sir George Buchanan, wrote *My Mission to Russia* (Boston, 1923). Grand Duke Constantine Constantinovich's conviction that the tsar's concessions were "torn from him by force" is included in *Krasny Archiv*, no. 40 (1931) and is quoted by Lincoln. Spiridovich details the interest of the palace security service in *Raspoutine*: the code name Blue Shirt was later changed by Okhrana agents to the Dark One. The account of Madame O's experiences with Rasputin is from Spiridovich, who, writing while several of Rasputin's acquaintances were still alive, granted some of them anonymity.

Anna Taneeva, the central figure in Rasputin's dealings with the imperial couple, who is introduced in Chapter 8, "The Heir," wrote her *Memories of the Russian Court* (New York, 1923) under her married name, Anna Vyrubova. She also appeared as a witness for the Commission of Inquiry. Both Spiridovich and Witte deal with her marriage to her naval lieutenant; apart from her own reminiscence, Vyrubova was examined by a doctor on the orders of the Commission of Inquiry in 1917 and found to be a virgin. The journalist G. P. Sazonov, whose servants found that Rasputin "didn't sleep at night but prayed," gave evidence to the Commission of Inquiry. The affectations of *tryn-trava*, "the inconsequence of consequence," are well dealt with in Lincoln's *In War's Dark Shadow*. The French ambassador to whom a lady admitted that Rasputin "disgusts me physically. . . . I admit he amused me" is Maurice Paléologue. Spiridovich noted that Rasputin attended church only when it was essential.

Gilliard's accounts of Alexis's hemophilia—"how I realized the secret tragedy . . ." —are included in his *Thirteen Years at the Russian Court*. Bernard Pares describes Alexandra's lack of sociability; he said that she gave guests the impression that she was always thinking, "When are you going to get out of my house?" Young Alexis's taste for protocol was recorded by Gleb Botkin in *The Real Romanovs*. The invitation to the tsar's sister to meet Rasputin—"Will you come to meet a Russian peasant?"—and its aftermath are recorded in *The Last Grand-Duchess: Her Imperial Highness Duchess Olga Alexandrovna* by Ian Vorres (New York, 1964). V. A. Teliakovsky's conversation with Korovine—"Who is this Rasputin?"—is recollected in his memoirs, *Vospominaniya* (Paris, 1924).

Spiridovich noted Rasputin to be "full of self-confidence" on his return to St. Petersburg in Chapter 9, "The Go-between." Simanovich discusses Rasputin's lack of financial acumen in *Rasputin i evrei*. The characterization of Vyrubova's childish mind is made by the tutor Pierre Gilliard; she herself described her relations with the imperial couple to the Commission of Inquiry. The entries in the *Kammerfurier* are noted in *Voprosy Istorii*, no. 10 (1964). A. A. Mosolov's *At the Court of the Last Tsar* (London, 1935) includes details of protocol. Madame Bogdanova is cited in Alex de Jonge's *The Life and Times of Grigorii Rasputin* (New York, 1982). Maria Rasputin and Simanovich provide similar evidence of Rasputin's family relationships. Prince Dzhevakov related his experiences with Rasputin to Spiridovich and in his memoirs, *Vospominaniya* (2 vols., Munich, 1923). The description of Rasputin's eating habits—"big pieces he tore like an animal"—is by Simanovich and accords only too well with other accounts. Spiridovich notes that Rasputin represented to Nicholas "his people of whom he is ignorant." Olga's discovery of "kindness, magnanimity, and an unbreakable faith in God" is from her *Memoirs*. Sablin gave his recollection of shipboard conversations with the empress to the Commission of Inquiry.

Berlandskaya's seduction on the Trans-Siberian, recounted in Chapter 10, "Testing the Flesh," is quoted in Alex de Jonge's *Life and Times of Grigorii Rasputin*. Lili von Dehn, who found Rasputin "a typical peasant from the frozen North," wrote *The Real Tsaritsa* (London, 1922) and gave evidence to the Commission of Inquiry. Olga's astonishment at her nephew's recovery—"I just could not believe my eyes"—is recorded in her *Memoirs*. The accounts given by Vyrubova and Spiridovich of the former's trip to Siberia differ in almost every respect other than that the visit took place.

The text of the report filed by Robert Wilton on his visit to see Iliodor is from *The Times*'s archives. Rasputin's boastful account of his interview with Nicholas, "You are the tsar . . . act like one," is from Iliodor. Rasputin was certainly as blunt as this to others, but other evidence suggests that he was normally deferential if also familiar with Nicholas. The fact that Father Pyotr risked Rasputin's rage by telling Iliodor that the starets was "nothing but a drunk and a troublemaker" suggests that it was already clear to an outsider that relations between Rasputin and the monk were deteriorating. This is confirmed by Iliodor's account of his interview with the novice Xenia.

Dmitri Merezhkovsky, who described "murders and adultery, blood and mud" as the hallmarks of the Romanovs in Chapter 11, "Friends and Enemies," was married to Zinaida Gippius. Andrei Bely was the pseudonym of Boris Bugayev, the leading Russian Symbolist, whose novel *The Silver Dove* was followed in 1913 by his masterpiece, *Petersburg*, which revolves around a bomb disguised as a can of sardines. The disillusioned Feofan gave evidence to the Commission of Inquiry, as did Tyutcheva, who gave testimony of her audience with the tsar and her subsequent dismissal. Yusupov wrote of his early acquaintance with Rasputin in *Lost Splendor.* The devotion of Akulina to Rasputin is recorded in Fülöp-Miller. Witte and Simanovich, among others, describe the odious Prince Andronnikov—the description of his flattering letters of introduction was given to his fellow fixer, Simanovich—who himself, with the prince's valet Kilter, gave evidence to the Commission of Inquiry.

The incident of the Tansin photographs and the droshky ride to Tsarskoye Selo is from Maria Rasputin. General Kurlov, who thought Rasputin a "downright maniac," was examined by the Commission of Inquiry. Rasputin's alleged attempt to hypnotize Stolypin was related by the latter to Rodzianko. Mandryka's mission to Tsaritsyn and its sequel are covered by de Jonge in *The Life and Times of Grigorii Rasputin.*

Anna Vyrubova gave evidence to the Commission of Inquiry that Rasputin's volume on his visit to the Holy Land, described in Chapter 12, "Pilgrim," was dictated, and printed by the publisher Filippov, but she did not say who prepared the draft. The claims of the vision in the Garden of Gethsemane are made by Maria Rasputin. Robert Wilton's account of Iliodor in Tsaritsyn is from the archives of *The Times.* The strange affair of Rasputin and Sazonov's approach to Witte is included in the former prime minister's *Memoirs.* Rasputin's dealings with the eccentric Bishop Varnava were investigated by the Commission of Inquiry and are detailed in *Voprosy Istorii*, no. 2 (1965). Vyrubova claimed that Rasputin foresaw the murder of Stolypin, in which Bogrov's sinister role is examined by Bernard Pares. Rasputin's host in Kiev relates entertaining him there in Shulgin's *Dni (Days)*. Vladimir Kokovtsov, appointed to follow Stolypin in such bizarre circumstances, and accorded such an acid audience by the empress, recorded his experiences in *Mémoires* (2 vols., Paris, 1933) with an English edition, *Out of My Past* (London, 1935).

Bishop Hermogen gave the interview cited in Chapter 13, "Scandal," to the newspaper *Russkoye Slovo* after Rasputin's murder. Iliodor included his account of the beating in *The Mad Monk of Russia* (New York, 1918). Rodzianko noted the fancy prices paid for copies of Novosyolov's attack, printed in Moscow as *Grigorii Rasputin i misticheskoe rasputstvo.* Kokovtsov described the political fallout and his cold reception by the tsar. The letters from the empress and her daughters to Rasputin were widely distributed in pamphlet form and are included in the context of the Commission of Inquiry in *Voprosy Istorii*, no. 10 (1964). Laptinskaya gave evidence to the inquiry. Rodzianko detailed the reaction to the scandal. Rasputin's version of his rift with Iliodor, as recounted by his daughter Maria, is no more (or less) reliable than that given by Iliodor.

. . .

The baleful glare Rasputin fixed on Kokovtsov in Chapter 14, "Miracle at Spala," which the prime minister recalled in *Out of My Past*, is almost identical to what Stolypin described to Rodzianko. It is striking that two premiers should have felt Rasputin was attempting to hypnotize them; lesser politicians did not make such claims. Rodzianko, who describes his interview with the tsar in *Krushenie imperii*, was no admirer of the tsar but was nonetheless as loyal as circumstances permitted and an acute observer. Guchkov's stinging attack on Rasputin was the more powerful for being delivered by an instinctive conservative. Dumbadze's rough treatment of Rasputin in Yalta is in Bernard Pares. The traumatic events at Spala were recounted by Vyrubova and Gilliard.

General Mosolov also includes a description in *At the Court of the Last Tsar*. He was present with the physician Eugene Botkin, the surgeon Professor Fedorov, and the pediatrician Rauchfuss. Since it was Mosolov's duty to prepare medical bulletins, he was kept informed of the crisis as it worsened. Fedorov told him the tsarevich was at the point of death without the other two medical men being present. "In my opinion, more energetic measures should be taken," Fedorov said. "Regrettably, they are rather dangerous. However, were I the only one to be treating him, I'd use them." Mosolov agrees that the bleeding stopped soon after receipt of the telegram from Rasputin. When he asked Fedorov whether he had used the dangerous treatment he had spoken of, the professor waved his hand and said, "If I used it, I wouldn't confess to it under the present circumstances!"

Rasputin's sudden alarm while walking on the riverbank in Pokrovskoye—"It is the tsarevich . . . he has been stricken"—was claimed by his daughter. The effect of his telegrams on the empress is stated by Vyrubova and by Mosolov. "Thanks to the mystical nature of the empress," the latter commented, "she was forced to believe in anything Rasputin said to her. The sly muzhik told her that the life of Alexei Nickolayevich and the existence of the house of the Romanovs—and the wealth of all Russia—depended on his prayers: after his death everything will go to wrack and ruin. This was told me by the lower staff in the service of the empress. I do not think that the tsar believed in it, but I admit that [after Spala] a kind of superstitious fear crept into his soul as well."

In Chapter 15, "Before the Storm," Rodzianko described Rasputin's behavior in the cathedral—surely calculated to enrage him—and Meriel Buchanan noticed the empress's nervousness during the tercentenary celebrations, while Kokovtsov noted the indifference that accompanied the imperial couple on their progress on the Volga. Simanovich described Rasputin's behavior in the Villa Rhode; his sympathetic account of Rasputin's virtues—here the absence of warmongering—is confirmed by Rasputin's press interview. Anna Akhmatova, the pseudonym of Anna Gorenko, was a fine poet, the wife of a naval officer later shot by the Bolsheviks, whose collections of lyrical poems include *Evening*, *Beads*, and *White Flock*.

Count Paul Benckendorff, who remarked that the tsar "neither wanted nor expected" his new premier to do anything, reminisced in *Last Days at Tsarskoye Selo* (London, 1927).

Dostoyevksy's *Idiot* describes Rasputin's street in 1868, the year the novel was published; his *Crime and Punishment*, published two years earlier, magnificently evokes a city that still retained echoes when Rasputin became a resident. Rasputin's "erotic exercises" with Laptinskaya, noted by secret police agents, appear in a long archive of Okhrana material, "Rasputin in the Eyes of the Okhrana," published in *Krasny Archiv*, no. 24 (1924). The experiences of the provincial lady Zhukovskaya are recounted by Fülöp-Miller.

The official account of the murder attempt in Chapter 16, " 'I've Killed the Antichrist!' " which is used here, is from *Omskaya pravda* (November 13, 1990). It corresponds in most details with that given by Maria Rasputin but makes no reference to Davidsohn. The journalist's own account, however, makes it clear that he was present in Pokrovskoye. The account of how the news was treated aboard the *Standart*—"people whispered no end"—is from Gilliard. Maurice Paléologue was present at the major celebrations of the Poincaré visit.

The outbreak of the First World War, the climactic event and nemesis of the thrones of Russia, Germany, and Austria-Hungary, is related in *The Guns of August* by Barbara Tuchman (New York, 1962). Serge Sazonov wrote an account of Russian involvement in *Fateful Years, 1909–16* (New York, 1928). Alexander Solzhenitsyn's *August 1914* (New York, 1972) gives wonderful insights into Russia's first days of war in novel form. The war minister, Vladimir Sukhomlinov—"I know few men who inspire more distrust at first sight"—survived the war, despite being charged with treason; even more remarkable, he survived the revolution and the Bolsheviks, and fled to Berlin to write his *Erinnerungen* (Berlin, 1924). The catastrophic Russian advance into East Prussia is the subject of *Tannenberg* by Sir Edmund Ironside (Edinburgh, 1925).

Mosolov gives his account of Rasputin's intervention at the bedside of Vyrubova, in Chapter 17, "Party Time in Moscow," in his *At the Court of the Last Tsar.* The secret police agents who guarded and observed Rasputin are a reliable source for his day-to-day movements. Their reports are included in "Rasputin in the Eyes of the Okhrana," published in *Krasny Archiv*, no. 24 (1924). Elena Djanumova's reminiscences of Rasputin are published in "My Encounters with Grigory Rasputin" in supplements to *Ogonyok*, nos. 47–49 (November 1992), translated for this book by Dr. Igor Bogdanov. Robert Bruce Lockhart's description of events at the Yar—"wild shrieks of a woman . . ."—are included in his *Memoirs of a British Agent.*

With the Russian Army by Maj. Gen. Sir Alfred Knox (2 vols., London, 1921) gives a vivid picture of Russia's war effort. Knox was a British observer and spent much time at the front. Pares also writes powerfully of the unfolding tragedy, as does W. Bruce Lincoln in *Passage through Armageddon.* The memoirs of Gen. V. T.

Gurko, *War and Revolution in Russia, 1914–17* (New York, 1919), give a Russian perspective; Field Marshal Erich von Ludendorff's *Meine Kriegserinnerungen* (Berlin, 1919) does the same from a German viewpoint.

Both Simanovich and Maria Rasputin mention Pkhakadze's threat to the starets, described in Chapter 18, "Vengeance." General Brusilov notes his experiences in *A Soldier's Notebook* (London, 1930). The details of Rasputin's daily life in Petrograd—"he pestered the caretaker's wife"—were recorded by Okhrana agents. They also followed him to Siberia. Vassilyev gives his account of the Sukhomlinov affair—"it's raining in Carlsbad"—in *The Ochrana*. Rasputin's relations with Varnava were investigated by the Commission of Inquiry. The poet Vladimir Mayakovsky—"You can't/Simply cannot/Bury him alive"—had set out to shock; when he was eighteen years old, in 1912, his work was included in a miscellany called *A Slap in the Face of Public Taste*. His passion for Bolshevism gave way to disillusion, and he shot himself in 1930.

Vassilyev's account of Rasputin's confession of immorality and its excuse—"Who is innocent before God is also innocent before the tsar"—is interesting, since the secret police chief was sympathetic to Rasputin and ridiculed the idea that the starets had khlyst leanings. The war minister General Polivanov—"the army is no longer retreating—it is simply running away"—wrote his recollections in *Memuary* (Moscow, 1924). The diary of Grand Duke Andrei Vladimirovich—"It was not my dear boy who did this!"—is published as *Dnevnik* (Leningrad, 1925). Robert Wilton's private letter—"the loathsome Rasputin"—is from the archives of *The Times*.

The extraordinary saga of the beatification of Ioann Maximovich in Chapter 19, " 'God Opens Everything to Him,' " was a subject of the Commission of Inquiry. It is detailed at length in *Voprosy Istorii*, no. 2 (1965) as "The Impact of Irresponsible Forces upon Questions of Church Governance." Grand Duke Andrei Vladimirovich details the public reaction in *Dnevnik*. Rasputin's own state of mind—"Sometimes there's peace in my heart for a couple of hours"—is recorded by Okhrana agents, as is the row with his father. Prewar Mogilev is described in Karl Baedeker's *Russia*. Brusilov's anger at Alexandra and Rasputin—"no better than criminals"—is recorded in *A Soldier's Notebook*. Elena Djanumova's fascinating descriptions of Rasputin are from *Ogonyok*.

The ensign's wife in Chapter 20, "The Idealists"—"Undress and go in here"— reported her conversation with Rasputin to the Okhrana agents. Vassilyev's *The Ochrana* contains much information on the training of the agents who shadowed Rasputin, including both External and Internal agencies. The Okhrana was of natural interest to the Bolsheviks, who imitated it while infinitely extending its repressive powers in their own Cheka secret police. Vassilyev's Okhrana documents were published in Petrograd in 1918 in V. K. Agafonov's *Zagranichnaya okhranka*.

Wilton's description of the fighting west of Riga—"more terrible than anything we knew or even suspected"—was sent by letter to avoid the censors and is from *The Times*'s archives. Norman Stone's *The Eastern Front, 1914–1917* (New York, 1975) gives a strong account of the crisis in supply and its eventual resolution.

The description of Manasevich-Manuilov—"stool pigeon, spy, sharper, swindler"—is by Maurice Paléologue, as is that of Rasputin's "piercing and caressing" gaze. Pares notes that Manuilov, "one of those parasites who moved about with confident dexterity on the fringes of the Press and the secret police," realized that "Rasputin was the one sure source of favor and ingratiated himself with him." The description of Rasputin's liberalism—"Life stops in the villages . . . noblemen have too much"—is from Simanovich. Although Simanovich had an interest in portraying his friend in a kindly light, there is strong evidence from other sources—notably comments by Okhrana agents on his treatment of petitioners—to show Rasputin's humanitarian streak. The tsar's dislike of Jews is from Witte.

The sources for Chapter 21, "Two Weeks in the Life of Grigory Efimovich," are Elena Djanumova and the Okhrana archive. The records of the secret police agents confirm Djanumova's visit with Filippova. Where possible the agents noted the age and social rank of Rasputin's visitors, here "wife of a hereditary honorable citizen," a rank below nobility. It is clear that they had informants within the apartment, most probably a maid, as well as the block's concierge and gatekeeper. Rasputin's dramatic intervention at Tsarskoye Selo is confirmed by Gilliard, no admirer, as well as Vyrubova. Galina Filippova, "Lyolya," told Djanumova of her experience with Rasputin—"a moment of love"—after her return to Moscow. The threatening incident in the Villa Rhode is recalled by Simanovich; the Okhrana agents in Petrograd did not accompany Rasputin to parties or into nightclubs, but they often kept watch outside.

The reference to diminishing powers in Chapter 22, " 'They Are Certainly Going to Kill Me, My Dear' "—"The Lord has taken my power from me"—is made by Maria Rasputin. From a Western viewpoint, Pares found Stürmer "a shallow and dishonest figure, without even the merits of courage." Ignatev was so angry about Stürmer's secret fund—"What's this?"—that Pares reports he told the tsar, "Such scandals were not to be tolerated in Russia." Pares records reports of Rasputin's heady sense of power—"I begat Pitirim and Pitirim begat Stürmer"—and the bizarre affair of the poisoned cat. Shavelsky, the chaplain who complained of "Rasputin's closeness to the tsar's family," gave evidence to the Commission of Inquiry. Vera Zhukovskaya's accounts are included in Fülöp-Miller. General Knox's observations on Polivanov and the supply situation are included in his *With the Russian Army*. Blok's comments are in Avril Pyman's *Life*. The hostile incident between Rasputin and Sazonov over Madame Lippert is recorded by Simanovich. It appears from Djanumova's account of the incident at the Strelna that Moscow Okhrana agents, unlike their Petrograd colleagues, made sure that they remained in sight of

Rasputin during his nightclub outings. The synod clerk Blagoveshchensky's accounts of his neighbor's goings-on are from *Krasny Archiv*, no. 5 (1924).

Rodzianko recalls his abortive visit to the tsar recounted in Chapter 23, " 'For Their Sakes, Go.' " Lili von Dehn records her impressions at this period in *The Real Tsaritsa*. Simanovich records the Rubinstein affair. The potential for harming the empress was clearly enormous; transferring funds to Germany in wartime was a treasonable offense. There are no references to this from other sources, and the Commission of Inquiry had no wind of it. Simanovich's relations with the empress have an element of boasting about them; he was close enough to Rubinstein to have known details of transactions, although there is no proof that any took place. The anti-German hysteria is recorded, and dismissed, by Vassilyev. Paléologue found Protopopov like an "excitable seal." Gen. P. G. Kurlov includes a sympathetic picture of Badmaev in *The Fall of Imperial Russia* (Berlin, 1923; reprint, Moscow, 1992). Protopopov gave evidence of his relations with Rasputin to the Commission of Inquiry. The outraged Pavel Miliukov—"a man who works with Stürmer"—wrote his memoirs, *Vospominaniya, 1859–1917* (2 vols., New York, 1955).

The atmosphere in Chapter 24, "A Tragedy Played in a Brothel," is powerfully invoked in Harrison E. Salisbury's *Black Night, White Snow*. Konstantin Paustovsky, who was sent to discover what provincial Russia was thinking, wrote *The Story of a Life* (New York, 1964), and Ivan Bunin is the author of *Memories and Portraits* (Garden City, N.Y., 1951). Pares credits Purishkevich with coining the phrase "ministerial leapfrog." The journalist N. A. Teffi, who describes "the most talked about man in Russia," wrote her memoirs, *Vospominaniya* (Paris, 1932), and is quoted by Alex de Jonge. The Okhrana political reports—"the industrial proletariat . . . is on the verge of despair"—were remarkably accurate. The censors kept such pessimism out of the press (including the foreign press, as Wilton of *The Times* frequently complained), but Nicholas received regular for-his-eyes-only reports of intelligence data, so there was no excuse for the blindness of the rulers. Protopopov, who complained that the throne "became the prisoner of stupid influences and stupid forces," of which he himself was a leading example, gave evidence to the Commission of Inquiry.

Details of Felix Yusupov's family, early life, and meetings with Rasputin in Chapter 25, " 'Vanya Has Arrived,' " are included in *Lost Splendor*. The account of the hypnosis attempt is similar to those of Stolypin and Kokovtsov. Purishkevich is an intriguing figure in his own right; Pares thought he had "a sparkling intelligence and a fearless spirit." Shulgin recollects his meeting with him—"Remember December sixteenth"—in *Dni*. Simanovich's claim to have had early warning of a murder attempt is confirmed by Okhrana reports of an atmosphere in which assassinations were expected. Although Simanovich says that he deposited several thousand rubles in Maria Rasputin's name, she denied receiving any significant sums after her father's murder.

The policemen who were first aware of a disturbance at the Yusupov palace on the night of the murder, in Chapter 26, "The Dead Dog," made full statements. These were passed to Vassilyev, who details them in *The Ochrana*. An outline was soon obtained by reporters from *Novoye Vremya*, but Vassilyev had access to the original depositions. The interview with Maria Rasputin—"soon after I went to bed"—suggests that her account of watching her father leave the apartment is incorrect. Yusupov's attempt to create an alibi—Rasputin's telephone call "insisting that I go with him to the Gypsies"—is noted in Vassilyev. The excuse that Purishkevich was "very drunk" is feeble; he was known not to drink.

The versions given by Yusupov and Purishkevich of the actual killing of Rasputin and their part in it in Chapter 27, "Confessional," correspond broadly with each other and with the autopsy. They do not, however, mention the presence of women in the palace. Constable Yefimov's description of a cry "as if uttered by a woman" appears in his deposition as recorded verbatim by Vassilyev. Wilton's unpublished notes on the affair, which he wrote up the day after the murder, were mailed to Wickham Steed, foreign editor of *The Times*, on December 20, 1916 (Wilton typed the Western calendar date January 2, 1917, on his letter). They are from *The Times's* archives. General Kurlov's account of the willingness of the conspirators to protect those involved is from *The Fall of Imperial Russia*.

Simanovich claims that the coffin described in Chapter 28, "Finis," had a glass panel, through which the embalmed face of the dead Rasputin could be seen. He says that an officer named Belyaev discovered that an icon signed by members of the imperial family was buried with the body. Belyaev knew that this would have great value for collectors and exhumed the body and stole it after the revolution. Simanovich also claims that the empress intended to turn Rasputin's apartment into a chapel-museum and gave him twelve thousand rubles to find a new apartment for Rasputin's daughters. He rented one at 13 Kolomenskaya Street from a Pole. It was well furnished and cost him twenty-five thousand rubles; when Vyrubova discovered that he had added thirteen thousand rubles of his own to Alexandra's money, she repaid him. But the girls were not happy at their new address and returned to Gorokhovaya ulitsa.

Index

ABOUT THE AUTHOR

BRIAN MOYNAHAN is a former foundation scholar of Corpus Christi College, Cambridge; he graduated in 1962 with first-class honors in history. He was for many years a foreign correspondent, and latterly European editor, with the London *Sunday Times*. He has traveled frequently to Russia and is the author of three previous books on Russian history: *Claws of the Bear*, *Comrades*, and *The Russian Century*. He is also the author of *The British Century*.

ABOUT THE TYPE

This book was set in Photina, a typeface designed by
José Mendoza in 1971. It is a very elegant design with
high legibility, and its close character fit has made it a
popular choice for use in quality magazines and art
gallery publications.

29282244R00266

Made in the USA
San Bernardino, CA
18 January 2016